Dirty Words in *Deadwood*

Postwestern Horizons

GENERAL EDITOR

William R. Handley
University of Southern California

SERIES EDITORS

José Aranda
Rice University

Melody Graulich
Utah State University

Thomas King
University of Guelph

Rachel Lee
University of California, Los Angeles

Nathaniel Lewis
Saint Michael's College

Stephen Tatum
University of Utah

DIRTY WORDS IN DEADWOOD

Literature and the Postwestern

EDITED BY MELODY GRAULICH
and NICOLAS S. WITSCHI

University of Nebraska Press § Lincoln and London

© 2013 by the Board of Regents of the University of Nebraska. Chapter 2, "Last Words in *Deadwood*," by Brian McCuskey, originally appeared as "Last Words in *Deadwood*: Literacy and Mortality on the Frontier" in *The Journal of Popular Culture* (2011) Wiley Online Library. http://onlinelibrary.wiley.com/doi/10.1111/j.1540-5931.2011.00876.x/pdf.

All rights reserved
Manufactured in the United States of America ∞

Library of Congress Cataloging-in-Publication Data
Dirty words in Deadwood: literature and the postwestern / edited by Melody Graulich and Nicolas S. Witschi.
pages cm. — (Postwestern horizons)
Includes bibliographical references and index.
ISBN 978-0-8032-6474-8 (pbk.: alk. paper) 1. Deadwood (Television program) I. Graulich, Melody, 1951– II. Witschi, Nicolas S., 1966–
PN1992.77.D39D58 2013
791.45'72—dc23
2013000344

Set in ITC New Baskerville by Laura Wellington.
Designed by A. Shahan.

We dedicate this book to David Milch; to the cast, writers, and directors of *Deadwood*; and to everyone else who helped to make for hours of viewing and intellectual pleasure.

CONTENTS

LIST OF ILLUSTRATIONS   ix

ACKNOWLEDGMENTS   xi

INTRODUCTION: *Deadwood*'s Barbaric Yawp:
Sharing a Literary Heritage   xiii
Melody Graulich

DEADWOOD EPISODES   lv

DEADWOOD CAST   lix

1. David Milch at Yale: An Interview   1
   Nathaniel Lewis

2. Last Words in *Deadwood*   18
   Brian McCuskey

3. The Thinking of Al Swearengen's Body: Kidney Stones, Pigpens, and Burkean Catharsis in *Deadwood*   44
   Tim Steckline

4. "Land of Oblivion": Abjection, Broken Bodies, and the Western Narrative in *Deadwood*   72
   John Dudley

5. The Final Stamp: *Deadwood* and the Gothic American Frontier   104
   Wendy Witherspoon

6. "Down These Mean Streets": Film Noir, *Deadwood*, Cinematic Space, and the Irruption of Genre Codes   124
   Nicolas S. Witschi

7. "Right or Wrong, You Side with Your Feelings"   141
   Jennilyn Merten

8. "A Brooding and Dangerous Soul": *Deadwood*'s
   Imperfect Music   165
   David Fenimore

9. Calamity Jane and Female Masculinity in *Deadwood*   184
   Linda Mizejewski

10. Queer Spaces and Emotional Couplings in *Deadwood*   208
    Michael K. Johnson

11. Who Put the Gun into the Whore's Hand?
    Disability in *Deadwood*   236
    Nicole Tonkovich

    BIBLIOGRAPHY   269
    CONTRIBUTORS   281
    INDEX   285

ILLUSTRATIONS

1. Al observes the Gem   xv
2. Al and Wu discuss "the San Francisco cocksucker"   xxvi
3. Al and Adams discuss the "Founding Document"   xxxvii
4. Sofia observes   xl
5. The team surveys Main Street   xlii
6. Alma teases Bullock   xliv
7. Bullock accepts his badge   xlvii
8. David Milch   2
9. Al and Silas checking a document   32
10. Successful surgery   58
11. Trixie   74
12. Al and Cy on the watch   99
13. Sofia   109
14. Charlie at Hickok's grave   112
15. Bullock with his stepson's casket   137
16. Al taking care of the preacher   142
17. Jane and the General   162
18. Wild Bill Hickok's funeral   174
19. Jane and Joanie   201
20. Joanie helps with the bath   229
21. Jewel with Doc   256
22. Al in his office   261
23. Preparing Jen's body   262

ACKNOWLEDGMENTS

We would like to thank three editorial fellows from the *Western American Literature* office for their considerable professional help. Diane Bush kept track of files, copyedited manuscripts, compiled an early bibliography, and consulted with authors. Jaquelin Pelzer helped with the final copyediting and bibliography, compiled cast and episode lists, formatted the manuscript, and proofread. Joshua Anderson caught errors in the final proofreading. All offered insights from their own *Deadwood* viewing.

We would also like to thank the two anonymous readers for the University of Nebraska Press for their extraordinarily attentive, detailed, and useful evaluations of the manuscript. Jennilyn Merten has our gratitude for her tremendous work in gathering images for this volume. And thanks to Brian McCuskey, always as quick witted as Al Swearengen, for our title.

As always Melody owes thanks to Sabine Barcatta, the superb managing editor of *Western American Literature*, for all her support. She would also like to thank her husband, Brock Dethier, who is not a television fan, for putting up with her endless repetitions of *Deadwood* lines and plot developments, and her colleague, Brian McCuskey, for giving her someone with whom to talk TV.

Nic expresses his gratitude to his fellow panelists and the members of the audience who attended the 2007 ALA and 2011 MLA sessions in which he presented his work on *Deadwood*, for the many excellent comments and questions that helped him strengthen and consolidate his argument. And his deepest gratitude is reserved for Meg Dupuis, whose sustaining spirit is an ever-present reminder to stay grounded and whose careful eye for interpretive detail and logic have always provided much-welcomed course corrections.

INTRODUCTION
Deadwood's Barbaric Yawp
Sharing a Literary Heritage

Melody Graulich

When discussing the genesis of Deadwood, *David Milch has often declared, "I did want to do a show on the American West, but I didn't want to do a Western. I've never really understood or cared for the conventions of the Western." This does not mean, however, that the series is free of conventions. As Melody Graulich demonstrates in her literary historian's approach to Milch's writing, the series is best "read intertextually," a feat accomplished by paying specific attention to the various "conversations" with a wide array of literary and cultural histories that Milch engages in (including, in fact, those of the genre Western). By way of introduction to this collection of essays, Graulich opens for consideration a number of Milch's conventional concerns, among them the "conversations" he has about character, point of view, and narrative perspective; about the use of humor and the grotesque; and about the power of language to both obfuscate and reveal deeply held truths. More importantly, though, Graulich's opening appraisal makes clear that as "a verbal and visual construct,"* Deadwood *is far from conventional. Ultimately, she affirms that the approaches offered by the essays that follow, while initially literary in focus, will rapidly expand to include the full range of critical insights and rewards that "close analysis and interpretation" can bring.* Deadwood's *literary conventions are those that come into view when an interpretive model informed by the tools of contemporary literary and cultural analysis are brought to the task, when, as Graulich concludes, the show's engagement with "imagination" is more fully accounted for.*

I too am not a bit tamed, I too am untranslatable,
I sound my barbaric yawp over the roofs of the world.
  WALT WHITMAN, "Song of Myself"

Mr. Warren spread out pretty much all the literary artifacts of American culture for me to study, as part of my working for him on that history of American literature. And in that I found the refraction, the perspective that I needed, to give me access to play the cards that I'd been dealt.

DAVID MILCH

When we rehearse, David sits down and gives his take on the scene. But he usually doesn't talk about the scene; he talks about where it sits in the larger picture. Nineteenth-century American literature is what he's steeped in, with big themes on a small level.

IAN MCSHANE

In September 2006 I was invited to participate in "Got Yourself a Gun: Frontier Violence in American History and Culture," a symposium on the HBO series *Deadwood* at the Lamar Center for the Study of Frontiers and Borders at Yale. The plan: the show's creator, David Milch, who had attended and later taught at Yale, would speak one night; the next day the "scholars" would comment extemporaneously on his remarks, and Milch would then respond. I was invited, I presume, because I had published in 1984 one of the first essays on violence against women in the U.S. West, in a collection called *The Women's West*, edited and widely read by western historians, who made up the rest of the panel. Along with its profane language (the number of times "cocksucker" was used per episode, as well as the average length of time between its use, had actually been tallied) and its "authenticity" in representing the frontier West, the series' shockingly vivid and repeated scenes of brutality against women had been a topic of discussion, among scholars, fans, and critics—and here I mean those who disliked the show—alike.

Although enjoined not to prepare remarks, I knew generally what I wanted to talk about—and it was not to speculate about the historical accuracy of Swerengen's stepping on Trixie's neck after slapping her around or Wolcott's murders of women at the Chez Ami. I wanted to speak as a *literary* historian, to talk about *Deadwood*'s many allusions to U.S. literature to argue that the series must be read intertextually. From 1975 to 1976 I had absorbed the anthology *American Literature: The Makers and the Making*, written and ed-

1. Al observes the Gem. "Sold under Sin" (*Deadwood*, 1.12).

ited by Cleanth Brooks, R. W. B. Lewis, and Robert Penn Warren, to study for my PhD-period exam, which focused on nineteenth-century U.S. literature.¹ I had learned from Mark Singer's *New Yorker* profile that Milch had assisted that great trio, who end their introduction with this line: "And special gratitude is owed to David Milch for long, devoted, and invaluable assistance" (Brooks, Lewis, and Warren 1: xx). In a later essay Lewis describes their collaborative process: "The selection of the poets afforded particular pleasure and difficulty, as we read aloud to each other in the Vermont cabin from our personal favorites. . . . The texts were preceded simply by condensed biographical sketches, most of them compiled by our gifted younger colleague David Milch, who had often made a fourth figure at our meetings" (572).² (Nathaniel Lewis's interview following this introduction explores these relationships more fully.)

I felt that *The Makers and the Making* offered me an intellectual intersection with Milch, who had majored in English at Yale, received an MFA from Iowa, and taught literature. But it had been always already clear from watching *Deadwood* that Milch, like literary historians, carries on constant conversations with Hawthorne and Melville, Twain, James, Faulkner, and Flannery O'Connor, as well as lesser knowns such as George Washington Harris's verbally rambunctious and socially defiant Sut Lovingood (1865), Thomas Bangs Thorpes's "Big Bear of Arkansas" (1841), said to be based on Davy Crockett, or Johnson Jones Hooper's confidence man, Simon Suggs, whose most famous line and "whole ethical system lies snugly in his favourite aphorism—'IT IS GOOD TO BE SHIFTY IN A NEW COUNTRY'" (1845) (12, capitals in original).[3] Milch's comment in the epigraph to this essay about playing the cards he had been dealt even echoes a key trope in a Western novel often, simplistically, accused of instigating the "mythic West," Owen Wister's *The Virginian* (1902), as does the poker scene in *Deadwood* where Cy reprimands McCall for calling Wild Bill a "son of a bitch," the same insult Trampas uses in a poker game against the Virginian (1.4).[4] Readers of Milch's *Deadwood: Stories from the Black Hills* (2006) and interviews, as well as those who have heard him speak, in person or in audio commentaries, know he frequently refers to and directly quotes authors; I read *Stories from the Black Hills* as Milch's literary and cultural analysis of his own series. More significantly for *Deadwood*, as he pays homage to *The Virginian* without ever citing the novel, he often develops ideas in terms that rephrase works that have obviously influenced him, without directly mentioning them. Consider this passage:

> When the disjunction between our own inconsequence and what we would like to feel about our vital connection to the universe gets to be too much, we try to resolve that contradiction through altered states. I always had the secret suspicion that history had tended toward my birth and would trail into tawdry inconsequence after I left. Yet the facts of the universe appear to mitigate against that conclusion. (Milch, *Deadwood* 67)

Anyone familiar with the American literary canon will recognize that Milch explains his tendencies to addiction (as well as those of *Deadwood* characters) through the words and philosophy of a writer who appears in *The Makers and the Making* as "the dominant figure" of the 1890s (2: 1625):

> A man said to the universe:
> "Sir, I exist!"

"However," replied the universe,
"The fact has not created in me
"A sense of obligation."

Stephen Crane (1899) (2: 1653)

Similar echoes reverberate throughout *Deadwood*, as we will see.

While others described it as "Shakespearean," *Deadwood*'s dialogue reminded me of the voices from *The Makers and the Making*, and I was far more interested in how it entered into cultural and literary than historical conversations, though like most literary critics influenced by the American studies tradition and by postmodern theory, I usually focus on intersections between literature and history. After all, Milch adapted Napoleon's famous line, "History is a set of lies agreed upon," to assert a central focus for the series: "Language is a lie agreed upon," a comment that stresses his sense that all meaning is contextual and collaborative (*Deadwood* 26). In the remarks to which we were to respond, he helped me by extending an allusion he often repeats—"Melville said that any great poem spins against the way it drives. So does any great character" (*Deadwood* 17)—and by mentioning Ethan Brand's "unpardonable sin." His reference to Hawthorne gave me a literary avenue into what I knew from talking with the other speakers would be one of the more contentious topics of discussion the following day, the series' "historical accuracy," and I went back to my hotel room and thought about Hawthorne.

And contentious it was. The first historian mounted his high horse—his many years of scholarly research in primary documents—to point out what he considered to be the numerous historical flaws in the show. Milch, who was scheduled to speak only after the rest of us had finished and who is, unsurprisingly, as articulate as Swearengen, thundered back, referring to him as "the pompous professor." Although I had read Singer's description of Milch's discourse, "intellectually daunting, digressive, arcane, wittily profane" (192), I was still stunned by his physical presence. No fools, the next two speakers demurred at discussing the show's "authenticity," and Milch let them be. Then it was my turn to try to quote Hawthorne from memory.

"Last night as I listened to David Milch," I began, "I was reminded of Hawthorne's famous injunction in the preface to *The House of the Seven Gables* (1851), his historical fiction about Salem, Massachusetts, that while the *Novel* 'is presumed to aim at a very minute fidelity, not merely to the possible but to the probable and ordinary course of man's experience,' the *Romance* 'sins unpardonably so far as it may swerve aside from the truth of the human heart—[and] has fairly a right to present that truth under circumstances to a great extent, of the writer's own choosing or creation'" (vii).[5] Hawthorne had much to say about what he meant by "romance," but for our purposes today, we can substitute for novel, history, and for romance, historical fiction.

"I thought also of the preface to *The Scarlet Letter* (1850), when the narrator, a 'Hawthorne' the author has created, rummages through the attic of the Custom House and finds a torn, ragged, and faded 'A,' which, for reasons he doesn't fully understand, he places over his heart. At which point he feels a searing pain, which leads him, indeed enables him, to begin his story of a fledgling community executing its righteous sense of justice on a defiant yet deeply scarred young woman. Milch's remarks suggest that Hawthorne and his *Scarlet Letter* were on his mind: *Deadwood*, he has said, is 'a reenactment of the story of the founding of America, and a reenactment, too, of the story of Original Sin. I suppose I accept Hawthorne's definition of Original Sin as the violation of the sanctity of another's heart' (*Deadwood* 12).

"Hawthorne's sympathy for this young woman, this 'sinner,' made *The Scarlet Letter* a rather scandalous book in its time. Hawthorne's wife, Sophia, said it 'sent her to bed with a grievous headache,' while an author deeply influenced by Hawthorne, Henry James, wrote that 'Emerson, as a spiritual sun-worshipper, could have attached but a moderate value to Hawthorne's catlike faculty of seeing in the dark' [both qtd. in Brooks, Lewis, and Warren 1: 445]."

At this point Milch laughed at Sophia's headache and made an appreciative *um-hum* at James's light/dark image. (Only memory serves me: the Lamar Center did not tape the proceedings.) Thereafter, Milch, seated next to me as I stood at the podium, began to chime in, dueting my quotes, commenting on what was written on authors' gravestones or what they said about each other, guffawing knowledgeably when I mentioned the too-little-known Sut Lovingood. Soon it felt as if we were in dialogue. I went on:

"The language of the U.S. literary tradition echoes—perhaps thunders—throughout *Deadwood*. When Wild Bill offers Alma Garret a warning after her husband's murder that she should return to the East, he asks her to imagine the sound of thunder, adding, 'I told your husband to head home to avoid a dark result. But I didn't say it in thunder. Listen to the thunder' (1.4). His comment identifies one kind of sensibility—'a great power of blackness'—that informs *Deadwood*, as well as hints at Hickok's melancholy, qualities Melville describes as central to Hawthorne's fiction ("Hawthorne and His Mosses," in Brooks, Lewis, and Warren 1: 836). Rather like James, Melville saw Emerson as one of the 'yes' men, in contrast to his famous assessment of his friend, echoed by Wild Bill: 'There is the grand truth about Nathaniel Hawthorne. He says No! in thunder; but the Devil himself cannot make him say *yes*. For all men who say *yes*, lie; and all men who say *no*,—why, they are in the happy condition of judicious, unincumbered travellers in Europe; they cross the frontiers into Eternity with nothing but a carpet-bag,—that is to say, the Ego' (review of *The House of the Seven Gables*, in Brooks, Lewis, and Warren 1: 444).

"Of course today Hawthorne is regarded as one of our greatest historical novelists. I wonder if he *really* found that faded 'A' in the Custom House attic. Is it in an archive somewhere? How 'authentic' is *The Scarlet Letter*? Does 'A' stand for authenticity? [My understanding of how labels of "authentic" and "inauthentic" had permeated western history and literary studies has been shaped by the work of Nathaniel Lewis and William Handley, which I discussed later in my talk and will explore later in this essay.]

"We heard David quote Hawthorne last night. In another context he's talked of Doc Cochrane as suffering from the same sense of seeing too deeply into human suffering that destroyed Hawthorne's Ethan Brand. Apparently he also quotes Hawthorne to define characters who pretend, or aspire, to be what they are not, such as E. B.

Farnum, for the actor who plays him, William Sanderson, recounts that David will 'say Hawthorne says this and that, you know, and that we're all imposters' (in Milch, *Deadwood* 30). Alma Garret, of course, parades down the streets of Deadwood to meet Bullock's wife in a bright red dress in the first episode of the second season, which is called 'A Lie Agreed Upon.' [Here Milch chortled loudly.] Which is another articulation of perhaps *the* key theme of the American Renaissance: appearance versus reality." [Recall Ian McShane's comment that Milch is interested in "big themes on a small level." In *Deadwood: Stories of the Black Hills*, Milch often comments on this theme: "Swearengen . . . recognizes the sham and pretense and emptiness of institutions unless vitalized by behavior," for instance (111); "What Al Swearengen is doing and what he thinks he is doing are two absolutely opposite things" (17). Al is one of those "great characters who spins against the way he drives."]

"Milch has repeated his allusions to literature often enough that *Deadwood* actors have internalized them, as in this one that extends Melville's line about a poem: 'David has said that he loves Melville, and Melville said the only great scene is actually about the opposite of what it appears to be about—and when we come to work, I feel that's exactly what happens' (Garret Dillahunt [Wolcott], 'Making Episode 12'). Melville emerges in season 2 when, after Wolcott arrives in town, E.B. gives Johnny and Dan a message for the ailing Al, 'Al, if you're not dead and already moldering, I send news to revive you. A fish to rival the fabled leviathan has swum into our waters. Get well soon and we'll land the cocksucker together. Your friend, E.B.' (2.3). [Part of this line introduces the episode description on the DVD.] The fishing trope continues throughout the season. Again near the end of season 3 in 'Leviathan Smiles,' Al sees Hearst's men riding into town and says, 'Fucking Leviathan Smiles' (3.8). Unlike Ahab, Al loses a finger, not a leg. These are only a few of many references to Melville in *Deadwood*, which I see as a retelling in many ways of *The Confidence Man*."[6]

"'Let the Masquerade Begin,'" Milch broke in, quoting from memory the last line of Melville's novel.[7]

I had more to say, some of which I will explore later, as did

Milch—notably and not surprisingly that he reads Cormac McCarthy, another author whose historical authenticity has been challenged but whose work, like *Deadwood*, is about the power of language and the imagination to create a world. But this is a fitting place to end this dramatic dialogue, which I hope demonstrates that Milch, without preparation but with an amazing memory, entered into my intertextual reading of *Deadwood*, happily channeling the voices included in *The Makers and the Making*. Afterward audience members asked me if we had worked together, rehearsed together, what was a spontaneous demonstration of the power of our shared literary heritage.[8]

I am obviously suggesting that I find *Deadwood* compelling and convincing as historical fiction. I follow the lead of William Handley, whose methodology was praised in an essay by Stephen Tatum:

> Handley's intertextual methodology combining formalist and historicist techniques purposefully blurs the boundaries between literary and historical discourse, and between popular or formula westerns and so-called "serious" western literature, so as to trouble the binary structures (for example, myth/reality; dominant/resistant; authentic/false) too often employed by western critics and historians in search of some authentic, "real" West or regional difference. (465)

The scholars writing in this volume, all literary or film critics, explore *Deadwood* as they would a novel by Hawthorne or a play by O'Neill (each one-day episode could, in fact, by read as a "long day's journey into night," echoing many of the themes of the play: fathers and sons, theatricality, drug abuse). They read it as an imaginative text, using the techniques of literary and cultural criticism, with close analyses of individual scenes or episodes, having moved beyond the "American literary studies of the West [that] have often been as resistant to theoretical matters, even to formal aesthetics, as the field of western history has been resistant to literary concerns" (Handley 1). Milch certainly read widely in historical documents, as he did while working with the authors of *The Makers and the Making* in order to understand literary texts within their histor-

Introduction xxi

ical contexts. Suggesting that intersection between research and historical fiction, he excerpts some of these primary sources in *Deadwood: Stories of the Black Hills*. But despite its grisly subject matter, *Deadwood* fits Hawthorne's definition of the "romance," far more concerned with "the truths of the human heart" than with fidelity to facts. (Later in this volume several authors will look at how other literary genres are at play in *Deadwood*.) I believe Milch became embroiled in defending the series' "authenticity" when the language he used to express those fundamental truths was attacked.[9] He makes his position clear when he says, "The truths of storytelling have to do with something other than verifiable fact" ("Imaginative Reality"). Many, in fact most, aspects of the series demand a literary reading of the series' aesthetic dimensions, conventions, and echoes of literary traditions.

For instance, while the series' costume designers carefully dressed Wild Bill in historically appropriate clothes and while he really was shot by Jack McCall in Deadwood, the reverberating significance of his death can only be fully understood symbolically, using the tools and insights of literary understanding, as Milch himself has suggested, focusing on character development (literal and symbolic), themes, cultural meaning, and viewer response. Because "Hickok fathered Bullock," "the death of Wild Bill allows Bullock to grow into manhood," Milch argues (*Deadwood* 197, 179). "Bullock is left with Utter and Jane. They're his foster parents" (201). Although a character such as the coward McCall sees Hickok only as a public figure, viewers come to understand the meaning of his death through the dramatized private responses of characters such as Jane, Charlie Utter, and Bullock, for whom there are no historical documents, only the knowledge of the human heart. "Death allows Doc Cochran and Jane to realize the fullness of their humanity and become part of the town," says Milch (179). Wild Bill's death "allows Deadwood to exist outside the shadow of Western myth," his death weaning "the viewer . . . from any preconception of what the West had been or what the experience of watching the show was going to be like" (179). "I wanted viewers to invest in Hickok the old idea of what the hero was and then deprive them of the hero.

The audience gets angry if you deprive them of their hero. . . . Then they discover in themselves the emotional resources to adapt to that environment and recommit" (Milch, audio commentary, 2.3).[10]

As critics will argue later in the volume, using various current critical approaches, the trajectory of Jane's story has far less to do with what is known, or not known, represented, or misrepresented, about Martha Jane Canary's life history than it does with the series' key themes. The actress who plays Jane, Robin Weigert, was "floored" one day when Milch said before filming a scene, "'What Jane is, essentially, is a wife and mother.' And I said, 'What? How do we get from this bullwhacker of the Old West to being the wife and the mother'" (in Milch, *Deadwood* 70). Like Hickok, Jane is initially a recasting of the legendary figure. However, her care of and for Sofia in season 1 foreshadows her interest in Deadwood's schoolchildren and her leadership of them, with Joanie, in the parade to their new schoolhouse in season 3, which represents her gradual—and partial—movement from outsider to insider. Like her concern for children, her nursing during the plague complicates viewers' understanding of her gender identification and, again, foreshadows her increasing participation in community activities. Despite her appearance, language, and behavior, Jane is initially—and conventionally—defined by her relationship to a man as she moons after the unavailable Hickok. By season 3, her gradual acceptance of Joanie's affections and caring represents the (limited) female empowerment that takes place throughout the series and also the value of shared emotional commitment, which we see expressed in numerous unions.[11] Jane's evolution, for which there is no evidence in the historical record, parallels the series' major theme of the movement from primitivism and individualism to community and mutual dependence. (Linda Mizejewski examines the differences between Canary's "real" life and Jane's plotline more fully later in this volume.)

With his background as a literary critic, Milch also understands how the series will be "read." He repeatedly acknowledges that *Deadwood*'s meaning will be a collaboration between many. The characters are a result of the actors "fleshing out" the role, as well as Milch adapting the role to fit the actors (Milch, *Deadwood* 12, 27–28), but repeatedly he emphasizes the readers' part in the process: "The viewer collaborates in Ian's creation of Swearengen" (27). He sees *Deadwood*'s meaning not as fixed but as a conversation between its creators and viewers. In passages like the following, he addresses the fallacy of intentionality: "I never thought of the name Swearengen as connected to his profane language, any more than I thought of Bullock as bull-headed, or Farnum as Barnum, or anything of the sort. It is the life of this fiction, of the world of *Deadwood*, that generates these similarities. Symbols generate their meaning out of the closed system of a fiction" (35). Discussing the meaning of Hickok's death, he concludes, "These are understandings that have come to me after the fact" (197).

Milch does not resist those who, in our students' jargon, go fishing for "deep hidden meanings." Within the series itself, characters, notably Swearengen, repeatedly try to "decipher" what things mean, what they symbolize, whether Wu's drawings, Hearst's notes, just about anyone's actions, or what people are trying to say. Swearengen is always happy when he can "identify a pattern in these events" (3.3). As Dority says to the recovering Al, "You'll have to gather all your fucking wiles, Al. There's developments that need interpreting at every front" (2.5). E.B. comes to Al and announces: "Something strange has transpired. I need you to construe" (2.9). Typically, Cy purposefully deceives, saying to Lila, "I ain't answerable for misinterpretations." (2.3). (Brian McCuskey will have more to say about the difficulties of "reading" meanings later in this volume.)

Deadwood also declares its literariness through its attention to the poetry and ambiguity of language.[12] Describing *Leaves of Grass* as a "language experiment," Walt Whitman wrote, "The subject of language interests me—interests me: I never quite get it out of my mind" (qtd. in Traubel viii). Nor does Milch, who describes "a world you create simply by the way people talk" (Milch and Carradine). In this sense *Deadwood* is also a "language experiment," not only creating a world by the way people talk but also self-conscious about language. Like all great literature, *Deadwood* is wonderfully quotable. Every viewer will remember favorite lines; for months colleagues in my (English) department chanted *Deadwood*isms as we passed each other in the hall. My favorite: Al to Trixie, before inviting her back to his bed: "Take half a day off if you feel like it. Go see that child. Well, venture out. Sally fuckin' forth" [1.11]; we also reenacted the "Wu/who/cocksucker" "conversation" between Al and Wu, in the rhythm of "Who's [Wu's?] on First?" [1.10]. Certainly Milch's coinage for Barnum's suckers, "hoople-heads," already all over the web, will one day make Webster's.

The characters repeatedly comment about language, particularly focusing on the many difficulties of communication. Here Milch again echoes one of the central concerns of the American Renaissance writers: ambiguity of meaning. The conversations of the two "allies," Al and Wu, ridiculous yet successful — in communicating information, helping a relationship evolve, and ultimately conveying affection — are only the most exaggerated expressions of this theme. Ellsworth gives voice to one of the series' key themes — the difficulties of finding language to convey feelings, or the inner reality — when he says to Alma, "Forgiving me my language; I ask you to consider my meaning" (3.1). Responding to speakers who favor indirection and sarcasm, characters frequently ask, "What did that mean?" or "What just happened?" (Adams 2.10). "What's the import of that expression [amalgamation and capital]?" asks Seth. Angry with Wolcott asking him if he's a "student of Hume," Charlie answers, "Do I look like I fucking know?" (1.9). "I ain't got one fucking scintilla what it means," says Dan to Al (2.10). Mildly threatened by Al, Merrick says, "I can imagine bleeding if first I've been made to understand" (3.1). Characters frequently feel called upon to rephrase their "point." Generally, though certainly not always, Al responds to his cohorts' lack of comprehension with bemused but biting sarcasm, while Cy conveys his characteristic aggression and contempt: to Lila, "Don't mistake me. I *want* to take the time to explain myself to you" (2.9).

Al has faith in his verbal abilities; miscomprehension results from the stunted understanding of his auditors. He provides evidence for Milch's assertion that language "was the only social force before

2. Al and Wu discuss "the San Francisco cocksucker." "Something Very Expensive" (*Deadwood* 2.6).

government. Those who could speak well became the leaders" (Milch and Carradine). Al's loquaciousness, exaggeration, and wordplay might exert power and control, but his insults to characters for whom we know he has affection (Trixie, Dan, Jewel, Doc, Silas, Wu, Bullock, even "the Jew") are a defensive way of sustaining relationships. For instance, while he is still suffering from her attraction to Sol, he uses this obscene and aggressive metonymy when he looks down on Trixie from the inside balcony in the Gem and says, "Why aren't you among the circumcised?" yet by this time he has facilitated her movement from whore to bookkeeper, from the Gem to Sol's bed (2.10). Milch says, "When Swearengen is talking his tone often works against the content of what he says" (*Deadwood* 25). His meaning exceeds his words, and as Milch says about his father in a quotation later in this essay, there is often "hospitality" in Swearengen's words, quite unlike Cy's. The pent-up Bullock is capable of direct and contrite apologies to Sol and Martha for saying the wrong things, but he doesn't have faith that his community will understand him. He says to Martha, "Words do the wrong jobs, piling on too heavy, at odds over meanings," before speaking only a few words in his campaign speech (3.1). For Hearst, who would "rather be off by [him]self," language is never a social act, only a means to intimidate and control (3.3).

Like Swearengen, Bullock, and Hearst, each *Deadwood* character speaks with his or her own inflection. "The language," says McShane, "is a way of saying who you are" (audio commentary 1.12). Joanie acknowledges her place in the camp in the following interchange: after using "fucking," Al says, "Pardon my French." Joanie: "Oh, I speak French" (1.3). But later she speaks in various emotionally vulnerable discourses, to Charlie, to Alma, to Jane (1.3). Ultimately the women, whom Paula Malcomson (Trixie) described as "really grasping to be heard" during the first season, find their voices (in Milch, *Deadwood* 88). While romantic Sol would "settle for a vigorous handholding" (2.2), Trixie integrates her past life with her current one in repeated sexual innuendos: punning on being his bookkeeper, she says, "Let me work on your column," their very relationship measuring the distance from her initial promise to Al: "I'll be good" (2.5; 1.1). Ellsworth delivers the series' first burst of inspired profanity to Al in "Deadwood," but by his death he, like Charlie Utter (befitting his name), is one of the characters most capable of expressing directly his caring for others.

As intriguing are the characters' comments on one another's ways of speaking. Swearengen to Merrick: "Ever wonder if you expressed yourself more directly, you would weigh less" (1.6). More nastily, Adams to Jarry: "You talk like you take it up the fucking ass" (3.1). Other comments are more indirect. Worried about protecting the camp against the plague, Al refuses to put up with E.B.'s usual flowery diction: "Don't play that shit where you make me drag your words out of you. Declare, or shut the fuck up" (1.6). Alma frequently puts Farnum in his place by trumping his highfalutin discourse with her own, then speaking the language of the camp: "Shit or get off the chamber pot" (2.4). Wanting Al back after his bout with the kidney stone, Johnny says, "Boss, talk any way you want as long as you're miserable and mean" (2.5). The drunken Merrick inarticulately compliments Dan: "I often find you the source of the many well put and witty things that you say" (1.6).

Rather ironically given *Deadwood*'s grandiloquent speech and the way Al talks over his subordinates' heads, in the tradition of the tall tale Milch mocks ostentatious language, used by characters and institutions who suffer from what Twain calls in *Life upon the Mississippi* (1883) "the Sir Walter Scott disease." This time a character is the exaggerated embodiment of the theme, E. B. Farnum, though Merrick also comes in for ridicule. When Merrick posts an announcement about the plague using the word "gratis," Al comments, "Is your intention to inform your fucking readership or make them feel like a dunce?" (1.6). Yet Merrick also serves as a critic of governmental discourse. When Jarry brings the camp a statement about claims, Merrick says, "Uh, if I discern this correctly, sir, this statement could be taken to mean, uh, nothing," adding, "What exactly will or won't qualify or mitigate the presumption of ownership eludes me" (2.5). When he puts up the notice, a group of indignant hoople-heads cluster round, asking, "What in fuck's that word sposta mean?" Merrick's definition only leads to threats, while Steve's is more satisfying: "New county commissioner give Merrick a statement mitigating us into an ass fucking" (2.5). (As befits an institutional setting, my department colleagues "mitigated" each other for a few weeks.) In *Deadwood* the relationship between politics and the English language is suspect.

Deadwood's language deserves an old-fashioned close reading, something essayists in this volume have begun to do. I have space for only one more point. In the series and in his comments, Milch repeatedly insists on language's fluidity, another topic important to both the yay- and the naysayers of the American Renaissance. With its changeable multiple meanings, Milch sees it as sustaining theme: "Which is to say language always generates meaning from context and what begins as seeming an unremitting and profane environment is just seeking a new way to organize itself. At the level of language I was trying to prefigure the theme of improvisation of society" (audio commentary 2.3). Here Milch, like Whitman, connects language to democracy and to a shared attempt to make meaning, always shifting, and to understand: "Language has no intrinsic meaning and no intrinsic value. It depends upon a consensus, as does the value of gold, and it is constantly redefining itself"

(*Deadwood* 19). The reference to gold's lack of intrinsic meaning recalls the debated meanings of literary symbols—the Scarlet A, Moby Dick, James's golden bowl—and the comparison emphasizes Milch's view of language as a social construct.

Not surprisingly Milch expresses no evidence of Harold Bloom's "anxiety of influence." (In his interview with Lewis in this volume, he indicates a preference for literary history over theory.) When I asked him how all those years of working on *The Makers and the Making* influence his imaginative vision, he answered, "I think it's so fundamentally and pervasively that it's almost impossible to speak of, to articulate."[13] Yet he gave it a try, describing how a community of scholars discussed how their work entered into a conversation with a literary tradition:

DM: The method was that we all sat and read.... And then talked about it and then sort of split things up and so on. So there were the materials. But then there was the experience of the sitting and talking about the materials, and that process was so predominately without any kind of ego attachment that the example of the humility and the tenacity and the perseverance, and the assumption of a good in the enterprise and a worthiness in the enterprise—that was what was most precious to me. You know there's a Santayana comment in "The Genteel Tradition in American Philosophy" about the intrinsic suspicion in America of the life of the mind....

Certainly I came to the idea of being an artist with all of those ambivalences and uneasinesses, and here in particular was Mr. Warren who... was an extraordinary poet and unapologetically, unabashedly leading a life of the mind and recognizing as a necessity the fact that one had to understand and incorporate into the fiber of your being that you were working in a tradition. That the idea that you would, that an artist could, create alone was every bit as self-deluding and narcissistic as the kind of, the philistine prejudice against writing, against being an artist at all. And so it put to rest at a level of habit, which is always the place to put things to rest: you just stopped questioning the fact that your work is part of a conversation, with everybody, with the work that has preceded you and you can pray humbly that it will be part of the conversation which ensues.

MG: That's part of the real pleasure for the reader, from a literary standpoint, to see that conversation going on in *Deadwood*.

DM: Yes. Yes. And it isn't meant to be an elegant parlor trick. That is, an arcane reference or, you know, only for the really initiated. That's not what it is. By the process of working on all of those materials, over a number of years . . . it became part of the air that one breathes. . . .

Ultimately, after all of that work, and all of those different writers we studied—and you know we studied the Indian, all of the Indian poetry and the black spirituals—for me, that was what the river was for Mark Twain.

MG: Or the sea for Melville?

DM: Absolutely.

MG: His Harvard and his Yale?

DM: Absolutely. I had the sea and I had the river. I knocked around a little bit but understand that everyone that you met on the sea and on the river was also legitimately met in the world of the imagination. All of that stuff could be drawn on, and you didn't have to say, well, this is highbrow and this is lowbrow and all of that horseshit. It [literature] is a great leveler. It makes all of your experience available to you. That was the great gift that both Mr. Warren and Mr. Lewis gave me.

As we have seen, Milch repeatedly pays tribute to "all that stuff [that] could be drawn on," mentions authors and texts that have influenced him. "The writer Katherine Anne Porter once said," he writes, "'There is no such thing as an exact synonym or an unmixed motive.' I think both of those things are true"; the extravagance of *Deadwood*'s language suggests that no simple synonym will do, while we seldom, perhaps never, meet a character with an unmixed motive (Milch *Deadwood* 90). Milch also sees his work as honoring writers who have taught him his craft: "[I consider] the judgment that they would make of the way that I work, that's the deepest tribute that I could pay to them, that I try not to be distracted by sterile ideas of novelty, I just try to serve the materials, and that's how all of those influences ad, mix, in a constructive fashion. And then sometimes when you're laying head to pillow at night, you think, 'Oh, maybe Twain liked that, maybe he would have liked that'"(Milch, personal interview). This is a wonderfully symbiotic moment, for as much as Milch takes pleasure in the idea that Twain would have liked his work, he also wants his work to give Twain pleasure. Like many readers influenced by Wayne Booth's *The Rhetoric of Fiction* (1961), he enjoys the company of the "implied author," enjoys conversing with him. Although his motif of orphans in *Deadwood* has been connected to Dickens, we could as easily see Swearengen, with his concrete and self-expressive language, his confused but sometimes heartfelt morals, his (almost) solitary meditations, and his initial decision to "light out for the territories" as what we hope Huck Finn will not become, and variations of the King and the Duke parade through *Deadwood*'s theatrical, deceptive, and violent world, offering their own versions of Shakespearean soliliquys.[14] For the remainder of this introduction, I will suggest only a few more of "those influences that ad, mix in a constructive fashion" into *Deadwood*. Other viewers will no doubt immediately think of dozens I have missed.

Through references to founding fathers and founding documents, in *Deadwood* and in *Deadwood: Stories of the Black Hills*, Milch implies that *Deadwood* is a microcosm of larger U.S. themes. "How would there be order in this environment in the absence of laws?" he asks. "In that regard, *Deadwood* was sort of a petri dish, it was a laboratory experiment in which was reenacted the entire American experience" (Milch and Carradine). And so, appropriately, although *Deadwood* is set in the frontier West, literarily it encompasses the whole nation. Most of the writers I have discussed so far were rooted in New England. Twain, however, unites the South with the West. Like his work *Deadwood* owes a good deal to what is known as the frontier region of the "Old Southwest," which introduces another genre to consider, the tall tale, described in a section on

Twain in *The Makers and the Making* as having "its own kind of poetry, . . . poetry [which] even in its wildest grotesquerie, was aimed at expression, not decoration" (2: 1278). Milch's father, a looming figure in his life, apparently told stories in tall-tale style: "There was a hospitality in the exuberance of [my father's] language. Exaggeration didn't bother him. He felt it was of the essence" (Milch, *Deadwood* 17). When Al tries to bribe Blazanov, the new telegrapher, with the offer of having his "prick sucked constantly," Merrick dissembles, "You encounter one of our wonderful, meaningless American traditions, Mr. Blazanov, the tall-tale conversation"; Al rejoins that customers enjoy his establishment, "be their preference for tall tale or otherwise" (2.8).

Southwest humor stories characteristically use a proper, educated, and verbally stilted frame narrator (think Merrick, though Farnum would be hilarious in this role, and perhaps embodies Milch's satire of it) who is simultaneously appalled and enraptured by the outrageous, uncivilized behavior and equally outrageous verbal virtuosity of a frontier storyteller (think Swearengen). As Brad Benz has written in a Chinese box of quotations:

> As Hughes notes, "the idiom of western expansion was tall talk, which in Boorstein's words, 'blurred the edges of fact and fiction,' and tall talk has generally been celebrated as a particularly American discourse." It's worth asking why Twain is not taken to task for stretching the truth. (249)

While Milch makes overt Twain's influence on *Deadwood*, when I met him at Yale he acknowledged that he knew the marvelous *Sut Lovingood Tales* (1867), by George Washington Harris, whose "Mrs. Yardley's Quilting" was reprinted in *The Makers and the Making*, where he was cited as an influence on Twain and Faulkner (Brooks, Lewis, and Warren 1: 1116). Among Southwest humorists Harris most pushed the boundaries of "decency," creating, in the words of the introduction to the story in *The Makers and the Making*, a "world of amiable brutality, grotesque high jinks, and crazy poetry" (1: 1115). Sut challenges all social proprieties, law, morality, and social institutions, in his actions and in his language. For Harris's time his treatment of sex was almost as startling, as audacious, as *Deadwood*'s. Here is the conclusion to a long passage in which Sut describes to the conventionally educated city boy George what goes on in the dark at quilting bees:

> "But then, George, gals and ole maids ain't the things to fool time away on. It's widders, by golly, what am the real sensible, steady-goin', never-scarin', never-kickin', willin spirited smooth pacers. They come close't up to the hoss-block, standin still with their purty, silky ears playin and the neck-veins a-throbbin, and waits for the word—which of course you gives after you finds your feet well in the stirrup—and away they moves like a cradle on cushioned rockers, or a spring buggy runnin in damp sand. A tetch of the bridle and they knows you want 'em to turn, and they does it as willin as if the idea were their own. I be dod-rabbitted if a man can't 'propriate happiness by the skinful is he is contact with somebody's widder and is smart." (1: 1118)

As the editors conclude, "The saga of Sut gives a gallery of other characters drawn with verve and astuteness; around him there is a whole society, a world grotesque but humanly recognizable. And Harris caught, created even, a language for that world. It is a language of vital rhythm and vivid images" (1: 1116). Surely this passage could as well describe *Deadwood*.

The grotesque often resides in southern literature. *Deadwood* is filled with such characters. It might take one to know one in Wolcott's description of the hotel owner, "a grotesque named Farnum," or in E.B.'s later recognition of Richardson as a "grotesque" (2.8; 3.3). After Swearengen's suggestion to "sheath your prick," Bullock fights him at the beginning of season 2, Milch says, "because it is his own soul speaking to him in the form of this grotesque little man. Bullock doesn't want to believe that his soul can be housed in that" (*Deadwood* 157). As with Al, the "grotesque" characters in *Deadwood* are often treated most sympathetically. Since at least the nineteenth century, writers have employed the grotesque to express, humorously and ludicrously, a sympathy for humankind and its generally painful conditions, an emotion much in evidence in *Dead-*

wood. Milch suggests one source for his vision when he says of Swearengen: "Something in him is impelled to enfranchise Jewel, to give her a place to stand. He can't understand why. He is moved by grace even as he disavows it" (*Deadwood* 19). "All my stories," wrote Flannery O'Connor, "are about the action of grace on a character who is not very willing to support it, but most people think of these stories as hard, hopeless and brutal" (275). (*The Makers and the Making* reprinted "A Good Man Is Hard to Find" ([1955]).) The grotesque and grace are often linked through humor: according to O'Connor, Simone Weil's "life is almost a perfect blending of the Comic and the Terrible, which two things may be opposite sides of the same coin. In my own experience, everything funny I have written is even more terrible than it is funny, or only funny because it is terrible, or only terrible because it is funny" (105). "Seeming absolute contraries contain each other," says Milch, and the conjoining of the comic and the terrible is central to *Deadwood* ("Wedding Ceremony"). Throughout *Deadwood* we see characters struggling to accept the compassion and caring of others, moments of grace—Trixie, Bullock, Swearengen, Joanie, Jane. Sometimes the light of grace shines over them all: I think of the moment when Trixie looks up to meet Al's eyes and smiles as they watch Doc and Jewel, wearing her new brace, dance around the Gem at the end of season 1 (1.12).

One of the more grotesque story lines begins in season 2, when characters debate whether Steve "fucked the sheriff's horse" or perhaps, as he says, only "beat off on it," and extends into season 3 (2.6). This story line could have originated in Faulkner's *The Hamlet* (1940), though Ike Snopes's love affair with a cow is recounted in romantic language, while Steve's rape of Bullock's horse displays the sense of inferiority and powerlessness he can't express in words. (Imagine a Milch adaptation of the Snopes trilogy!) Milch clearly shares one of Faulkner's central tenets, stated in his Nobel Prize address in 1950: great writing concerns itself with "the problems of the human heart in conflict with itself" (qtd. in Brooks, Lewis, and Warren 2: 2546). He frequently mentions Faulkner, suggesting he had him in mind in creating scenes. When Lila tells the outraged

Cy that she believes God loves us and that she prays for him every night, Milch comments, "That's a tough one for a guy like Tolliver to feel someone's praying for him. *Light in August*—it's a great novel by Faulkner—the fundamental turn in it is where a woman [Joanna Burden] starts praying over this guy [Joe Christmas]. He kills her" (audio commentary 3.2). Perhaps Lila survives because of her economic value to Cy. In season 1 Johnny Burns tries to prevent the immigrant upstart Wu from walking in the front door of the Gem. In Faulkner's *Absalom, Absalom!* (1936), Thomas Sutpen's grand "design" to build a dynasty originates when he, believing the stories America likes to tell about itself, presumes to approach the front door of the Pettibone mansion and is turned away. Significantly, Al tells Johnny to let Wu in, and before he later sends Wu out the back door, having made a deal with him, he pats him gently and fondly on the back (1.10).

The writer Milch still calls his mentor, Robert Penn Warren, was deeply southern in outlook and wrote particularly about the southern frontier. Joseph Millichap has argued the influence of Warren's work on *Deadwood*, focusing particularly on shared "Naturalistic visions" and a thematic focus on "the exploitation and betrayal of youthful innocence" (107, 108). Frequently quoting Warren's poetry, Milch suggests that Swearengen's character originated in one of his poems, "Audubon" (1978), "about his father, where the father says, 'I longed to know the world's name.'" As Milch explains, "Swearengen affects a kind of ruthless pragmatism, but in fact his whole being yearns toward knowing the world's name. It embarrasses him" (*Deadwood* 19). The example he offers of what Al "wants to understand" is, significantly, Jewel. "He's fascinated by Jewel, the cripple. But he can't acknowledge that in his behavior. . . . The real reason is that there is a miracle embodied in Jewel, that she seems so wounded as to be disqualified, and yet she isn't" (19). Jewel, who insists on her own humanity, is one of the few characters who gets away with talking back to Al. His acceptance of her smart mouth is certainly a miracle, but Milch's use of the word suggests that Jewel renders visible to Al some act of grace he wants to understand. As Warren wrote, "The grotesque is one of the most obvious forms art may take to pierce the veil of familiarity, to stab us up from the drowse of the accustomed, to make us aware of the perilous paradoxicality of life" (qtd. in Adams and Yates xi).

Although most critics, including Milch, consider Warren's poetry his greatest achievement, his best-known work is a historical novel based on a "real life" figure, *All the King's Men* (1946). Certainly Willie Stark, a charismatic leader who commits morally unjustifiable acts to build a better society, anachronistically fathers Al Swearengen. Stark is killed by the morally rigid Adam Stanton; fortunately for Al he was able to seduce his "Adam," Silas Adams, and avoid being murdered. In our interview Milch acknowledged the important influence of *The American Adam*, by his longtime office mate and advisor, R. W. B. Lewis, as he has in speaking about *Deadwood*:[15]

> Gold was a second chance, a fresh state that had nothing to do with the Indians. In this New World, Silas Adams is Adam. The reason that Dority has such misgivings about Adams is that he intuits that he is Swearengen's natural successor. . . . Adams is the educable primitive self, a political opportunist who is also something more. . . . Adams is waiting for his father, and he finds him in Swearengen, who is a man not afraid to act, but who keeps on going back to discover the source of his actions. They both share a curiosity about how things work. (*Deadwood* 143)

If Silas is Adam, then Al takes on an ironically powerful role as the creator of the universe of *Deadwood*. (In the beginning was the word?) Lewis identifies various Adamic figures, but a key characteristic is innocence. Certainly innocence (Sofia, the Reverend Smith, William Bullock, the Chinese prostitutes, Johnny Burns, Jane, even Alma) and experience are central themes in *Deadwood*, as both a human and a social trait. Silas is hardly an innocent, but perhaps he is, in Lewis's words, "advancing hopefully into a complex world he knows not of," a characteristic of the Adam created by Melville, who was, according to Lewis, "engaged in a long quarrel with himself" (*American Adam* 127, 129) — as are Swearengen, Bullock, Trixie, Jane, Joanie, and many others, all of whom share Faulkner's "problems of the human heart in conflict with itself."

3. Al and Adams discuss the "Founding Document." "Boy-the-Earth-Talks-To" (*Deadwood* 2.12).

In creating his characters Milch might agree with Emerson that "a foolish consistency is the hobgoblin of little minds" ("Self Reliance," in Brooks, Lewis, and Warren 1: 715). The large-minded—and large-hearted—"Al is a very good man with none of the behaviors of goodness" (Milch, *Deadwood* 17). But Milch's vision of the conflicted human character is much darker than that of the "spiritual sun-worshipper." While he believes that "seeming absolute contraries contain each other" ("Wedding Ceremony"), no *Deadwood* character could rest as comfortably in his contradictoriness as does Whitman: "Do I contradict myself? / Very well then I contradict myself / (I am large, I contain multitudes)" ("Song of Myself," in Brooks, Lewis and Warren 1: 979). Much of *Deadwood*'s dark viewing pleasure results from watching characters we have come to know and care about struggle with their internal conflicts. Sharing Hawthorne's—and Melville's—"catlike faculty for seeing in the dark," Milch does not envision these moments as merry and expansive. Yet, contradictory himself, he believes that "the human heart yearns to be lifted up" by stories "about our brothers and sisters" (Milch, *Deadwood* 11).

The American Adam, of course, is much concerned with "original sin," a concept Milch uses psychologically—in his borrowings from Hawthorne about "the violation of the sanctity of another's heart" and in comments such as "the failure to respect the common humanity of our fellow travelers is to me the fundamental sin" (Milch and Carradine)—and symbolically: "Taking the gold from the Indians is our original sin. That's what comes before. *Deadwood* is the story of what comes after" (Milch, *Deadwood* 12, 53). According to Milch, when Bullock kills the Indian, "he got kicked out of the fucking Garden" (*Deadwood* 201). Both usages render history aesthetically, producing a historical romance. He elaborates: "The men who came to Deadwood craved a new beginning a chance to break their ties to civilized institutions and forms of meaning," but they soon recognized the need to develop a new society (*Deadwood* 15). Moving from the frontier story as emblematic of the American story, Milch extends outward: "The American story is a microcosm of the more universal story, the original sin" (Milch and Carradine). He grounds that "universal story" and his "big themes" in the muddy streets of Deadwood because he believes that "the way to get to the most general or universal portrayal is to be rigorously specific. If the details are right and the emotional life of the characters and the situation are both right, they begin to attract to themselves more general truths and more universal themes" (Milch and Carradine).

Viewed this way the shockingly original *Deadwood* fits quite comfortably into the early paradigms of the field of American studies, a field Lewis greatly influenced, then focused on the "myth and symbol" school; on "the American character"; on regional literature; on using literature, elite and popular, to understand cultural history; on reading texts in conversation with one another. Milch no doubt sat in on some of the many discussions Brooks, Warren, and Lewis must have had about the themes of innocence and experience in U.S. literature. One wonders if the telegraph's portentous arrival in Deadwood owes something to Leo Marx's *The Machine in the Garden* (1964); if Milch's choice to make Calamity Jane a major character allows him to revisit Henry Nash Smith's *Virgin Land* (1950); if any of his characters achieve the "regeneration through violence" described by Richard Slotkin (1975); if his insistence on the development of community as a key western theme reveals a reading of Wallace Stegner, who expressed the following sentiment in multiple genres: "When [the West] fully learns that cooperation, not rugged individualism, is the quality that most characterizes and preserves it, then it will have achieved itself and outlived its origins. Then it has a chance to create a society to match its scenery" (*Sound* 38). (Milch cannot be accused of buying into "American exceptionalism," one of the attacks against early American studies scholarship, since the themes he spins out in *Deadwood* he originally planned to explore in ancient Rome.)

When Milch left Yale "to write *Hill Street Blues*," circa 1980–81, he and Lewis had planned another collaboration, "had signed a contract . . . to do the biography of the James family, which [Lewis] finally published years later and very graciously acknowledged having issued from [their] original ideas" (Milch, personal interview).[16] The research for this book left a deep impression, evidenced by Milch's frequent references to both William and Henry James, whom he discusses at some length in Mark Singer's profile. Perhaps he also made a suggestion to Molly Parker (Alma), who, seeking to understand the pressures on Victorian women, mentions that she's "been reading the diary of Alice James" (audio commentary 2.1).[17] He calls on Henry to help him address the gap between representation and "real life": "They once asked Henry James about a character, in 'The Spoils of Poynton' [1897]. He was so good but does such a character exist in real life? And James said, 'So much the worse for real life'" ("Imaginative Reality"). Many have pointed to James's "The Turn of the Screw" as the source of the names of the con couple, Flora and Miles, in "Suffer the Little Children," which Millichap argues raises the theme of innocence and experience, certainly a persistent theme in James's work. The presence of the innocent Sofia looking on silently at adult desire and duplicity recalls *What Maisie Knew* (1897). Confidence people abound in James's novels—Mme Merle is a prime example—characters who pretend to be what they are not, to feel what they do not feel, who dissemble with indirect and ambiguous language. I suggest that while the American studies tradition influenced Milch's represen-

4. Sofia observes. "Sold under Sin" (*Deadwood*, 1.12).

tation of character and cultural symbolism, James's aesthetics, particularly his insights about point of view, inform *Deadwood*.

Consider, for instance, James's use of dialogue and interior monologues. In James's novels there is always a subtext, often concealed within dialogue, which is often characterized by indirection. Consider: Al to Trixie: "How's the Jew going?" . . . Trixie (as if disgusted): "He stares in my eyes when he fucks me . . . " Al: "Jesus Christ" (2.6). I could spend two paragraphs dismantling the emotions, the cover-ups, the cultural references, the innuendoes, and the wordplay in these few words. Characters sometimes delude themselves in their inner thoughts, but they also come to understand themselves and their histories in internal monologues. Perhaps it appears ludicrous, grotesque, to compare "Isabel Archer's vigil before the fire" in her villa in Rome when she comes to realize how her husband and dear friend have lied to and used her, described in *The Makers and the Making* as, a "characteristic moment . . . of self-confrontation," to Swearengen's soliloquy about his mother and the orphanage as Dolly sucks him off (Brooks, Lewis, and Warren 2: 1374; 1.11). But Milch and James put the moments to similar uses.

But even more significantly, for his themes—surveillance, deception, disconnection, interpretation, insight into human nature—and for his set, Milch takes as his blueprint one of James's most famous comments about storytelling.

> The house of fiction has in short not one window, but a million—a number of possible windows not to be reckoned, rather; every one of which has been pierced, or is still pierceable, in its vast front, by the need to the individual will. These apertures, of dissimilar shape and size, hang so, all together, over the human scene that we might have expected of them a greater sameness of report than we find. They are but windows at the best, mere holes in a dead wall, disconnected, perched aloft; they are not hinged doors opening straight upon life. But they have this mark of their own that at each of them stands a figure with a pair of eyes, or at least with a field-glass, which forms, again and again, for observation, a unique instrument, insuring to the person making use of it an impression distinct from every other. He and his neighbors are watching the same show, but one seeing more where the other sees less, one seeing black where the other sees white, one seeing big where the other sees small, one seeing coarse where the other sees fine. (*Art of Fiction* 46)

Of course this passage about narrative point of view owes a debt to chapters 17, "The Hotel," and 18, "The Boarding House," of Hawthorne's *The Blithedale Romance* (1852), in which the cold, prying, unreliable narrator, Coverdale, observes through his hotel window the tribulations of his friends in the boardinghouse across the street as if they were "actors in a drama" (145).

Many characters stand at windows in *Deadwood*—first and second story—or posture on balconies, each with his or her unique point of view about "the show" they're watching. This theme is overt in a comment from Seth to Martha about their new house: "I think you may laugh to see the mullion windows with their view of the camp from out the parlor. Being unfinished, they look like unfocused eyes" (2.1). Although Alma's red dress has provoked Martha's initiation, it will take a few episodes for her inexperienced eyes to see what's going on in the camp. The series' many observation scenes

5. The team surveys Main Street. "A Lie Agreed Upon, Part I" (*Deadwood* 2.1).

establish gender, class, and racial positions. For instance, Alma most often peers out from her hotel window while Trixie watches from the sidewalks. The men own the town from the balconies, as Hearst soon recognizes. Wu watches from his doorstep. Al brings the (dead) chief out on his balcony to watch Nuttall ride his new technology, his bike, apologizing to the chief that he will "have to suffer the low vantage" (2.8).

Although I agree with John Dudley, whose essay appears later in this volume, that these settings indicate a concern for surveillance, control, and power, they also announce the series' obsession with point of view. In *Deadwood* we encounter a remarkable number of individualized characters with diverse viewpoints on events, as if Milch, playing Monopoly, is trading in James's house for a town. Their points of view are established through language, but we also watch characters watching one another, the skilled actors offering us access to what they're thinking. The visual play capturing multiple points of view on "the show" could be demonstrated by a close reading of many of the final scenes of episodes, which focus on the establishment of community—"Advances, None Miraculous," where the town worries over the injured William Bullock (2.10), or "I Am Not the Fine Man You Take Me For," where the election speeches take place and where the mutilated, much observed Swearengen must lean on Bullock to help him save pride as he staggers from Hearst's room to the Gem (3.2). For a closer analysis I will briefly look at the two concluding episodes of season 1, where Jewel is one of the scrutinized: "Jewel's Boot Is Made for Walking" and "Sold under Sin" (1.11 and 1.12).

From Al's window Trixie spies Jewel walking through the streets; both wonder where she could be going, not just out of curiosity or control; their reason for concern is established when Trixie says to Jane, "Why [Jewel] is around is his sick fucking way of protecting her," not unlike his sick fucking way of protecting Trixie (2.3). We next see her from behind a wagon driver, who yells, "Get out of the way!" She is entertainment to a man imitating her walk to get laughs from a crowd. Jewel apparently ignores him, as she does a group of men who, without offering help, watch her fall into the mud and struggle to get up. Only a Chinese woman working on a sidewalk meets her eyes, but she is as powerless as Jewel appears to be. The street "show" ends in the sanctuary of Doc's office, but even he berates her before he hears her desire, her need from him. Finally he identifies with her, pointing out that "everybody's got limits. You draggin' your leg is yours" (1.11). Later he comments on his own limits as a doctor (2.2) and repeats the line—"as having limits like the rest of us"— to the woman in the camp perhaps most unlike Jewel, Alma Garret (3.3).

In the next episode, in the final scenes of season 1, the viewer looks at the house, or town, of fiction, reviewing many of the points of view that have observed tonight's show. (Ian McShane calls this medley a "curtain call" [audio commentary 1.12].) Crook's men depart the town, carrying Alma's unconscious father on a horse, a victory for Al and the camp, who will be "left to go their own way." Seth and Al, having just agreed to be allies, watch from Al's balcony. The camera cuts to a series of characters watching from street side: Sol alone; Trixie alone, joined by Adams; Dan joined by Johnny; Utter alone; Farnum joined by Merrick. Then the camera watches from behind a hoople-head, who "speaks" for many camp denizens by mooning the departing troops. Alma, still warm from a session

6. Alma teases Bullock. "Sold under Sin" (*Deadwood* 1.12).

of lovemaking with Bullock (who has promised to return), watches from her window across the narrow street. Gazes meet. As Seth and Al talk, we hear piano music from inside the Gem, the music so loved by Reverend Smith, whom Al has gently dispatched. We follow Al to the interior balcony, where he sees Doc Cochrane, happy to be relieved from the Reverend Smith's suffering and emotionally protected by Al, dancing with Jewel in her new boot. At the bar Trixie and Dan exchange a look of mutual happiness at their dance. Feeling Al's eyes on her, Trixie looks up and smiles, trying to share her pleasure. Burdened with the memory of his mercy killing of Smith, to spare Doc and the rest of the community, smarting from Trixie's desertion, Al rebuffs her with a heavy sorrowful gaze, then when she turns away, back to Jewel and Doc, looks down at his folded hands in regret. The camera moves behind Al; with him we watch two people ignore their "limits" to cavort, each "nimble as a forest creature" (1.12). Through all these eyes, we experience "the yearning of the spirit toward community" (Milch and Carradine).[18]

Cleanth Brooks suggested that the truths of history depend on a correspondence to an externally verifiable reality, whereas the truths of storytelling depend on an internal emotional coherence.

DAVID MILCH

In real life, Sol never married, but I don't think you let the facts get in the way of truth necessarily.

JOHN HAWKES (Sol Starr) discussing his hopes for Sol's relationship with Trixie

In their introduction to *True West: Authenticity and the American West* (2004), William Handley and Nathaniel Lewis note how often readers and critics of western American literature "make unexamined assumptions about what is authentic, what is real, what is true" (1). Quoting Don D. Walker, who "wrote that 'western literary criticism has for a long time been dominated by the historian's way of judgment,'" they suggest that too often "'history' overwhelms 'literature' with the effect that the inevitable fissures and fractures, inherent in any literary tradition, seem to disappear behind a simple question: is the work true?" (9). In *Unsettling the Literary West: Authenticity and Authorship* (2003), Lewis pushes this point further: "When encountering a western work, readers tend not to engage 'literary' issues (such as narrative aesthetics, forms of signification, or intertextuality) but to question its realism" (2). While arguing that "the literary and the historical are inseparable whenever we read the West" (9), Handley discusses in *Marriage, Violence, and the Nation in the Literary West* (2002) Forrest Robinson's assertion "that historians fail to take into account the postmodernist awareness of the discursive, constructed nature of all representation, including the historiographical" (226). In so doing they undervalue "literary complexity" (233).[19]

Deadwood is a representation of the frontier West. Despite my analysis of its literary conversations with its predecessors, it is a strikingly original one. Too much of the reaction to the series has focused on the question of historical accuracy rather than on its literary complexity. With its emotional coherence, its compelling characterizations, its compressed structural brilliance, its moral ambiguity, its language experiments, its interpretation of the past and its relevance to the present, and its engagement with its literary forebears, *Deadwood* is an aesthetic triumph as historical fiction. Like much great literature *Deadwood* makes a case for the humanistic value of storytelling. As Milch says in answer to the question of how he turns his research into fiction,

> You forget [the reading you've done] and to allow it become an imaginative reality. The truths of storytelling are not the truths of reportage. The truths of reportage finally depend upon their correspondence to an externally verifiable reality. The truths of storytelling may incorporate the so-called real event but they don't depend for their effect on the fact that a researcher can corroborate that an event occurred. They have to come alive in the imagination of the viewer. ("Imaginative Reality")

Deadwood is ultimately about the imagination, a verbal and visual construct, a literary masterpiece, richly rewarding close analysis and interpretation. We take on that project in this volume because it has come alive in our imaginations. Sally fucking forth into the literary landscape of *Deadwood*.

Although *Deadwood* is a collaborative project, with many writers and many voices involved in the production, we have chosen to focus on Milch as the primary creative force behind the series. For a detailed discussion of his role as "auteur," see Horace Newcomb, who points out in "Deadwood" that as "'creator and executive producer,' . . . Milch reviews every script; all go through his edit, alteration, and approval, dictated or otherwise formed. And it also remains part of the executive producer's role to oversee all other elements of the production process, from performance to final editing" (193). Although he notes out that crediting Milch for *Deadwood* or David Simon for *The Wire* is part of contemporary TV culture, he argues that *Deadwood*, more than other series, "is fully realized, created, from Milch's vision"(96). A viewing of the special features at the end of season 2 suggests that the actors agree. "I don't think

7. Bullock accepts his badge. "Sold under Sin" (*Deadwood* 1.12).

anything goes on on this set that David doesn't affect, alter, correct, delete, or add," says Stephen Tobolowsky (Hugo Jarry). "No scene starts until David shows up," says Jeffrey Jones (A. W. Merrick). "David will show up and do a little background on the scene, show what is at stake in the scene, what the connections are, and throw a few curve balls in, in fact make some changes on the spot. . . . There's always some other depth, some other dimension, that he illuminates" ("Trusting the Process"). Viewers recognize the truth of Jones's assertion when observing Milch in "Trusting the Process" or "Mr. Wu Proves Out," as he suggests new lines to actors, ways of speaking and inhabiting space, how to conceive of their characters. In an audio commentary to "Sold under Sin," Timothy Olyphant (Bullock) describes how Milch "made up" all the dialogue in a scene between him and Ian McShane "right there," as they were rehearsing, but that he, Oliphant, added a line about the sheriff badge, "I *know* where it goes" (1.12). Milch persistently emphasizes the collaborative nature of the process. "When you go down to the set, you always want to be willing to respond to either the suggestions of an actor or the director," he says in "Mr. Wu Proves Out," where we watch his hands-on involvement in a key scene, watch him get excited about Keone Young's suggestion that Wu should cut off his queue to symbolize his acceptance of being an American, a gesture incorporated into the end of the episode (2.12).

Generally the authors in this volume checked their own notes against the transcriptions prepared by Cristi H. Brockway. However, occasionally authors, hearing different words or intonations, made small unnoted modifications to these transcriptions. Whenever possible we have taken Milch's written lead; for instance, we use the spelling "hoople-head" as Milch did in *Deadwood: Stories of the Black Hills.*

Rather than repeat the names of episodes and actors, again following Milch's lead, we have chosen to cite episodes by season and number—1.4, for instance, or 3.9—and omit the names of actors from individual essays. Instead we provide a list of episode names and numbers and a list of characters and actors immediately following this introduction.

While many introductions provide brief summaries of the essays in the volume, we have chosen instead to write headnotes to essays, drawing parallels between them. We have grouped the essays, all of which are richer than this categorization, into three loosely defined groups: the first employs poststructuralist criticism; the second explores genre; and the third examines *Deadwood* through the lenses of current critical approaches.

Notes

1. Throughout this essay I refer to the two-volume *American Literature: The Makers and the Making,* first published in 1973. Whenever possible I have cited from it because Milch worked on it, and we can be sure he has a copy on his bookshelf. The authors write in the "Letter to the Reader," "our mode of working was social; that is we read and we talked" (1: xi). Milch was a consistent participant in these conversations. The anthology was a perfect vehicle for studying for my exams because it is as much a literary history as a collection of pieces and excerpts. "Though we began by thinking of an anthology with relatively brief introductions and headnotes," the authors write, "we found, as the work proceeded, that this plan would not accommodate a discussion of the urgent issues that kept arising. Eventually we found that we were being driven to write a history"

(1: xiii). As a result the introductions to sections and to major authors are often twenty (large) pages long, ambitiously drawing parallels and connections between authors and literary styles. The anthology was also one of the first to dismantle distinctions between high, popular, and folk culture, including not only works by such figures as Thorpe and Harris but also sections on spirituals, folk songs, "Indian Oratory" and poetry, speeches, and diaries. While the authors have sometimes been critiqued as exemplars of the New Criticism, by the time they wrote *The Makers and the Making*, they had combined close reading with cultural criticism. Lewis in particular was influential in the emerging field of American studies.

Although Lewis's later *Yale Review* essay points out a few sections written primarily by one author, the anthology does not identify individual authors of introductions. I therefore refer to "the authors" when citing the text.

2. Mark Singer initially reported on Milch's work on the anthology. Joseph Millichap has suggested generally "how much [Milch] is influenced by the great traditions of American literature" (104). My analysis is more extensive.

3. Others have, of course, noted *Deadwood*'s literariness. Many have commented on the "Shakespearian" qualities of *Deadwood*'s dialogue, notably Brad Benz in an essay on language in the series. Sean O'Sullivan has adapted ideas about "serial fiction," most particularly Dickens's, to discuss *Deadwood*'s second season as an "allegory of seriality" (118). Millichap examines Milch's debt to Warren. Horace Newcomb compares Swearengen to Milton's "heroic Satan" (97). Many have also commented that the names of the unfortunate con artists in "Suffer the Little Children," Miles and Flora, reference James's *The Turn of the Screw*.

In this essay I focus on Milch's debts to American literature, but I in no way mean to suggest that these are his only influences. His "favorite character" in literature is Falstaff, "whose capacity for language, the exuberance of whose expression was such that every experience, in the method of its expression, ultimately had a joyful effect," as does, paradoxically, the violent and often obscene language in *Deadwood* (qtd. in Singer 205). In *Deadwood: Stories from the Black Hills*, he says, "The writers who are alive to me, whom I consider my contemporaries, are writers who lived in another time — Dickens and Tolstoy and Dostoevsky and Twain" (12). He points out that the language used by *Deadwood* characters stems in part from their reading: the Bible, Shakespeare, and the Romantic novelists (25). He observes, "That encounter between the Doc and Jewel is a bit based on a scene in *Madame Bovary* with the hunchback Hippolyte. Her mope husband does an operation on the guy in order to impress Emma and fucks the hunchback up worse than ever" (*Deadwood*

181). Cochrane has a complicated literary heritage: "The doctor is a figure out of Conrad. Whereas Dr. Monygham in *Nostromo* broke under torture, this doctor broke in the Civil War. He's kind of an exile, like most of the characters in *Deadwood*" (Thorburn). Nevertheless, he discusses and obliquely references primarily U.S. authors.

4. See the end of the chapter "Quality and Equality," where the Virginian uses a "how you play your cards" metaphor to define the concepts to Molly Wood; the end of "The Game and the Nation—Act First," where he discusses Henry IV's poker skills; and the end of "The Game and the Nation—Last Act," where he acknowledges that good as the Virginian is, Queen Elizabeth would have beat him at poker. (Milch attributes this metaphor to William James in Singer 205.) As I have argued in "What if Wister Were a Woman," the poker and bluffing conceit operates throughout the novel, which depends significantly on the tall-tale genre and which explores wordplay, meaning, and language. Of numerous examples I could quote, the following line from the Virginian to Molly is echoed by Ellsworth to Alma (quoted later in this essay): "'I ask your pardon if I say what I have a right to say in language not as good as I'd like to talk to yu' with'" (82). Perhaps coincidentally, Falstaff is one the Virginian's favorite literary characters; he talks about him with the narrator ("The Game and the Nation—Act First") and with Molly ("Grandmother Stark"). Set during the "dawn of a neighborhood," *The Virginian*'s characters also take matters into their own hands to bring law and social order to land that originally belonged to Indians, who are shoved offstage much as they are in *Deadwood* (60).

5. I have incorporated some of my original talk into this introduction as a way of demonstrating Milch's extemporaneous engagement with U.S. literary traditions. I had typed up some key quotes to bring with me, but I actually did write up what I had to say after hearing Milch speak, so many of the non-*Deadwood* quotations were from memory. For instance, I actually said, "While the *Novel* must exhibit the utmost fidelity to fact, the *romance* sins unpardonably when it swerves from the deeper truths of the human heart." I have replaced my imprecise quotations with exact ones and cited them when possible. I have occasionally added comments to flesh out the argument, enclosed in brackets.

6. In *Deadwood: Stories of the Black Hills*, Milch suggests that his understanding of Ahab informs his thinking about Swearengen, who "can't figure a way out. He thinks, 'I don't understand what it is that is moving Hearst, but sometimes you never understand and you have to act anyway.' He should be able to figure things out and then act. . . . Ahab spends so much time trying to understand the whale and finally he says, 'I know not what the whale may mean but I must call it evil'" (164).

Seeking to explain Dority's sadness after fighting Hearst's henchman, Captain Turner, Milch turns immediately to a Melville poem, "The College Colonel," about a "kid who comes back home from the Civil War to his little village in Massachusetts," to explain how "the entire truth of what life is like absent civilization has come home to" Dority (*Deadwood* 169).

7. I wish I had thought to mention to Milch that I purposefully took the PhD oral exams, for which I used *The Makers and the Making*, on April 1, the day, significantly, that *The Confidence Man* takes place.
8. When I later visited Melody Ranch and watched Milch and some of his crew working on a scene from *John from Cincinnati* I realized that we were extemporaneously cowriting my talk in much the manner that he writes his scripts, elaborating on and extending each other's comments. See Singer for a fuller description of this collaborative process, which can be observed on some of the special features on *Deadwood* DVDs, notably "Making Episode 12."
9. For Milch's discussions of issues surrounding the historical authenticity of *Deadwood's* language, view Milch and Carradine, "The New Language of the Old West." See also Benz.
10. Opening with only a brief reference to the historical record, Douglas L. Howard devotes an entire essay, so titled, to "Why Wild Bill Hickok Had to Die."
11. In fact, *Deadwood* persistently plays with pairings on many levels, some partnerships, some alliances (a favorite word of Al's), some oppositions, many shifting and various: Swearengen and Dority, Swearengen and Trixie, Swearengen and Tolliver, Swearengen and Bullock, Swearengen and Hearst, Swearengen and Wu, Dority and Burns, Bullock and Star, Star and Trixie, Alma and Trixie, Jewel and Trixie, the Doc and Jewel. And then there are the doubled pairings: Swearengen/Trixie and Tolliver/Joanie; Bullock/Star and Wild Bill/Charlie; Alma/Bullock and Alma/Ellsworth. Some are more unlikely: Martha/Jane (Martha Jane Canary).
12. In popular culture the western hero has usually been seen as distrusting language, as silent and violent. See Jane Tompkins, *West of Everything*, for a version of that argument. Others, notably Lee Clark Mitchell, "When You Call Me That, Smile," and myself, "What if Wister Were a Woman?," have argued that the seminal popular western is in fact all about talk, and we can see Milch extending this tradition. Later in this volume, Jennilyn Merten discusses the relationship between language and emotion in the series.

Milch has commented on the film evolution of the silent western hero, which he argues is a result of the Hays Code, which forbade the kind of language used on *Deadwood*.

Introduction li

It's my experience that a good storyteller can find a way to internalize and neutralize the pernicious effect of those kinds of extraneous, controlling statutes or strictures by finding equivalence within the story that obey the terms that are . . . laid down within the code without doing violence to the emotional integrity of the character or of the story. So, if characters can't say anything obscene, you try and conceive a character for whom obscenity is a kind of fallen or pathetic expression of weakness. I believe that was the source of development of the laconic cowboy. . . . A man of few words but deep and complicated morality. (Milch and Carradine)

13. In February 2007, at David Milch's invitation, I spent a day at Melody Ranch, touring the *Deadwood* set (which was still up, though the interiors were being used to film *John from Cincinnati*), observing the writing and filming of a *John* episode, and conducting a short interview with Milch. These are excerpts of that interview, in which he also discussed work by William James, Theodore Dreiser, and Sherwood Anderson.

    Milch sometimes jokes about his debts to authors: "I try to be very careful about who I steal from. I only steal from the best. Nathaniel West wrote, I thought beautifully, about that syndrome [those who feed off celebrity, in relation to Wild Bill]" (Milch and Carradine).

14. In Singer's profile Milch comments, "Mark Twain used to say that when he would formulate a character he would suddenly realize he was meeting them for the second time; he met them the first time on the river" (196). As he often does, he uses this anecdote to provide language to describe his engagement with the Bullock character: "'I knew that there had to be a Bullock, and when I read about him it was like'—he snapped his fingers—'I met him on the river'" (196).

15. Here is the transcription from the interview:

    MG: What about R. W. B. Lewis? I see "the American Adam" lingering behind *Deadwood*.
    DM: Sure. Oh absolutely. Absolutely.
    MG: With Silas Adams and original sin.
    DM: Yeah. Yes, absolutely. And you know, Dick and I shared an office for ever so long, even after the work on *The American Literature: The Makers in the Making*.

    I don't have the space here, but an extended reading of *Deadwood*'s characters and themes in relationship to Lewis's representation of the various avatars of the American Adam would yield some interesting insights.

16. Lewis writes in the first paragraph of his acknowledgments:

    To David Milch I owe a very large and special debt of gratitude. This work began in fact as a collaborative venture with my former student, colleague, and office-sharer, the venture itself being an offshoot of a proposed television series on the James family. The series was first conceived by David Milch, and we worked it up together into twelve episodes. It fell by the wayside, however, and the collaborative biographical enterprise was eventually given up as impractical. But the book I went on to write contains—however transformed in definition and style of expression—many ideas, findings, and emphases originating in discussions and trial runs with David Milch. It is an enormous pleasure for me to record this debt, even as it is next to impossible for me to measure it. (671)

In *Edith Wharton: A Biography* (1975), Lewis wrote, "David Milch has been another *sine qua non* of this book. . . . As grateful as I am for [his practical assistance], I owe Mr. Milch even more for the wealth of suggestions he made out of his extensive literary, psychological, medical, and legal knowledge" (573). Like Alma, Wharton was pressured into marriage with a man she did not love and later found sexual fulfillment outside the boundaries of convention.

17. Milch planned to turn to another woman author to help him write Alma's future: "Alma had lied about her reason for coming out to *Deadwood*, which was to become a writer, and I hope to mine a lot of Willa Cather's experiences for her character" ("Trusting the Process").

18. After I wrote this line, which I worried was a stretch, I was pleased to hear Ian McShane comment about this scene, "This is the epiphany. I love this. . . . He [Milch] gives every character a view of the Army leaving. So you're left with a sense of community. This is Deadwood. This is what the show's about" (audio commentary 1.12).

The language Milch uses to describe community could come directly from John Steinbeck, who frequently used concepts he borrowed from ecology; in *Cannery Row* (1945), for instance, the community is described as a biological organism, with its own internal interdependent relationships. "Our best nature is when we find ourselves part of some larger organism," says Milch. "The emotional ecology of the Gem and to some extent the whole camp is disrupted by Swearengen's disempowerment" (audio commentary 2.3).

19. Handley refers to Robinson's pioneering work in "Clio Bereft of Calliope: Literature and the New Western History" (1997), in which he explores "the failure of historians to consult literature—either as a source of information, a model for historical interpretation, or a laboratory on language and meaning" and argues for the blurring of "the boundaries separating history and literature" (88–89). In the same special issue of *Arizona Quarterly*, Krista Comer makes a case "for the very active role that literature makes in the making of history," for the importance of exploring "the ways that cultural works themselves shape, influence, and prevail upon history" ("Literature, Gender Studies" 121, 127). Both argue

that when the New Western historians dismiss western literature as "mythic," they overlook a long revisionist tradition in western literature *and* historical writing, a tradition highly critical of western expansion, a tradition *Deadwood* extends. More recently Lee Clark Mitchell has argued that "the relationship between history and literature will vex western studies so long as truth is associated with narrow notions of historical pattern rather than literary insight. And to the extent that literary critics buy into this logic, western literature becomes a pale imitation not only of the actual West but of its recorded history. Style and narrative inventiveness are the first to fall by the wayside, but even subject matter limps along, victim of narrow conceptions of what constitutes the 'authentic'" ("What's Authentic?" 104).

DEADWOOD EPISODES

Season 1

Episode 1: "Deadwood." Directed by Walter Hill. Written by David Milch.
Episode 2: "Deep Water." Directed by Davis Guggenheim. Written by Malcolm MacRury.
Episode 3: "Reconnoitering the Rim." Directed by Davis Guggenheim. Written by Jody Worth.
Episode 4: "Here Was a Man." Directed by Alan Taylor. Written by Elizabeth Sarnoff.
Episode 5: "The Trial of Jack McCall." Directed by Ed Bianchi. Written by John Belluso.
Episode 6: "Plague." Directed by Davis Guggenheim. Written by Malcolm MacRury.
Episode 7: "Bullock Returns to Camp." Directed by Michael Engler. Written by Jody Worth.
Episode 8: "Suffer the Little Children." Directed by Daniel Minahan. Written by Elizabeth Sarnoff.
Episode 9: "No Other Sons or Daughters." Directed by Ed Bianchi. Written by George Putnam.
Episode 10: "Mr. Wu." Directed by Daniel Minahan. Written by Bryan McDonald.
Episode 11: "Jewel's Boot Is Made for Walking." Directed by Steve Shill. Written by Ricky Jay.
Episode 12: "Sold under Sin." Directed by Davis Guggenheim. Written by Ted Mann.

Season 2

Episode 1: "A Lie Agreed Upon, Part I." Directed by Ed Bianchi. Written by David Milch.

Episode 2: "A Lie Agreed Upon, Part II." Directed by Ed Bianchi. Written by Jody Worth.

Episode 3: "New Money." Directed by Steve Shill. Written by Elizabeth Sarnoff.

Episode 4: "Requiem for a Gleet." Directed by Alan Taylor. Written by Ted Mann.

Episode 5: "Complications" (formerly "Difficulties"). Directed by Gregg Fienberg. Written by Victoria Morrow.

Episode 6: "Something Very Expensive." Directed by Steve Shill. Written by Steve Shill.

Episode 7: "E. B. Was Left Out." Directed by Michael Almereyda. Written by Jody Worth.

Episode 8: "Childish Things." Directed by Timothy Van Patten. Written by Regina Corrado.

Episode 9: "Amalgamation and Capital." Directed by Ed Bianchi. Written by Elizabeth Sarnoff.

Episode 10: "Advances, None Miraculous." Directed by Daniel Minahan. Written by Sara Hess.

Episode 11: "The Whores Can Come." Directed by Gregg Fienberg. Written by Bryan McDonald.

Episode 12: "Boy-the-Earth-Talks-To." Directed by Ed Bianchi. Written by Ted Mann.

Season 3

Episode 1: "Tell Your God to Ready for Blood." Directed by Mark Tinker. Written by David Milch and Ted Mann.

Episode 2: "I Am Not the Fine Man You Take Me For." Directed by Dan Attias. Written by David Milch and Regina Corrado.

Episode 3: "True Colors." Directed by Gregg Fienberg. Written by Regina Corrado and Ted Mann.

Episode 4: "Full Faith and Credit." Directed by Ed Bianchi. Written by Ted Mann.

Episode 5: "A Two-Headed Beast." Directed by Daniel Minahan. Written by David Milch.

Episode 6: "A Rich Find." Directed by Tim Hunter. Written by Alix Lambert.

Episode 7: "Unauthorized Cinnamon." Directed by Mark Tinker. Written by Regina Corrado.

Episode 8: "Leviathan Smiles." Directed by Ed Bianchi. Written by Kem Nunn.

Episode 9: "Amateur Night." Directed by Adam Davidson. Written by Nick Towne and Zack Whedon.

Episode 10: "A Constant Throb." Directed by Mark Tinker. Written by W. Earl Brown.

Episode 11: "The Catbird Seat." Directed by Gregg Fienberg. Written by Bernadette McNamara.

Episode 12: "Tell Him Something Pretty." Directed by Mark Tinker. Written by Ted Mann.

DEADWOOD CAST

Seth Bullock. . . . . Timothy Olyphant
Al Swearengen . . . . Ian McShane
Alma Garret. . . . . Molly Parker
Sol Star . . . . John Hawkes
Trixie . . . . Paula Malcomson
Cy Tolliver . . . . Powers Boothe
Calamity Jane. . . . . Robin Weigert
Joanie Stubbs . . . . Kim Dickens
Charlie Utter . . . . Dayton Callie
Doc Cochran . . . . Brad Dourif
Tom Nuttall . . . . Leon Rippey
Silas Adams . . . . Titus Welliver
Wild Bill Hickok . . . . Keith Carradine
William Bullock . . . . Josh Eriksson
George Hearst . . . . Gerald McRaney
Martha Bullock. . . . . Anna Gunn
Ellsworth . . . . Jim Beaver
Johnny Burns . . . . Sean Bridgers
Con Stapleton . . . . Peter Jason
Jewel. . . . . Geri Jewell
Jack Langrishe . . . . Brian Cox
Sofia Metz . . . . Bree Seanna Wall
Francis Wolcott. . . . . Garret Dillahunt
Samuel "Nigger General" Fields . . . Franklyn Ajaye
Pete Richardson . . . . Ralph Richeson
A. W. Merrick. . . . . Jeffrey Jones
Hugo Jarry. . . . . Stephen Tobolowsky
Brom Garret. . . . . Timothy Omundson

Mr. Wu	Keone Young
Leon	Larry Cedar
Harry Manning	Brent Sexton
Reverend Smith	Ray McKinnon
Aunt Lou Marchbanks	Cleo King
Odell Marchbanks	Omar Gooding
Maddie	Alice Krige
E. B. Farnum	William Sanderson
Dan Dority	W. Earl Brown
Miss Isringhausen	Sarah Paulson
Blazanov	Pasha D. Lychnikoff
Wyatt Earp	Gale Howard
Morgan Earp	Austin Nichols
Eddie Sawyer	Ricky Jay
Andy Cramed	Zach Grenier
Hostetler	Richard Gant
Steve	Michael Harney
Jack McCall	Garret Dillahunt
Dolly	Ashleigh Kizer
Flora Anderson	Kristen Bell
Miles Anderson	Greg Cipes
Mose Manuel	Pruitt Taylor Vince
Jen	Jennifer Lutheran
Shaughnessy	Dan Hildebrand
Clell Watson	James Parks
Magistrate Clagett	Marshall Bell
Gustave	Gordon Clappe
Otis Russell	William Russ

Dirty Words in *Deadwood*

1 David Milch at Yale
An Interview

Nathaniel Lewis

Art and Tradition. Philosophy and Religion. Literature and Storytelling. Fathers and Sons. These are some of the topics that interest David Milch, and they are among the topics through which he and Nathaniel Lewis maneuver in their conversation about Deadwood. *Whereas Graulich begins with a literary historian's eye for narrative and language, Lewis approaches the series and its creator with a mix of aesthetic and personal concerns, deftly shifting from* Deadwood's *thematic representations to Milch's recollections of working with Lewis's father at Yale in the 1970s and early 1980s and back again. Through their conversation Lewis and Milch affirm that* Deadwood *exists as a diversely creative work, available for interpretation on a number of levels. Chief among them, perhaps, is Milch's stated interest in dramatizing "that we're all members of one body," even as an inhumane "failure to respect the integrity of the individual" will result from "any kind of formulaic approach" to society or art. Milch renders this last judgment in a comment about the rise, during his time at Yale, of deconstruction as a mode of interpretation; his core insight, as Lewis keenly observes, applies equally well to the multivalent and unconventional aspects of* Deadwood.

David Milch began his undergraduate studies at Yale in 1962. After a series of what he calls "fits and starts," he became an English major, mentored in large part by Robert Penn Warren and my father, R. W. B. Lewis. In the 1970s Warren and my father, recognizing David's brilliance and promise, invited him to become their colleague at Yale. During the decade or so that he spent at Yale, David taught writing and literature and assisted Warren, my father, and their colleague Cleanth Brooks on their anthology, *American Literature: The Makers and the Making* (1973).

In February 2009, during a trip to New Haven for several events

8. David Milch. "Making of Season Two Finale: 'Boy-the-Earth-Talks-To': Mr. Wu Proves Out." Bonus Features. *Deadwood: The Complete Second Season.* 2006. DVD.

at Yale, David sat down with me to discuss *Deadwood*. But because David has been part of the Warren and Lewis families from his earliest days in New Haven, our conversation inevitably moved between the personal and the professional—between the office David shared with my father in Calhoun College (Yale) and the Gem Saloon, between the Warrens' Vermont home and *Deadwood*'s Grand Central Hotel.

LEWIS: Let's start with a couple fairly straightforward questions, and then I hope we can get into some interesting territory. I've heard you say a number of times, when describing the origins of *Deadwood*, that you originally intended to do a show on ancient Rome—and that this idea had to be scrapped because HBO already had a series on Rome in the works. I gather that you kept a number of the central themes but changed the place and time. Out of all the different sites and historical moments you picked Deadwood. Why?

MILCH: I felt that it was a kind of laboratory reenactment of the larger patterns of our settlement or taking of the land, however you want to put it, and that there was a telescoping of the accessibility of that theme. This was land, literally, which had not been settled by whites at all, going into, say, 1870. But in addition to that, the first resources of what we'll call modernity were simultaneously available, so it was as if you could do the two hundred some odd years of the experiment all at once. And that appealed to me enormously. The discovery of the gold was, for a dramatist, such a kindling point. And so I had at it.

LEWIS: That tension between the past and modernity is brilliantly depicted in *Deadwood*. And thinking along those lines in terms of your own relationship to American literary and cinematic traditions: I've read a number of people argue that *Deadwood* is a radical departure from not only the Hays Code Western but from the genre itself. But I tend to see it as a reworking, and in many ways a very fond reworking, of John Ford, Sam Peckinpah . . .

MILCH: Absolutely, absolutely. I think that the strictures of the Hays Code were such that to me the revisionism was those strictures imposed upon wonderful work; the ingenuity of Ford and the other masters was in being able to sustain a kind of realism in spite of that through the creation of laconic or stoic characters, who therefore were not forced to depart from the realities of the situation by speaking too much. I felt that it wasn't so much that I was concerned with being within the tradition but that I was able to draw on my affection for it.

[At this point our conversation was interrupted, and when we picked up again, the conversation had turned to the working friendship between David and my father during the seventies and early eighties. They shared an office at Yale for much of that time, as David remembers with amusement and, perhaps, a little incredulity.]

MILCH: I used to jump into the moat and climb in through the window because I never had a key, and your dad was the only person, I think, who could have tolerated that kind of stuff. He seemed to understand it perfectly.

LEWIS: He did. In one sense I think he understood those times, the midsixties through the midseventies, very well. But he also had a heartfelt faith and wonder in you that, though not necessarily paternal, was in many ways the same faith and wonder that he had in his children—and it had little to do with your brilliance or your character . . .

MILCH: Or lack thereof . . .

LEWIS: But he believed in you.

MILCH: Well, you're very gracious to say that. In *Gatsby* the narrator remarks that one of Gatsby's great gifts was that he thought the best of people. And that was your dad. And it was very much a choice on his part. It was not that he was incapable of imagining the alternative, quite the opposite, but had it not been for that faith, I know my life would have been very, very different, because there was a great deal of evidence accumulating on the other side. And your dad understood so much about the vagaries of the heart, so it was just blessed good luck on my part.

LEWIS: That's another way of saying that he had his demons but also really a remarkable kind of strength to ignore them or to live with them. His discipline was incredible: early every morning he was at the dining-room table, writing; every evening he had cocktails with my mother and talked over his day's work. He loved his work. I don't think he ever took a day off.

MILCH: And that was, I can say for both of us, the bridge to the world, which had to be maintained every day or it would fall into disrepair, and from which there might be no return.

I'm an alcoholic, I'm every kind of addict that there is, and I can say that when I saw in my boy the beginnings of that, I was terrified. And then as I saw him come out of it a little bit, it was a sort of redemption. If you feel like you're cursed yourself, you can probably live with that, but if you feel you've cursed the next generation . . . To see someone more or less surviving, or at least soldiering on—I think your dad enjoyed that very much, and enjoyed seeing all of my fallibilities play themselves out. They don't call it the Divine Tragedy—they call it the Divine Comedy.

I would say that the tradition in which I felt myself working when I wrote *Deadwood* had much more to do with all of that . . . If we tried for a moment to believe what Joyce said, "paternity is not so much a matter of blood but an apostolic succession," then I felt much more that I was with your dad and with Mr. Warren and with Mr. Brooks, in their hospitality. They experienced the tradition in every way, in every form, and were hospitable to it in every way. I can remember Mr. Warren coming to see the first god-awful film I had worked on, in 1972, and the despair which he must have felt must have been just about complete. And yet he would not have thought not to be there.

And so in *Deadwood* the tradition of a hospitality to looking at things new, that was the tradition that I felt I was working in, trying to reencounter them, not for the sake of novelty, but just to try to imagine how it must have been. And that was the bravery that I experienced in your dad and Mr. Warren—not quite so much in Mr. Brooks because he felt that he came armed with a Christian perspective—and they kind of walked in bare-assed naked. There was a fierce intelligence and vigor to what Mr. Brooks did, but I felt that with your dad and Mr. Warren it was *de nouveau*. When your dad and I started to work on the James family, the excitement was tremendous. We were coming to it with no holds barred, and you can imagine what a wonderful example that was for a young writer.

So it was when I was working on *Deadwood*, even though *Deadwood* as a Western on television seemed so out of the blue. You know Mark Twain used to say, whenever he would be working on a character, that when the character would finally come alive—he would say, "I met him on the river." And I felt as if all of these characters I had met on the river with your dad and Mr. Warren.

LEWIS: There has been a lot of commentary on the language of *Deadwood*, but I am equally struck by your attention to *character*.
MILCH: Yes. Let me analogize a little bit with my experience with your father and circle back to the interest in character. Santayana, I believe in the essay "The Genteel Tradition in Amer-

ican Philosophy," after analyzing the hold that gentility had come to have on American letters, remarked in passing what a curiosity it was that two brothers, Henry and William James, had, in very different ways, loosened the hold of gentility. Your dad and I talked about that and lived into it. I don't know if you recall but I began to write a series that was going to be twelve episodes about the James family, trying to imagine the combination of circumstances: the paradox of being inheritors of gentility, the Calvinist perspective of their grandfather, and the enormous amount of energy that was liberated by that (you couldn't know if you were saved, but if you were rich it was a pretty good hint!), his connection with Union College—you know the story. But then the intensely specific: the father, Henry James Sr., being tutored by a man of science—his tutor when he was a little boy was Joseph Henry, who later founded the Smithsonian. In the midst of an experiment in which he was learning how changes in temperature caused air to rise, they were flying a fire kite, and the kite went into a barn, and the barn caught fire, and the boy ran ahead and was trapped in the fire, and science couldn't save him. He lost his leg in that fire, and literally did not have a leg to stand on in encountering what was happening in America—and that paradox was what saved the boys from living into the usual sequence of gentility. He developed a panicky but resourceful compulsion to flee the hold of what was happening in America, kept taking the boys from one place to another, and radically misunderstanding the nature of the experience. Henry wrote to William when William started to have children, "Above all, don't make the mistake with your children of our own torn and uprooted childhood."

So the experience of starting, say, with an essay by Santayana and going back and back and back and trying finally to let the characters—which was the way I conceived of them, the father and all the James family—come alive and speak, without the prism of criticism, this was exactly what I felt I was doing when I went on to work on *Deadwood*.

LEWIS: Part of what you're saying is that too much security or "gentility" is disrupting to the artistic imagination. My father and Red Warren were certainly hospitable, to use your word, but they were not interested in followers, they were interested in . . .

MILCH: They were interested in the *work*.

For an artist, for a storyteller, the reason that the idea that "paternity is not so much a matter of blood but an apostolic succession" is so important is because that is really all you have. When you're trying to let the story come alive, you have only the example of bravery as witnessed in the lived experience of others. "Followers" is another version of an audience, confirming the validity of what you're doing, and you know as an artist that the only confirmation is if the world comes alive. And it's reborn every day, and what you did the day before is no guarantee of what will happen in the day's work. The combination of your dad and Mr. Warren and to some extent Mr. Brooks, for an aspiring writer, was magical, simply because they were so different in the way that they comported themselves personally—and that difference served to cancel out for me any thought that there was one way. And so, as fallen and as incoherent as my life was at that time, I knew it was no excuse. Your dad knew a way out of hell and didn't proselytize—but he showed it.

LEWIS: We're talking about the relation of the artist to the literary and historical past, what Eliot called "tradition and the individual talent." Paradoxically or not, that sense of being orphaned or uprooted that you're describing in yourself in many ways constitutes an important American tradition. Do you feel that as you came into awareness of models and paths, that it was not to reject a past but to see that what had looked like isolation, loneliness, despair, whatever word you want to use, was actually central to one of these American stories?

MILCH: Gradually, to come to understand that was a liberation. But there are certain rooms, by which I mean the rooms of recovery, where there's a formulation about the personality construct that expresses itself toward that kind of behavior by saying, "I'm the piece of shit at the center of the universe" [laughter]— that combination of no self-esteem with self-centeredness. To realize that part of that self-centeredness is to think it started with you, and with no proselytizing whatever, is to live into the realization that there was a tradition.

You know, when I was a kid, it was understood that the mark of excellence in a writer was not so much his writing but how well he wrote drunk. You were supposed to be an alcoholic. When I left Yale, my teacher at Iowa was Richard Yates, who was a fall-down drunk, and Kurt Vonnegut was a drunk, and Vance Bourjaily. And I can remember starting to sleep in the streets at Iowa and thinking to myself, "You know, I wonder if I've got a problem here." Then I said, "Naahhh"—this is what you were supposed to do. That was such a curious and potentially lethal combination.

What I really was up to that point was a full-time drunk. I had been admitted to Yale, so I had to find the absolutely most useless major, so I was an African religion major. When my best friend was killed in an auto accident between our sophomore and junior years, I began to write about that—his family—and then I thought, well jeez, maybe I could be an English major—and just in that sort of fits and starts, with no thought and no recognition of the tradition, nothing. Because it wasn't enough that you were supposed to be drunk, you were supposed to be actively hostile toward any idea of utility, reading, or anything else. Even when I graduated: what my father really liked about the graduation was that as I got my Phi Beta Kappa key, I passed out.

So in that connection I think of *Deadwood*, in which the image of the saloon—and compulsions of gambling, whoring, and so on—is the matrix out of which governance grows: the fact that a guy like Swearengen is able to recognize in the compulsions of Bullock the possibility of a benign mutation of his own obsessions. Not that Swearengen understands that consciously; he thinks he hates Bullock—but he knows that if there can be some sort of collaboration, that that's the possibility of civilization, however fallen it will be. One of my favorite scenes in *Deadwood* is in the second season when he and Dority and Johnny Burns are up on the balcony and they see way off in the distance they're starting to set up the telegraph wires. Swearengen is morose, and he says, "Messages from invisible sources, or what some people think of as progress." And Dority, who has a cheerful mentality, says, "Ain't the heathens use smoke signals?" And Swearengen says, "How's that a fuckin' recommendation?"

What you see in Swearengen is a guy whose intuitions, which are all constructive, have to navigate through all of these obsessions, which are all fanciful. And by "fancy" I mean as opposed to truly imaginative associations. When they get together to form the government, he says, "Well, serve 'em something," and it turns out they have some canned peaches. Thereafter, whenever there's a town meeting, Swearengen insists that there has to be canned peaches because he doesn't know what made the first one work. And even when a guy goes into an anaphylactic shock, he says, "Keep serving them the goddamned peaches." That's the way we are in trying to evolve a government. We don't know why what works works, so we develop all these mystic attachments to things which are really just fanciful and accidental. But I think that if finally God were asked to explain "what the hell do you leave humans around for?" he'd say, "Because they make me laugh." They're so lost, humans are, and yet there's this tenacity that expresses itself in incoherences of every single kind. In a way, look back at that office that your dad and I shared, the chaos of both of those desks, and me climbing in through the window—and yet the work got done.

LEWIS: One of my favorite things about *Deadwood* is your capacity to manifest a stunning presence, visually explosive, which is always troubled by invisible ghosts on the margins. The isolation of Deadwood Gulch is really complicated by Yankton and Montana, and more broadly by each character's past. I wonder if you could comment on your sense of the ghostly or spectral surrounding that vibrant presence.

MILCH: It's a lot like life, isn't it? We're all past haunted, and yet what makes God laugh, to recklessly pursue that idea, is that against all of that hauntedness, we keep going. What I enjoyed about the scene when Swearengen is talking about his past is the way he was trying to explain it to himself. He could not accept the fact that it was his past. What he said was, "You've changed the way you're sucking my prick—because I'm not the kind of guy who doesn't get a hard-on."[1] So here you see the tremendous weight not only of the Freudian implications of having had his middle finger cut off by modernity—which is Hearst—but also by what his mother had done, and the idea that he was being held back from rejoining her on a ship where clearly she had gone to get away from him. But in his imagination she had changed her mind and wanted him to break free, and he was being held back. And the conclusion of that scene, where finally he comes back to the present, reminds me of "Little Gidding," in which Eliot says, "We shall never cease from the journey, and the object of all shall be to arrive at the place where we began and know it for the first time."[2] The place where we began is the scene with that girl. At the end he says, "They hold you down from behind, then you wonder why you're helpless." And she says, "I don't like it either, when they hold you down." And he says, "I guess I do that when I hold your fuckin' hair," and she says, "No," and he says, "Well bless you for a fuckin' fibber." And that is how we go on, telling lies to ourselves.

And that's the blessing of art. Kierkegaard said, "Life has to be lived forwards, and it can only be understood backwards." For me I show up every day and I refuse to plan what I'm going to write. I try to put the characters in this situation and then see what happens. There's a prayer that one says at the beginning of the day, which is "I offer myself to thee," and that can be either God or art, "to build with me and to do with me as thou wilt. Relieve me of the bondage of self that I may better do thy will." And I try to be available to the possibilities of the characters in that moment, without superimposing "this is how it should end" or "this is where it should go." It imposed on everyone else because they never had the scenes before we began to shoot, but it did, I think, subordinate, as much as possible, everything except for the vital energies of these materials in all their contradiction. And so then all of those things began to superimpose themselves: the past and the present, the simultaneity of all those things—and that's as close as I get to fun. [Laughter]

LEWIS: You're talking in a sense about what a Buddhist might call the thusness of art, its presentness or presence. I know that you've cited often Robert Penn Warren's lines about the "pain of the past"...

MILCH: "This / Is the process whereby pain of the past in its pastness / May be converted into the future tense / Of Joy."

LEWIS: What I love about that line, and also the lines you cited from "Little Gidding," is that they're not giving you an easy present. That is, you're working in between the pain of the past and the possibility of a future joy. We might say that art is the thusness that you have.

MILCH: Exactly. I think that every principle of organization of human behavior is a thusness—but so many of the thusnesses bring their own set of jokes, distort government, all sorts of things. And the reason that I was so interested in *Deadwood* in terms of the gold is that gold is a lie agreed upon. It has no intrinsic meaning; it's just the energy that is liberated through the collective embrace of an illusion. And there's a tremendous organizing power in that. The very neutrality of the symbol allows all sorts of the defects of the heart to be accommodated there and to express themselves through the symbol.

One episode was called "Unauthorized Cinnamon," in which Hearst is talking to Odell, the son of his cook, and he says that gold is the chance to "help your people" because of "our agreement that gold has value." There's an irony within that irony, of course. You've probably heard me say that I think that our fundamental identity is collective rather than individual, or to use your term our thusness is collective rather than individual. And yet all of the appurtenances of civilization, particularly of modernity, go toward making us feel like individuals. Art is, I believe, the gift that whatever spirit informs the universe gives us that allows us to organize and still to have a collective thusness rather than an individual thusness.

LEWIS: Thinking back to Henry James, I'm teaching *The Golden Bowl* this week, and it strikes me that so much of what you're saying about *Deadwood* is true of that novel, right down to the symbolism of the gold . . .

MILCH: The gold!

LEWIS: And both the novel and *Deadwood* convey complex characters caught in a compelling but fragile narrative structure that's constantly being undone by their legacies of the past, or by forms of desire . . .

MILCH: Yes, and I think ultimately the seeming undoing is in fact a revelation of a deeper unity. So that when the little boy is dying, ultimately that's an opportunity. So when his mother is just about to let him go, when he's in the coffin, and then she runs back in, and feels she can't let him go, and finally lets him go again, she finally understands that that's the way she can stay with him — by realizing that the *seeming* separation is the illusion.

LEWIS: It's a beautiful turn because common sense would suggest just the opposite.

MILCH: Exactly — and that everything makes us feel that without a sense of ego, without a sense of our individuality, we ain't going to spend too much time around here — and yet understand our deepest identity as being in the collective. That's why I had the minister preach from Paul, saying, "If the hand shall say, because I am not the foot I am not a member of the body of Christ." Just because it misunderstands doesn't mean it's not a member of the body.[3]

He has a tumor. There's something called Capgras syndrome, where the pressure of the tumor affects the temporal lobe in such a way that if a kid get hits on the head, sometimes he'll see his parents and he'll say, "What did you do with my parents?" and they'll say, "What do you mean?" and he'll say, "Well you *look* like my parents." That's because there has been some trauma, and the emotional associations that he has with his parents are lost, so it looks to him that, though they have the appearance of his parents, they must be impostors. There's a moment when Bullock and Star, in trying to allay the minister's terror, say, "I'm from Etobicoke, Ontario," and "I'm from Vienna, Austria." By a series of lived associations he remembers, and that sense of isolation, the terror of isolation—where I see the world but I have no emotional attachment to it—is allayed. But we live into that tension every moment.

LEWIS: It's brilliant to apply that to the American West, which in many ways is a history of trauma that is then erased by mythologies of forgetting: the West as the land of the future . . .

MILCH: Manifest destiny . . .

LEWIS: And so the remembrance of the past may provide some deeper access to the troubled present, but it is bound up in national myths of trauma and forgetting. To try to come to terms with these traumas, past and present, seems enormously complicated.

MILCH: You know, we were not unique in the postulation of those myths. When a culture intuits that it's about to be overwhelmed, there's a tendency to postulate an alternate reality as transcending the seeming futility of the present. So when the Indians came to understand, at least intuitively, that their culture was about to be overrun, there came Wovoka and the Ghost Dance, in which they were impervious to the bullets which seemed to kill them, and therefore were able to walk right into the gunfire. Or consider the parallels with the Islamists who, as they experienced the influx of the West and modernity, postulated this reality where if I kill myself I immediately go to the true reality.

We are capable—and it's the terror of our species—of the most suicidal mythologies, one of which, as Conrad understood better than anyone among our storytellers, is the idea of our superiority: that it is just as suicidal to deny the humanity of the Indian, ultimately just as suicidal, as to walk into bullets. Thus we have the image of Kurtz thinking that he's going into the jungle to convert the natives to Christianity and within two years understanding that what he really wanted was to see human heads on the spike.

LEWIS: I think you're saying that individual ego gets caught up in cultural mythologies, overwhelming our understanding of history and literature, complicating tradition. You spoke earlier of "the prism of criticism" as a problem. Going back to your own relationship with Yale and New Haven, and your relationship with tradition: my father and Red Warren and Cleanth Brooks were coming out of a tradition that was being challenged at Yale during the 1970s and early eighties. You were there for some of the theory wars, the arrival of deconstruction, and dramatically new ways of responding to tradition and the written word. Did you feel those tensions?

MILCH: You know, Hillis Miller had the office right on the other side of the door, as part of the same suite. It was a wonderful thing to see the civility that obtained between Prof. Miller and your dad, who could not abide each other's perspectives. That was precious to me because I hated those who were supplanting the Red Warrens and R. W. B. Lewises; I hated in terms of what we were just talking about: there was no thusness. It was turning things into a kind of parlor game and trying to find new words simply for their novelty, which obscured the meaning of things—there was this secret code. And yet so long as the dialogue remained civil, I don't think anyone minded; certainly I didn't have a problem with it. But invariably there is a terrible danger when you impose any kind of convention. That's why I pray: relieve me of the bondage of self, of the idea that there is a new approach, a new code, that will reveal the true dynamics, which are totally different from the apparent dynamics of things. All of that horseshit ultimately is an excuse to be inhumane.

At one level what is inhumane is the failure to respect the integrity of the individual work, and then in another regard just drop "work" out of the last sentence: it's the failure to respect the integrity of the individual, and that's the danger of any kind of formulaic approach. That was the blessing of working with your dad and Mr. Warren and Mr. Brooks: you go back to the thing itself, and you encounter it on its own terms, and you pray to be relieved of the bondage of preexisting expectations or interpretation. So at one level I knew it was time to go, but it was time to go when all of that stuff started to take over simply because I had been blessed to receive the teaching that I needed, and now it was time to teach myself. I use that in both senses, because you aren't an artist if you don't recognize the tradition and try to pass it on. And so I always have beginning writers with me who are my interns, and in that regard I try in a small way to honor the gift that I was given by your father and Mr. Warren.

LEWIS: And in so many ways everything you're saying applies to *Deadwood*, for example the various impositions of certain kinds of codes or orders that are ultimately never going to be as perfect as they seem like they're going to be . . . And I'm reminded that I've read in a few different places about the moral relativism of *Deadwood*. But one could just as easily argue that you're not pursuing inhumanity but the depths of humanity.

MILCH: And that morality can never be anything but relative because morality presupposed subject-object relationships, dualities. The whole argument of *Deadwood*, and of the Reverend's speech, is that we're all members of one body. To go back to the Jameses for a moment, it was William James who introduced me to the work of Feuerbach, who argued that we are literally each of us the sense organs of some larger entity, and in that the community of spirit.[4] I'll leave it to Feuerbach and others much more learned than I to verify the truth of that assertion as a cosmology, but I can tell you that in art it is absolutely true. Your dad, among his kindnesses to me, sponsored my teaching college seminars, and the title which he gave to the seminar was "Strategies of Indirection, the Tactics of Fictive Persuasion." And in art we are certainly the sense organs of some larger entity. It's the tactic of art, and the content of art, and that's enough for me.

LEWIS: We've been talking about the relationship between the present, past, and future, and it seems to me that in *Deadwood*, on the one hand, there's a sense of the West as directing modernity, but on the other hand, there's this sense that the West is always already past—that even Lewis and Clark, as they're seeing these landscapes for the first time, are imagining them as gone. Were you consciously working through that in *Deadwood*?

MILCH: The place of death, the place where the sin of murder is committed, becomes the schoolhouse, in which there is this sort of mystic insistence that the tree be allowed to grow through the roof. So that when Jane is playing "Duck Duck Goose" with the children, she's rediscovering a childhood that she never had. It's understood that all of the corruption of the past has to be absorbed if the present is to be understood as the present, that it contains all of our past sinfulness without remediation.

And yet as paradoxical as it seems, life does go on. The world is not going to end when America ends. Again to recur to Fitzgerald, the beating on, the boat against the current, borne back ceaselessly to the past. To recur to one of the things we said at the beginning, it was a reenactment of original sin, simultaneous with a vision of the end of things. That's the truth of every day, whether we realize it or not: ultimately to be able to see in the end of things not the end but the end of *things* and the continuing rebirth of thusness.

Notes

1. Swearengen says: "It's you that's changed the level of your suction somehow; that's the sum and substance of it."
2. We shall not cease from exploration
   And the end of all our exploring

    Will be to arrive where we started
    And know the place for the first time.
3. At Wild Bill Hickok's funeral (in "The Trial of Jack McCall"), Reverend Smith refers to Paul's letter in 1 Corinthians: "He tells us, the eye cannot say unto the hand, I have no need of thee. Nor again the head to the feet, I have no need of thee. . . . He says that there should be no schism in the body but that the members should have the same care, one to another, and where one member suffers, all the members suffer with it."
4. Ludwig Andreas Feuerbach (1804–72), German philosopher.

2   Last Words in *Deadwood*

Brian McCuskey

"I was interested in how people improvised the structures of a society when there was no law to guide them," David Milch told Mark Singer. One way, Brian McCuskey argues, is by writing, by making a "transition from orality to literacy, from oaths and handshakes to contracts and signatures." Chronicling a "pivotal moment in frontier history," the series, he argues, "tell[s] the story of Deadwood putting itself on paper, as a line item in the county register and a dot on the territory map." This process, of course, has everything to do with the evolution of capitalism, and Milch's representation of it cuts far deeper into American cultural history than does John Ford's depiction of a newspaper reporter in The Man Who Shot Liberty Valance *who is told to "print the legend."*

McCuskey finds numerous examples of a surprising trope in the series, writing "as both an act of representation and an object of interpretation." He is the first of a series of critics in this volume to use poststructuralist theory to make sense of the series' "paper trail." It is perhaps ironic that David Milch worked at Yale at the precise time when Jacques Derrida and the Yale School first rose to prominence; in his interview with Nathaniel Lewis, he even hints at his dislike of the implications of deconstructive analysis. However, by turning to Derrida's discussions of "paper ghosts" and his linking of "writing, transcendence, and death" to explore the "self-negation that haunts all forms of writing," McCuskey ably demonstrates that Derrida's methods provide insight into the goings-on in Deadwood.

First Words

After an establishing shot of a Montana territory jailhouse at night, the series opener of HBO's *Deadwood* cuts to a close-up of Seth Bullock's hands: he dips a pen into ink with his left, switches it to his right, and puts it to page. The camera tilts up, revealing the sling on his injured right arm and resting on his face. From behind bars comes the first line of dialogue: "Is that some sort of a letter, Marshal?" asks the imprisoned horse thief. "Journal," replies Bullock. "Journal," repeats the prisoner, surprised: "Good" (1.1). His surprise reflects our own: we may not know Bullock yet, but we do know plenty of other western marshals — Will Kane, Wyatt Earp, Rooster Cogburn, Matt Dillon — and they do not, as a rule, keep diaries. The prisoner again interrupts Bullock: "You know, I was going to Deadwood, same as you." Now his impatience reflects our own: we do not watch Westerns — or subscribe to HBO, for that matter — to watch rugged leading men sit quietly writing. Bullock finishes his entry, puts down the pen, tucks the journal into his coat pocket, and resigns himself to the necessary exposition:

THIEF: No law at all, in Deadwood? Is that true?
BULLOCK: Being on Indian land.
THIEF: So then you won't be a marshal?
BULLOCK: Taking goods there to open a hardware business.
    Me and my partner. (1.1)

Returning to this scene after spending three seasons in Deadwood, we know all this already, so let us instead consider a nagging question. Whatever happened to that journal? It never reappears in Deadwood, hidden away for thirty-six episodes in the long black coat that Bullock wraps tightly around himself. Perhaps the journal, as a symbol, conveys enough meaning in this first scene that it can safely retire offstage, its work done. It does underscore the first plot point — Bullock closes the book on his old life as a lawman in Montana in order to start fresh as an entrepreneur in Deadwood — and it also suggests everything we will need to know about the psychology of our morally conflicted protagonist, as literate and thoughtful as he is violent and impulsive. Bullock yearns to understand and express his inner self, but that self remains mysterious and dangerous, something best apprehended in a jailhouse at night, described in sentences that no one else may read, confined to a black book — seen just once, by a condemned man — and carried next to the heart.

The journal, however, reveals as much about Bullock's environment as it does about his character: out here in the territories, far from civilization, the act of writing is remarkable, drawing the attention of both the camera and the thief. The thief's attention wanders almost immediately—all he can manage to say is "good" before changing the subject to Deadwood—but the camera carefully frames and tracks Bullock until he completes the day's entry. The scene thus splits off the thief's perspective, in which Bullock's writing is peripheral, from our own, in which the writing remains in focus, as important to us as it is to Bullock. In the nineteenth-century West it is hard for even a marshal to get much writing done—his arm shot, his concentration likewise—but the journal affords a glimpse of a more civilized future, when the establishment of law and order will in turn permit the rise of literacy, education, and culture. As an audience seeking excitement, we are glad when Bullock stands from his desk to prove himself foremost a man of action, but if the badge on his coat gives him license to kill, then the journal in his coat licenses us to enjoy the killing, since we know that it paves the way for schools and libraries. The end of the scene underscores this point: after Bullock thwarts a lynch mob by hanging the thief himself, brutally but "under color of law," he carefully notes down the thief's last words for his sister. His partner, Sol Star, waving a shotgun from a wagon loaded with hardware goods, covers Bullock as the mob grows angrier: "Move the fuck back, while my partner . . . while my partner's taking his sweet-ass time writing whatever the fuck he's writing over there!" Bullock then shames the mob into accepting the note for delivery; having done what little he can to civilize Montana, he leaps on the wagon with Star and lights out for the Black Hills.

In following Bullock to Deadwood, this essay argues that writing—as both an act of representation and an object of interpretation—remains a focus of the series, whose creator, David Milch, continues to ask questions about the status and value of the written word on the frontier, questions that tend rudely to interrupt the civilizing process: "Is that some sort of a letter, Marshal?" As Deadwood evolves from unofficial camp to incorporated town, one visible sign of progress is all the paper that accumulates; like Charlie Utter in his freight office but with more patience, we must sort through the letters, newspapers, telegrams, banknotes, receipts, titles, warrants, notices, speeches, contracts, and treaties that pile higher episode by episode. Al Swearengen may prefer to do "no fucking paperwork" while running Deadwood from the back office of his saloon, but the course of history is against him (1.11); if he and the other principals are to survive the political transition from camp to town, they must make a corresponding transition from orality to literacy, from oaths and handshakes to contracts and signatures. In his analysis of the development of democracy in the early years of the United States, Larzer Ziff describes this transition as "the powerful drift from immanence to representation in both literature and society" (xi); the written word allows individuals to abstract themselves from their bodies and to enter as citizens into political, social, and economic relations that transcend the here and now. As Deadwood joins the republic a century later, it immediately drifts in the same direction.

Chronicling the birth of civilization in the Black Hills would be ambitious enough, but what interests Milch more than the general rise of literacy within the camp is the acute growing pains experienced variously by its individuals. Borrowing from Herman Melville, Milch has said that a good dramatic scene "spins against the way it drives"; that is, the subtext of psychological tension and emotional friction tends to warp the overall trajectory of the scene, bending the plotline into a more interesting and pleasing dramatic arc (Milch, "TV's Great Writer"). The same can be said of the entire series: near the end of the third season, the children of Deadwood march single-file behind their teacher toward the new schoolhouse, but for the adults watching the procession, the route to literacy has been more roundabout, full of complications and difficulties. "If there was a drift toward representation," Ziff argues, "there was always an undertow of immanence" (xi). The adults do not find it as easy as their children to exchange a preliterate sense of self, securely anchored to the old familiar body standing here and speaking now, for a newly written self that seems alien because of its indifference—and even hostility—to the presence of the person who sits and writes. Exploring this pivotal moment in frontier history,

Deadwood dramatizes the specific psychological effects of a general philosophical paradox described by Jacques Derrida: "the value or effect of transcendentality is linked necessarily to the possibility of writing and of 'death'" ("Signature" 316). On the one hand, writing extends "the range of the voice and of gesture" for the writer, who may then overleap "an empirical boundary in the form of space and time" (311); on the other, because writing thus presumes "a break in presence" of the writer, whose words no longer need him, his demise is "inscribed in the structure of the mark" (316). Precisely the transcendental assumption that Bullock makes in the first scene—that a journal or a letter can conserve and preserve the self, saving it from dissolution and death—does not hold in grimy Deadwood, where the literacy and mortality rates seem to correspond directly. Not much point keeping a journal in a place where written words are always last ones.

The Paper Trail

The series tells the story of Deadwood putting itself on paper, as a line item in the county register and a dot on the territory map: "We study for our fucking lives," says Swearengen at the end of the second season, reading through the proposed terms of annexation to the United States (2.12). That "founding document" represents a new beginning for the camp, now a town, but it also marks the end of a very long paper trail that stretches all the way back to the twenty-dollar rent that Star and Bullock pay Swearengen upon arrival in Deadwood (2.12). Swearengen receives their money along with gold from the prospector Ellsworth, who keeps a running tab in the saloon: the mix of notes and nuggets in Swearengen's cash box shows the local economy in transition, with paper currency floating in from outside Deadwood to circulate alongside the precious metals mined from its streams. Up to this point prospectors have had little choice but to exchange their gold directly for women, whiskey, and poker chips: with no bank in town, and with Swearengen's road agents on the prowl, they must both assess and secure the value of the day's haul through the medium of saloon credit. Only Swearengen accumulates capital, since the prospectors must quickly spend rather than save their profits, but his wealth will grow only as fast as those prospectors can physically carry gold from strike to saloon. For his wealth to grow exponentially rather than linearly, Swearengen must relax his stranglehold and allow Deadwood's economy to modernize and expand through banking, which converts gold into paper—not only currency but also deposit receipts, promissory notes, and loan agreements—and thus encourages long-term investments in business and property rather than immediate gratifications of the flesh. It may seem to run counter to Swearengen's business interests, but allowing the widow Alma Garret to found the first bank in Deadwood proves him a shrewd speculator. The faster the bank converts gold into paper, the faster the value of the camp will grow, and the more eager the territory will become to annex it—on terms that will pay dividends for Swearengen.

 The civilizing process converts not only the gold but also the land itself into paper. In the first season, as Magistrate Clagett explains, the statutes of the Northwest Ordinance guarantee "that a citizen can have title to any land unclaimed or unincorporated by simple usage" (1.9). Ownership depends on someone personally occupying and actively improving the land, as Ellsworth explains to Alma: "Well, anyways, I'm glad to keep your title good working the surface" (1.9). When the territory annexes Deadwood as a whole, however, the prospectors will have to exchange their informal claims for formal deeds: words rather than work will keep the titles good. That moment of conversion—from turf into text—unnerves the prospectors, who worry that the politicians in Yankton, capital of the Dakota Territory, will exact a steep commission by stripping them of their property. Worry turns to panic in the second season after Francis Wolcott, agent for the capitalist George Hearst, conspires with Yankton to circulate a rumor that the claims will be invalidated; Wolcott then enlists Cy Tolliver, Swearengen's business rival, to buy up claims cheaply from prospectors eager to sell out. Whereas the conversion of gold into notes helps to grow the wealth of the local community, the conversion of land into deeds has the opposite effect. Once Tolliver duly signs over the stack of claims to Hearst, much of the Black Hills can be folded up and tucked into the wallet of one man who has never even been there in person.

As the hills go into Hearst's pocket, Swearengen struggles to keep the camp itself in his own: he has the same fear of losing political influence to outsiders that the prospectors have about property ownership. Each morning he stakes his claim on the town by appearing in person on a balcony overlooking the main thoroughfare; each evening he keeps his title good by working over anyone stupid enough to challenge him. In the first few episodes, Swearengen commands a bird's-eye view of both friends and enemies as they scurry and whisper in the street below; the comings and goings of the stagecoach alert him to any new developments in camp. However, as soon as outside parties start taking a political and economic interest in Deadwood, Swearengen's far-sighted vision becomes useless, because now there is no one to watch: those parties never appear in Deadwood, exerting pressure through the growing postal service as well as the new technology of the telegraph. "Invisible messages from invisible sources," he complains, "or what some people think of as progress" (2.1). To counter opponents who represent themselves in writing rather than present themselves in person, a strategy that "blinkers [his] judgment of motive," Swearengen must learn to apply his powers of interpretation to scrutinizing letters instead of faces and deciphering messages rather than gestures, so that he can continue to survey the increasingly abstract political landscape (2.1). When Charlie Utter opens his freight office in the first season, Swearengen snaps, "Nice sign, blocking my fucking view," but his visual field will soon have to expand to include written signs, which bear watching even more closely than actual people (1.9). By the start of the second season, when he receives a "pricey little personal note" from the governor, Swearengen has so much reading to do that he resorts first to a magnifying glass and then to a pair of spectacles, which he wears grudgingly for the rest of the series: "Yes," he sighs, "it has fallen to this" (2.1).

At the same time, Swearengen must learn not only to read but also to edit documents, to apply pressure back against his invisible enemies: the "instruments they use to fuck people up the ass," he says of governmental propaganda, "can be turned against them"

(2.9). He may miss his old instruments—"Don't I yearn for the days," he laments, "when a draw across the throat made fucking resolution?" (3.1)—but the time has come to slash copy rather than arteries. Behind his massive desk Swearengen immerses himself in the paperwork necessary to secure his own and the camp's interests, not only revising the terms of annexation but also replying to messages from Yankton, addressing envelopes stuffed with bribes, editing articles and publishing letters in the *Deadwood Pioneer*, and drafting the structure of an ad hoc local government. For all his grumbling, Swearengen proves a quick study, gifted with a "keen editorial sense," as journalist A. W. Merrick sniffs, at first annoyed by the interference (1.6); however, when the war of words escalates between Deadwood and Yankton, Merrick cheerfully collaborates with Swearengen, using the power of the press to circulate rumors and waft suspicion. Swearengen never overcomes his distaste for paperwork—yelling at Merrick that he wishes there were "any part of your rag I could just fucking read without having to evaluate how it fucking wafts!" (3.11)—but his editorial sense grows keen enough for him both to "parse Yankton's proposal" and to dictate its terms (2.12). Once Deadwood joins the territory and holds elections, currency will pile up in Swearengen's safe faster than ballots in the box—faster even than the mail on Utter's floor, the telegrams on Blazanov's desk, the back issues in Merrick's office, the receipts in Alma's bank, and the warrants in Bullock's file. No wonder that the town goes up in smoke in 1879; by then the paper trail ends in a firetrap.

The Dotted Line

All that paper constitutes the thin skin sloughed off a growing body of representations that would otherwise have no substance: the abstract system of economic, political, and social relations that will soon govern the circulation of wealth, the ownership of property, and the distribution of power in Deadwood. Entering into those relations is simple enough, because all the system requires is your name on the dotted line—here, and here, and here again. "Paper," says Derrida, speaking of its history in relation to the law, "often became the place where one took possession of oneself and became a legal subject," whose identity and agency "rested on the ideal assumption of self-identification by a signature on a body of paper" ("Paper" 15). To emphasize this point, *Deadwood* repeatedly enlists its audience to witness the signing of documents; its signature scene *is* the signature scene—there, and there, and there again. The series begins with Alma signing her proxy over to Bullock and ends with her signing her property over to Hearst, and in between there is a lot of "wrist business," as bartender Johnny Burns calls it, of "brief but crucial importance" (2.9). We witness Commissioner Jarry signing the articles of incorporation, Trixie the prostitute signing bank receipts first as a depositor and then as a teller, Leon the junkie signing his own bank receipt, hotelier E. B. Farnum requesting Sol Star's "John Hancock" for the receipt of camp funds, Bullock cosigning a property loan with the town drunk Steve Fields, the livery owner Hostetler writing his will on a chalkboard, Steve signing on the same chalkboard a confession that he molested Bullock's horse, the con artist Alice Isringhausen signing a confession of blackmail, and Star signing the deed to henchman Silas Adams's house. Even the hoople-head extras in the background get in on the act, signing up for jury duty, signing in at the vaccination tent, and signing away their claims.

All these signatures—and there is still more wrist business we hear about secondhand—are signs of progress and civilization, although each scene tends to spin against the way it drives: for example, to seal their deal, Adams spits in his palm and extends it to Star, who declines to shake hands according to a camp ritual that has already been repeated many times in the series. "Oh, no," he says, pointing to the inkwell and pen. "That's what these are for" (3.2). As a former lawyer, Adams should know better, but on the other hand, perhaps he does: a signature may not yet stick properly, not in a place so new to law and order. The same doubt about signatures arises elsewhere: when Steve signs the loan to purchase the livery, he presses down so hard—as if trying to engrave rather than ink his name on the paper—that he breaks the nib of the pen; Leon makes a similar gesture, handing his receipt to Alma only after carefully blowing his signature dry. Alma rolls her eyes, but she must make allowances for customers used to backing their word by making it flesh—swearing, spitting, shaking—rather than making a mark backed only by paper. Even Bullock, who puts his full faith in the bank, finds outside the bank that paper is too flimsy to support his signature; when he hesitates about how to cosign the livery loan in the street, Trixie must turn around, lean over, and literally back his signature.

The stock of the paper and the permanence of the ink are crucial because, for the signature to work as it should, all parties must accept that it will represent the signer now and in future—or rather, as Derrida insists, in a now that is forever, because it "marks and retains his having-been present in a past now, which will remain a future now, and therefore in a now in general, in the transcendental form of nowness" ("Signature" 328). The signature's games with time and infinity give rise to further confusion in Deadwood, particularly for Steve and Hostetler, who stubbornly refuse to meet but who also each refuse to sign the livery papers before the other does so; they understand that "a handshake signaling the transaction's completion" is no longer "absolutely required," as Alma says, but they do not understand that the sequence in which they sign is absolutely irrelevant (3.5). Bullock finally breaks the deadlock by staging the transcendental nowness of the signature as a farce: the two men synchronize their watches and sign simultaneously but separately, on opposite sides of the camp, when Bullock fires his pistol at exactly ten o'clock. As soon as one crisis is surmounted, however, another immediately arises: Steve demands that Hostetler return to him the chalkboard on which he signed his confession of bestiality, but when they find the board, it has already been accidentally wiped off, which causes Steve to suspect a trick and to call Hostetler a liar. "I don't know it's the actual board," Steve whines. "There's no more fucking writing on it!" (3.5). Insulted, Hostetler flies into a rage, but Bullock still tries to mediate between the men: "This is the board! For Christ's sake, what difference does the rest of it make?" Steve will never be satisfied, however, because the "actual" board with writing on it can never be produced; now blank again, this board will always differ from that one—which is to say, from itself. Signing in chalk rather than ink produces a nasty paradox: precisely because the signature was so easily wiped away, it can never be erased. It remains forever inscribed on what Steve calls "the true fucking board," which exists only in that transcendental nowness, where neither party to the signature will ever be able to clear his name (3.5). Hostetler realizes that the only way out is death; blowing out his brains all over the wall, he cleans the slate.

Steve lives on, but poetic justice soon catches up with him: a horse kicks him in the head, and he spends the rest of the series in a catatonic stupor. Steve thus cannot avoid paying extra interest on the price that a signature always exacts in return for transcendence: "By definition," says Derrida, "a written signature implies the actual or empirical nonpresence of the signer" ("Signature" 328). The signature does not merely stand for the signer, so that he *need not* be present anymore; rather, he *cannot* be present anymore, because the signature now functions—assuming his identity, exercising his agency—as if he were absent. Like Steve, the signer is no longer quite all there; to take possession of oneself on paper is to lose possession of oneself in person. Steve is so far gone that he has no more signatures left in him; because the new owner "couldn't authorize it," Star takes it upon himself to reorder supplies for the livery (3.10). Steve's helpless condition exaggerates the dissociation of represented and immanent selves that everyone else in Deadwood will also experience to some degree—the "situation being fluid," notes Star, "and not likely to get less so for a while" (3.10). Signing one's name may not always cause brain damage, but it does often produce dizzy spells, whether you are a lady like Alma, who fails to recognize her own initials on a currency receipt, or a prostitute like Trixie, who gasps when she mistakenly appends "—the whore" rather than her surname on a deposit slip (2.9). Even if one does get one's own name right, as when Hostetler chalks his will on that same confounded board, the self divides just as fluidly to produce alienation from rather than identification with the signature: "This isn't my will," he snarls only the next day, before erasing the board to start fresh—with Steve's confession (2.6).

A will, of course, implies the ultimate nonpresence of its signer, but death necessarily taints all signatures; once completed, the transaction no longer absolutely requires either a sound mind or a sound body. Alice Isringhausen, the femme fatale who seduces Adams, finds herself in a tight spot: Swearengen will kill her if she does not sign a letter of confession, but he also may well kill her if she does, since her signature would immediately make her expendable. Alice's predicament, in which she cannot be sure she is not signing her own death warrant, signifies a larger existential question that obtains during this period of transition from immanent to represented selfhood. Derrida speaks of "the paper ghosts that we have learned to trust" ("Paper" 15)—all the documents that embody us as twenty-first-century legal subjects—but the residents of nineteenth-century Deadwood have not yet learned to trust that such documents will conditionally represent rather than completely replace them, turning not paper but people into ghosts, immaterial in both senses of the word. Here is another reason to blow the ink dry, to bear down hard on the pen, to sign the document on someone's back, to spit and shake hands: to reassure oneself that one's body still carries some weight, that one's presence still matters, even as material reality gives way to an ethereal textuality. Thus Steve begins "the biggest day of [his] goddamn life," on which he signs for the livery, by taking a bath and combing his hair; before he can represent himself in writing for the first time, he feels compelled to make himself presentable (3.5). Self-presentation has everything to do here with self-preservation: even if the signature implies nonpresence, the act of signing at least requires that the signer be present, so that the growing body of representations cannot wholly dispense with the living bodies of individuals. Alice exploits this loophole by dragging out the act itself over two episodes—negotiating terms with Swearengen, calling for Bullock as a witness, signing first in a false hand—to avoid being dragged off to decompose in Wu's pigsty, where nonpresence awaits with teeth.

Swearengen counters the last of Alice's dodges by comparing her signature to the one on the hotel register and making her sign again, but not before Alice baits him: "Mightn't this be my true hand, and my hand to the hotel register false?" (2.10). Her cheeky question gives rise to two philosophical conundrums: the first, whether it is possible to forge one's own signature, is actually less problematic than the second, whether it is possible *not* to forge one's own signature. Derrida points out that a signature involves a paradoxical duplication of originality: "In order to function, that is, in order to be legible, a signature must have a repeatable, iterable, imitable form; it must be able to detach itself from the present and singular intention of its production" ("Signature" 328). A signature can only be copied, not authored, even by its signer; what counts most is that the names on various documents look the same, not that they were all put there by the same person. Swearengen knows this because he has already glimpsed a future in which it is not his signature but simply his name—written in any hand—that allows the body of representations to take possession and then dispose of his own; in the first season his name shows up on a murder warrant from Chicago, to be served as soon as the camp where "warrants don't count" becomes a town where they do (1.1). Magistrate Clagett, composing a list of Yankton officials to be paid off, demands an additional bribe to lift the warrant. Swearengen balks, but Clagett ignores him: "If you don't mind, I'll continue writing" (1.9). The magistrate thus pointedly reminds the cutthroat that a pen is now the weapon of choice in a rapidly modernizing West, where a single stroke—writing a man's name on this line, or on that one—either marks him a made man or makes him a marked man. It's bad enough not to be sure if you are signing your own death warrant; even worse not to know whether someone else is signing it for you.

The looming problem, however, is that the body of representations has already grown large enough to detach itself from the hands that put pen to paper, taking on an independent and immortal life of its own: "I didn't generate the warrant," Clagett says later, adding smugly, "My disappearance won't quash it. You can't murder an order, or the telegraph that transmitted it, or those that are content to put food on the table simply by being its instruments" (1.12). The warrant may threaten to deprive Swearengen of his personal liberty, but the network of official documents and bureaucratic records will soon also deprive everyone of identity and agency, even officers and bureaucrats themselves, now instruments rather than individuals. Clagett makes the mistake, however, of selling the warrant privately rather than serving it publicly; Swearengen, realizing that this particular paper trail dead-ends in a coat pocket, immediately kills the magistrate and lifts the warrant himself. Score one for Swearengen here at the end of the first season, but he has had a narrow escape; as soon as the telegraph poles go up at the start of the next season and invisible messages start circulating, he takes special measures to preserve himself from nonpresence. Not even a generous bottom line can compensate for the existential deficits of the dotted one: Swearengen strikes his name from the founding document, although it means turning down a fifty-thousand-dollar bribe; later he has Jarry sign the document but does not do so himself, instead shaking hands with Bullock (2.12). Swearengen does make one concession, however, to what other people think of as progress: this time, no spit.

Death Sentences

Swearengen does his best to avoid not just signing his name but writing anything at all: he may study, parse, and dictate, but he prefers to enlist other men—Bullock, Merrick, and Adams—as amanuenses. His reluctance may be read as a sign of gender trouble: while drafting the founding document, for example, he urinates in a chamber pot while Adams sits at the desk, transcribing his boss's words. The difference between what the two are holding in their hands suggests that the civilizing process will change the ways in which men conceive their masculinity and exercise their power; Swearengen's reluctance to exchange one instrument for the other suggests that men will at first experience such progress—the substitution of written fluency for physical potency—as a shameful loss. "Is the pen a metaphorical penis?" ask Sandra Gilbert and Susan Gubar at the beginning of their study of nineteenth-century literature (3); the answer for writers back in Boston or London may be "yes," but not out here in the territories. Real men certainly do not

9. Al and Silas checking a document. "A Lie Agreed Upon, Part I" (*Deadwood* 2.1).

write, and those who do will suffer both castration anxiety and homosexual panic: bad enough that both his eyesight and his prostate are failing, but Swearengen must worry also whether his choice to go after Hearst in print rather than in person means that he "mightn't be fucking queer" (3.3). The suspicion that all this paperwork will unman him dogs Swearengen throughout the series, even though he loses nothing worse than a finger, and his language is both contemptuous and homophobic when he describes how government officials use the press "to fuck people up the ass" (2.9), or mocks the governor's "pricey little personal note," or archly ridicules the notion that he would look something up in his "yesterday's diary" (1.5). Instead of a diary, Swearengen keeps a prostitute, who fellates him each night while he recounts the day and reminisces about his past. The sex act not only compensates for the pain and shame of his childhood but also substitutes for the embarrassing act of writing itself; like Adams, Dolly takes Swearengen's dictation to make him feel more of a man. In both cases the dysfunction he experiences is not only a symptom of his age but also a sign of his times. The advance of civilization has already begun sapping him, although he remains stronger and straighter than the literary, clerical, and administrative men around him, who are as limp (the indifferent Merrick and the naive Blazanov) or bent (the effeminate thespians Langrishe and Bellegarde, and the tittering, bubble-blowing Jarry) or both (the impotent and depraved Wolcott) as they are modern.

The damage that writing does to male sexual potency, however, is only one symptom of its enervating effect on bodies in general. The signature may be "the point at which both presence and writing are in question" (Derrida, "Signature" 327), where anxieties about death tend to cluster, but those anxieties soon float free to haunt all texts in Deadwood, not only public documentation but also private correspondence, where further questions about presence and writing arise. One running motif in the series is the identification of corpses—the john shot by Trixie, the road agent Ned Mason, Odell Marchbanks from Liberia, the murdered Cornishman—by the personal letters found in their pockets, a grim reminder of the link between writing, transcendence, and death. Writing allows friends and family members to cross space and time in their communications and relations with one another, but only because it can function entirely in their absence, generating meaning with reference to a larger system of signs rather than to the special relationship between these specific persons. In fact, writing must always function as if the correspondents were already dead and someone else, anyone else, were reading their letters: "A writing that was not structurally legible—iterable—beyond the death of the addressee would not be writing," Derrida argues, because it must first constitute "a communicable, transmittable, decipherable grid that is iterable for a third party, and thus for any possible user in general" ("Signature" 315). He then adds that "what holds for the addressee holds also, for the same reasons, for the sender" (316). To write letters, then, is to admit and confront the possibility of one's own death, as Wild Bill Hickok does instinctively in the postscript to his wife: "Agnes, darling, if such should be we never meet again, while firing my last shot I will gently breathe the name of my wife, Agnes, and with wishes even for my enemies, I will make the plunge and try to swim to the other shore" (2.5). Hickok's letter only makes explicit what Derrida argues all writing does implicitly: refer at last to the death of the writer, who in this case is also a man so sick of being written about that he hastens his own destruction.

Furthermore, as the shift here from "Agnes" the second-person addressee to "Agnes" the third-person referent suggests, to write letters is to anticipate the post-postscript moment that *Deadwood* dwells upon, when strangers—even enemies—will read the words that once bound together two loved ones but now serve the grubby purposes of third parties. In the exemplary case of Hickok, that moment is prolonged and exaggerated over the first two seasons, as his letter passes from one stranger to the next, each of whom defiles it in a different way. The drunken hotel clerk forgets to mail it, finds it in the soiled pants he left under a rock (1.9), and then gives it to Farnum, who studies the envelope under a magnifying glass and sells it on speculation to Wolcott (2.3), who in turn opens it and, finding nothing of financial value, amuses himself by reading it aloud in bed to a prostitute and making fun of Hickok's spelling (2.5). Here is a sordid corollary to Derrida's argument about writing, transcendence, and death: one man's love letter is always already another man's sex toy.

In reading the letter aloud, however, the jaded couple experiences together an unexpected emotional and erotic charge; the dead man's words move the prostitute nearly to tears and awaken in Wolcott a healthy sexual impulse. "Are you a man who needs his trousers rubbed?" she asks softly, since usually he can climax only if dry-humped; he answers, "I am a man who needs his trousers taken off," a response that seems to surprise him as much as her (2.5). Driving at first toward death and Derrida, the scene of foreplay spins away here toward the life-affirming transcendentalism of Thoreau, who famously declared in *Walden* (1854) that the written word is "at once more intimate with us and more universal than any other work of art," because it may "not only be read but actually breathed from all human lips;—not be represented on canvas or in marble only, but be carved out of the breath of life itself" (69). Given voice, Hickok's words not only relay his message but also restore something of his lost presence, producing an intimate experience of universal connection that twice prompts Wolcott to be a better man, if only very briefly: once with the prostitute, and once with Charlie Utter, to whom he again reads the postscript—gently breathing the name of Agnes, just as Hickok once did. "It's clear he would want her to have it," Wolcott says, giving the letter to an emotional Utter (2.7). Utter pledges to take it directly to Agnes himself, because he cannot bear the thought of its continued circulation and contamination: "God knows who [Wolcott] fucking bought it off of, or how many hands it passed through" (2.9). Delivering the dead letter to its rightful addressee, whose lips alone may then give breath to the words of her husband, Utter soothes his own grief by making a private gesture of faith in writing as "the work of art nearest to life itself," in Thoreau's phrase (69).

Merrick makes the same gesture of faith, although more publicly, by framing and hanging that quotation from *Walden* in his office (3.2); of course, an idealistic newspaperman has his own mixed psychological motives for mystifying the written word as a spiritual vessel rather than a tombstone. Although he loves to deprecate himself as an "ink-stained wretch" (1.2), Merrick also exalts his "sacred responsibility" (3.2) to shepherd public discourse into the new medium of print, where it will not only flourish but be transformed. One effect of print on public discourse, as Michael Warner has argued, is to replace "an ethic of personal presence" (22), which persists in relation to private correspondence, with a radically different "principle of negativity," which dictates that citizens entering the public sphere prove their lack of self-interest by checking individual personhood at the door (42). The self-negation that haunts all forms of writing functions here as a sign of virtue rather than a source of anxiety; so that his arguments may be considered rationally and objectively, the published writer absents himself from his printed words, which no longer bear even the traces of a singular hand. At this pivotal moment in Deadwood's history, however, public discourse raises questions about presence and writing that trouble even the forward-thinking Merrick. Reading aloud a draft of his forthcoming interview with the founder of the new bank, Merrick concludes with a frown, "Mrs. Ellsworth being so elevated, so sweetly radiant in spirit, I wonder if her words resonated with me at the time as being more poetic and compelling than now they seem in cold transcription, and with the lady herself absent" (3.5). And what holds for the interviewee also holds for the interviewer, whose personal presence matters less and less as his audience grows more and more anonymous, its members as faceless to him as he is to them. This is why Merrick both deprecates and promotes himself: on the one hand, the impersonality of printed public discourse demands that he, as its custodian and chief contributor, "bracket the particularities of his life" (Warner 72). On the other hand, to compensate for that displacement of self, he feels compelled to get in everyone's face, making his presence felt by perambulating up and down the boardwalk, holding forth windily to anyone who will listen, and introducing himself to newcomers just off the stage. Especially when he pesters Al for a response to the latest issue of the newspaper, Merrick betrays anxiety that his words will not resonate fully with their readership unless the writer also busily presents himself in person; because the cold transcription of print heralds his own death, he reassures himself by displaying the famous passage from *Walden*. Tellingly, however, Merrick omits its first sentence, in which even Thoreau concedes that writing, however sacred, is only ever a remnant of life: "A written word is the choicest of relics" (Thoreau 69).

The self-negating effect of public discourse troubles not just journalists but all citizens who write themselves into that discourse only to suffer even worse doubts than Merrick. "I'd sooner be hanging from those hustings than stand on them giving a speech," says Bullock, acknowledging a fear of public speaking that also afflicts other candidates in the coming elections (3.1). The problem is that the hybrid form of a speech—the oral rather than print publication of a manuscript, itself a cross between letter and document—brings the preceding ethic of personal presence into direct conflict with the emerging principle of negativity. On the one hand, the speaker presents himself before the audience, pronouncing his own handwritten words in his own voice; on the other, as the phrase "giving a speech" suggests, those words actually constitute a text that exists apart from the speaker, who presents it rather than himself, now a public citizen rather than an individual person. Even a drunken hoople-head can sense how much potential for slippage between speaker and speech obtains here—and in fact one drunken hoople-head does, mounting the hustings before dawn to deliver a mock address that begins, "I am not the fine man you take me for" (3.2)—but no one feels the slippage more acutely than the speaker himself, having to recall or read out his own scripted words, which no longer come to him naturally or belong to him integrally. To breathe life into another's words, as Thoreau recommends, is to experience a moment of connection that transcends time and space; to have to breathe life into one's own words, however, is to experience a moment of dissociation—split between first-person writer and third-party reader—that portends death. Bullock may exaggerate when he equates speechifying with being hanged, but only slightly, as that drunken hoople-head discovers; in mid-speech, he slips, plunges off the hustings, and breaks his neck.

To emphasize that the fear of public speaking originates in the writing of the speech, even if it culminates in the delivery, the first two episodes of the third season focus on the candidates' nervousness as they prepare their remarks. Paradoxically, the preparation worsens rather than soothes the mounting anxiety: the more Bullock revises his speech, the more estranged he becomes from his own words, which seem to be "doing the wrong jobs, piling on too heavy, or at odds over meaning" (3.1), until he must turn to his wife for editorial assistance. The other candidate for sheriff, Harry Manning, reads over his own pages, growing sicker and sicker to his stomach, until he loses control of his bowels; Utter, who will be called upon publicly to endorse Bullock, is only slightly less phobic, scripting even simple phrases like "thank you" on his increasingly sweaty palm. Star is cooler, but he meets with Utter and Bullock to go over their speeches at the last minute and mutter key phrases aloud; even the experienced Merrick, who will preside as moderator, jots down his introduction and practices it on the cutthroat Dan Dority at the bar. All of this rehearsal is symptomatic of the struggle to reintegrate the speaking subject with the written word; only Farnum, a mayoral candidate, seems immune to such anxiety, but not because he is the incumbent. Twice he extemporizes his stump speech, the first time denouncing Bullock and the second time insulting Star; however, his colorful ad hominem arguments indicate that he is not really participating in public discourse at all, in the rational and impersonal way that Warner describes, but instead just venting repressed animosity. That is, Farnum is not giving a speech so much as raising his voice and speaking his mind; however unbalanced that mind, at least he is spared the feelings of dissociation that hang up the other candidates. To calm their nerves and restore their sense of self-presence, even Farnum's opponents adopt his approach when they actually mount the hustings; instead of giving their scripted speeches, they speak informally about their own personal emotions ("I'm glad we're in the camp," says Bullock, "even on the sorriest of days") and individual histories ("I've always loved fires," says Harry, "since I was a boy") rather than take the dizzying plunge into formal public discourse (3.2).

Return to Sender

Standing with Hearst on the hotel's second story, Swearengen keeps his distance from the speeches, just as he keeps his distance from either official documents or personal letters—"I don't notify fucking family," he barks at Bullock (3.12)—and instead restricts himself, just as Hearst does, to brief and occasional notes. Like Farnum, Swearengen is "a stickler for self-delivered messages" that bypass questions about writing (1.7); unlike Farnum, however, his deep voice and fluent speech give him a powerful presence well out of proportion to his only average height. The actor who plays Swearengen, Ian McShane, emphasizes the way in which "the voice has this innate churning rhythm to it" (Milch, *Deadwood* 22): the strings of plosives and fricatives and the layers of syntactical inversions and the lacings of profanity thicken Swearengen's speech until it accumulates an almost material density—even a froth and spray of spit—more satisfying than paper imparts to the written word. Milch has said that profanity allows the characters "to raze the English language" and "to break their ties to civilized institutions and forms of meaning" as they start fresh in the Black Hills (*Deadwood* 15). As civilization overtakes Deadwood, however, profanity then allows its residents to resist the subversive effects of writing on their sense of self, not only by defending what Ellsworth calls his "full range of expression" against the restraints of polite or official discourse (1.6), but also by freighting their speech with sexual and scatological references to bodies that might otherwise go without saying. One may, as dimwitted Johnny often does, find it hard to parse what exactly Swearengen has just said, but there is never any doubt—least of all on his own part—that Swearengen is standing here, speaking now, so fully self-present that he has no need to weigh or mince his words.

Swearengen thus resembles "the figure of preliterary man, primitive or savage and frequently an Indian," whom writers such as Thoreau, Emerson, Whitman, and Melville invoke "as a standard of authenticity" (Ziff 188); certainly much of his appeal as a character derives from his will and power to cut ruthlessly through all the paperwork that complicates the civilized lives of HBO subscribers. However, even if he groans that civilization has "fallen to this," Swearengen is not at all sentimental about the past, which was never innocent; the cultural drift from immanence to representation does not precipitate a descent so much as initiate a slide from one set of problems to another. The series may emphasize the ways in which writing undermines self-presence, producing various psychological complications and difficulties, but the series also at times reverses its spin, suggesting ways in which unmediated self-presence causes moral lapses and excesses that writing can correct. The chief example here is not Swearengen, even though he occasionally talks aloud to the severed head of an Indian, but Hearst, who takes far too literally the Indian name he received in childhood: "Boy-the-Earth-Talks-To" (2.12). Projecting his own gold lust onto the natural world, which then seems to tell him "where the color is," Hearst immerses himself so completely in the sound of his own voice that he loses touch with humanity and becomes a monster of egotism (2.12). "Comprehending such a language," warns Langrishe, "can cost a man his own kind's sympathies," but Hearst prefers his "solitary life" in which he can indulge the grand delusion that he is the particular addressee of the earth's messages rather than the sender (3.12). Hearst thus takes to psychotic extremes the auto-affective experience that Derrida calls *s'entendre parler*, or "hearing oneself speak," through which the speaker both articulates a purely interior self and maintains its distinction from the external world that otherwise mediates it ("Voice" 79). No longer aware that he is hearing himself speak, Hearst loses that distinction entirely, becoming what Benjamin Franklin called "a King in *Soliloquy*" who "fancies himself conquering the World" (21).

A telling symptom of Hearst's megalomania is his antipathy to writing, which would introduce a break in presence that would in turn interrupt the fantasy; according to Derrida, the closed circuit of *s'entendre parler* is "broken when, instead of hearing myself speak, I see myself write" ("Voice" 80). Removed from his own written discourse and thus made a third party to it, Hearst would then have to admit the possibility that those messages from the earth have been self-delivered all along. "You wrote a letter on my behalf," protests Wolcott, when Hearst questions him about his criminal history; Wolcott quotes the letter from memory and asks, "What did you think that was about?" (2.12). "I didn't think about it!" snaps Hearst, angry at having his own words recited back to him and thus having to think now about their meaning then; repositioned as addressee rather than sender of the letter, Hearst cannot help but perceive its signs of his denial. Wolcott presses his advantage, repeating the earth's words aloud in order to question where they originate and what they mean: "Suppose to you it whispers, 'You are king over me. I exist to flesh your will," and to me, 'There is no sin.'" In no mood for critical detachment, Hearst fires Wolcott, but he cannot so easily dismiss the disruptive effects of self-representation on his otherwise universal ego. The next time Hearst picks up a pen, he avoids writing and instead draws a picture, a seating diagram of the saloon, from which Swearengen must puzzle out his intentions. Even when Hearst does follow up with a very short note to arrange a face-to-face meeting with Swearengen, Dority observes that it is "written in an awkward hand," as if its author were uncomfortable representing himself on paper (3.2). To compensate for this weakness, Hearst makes other writers feel awkward by twisting their words back against them; standing up and stepping closer, he imposes his physical presence on his enemies until they doubt their textual representations, which suddenly seem too flimsy to convey meaning. "I began to read to him my proposal," cries Alma, unnerved after Hearst bullies her, "but I was more and more afraid I was only chanting sounds" (3.3). In the same episode Bullock tries to put Hearst "on notice," writing up a list of criminal charges that includes the murder of a Cornish miner, only for Hearst to deconstruct the document: "With such disagreement among statements, Mr. Bullock, on what basis could an inquiry justifiably go forward?" "I identify a pattern in these events," counters Bullock, but Hearst advances his aggressively poststructuralist argument—"Why in fuck should I care what pattern you identify or don't?"—and forces Bullock to retreat (3.3).

Fed up, Bullock finally arrests Hearst on a trumped-up charge of drunkenness and drags him to jail by the ear, perhaps making it harder for him to listen to the earth but accomplishing little else; in fact, Hearst deliberately provokes the confrontation, since the sheriff then appears more prone to violence than he does. However, while Utter advises gunning down Hearst "as Wild Bill would have done," Bullock risks his masculinity and adopts instead what Langrishe calls "a strategy in counterpoise" that better befits the modernizing West: he writes a personal letter of condolence to the family of the murdered Cornishman, which he gives to Merrick to read aloud at a camp meeting and then publish in the newspaper (3.7). While Swearengen admires the "nice fucking letter," he is nonetheless "mystified [he] was moved to endorse it," since it does not accuse or even mention Hearst, but Langrishe assures him that the strategy is "cunningly sophisticated" (3.7). Rather than directly charge Hearst with a criminal offense to which there are no witnesses, the letter implicitly rebukes him for a moral offense of which the letter itself is witness: Hearst's failure to write it. "The letter's contents is witness that Bullock wrote a nice fucking letter, and it proves that that's the sort we are here, the caring sort that would write a letter of that ilk," Dority explains to Johnny; "furthermore, we don't give a fuck who knows it, George fucking Hearst included" (3.7). The letter writes off Hearst as a missing link in the civilizing process: because the medium is the message, it can go without saying that Hearst is not only preliterate but also subhuman, too primitive to write nicely and too savage to converse with anyone but himself and the earth. "Was the Sheriff's making his letter part of the public record meant to embarrass or reproach me?" demands Hearst (3.7). Merrick demurs, but the answer is yes, and Hearst knows it: "I suppose I should have written them myself" (3.7). Too late: everyone now acknowledges "the pretense to civility in a man so brutally vicious," as Alma declares, to be "vapid and grotesque" (3.12). Hearst may end up owning the town, but his methods debar him from the public discourse of civil society; instead, he resorts to buying up its print medium and hiring other writers to represent him in his absence. "I've stopped reading your paper, Merrick," he gloats as he rides out of town, on his way to fathering a publishing empire. "I'll have my people here start another one, to lie the other way" (3.12).

In contrast, the letter inscribes Bullock within public discourse as the representative figure of literate man, whose character is endorsed by even the most violent members of the camp as its new standard of authenticity; by voluntarily negating himself through print, where his words then represent the community as a whole, Bullock civilizes Deadwood by becoming its first genuine citizen. At this early stage of the civilizing process, however, literacy will cost the sheriff his own kind's sympathies: while the rest of the camp participates in Amateur Night, a communal celebration of immanent selfhood in which ordinary folk show off what their bodies and voices can do, Bullock sequesters himself to write, returning once again to a jailhouse at night (3.9). This time he is entirely alone, with no thief to interrupt him; he can write for as long as he likes in the peace and quiet it has taken him three seasons to earn. This time we cannot see what he is writing, because the lamp on the desk illuminates the room but blocks our view of his hands; we can see only that he is writing, an act even more dazzling than the performances taking place outside. Cutting away to the theatricals and then returning to Bullock, the camera moves back to a long shot from outside the jail; we watch him through a window that reflects and superimposes the images of passersby, as if his writing were already depriving them of presence and accelerating the drift from immanence to representation. From this distance we can only speculate about these last written words. Is that some sort of a letter, Sheriff? A journal? A speech? Whatever the answer, we can be certain that it is the founding document of the future from which we now look back at him, through the glass of the television screen that reflects our own ghostly images; we are sitting at the far end of the paper trail on which he is just setting out.

3 The Thinking of Al Swearengen's Body
Kidney Stones, Pigpens, and Burkean Catharsis in *Deadwood*

Tim Steckline

"Deadwood is a show about how order arises out of the mud," says Milch (Deadwood 135). Describing Deadwood's main street as "a mixture of mud and animal feces puddled with snowmelt and urine and spit," Tim Steckline considers whether order ever really comes to Deadwood and what blocks its emergence.

As Brian McCuskey turns to Derrida to make sense of "paper trails," Steckline turns to Kenneth Burke and his theory of "catharsis" to analyze Deadwood's polluted street, challenges to propriety, and various "social pollutions." Through consideration of the importance of "social catharsis" to the emergence of a "body politic," Steckline addresses, often wittily, Deadwood's grotesque treatment of human bodies and their various emissions, making sense of characters' usually futile efforts to "clean up," literally and symbolically. Although bodily purgations, he notes, are often blocked, offering no social catharsis, surely there are enough deaths to offer the kind of ritual scapegoats or tragic victim that Burke also identifies as crucial to "free flow" through the streets to achieve civilization and order. Steckline's trope leaves him less confident than McCuskey that social order has been or will be achieved. Ironically, HBO's decision to "block" a fitting conclusion to the series prevents us from ever finding out.

The town of Deadwood, South Dakota, is a twenty-minute drive from my front door. I have visited the place episodically ever since my grandmother took me there when I was seven years old. I was a young tourist, so the mythological Deadwood of gamblers and gunfighters and miners and Calamity Jane was the first Deadwood I came to know with my heart. By luck and fate I now live and work near the historical yet mundane Deadwood. One thing I have learned from some glancing familiarity with this town so singularly touched by history is this: Deadwood Gulch is a gut, a short, narrow defile with an intake orifice at one end and an outlet orifice at the other. (This is but one of several compelling reasons that Deadwood Gulch is a scary place to be when it periodically catches fire.) In 1991–92 the Deadwood Historic Preservation Commission ticketed the expenditure of some of its share of gambling revenues upon the restoration of brick streets to the downtown area (Wolfe 18, 21; "Deadwood Officials"). Brick streets hearken to Deadwood's genteel Victorian style of 1907, not to the halcyon boomtown sprawl of the 1870s celebrated in the town's mythos. If the historical commission was trying to re-create the frontier Deadwood that Wild Bill Hickok and Calamity Jane walked, the streets would look more like those in David Milch's *Deadwood*: a mixture of mud and animal feces puddled with snowmelt and urine and spit.[1] The narrow, crooked thoroughfare, always choked with horses, mules, oxen, freighters, and people afoot, was a difficult passage, when not utterly blocked.

Students of literature are familiar with Aristotle's ideas about the working through of emotional catharsis in tragic drama. Tragic figures are compelled to victimage by the plot and the inescapable fates of their characters. The emotions of pity and fear aroused in an audience by the drama's imitative depiction purge them of their excessive passions (Kruse 162–64). Language theorist and literary and social critic Kenneth Burke has extended this analysis of catharsis. Catharsis in the classical tradition, which Burke calls "grand catharsis," requires victims, though not necessarily tragic victims, for only a fragment of Aristotle's work on catharsis in its tragic context has survived, and other sorts of victims may well have been part of his taxonomy. Through a "Cult of the Kill," society can be purged of its *katharma*, persons who are "social pollution."[2] Burke insists that such social catharsis is mirrored by a bodily catharsis, enacted both physiologically and symbolically: "The purging of 'pollutions' from the body politic can be expressed directly or indirectly by the imagery of bodily purgation" ("On Catharsis" 359). He specifies among these images every bodily emission from a flow of tears to a stream of urine.

Because such emissions are infantile and socially taboo, or "dirty," they are not spoken of in polite society. Their points of exposure to the world are of a "privy nature" and are therefore kept covered by clothing "below the belt," and when in use they are by discretion hidden away in private rooms (Burke, *Grammar* 300–303). Such cloacal motives advise us to talk about bodily purgation only in furtive or roundabout ways or not at all in polite society. *Deadwood* has been noted for its convention of breaking taboos, but its liberal deployment of profanity has been the most prominent subject of discussion. Certainly a dramatic enactment of catharsis can be expected to exhibit the signs of repression and shock that mark our abhorrence for those parts and products of ourselves that must be rejected yet cannot be forgone. Whether these emissions are physiological, symbolic, or social, their public representation will generate a primitive revulsion toward such profanity before one can examine them in all their earthiness.

This emphasis on the saltiness of the language has obscured other socially forbidden material that regularly surfaces in the dialogue and mise-en-scène. The routine airing of profanity is but one symptom of social and physiological motives much more profound than any critique of the verisimilitude of Victorian cussin' in a mining camp melodrama. From an analysis of the imagery of bodily and social purgation, a general pattern of *deferred* or *arrested* catharsis emerges, which suggests that purgation in *Deadwood* is as blocked as the traffic through Deadwood's main street.

Burkean Catharsis and Cleansing Agents

Burke traces the efficacy of catharsis to its having "three empirical non-linguistic sources to draw on: the human body, the 'world's body' (the natural scene), and the body politic." The interchangeability of terms for these three realms permitted Aristotle to make the metaphorical link between social catharsis and the medical catharsis of humors that he had learned from his father, a practicing doctor, when he came to explain how dramatic catharsis works in a tragedy (Burke, "On Catharsis" 338–54). A tripartite process dictates the logic of catharsis whether social, medical, or dramatic:

guilt	→	victimage	→	redemption
disease	→	purgation	→	recuperation
unclean	→	cleansing	→	cleansed

Social catharsis requires a victim to restore social order, whether that victim be a tragic hero, a deserving villain, a blameless scapegoat, or multiple nameless, "expendable" victims ("On Catharsis" 361; "Dramatism" 450). But bodily catharsis figures its purgation in emissions, so the tears that are brought forth by fits of grief or laughter are a noble form of tragic or comedic cleansing. Less noble is the wide range of other emissions, such as bleeding, vomiting, perspiring, expectorating, lactating, menstruating, or ejaculating. Burke refers to the three most powerful and universal means of bodily purgation—defecation, micturition, and coition—as the "Demonic Trinity." These three are especially significant in Western culture because of their association with privacy, propriety, and guilt, despite their parodic inversion of the Holy Trinity ("On Catharsis" 354–57; *Grammar* 301–2). The Father, the Son, and the Holy Spirit are corporealized by sight, speech, and hearing, all of them not only above the belt but uncovered by virtue of being in the neighborhood of the head. The Holy Trinity's demonic counterpart is hidden and repressed, "down there" in the dark recesses of our underwear, but if we would "deal with 'fundamentals' and get to the 'bottom' of things," we must surface the imagery of the Demonic Trinity and read it aloud. Advises Burke: "An acceptance of the universe on this plane may also be a roundabout way of 'making peace with the faeces'" (*Grammar* 23). Let us consider *Deadwood* as an attempt to make such a peace. Or as Preacher Smith puts it in his eulogy over Wild Bill Hickok:

> St. Paul tells us, by one spirit are we all baptized into one body. . . . For the body is not one member, but many. He tells us, "The eye cannot say unto the hand, I have no need of thee." Nor again, the head unto the feet, "I have no need of thee." Then much more those members of the body which seem to be more feeble, and those members of the body which we think of as less honor-

able, all are necessary. He says that there should be no schism in the body, but that the members should have the same care, one to another. And whether one member suffers, all the members suffer with it. (1.5)

Although Milch's Deadwood is generally frustrated in its attempts at catharsis, some fragmentary purgations must take place to prevent Deadwood from drowning in its effluents. For instance, when George Hearst becomes so infuriated with E. B. Farnum's obsequiousness that he spits twice directly in Farnum's face, he warns, "[I would] regret my coming back and finding that you had cleaned your face." After Farnum has been paralyzed for some time, he shows us the inverse side of his overaccommodating style in dealing with his social superiors in a vindictive monologue:

> That I have not wiped his expectoration from my cheek is understandable. I'm threatened with death if I do. That I stand immobile for these hours speaks of a flaw in my will. Surely this is not the culminating indignity. There remains, for example, receiving his regurgitations, swallowing his feces. Would I stand stoic still? I am going to fuck you up. I'm gonna fuck you up. And I'm the kind of cunt that you let close. (3.11)

We know from his prior actions that Farnum is just blowing off steam here and will constitute no real threat to Hearst. Hearst can treat Farnum as a "less honorable" member of the social body, and Farnum will only spit back in private, even as he foresees a long series of such indignities in the future, leading to a culmination in a garbage heap. Frustrated social catharsis would seem to work well enough if everyone were to seethe ineffectually as Farnum does, but the pollutants are dammed up. Arrested release means no cleansing, no redemption.

Rather than obstructing catharsis, most characters manage their day-to-day frustrations through a great many fragmentary purgations. A social code in Deadwood, we learn early on, is that every time two parties shake hands to solemnize a deal, they share interjected gobs of blended expectorant. They also share a moment of small but incremental catharsis. Most cleaning up comes in regular and cumulative cleanup routines. Burke said of the cathartic process that "if there is a cleansing, there must be persons or things that do the cleansing, and there must be offscourings that result from the cleansing. Implicit here, in turn, is the idea of the need to dispose of the offscourings, or in some way to neutralize their bad effects" ("Catharsis- Second View" 123). Identifying the characters who make up the "cleanup crew" in Deadwood, the persons who do the cleansing, is a good place to start our investigation.

Let us begin with Jewel, the palsied factotum of the Gem, who, when not emptying chamber pots or spittoons or cleaning up after Swearengen's eliminatory accidents, must scrub the blood of the Gem's latest victim off the floorboards. Jewel's frequent appearance near the end or beginning of episodes semaphores her importance to the rounding out of the cathartic process. Nor should we overlook her lesser equivalent at the Simpson Hotel, the aged, enfeebled, and much-abused Richardson. During town crises, as when William Bullock is dying or after Trixie has shot Hearst, Richardson prays for protection from the violence of the camp by supplicating a rack of moose antlers with an antler from the head of a white-tailed deer. These two elemental agents, Richardson and Jewel, are at the hub of characters who clean up Deadwood, but these two stand apart by their status as full-time practitioners of literal custodial cleaning.

The practitioner of medical catharsis for the town is Doc Cochran, who purges and cleanses the ill and injured insofar as that is possible under frontier conditions. Part of the logic of catharsis is Burke's "principle of vicarage," the insight that the cleanser in the act of cleansing must take on some uncleanness himself or herself ("On Catharsis" 367–68; "Catharsis—Second View" 123–26). Jewel's clothes, for instance, are perpetually smeared or stained by body fluids and layered in dust. This holds true as well for Doc Cochran, who suffers from his own diseases and addiction and who must sometimes purge himself before returning to his duties with the cleanup crew.

The same could be said of the prostitutes at the Gem, the Bella

Union, and the Chez Ami. When they are not relieving the tensions of Swearengen, Tolliver, and the working-class males of the camp, they are laundering their pitiful few clothes, administering a bath to a customer, or taking baths themselves. The opening montage makes sure that the viewer sees a prostitute taking a tub as the credits roll to begin each episode. Their ritual hygienic cleansing is a parody of the libidinous release they render for a fee, which is a parody of true erotic catharsis.

Most notable of the prostitutes is the upwardly mobile Trixie, who commits the first action of the series to occur in Deadwood by cleansing the town of a physically abusive trick with her derringer pistol. She later helps Alma Garret purge herself of her opium addiction and, on another occasion, offers to supply Alma with the drastic purge of an abortifacient. It is Trixie who attempts in the third season of the program to cleanse Deadwood of the ultimate pollution of Hearst, again with her pistol. In all these illegal and perhaps immoral purgative actions, Trixie takes upon herself the taint of pollution, becoming a *katharma* of the society by virtue of performing her office as camp cleanser.

By way of illustration, after Swearengen arranges the medical, legal, and custodial cleanup of Trixie's inaugural killing in the first episode, he isolates her in his office like the unclean agent she is. With his foot on her throat, Al says, "What's it gonna be, Trixie?" The bruised and cornered woman croaks, "I'll be good" (1.1). And she is "good," too, up until she shoots George Hearst at the bookend of the third season. The compound status of the cleansing agent is evident in this, our first, meeting with Trixie, whose character is a constitutional confusion of killer and victim, wounder and healer, doctor and patient, subject and other, good and evil, action and passion. In this case Trixie's "I'll be good" is a contractual pledge to be Al's spy and agent, which makes every action of hers henceforth, even the most seemingly sincere or spontaneous, suspect. Neither Sol nor Al nor the viewer can trust her motives because her nature as a cleansing agent is thoroughly mixed. She is the alembic of Deadwood, perhaps even more beyond good and evil than Al.

Trixie's purgative duties are allied to those of Sol Star, who in the first episode gives away a complimentary chamber pot as the first transaction of his and Seth Bullock's hardware business, a relaxative amenity traded to buy time from the impatient miner who is blocked in the street while Star unloads his new inventory from a double-parked freight wagon. In the third season, when the Earp brothers aggravate Sheriff Bullock by leaving "two hundred dollars' worth of merchandise in the middle of [their] store, like an interrupted shit," Sol's duty is to clear the blockage as expeditiously as possible (3.5).

As long as we are considering social catharsis, we must arraign Swearengen's two able henchmen as key members of the cleanup crew. "Dirty" Dan Dority is aptly named because he cleans up Al's messes by fighting or killing at Al's behest. In a gory hand-to-hand battle in the puddled street, at the point of losing his own life, Dan just manages to beat to death the hulking Captain Turner, Hearst's chief Pinkerton enforcer. When Al lies in shock from uremic poisoning, Dirty Dan saves his boss's life by kicking in a locked door. Al's other associate is Silas Adams, the "clean-cut" counterpart to and rival of Dirty Dan. Somehow Silas arranges to keep his hands clean when he executes errands for the owner of the Gem. Charley Utter plays a similarly custodial role for Seth Bullock, albeit with more finesse and in more varied capacities. The Pinkertons shuttled through the camp by Hearst, and for that matter his advance geologist, Francis Wolcott, are perverse doubles of Dirty Dan: their clothes and coiffures are neater than his, but they seem only to make more messes.

No analysis of the cleansing of Deadwood would be complete without the mention of Mr. Wu's pigpen, which merges the alimentary and the eliminatory functions of the town in one grotesque locale. Wu's pigpen serves as the cloaca of Deadwood—an open secret, devil's work hidden away among the Celestials, the purgative outlet for those whom the mining camp can no longer stomach. Wu's pigpen encompasses in its concentrated miasma the slops of the streets pureed with the denizens of the edifices, the fetid with the hygienic, the human with the animal, the civilized with the feral, the hidden with the obvious, the sacred with the profane. In the third episode of the first season, Farnum promises Swearengen, "I'm not getting 'et by the pigs—in case there is a resurrection of the flesh" (1.3). In the first episode of the third season, as if in a long-delayed answer, Al confounds Farnum with a chiliastic warning in his Victorian thug's diction: "Gabriel's trumpet shall produce you from the asshole of Mr. Wu's pigs" (3.1). Redemption was never more gustatory.

Occluded Erotic Catharsis

Despite a great many fragmentary and incremental catharses, the accumulation of these purgative moments is not sufficient to produce a thorough cleansing. The failure of erotic outlets in Deadwood demonstrates this frustration. The plot is a plague of interrupted and stunted love affairs. Venereal or seminal catharsis is delayed until it cannot wait one minute more.

The cortege of star-crossed couples, the occluded ones, is led by the season-long polite simmer of the passions of Seth Bullock and Alma Garret. Their heated and overdue coupling climaxes the first season but must be suspended as soon as it ignites because of the inconvenient arrival of Seth's wife, Martha. The child Alma and Seth beget of their shared emissions eventually proves to be a miscarriage. Their catharsis is truncated and barren.

Seth's resumption of his marriage to Martha remains formal and constrained. In contrast to the irresistible passion that Alma inspired in Seth, the married couple stiffly and scrupulously discuss closing their bedroom door, so that they might have a long-deferred conversation. They awaken in the middle of the night, and Seth apologizes for falling asleep with his boots on:

SETH: Only I'd intended to be awake last night so we could talk. Which, what with how it's been, we have not done. In the peace of the evening, as I would like, since your arrival.
MARTHA: I would enjoy to converse in the stillness after a day like that.
SETH: Tonight I will have two cups of coffee and I will not fall asleep.

MARTHA: In the morning, in the quiet before we each take up our work, is also a pleasant occasion for such intercourse.
SETH: Yes . . .
MARTHA: Would you like to start a discussion this morning?
SETH: I wouldn't want to disturb the boy.
MARTHA: William sleeps soundly. If you will see to the bedroom door, Mr. Bullock? (2.4)

The polite strain of this exchange, all done back-to-back and each on his or her own side of the bed, does not promise much of a purgation. When Martha inches her left hand across the bed toward her husband, Seth pretends not to notice it. Seth has adopted the widowed Martha out of duty to his deceased brother, so he is a stand-in husband for a dead man. Duty proves to be insufficiently purgative.

Trixie and Sol Star persist in their own sputtering tryst, although the viewer is left uncertain whether Trixie's part in the affair is that of Sol's lover and bookkeeping student or that of a spy and cat's paw for Swearengen. Both Sol and Trixie are part of the cleanup crew, and both must regularly handle "filthy lucre," so these two usually wallow in pollution.[3] Sol says in defense of his pecuniary habits, "If money had to be clean before it was recirculated, we'd still be living in fucking caves" (2.2). This shared familiarity with the role of the cathartic reagent does not make for a smoother road to romance, however. When Trixie offers the ailing Sol a course of fellatio for what ails him (a gunshot wound), he can only say, "I'd settle for some vigorous hand holding" (2.4). Not long after this incident Sol adds his hand to the deputation backing Bullock in a showdown with Al, only to be diminished by Calamity Jane's ridicule of the size of his pistol: "The hardware jew with less than full force—now they'll be quakin'" (2.2). She may be speaking for Trixie, who typically berates Sol in the company of others.

The occluded erotic release is most crudely depicted in the relationship between Francis Wolcott, Hearst's stalking horse of a geologist, and Carrie, the prostitute he has stalked from San Francisco. "This place smells like shit," Carrie declares as she arrives off the muddy boulevard at Joanie Stubbs's bordello (2.4). It does not smell of love. Her first request of Wolcott when she steps from the stagecoach is not to be looked at until she could take a bath. Once Wolcott begins to arrange appointments with Carrie, their coition is simulated through his clothing while Wolcott toys sadistically with her mind. "I'm too quick," Wolcott says to acquit his premature catharsis. "You can't be too quick for me," guarantees Carrie (2.4). The stony relations of these two decadently indifferent agents of other players comes to an end in a throat-cutting spree with a razor, followed promptly by Wolcott's suicide by hanging, a strangled and unerotic catharsis.

The marriage of Alma Garret and Ellsworth is originally a union born of convenience. His proposal is one long embarrassing gaffe—he offers his tolerance for vomiting as his main qualification as a husband: "Anyways, I'm acquainted . . . with certain experiences . . . throwing up mornings, as an example. . . . And I'd say—not claiming credentials for raising a family, as my time with them was brief . . . but I'd hope it'd testify to a willingness as a candidate for marriage, and so forth. Offering myself . . . completing the sorry presentation" (2.8). But by the third season we see some warmth and small effusions of affection creeping into their relations. Just as this unlikely couple prove themselves worthy of a real romance between two civilized persons, Ellsworth is abruptly assassinated by Hearst's agents. Erotic catharsis is arrested again, this time across the gulf of death.

The romance of Calamity Jane and Wild Bill Hickok is a love affair staged all in Calamity's imagination, and so is one more love affair unconsummated, and, what is more, never even commenced. But the closest thing to a truly purgative coition in the entire series is the passion between Calamity and Joanie Stubbs during season 3. After months of cohabiting with Joanie, Jane dreams that Joanie kisses her. When she narrates the dream to Joanie the following afternoon, the kiss comes true. In the final episode Joanie tells Jane that she wants to be as dependable as Charley Utter "in a tight. . . . I want to be that to you, even when we don't get along" (3.12). Then she pulls out the buffalo robe of Wild Bill Hickok's, acquired from Charley that afternoon, and smothers the overjoyed Calamity in both her fantasies at once. Of course, this is a love "that dare not speak its name," even in a moral sewer like Deadwood. When Blazanov warns the pair, "I'll not have vileness or uncleanness on these premises," they move on to another nest (3.12). So this private drama of redemption is neither deferred nor arrested, only kept in a closet.

The cleansing release that catharsis should bring is rare in Deadwood, especially if one depends on erotic release. The failure of purgation underlines the way pity and fear circulate in Deadwood without much outlet. Burke has often insisted that catharsis is a good place to examine "the thinking of the body," because it bridges the animal and symbolic sides and the corresponding material and spiritual realms of the human experience. If the love lives of the adults of Deadwood are frustrated, this deferral and arrest of purgation should carry over into the other, more-excretory powers of the Demonic Trinity. Swearengen's body seems to obsess especially on an unstemmed flow, whether of words or water.

Blockage by Kidney Stone

The clearest depiction of arrested catharsis as both master trope and turning point for the plot of *Deadwood* is the saga of Swearengen's never-ending kidney stone. This nacreous cork literally stoppers his bladder for most of three episodes early in the second season. By the time he survives the crisis and passes the stone, his position in the power structure of the town has changed significantly.

The first clue to Swearengen's blockage is a comment he lets slip after a brief confrontation with Dirty Dan: "It feels like a cannonball shoved up my ass" (2.2). Later the same day, the phalangeal and oral ministrations of Dolly, one of his employees at the Gem, to Al's prostate and penis not only fail to bring him release; they provoke the first twinges of pain. "Even this gives me no pleasure," he laments as Dolly labors away.

By the following morning Swearengen is paralyzed and mute on the floor of his locked room. Visitors are blocked from disturbing him by his associates downstairs. Dan turns away Eamon, who is insulted as "Cropear" because of his mutilated head, and later refuses Wu, whose English Dan finds incomprehensible. An auditor without ears and a speaker without English become the interlocutory correlates of the mute Swearengen's blockage. When the flow of urine is arrested, Al's stream of words is pinched off along with it.[4] The stone that Al's body has secreted has secreted Al in his locked room. Dirty Dan lets Silas know the situation, but neither can hide his concern about Al's stifling condition:

DAN: Listen, Adams, Al is fucked up bad, maybe dying.
SILAS: Jesus.
DAN: Goddamn right, Jesus. Those stones done plum blocked off his piss passage.
SILAS: Fuck. . . . Okay. All right.
DAN: It's all backed up in him. Shit, he's got piss in his lungs.
SILAS: Can he talk?
DAN: Fuck no, he can't talk. He lays there and shivers and stares at nothin'. Aw, he screams when Doc abuses him with them fuckin' prick poles of his. (2.4)

Doc Cochrane, with the assistance of Dirty Dan and Johnny in restraining Al, performs a frontier catheterization on Al. The pain is tremendous, and Al's screams pierce the streets of the camp like a wire penetrating the crowd. The word *catheter* may spring from the same etymological root as *catharsis*, but the procedure fails to purge Al of more than a few drops of blood mixed with urine. The presence of a kidney stone is confirmed—"I can feel the fuckin' click of the gleet," says Doc—but no release comes (2.4). Unnerved by the screams, Trixie interrogates Johnny while she smokes off her jitters in the street:

JOHNNY: He put something out of himself, Trixie. That's something anyway.
TRIXIE: Is it out of him?
JOHNNY: That instrument's out of him.
TRIXIE: And what of the fuckin' stone?
JOHNNY: I didn't see no fuckin' stone come out. (2.3)

The impasse drags on while Doc works up his own nerve to cut the renal calculus out. Although he can convince none of the others nursing Al that surgery is the only resolution to his crisis and is doubtful that the winks of Al's pain-slitted eyes mean he assents, Doc Cochran finally takes the initiative. His instruments sterilized, hands shaking, Doc prepares to make the first cut for an operation that two in ten patients survive but is suddenly inspired to give less invasive methods one last try. The crew of cleansing agents holds Al upright, braces him with a continual draught of salts, and urges him to pass the stone while Trixie milks blood and urine out his urethra. Once the calculus drops enough, Doc inserts a lithotrite, the urologist's calipers for reaching and crushing a kidney stone, and delivers Al from his tribulations.

Immediately after this most exhausting of crises and most purgative of releases, the shots that follow are revealing. Doc has escaped performing a surgery he had little confidence in, and had only slight familiarity with, so his sense of deliverance is second only to Al's. Doc leans in to hug the recuperating barkeep and in an extreme close-up sincerely intones, "God bless you, Al! Thank you for saving me" (2.4). He shares redemption with Al, albeit via a different way of catharsis. But so do the others, as an overhead camera frames the four exhausted priests of this purgative ritual collapsed in a love knot with Al at the heart. This tableau completes the cathartic action most pivotal in the overall plot of the series and marks it with this visual stasis of drained bodies. As if to resonate with Al's salvation, the shots that succeed the tableau include Commissioner Jarry in a tub enjoying a bubble bath at the Bella Union and Dirty Dan slicing Eamon's throat and then dispatching Johnny to deliver the victim to Wu's pigpen. These images of, first, hygienic catharsis and, then, social catharsis make Al's cleansing a generalized motive of the camp. It also makes the earless scapegoat the dramatically fitting sacrifice for the recovery of Al's voice and with it his power over Deadwood. (The burlesque of this blood sacrifice lurks in the title of this episode, "Requiem for a Gleet," as Al's stone is eulogized for its sacrifice but not the incidental human, who becomes offal in the conversion.)

10. Successful surgery. "Requiem for a Gleet" (*Deadwood* 2.4).

The equation of verbal expression with control over urination takes on additional weight when we test the transitive equation of both with a third factor, ambition. In "*Somnia ad Urinandum*," an essay on the symbolic working out of physical and social barriers, Burke notes the frequent literary associations of attempts to resist bed-wetting with "total verbal blocking." The common blockage of the verbal and the excretory streams proceeds from a single problem reducible solely to neither the symbolic nor the material world but rather proceeding from the tangle of symbolic and material motives that drives all human acts of control.[5] Freud described this difficulty in more than one place, but when he did so he most often attributed images of urinary potency to insecurities about power. Freud deduced the logic of the association in a bulky footnote in *Civilization and Its Discontents*, as this biopsy of a snippet illustrates:

> It is as though primal man had the habit, when he came into contact with fire, of satisfying an infantile desire connected with it, by putting it out with a stream of his urine. . . . Putting out fire by micturating—a theme to which modern giants, Gulliver in Lilliput and Rabelais' Gargantua, still hark back—was therefore a kind of sexual act with a male, an enjoyment of sexual potency

> in a homosexual competition. The first person to renounce his desire and spare the fire was able to carry it off with him and subdue it to his own use. By damping down the fire of his own sexual excitation, he had tamed the natural force of fire. . . . It is remarkable, too, how regularly analytic experience testifies to this connection between ambition, fire and urethral erotism. (Freud n37)

Al's inability to exercise control over his verbal expression requires its physical counterpart in his inability to pass water. With the temporary arrest of both, he begins to lose his grip on the secret levers of power in the gold camp, despite the relief that sweeps him up briefly upon his recovery. The arc of one major plot that the viewer has followed through the first season and into the second has been Swearengen's rise to a consolidation of power amid the anarchy and lawlessness of early Deadwood days. Up to this point the competing phallus that seemed the most likely to thwart his ambition has been Seth Bullock, though that competition proves manageable in episodes to come. But the number of threats to Al's ambition will hereafter multiply. At least five significant declines in his fortunes begin during or about the time of his paralysis.

The initial symptoms of Al's kidney stone arrive within twenty-four hours after a mortifying brawl between Al and Bullock in the fecal soup of the street. Al's eye is still swollen nearly shut when he is stricken with uremic poisoning, and his ribs have been injured from his roll off the balcony while clutching Bullock. The serious physical damage to Al proves to be not nearly as crucial to the plot as the rapprochement with Bullock to which he resigns himself after the fight. Before the fight Al was not sure he wanted a sheriff in Deadwood or, if a sheriff was unavoidable, whether Bullock was the one of whom he approved. But after the fight he accepts Bullock's standing as the law in Deadwood, for all his faults in Al's eyes. This is no small concession, for Bullock represents one of a handful of five phalluses competing for dominance in Deadwood.

Al is threatened and diminished by two technologies that enter Deadwood during the time of his incapacitation. The arrival of telegraph poles and the wire that will link the town with the world outside is one such threat. It will make Al more vulnerable to being found by the law, if the hints that he is evading earlier crimes in Chicago and elsewhere are true. Another threat is the stamp mill that begins operation while Al is sweating on his floor. The mill is another advance toward independence by Alma Garret, as her bank will open in the year to come. Her power proceeding from these two sources will be hard to abate from this point onward. Both technologies, poles and stamps, come in the form of phalluses, and both promise competition for control, but the stamp mill masses iron phalluses in a crushing array, and what is more threatening to Al, these massed gangs of phalluses are owned by a woman.

Two other changes occur as Al recuperates, the appearance on the scene of two persons who will be more direct threats to Al's hegemony in Deadwood. Al's decline coincides with the arrival on the stage of Wolcott, the agent of the phallus that will depose Al from power in the camp, George Hearst. Hearst's ascension to dominance will be signaled physically by his eventual severing of Al's middle finger in the third season. This action ensures that Hearst will always be one digit up on Swearengen. That hard lesson is still a season away when Wolcott arrives, but Hearst's mercenary methods are meanwhile communicated in faithful form by Wolcott. Wolcott is a harbinger of Al's final decline.

The fifth unfortunate blow to Al's independence is the untimely arrival of Hugo Jarry, the Lawrence County commissioner sent out from Yankton, the territorial headquarters. He immediately begins floating false information about possible changes in the law regarding pending claims, a stratagem clearly aimed at panicking landholders into selling out too cheaply. Wolcott, not normally softhearted himself, remarks about Jarry's reptilian resolve, "I am a sinner, who does not expect forgiveness. But I am not a government official" (2.10). Jarry is unpopular in open-minded Deadwood, and his incompetence will likewise limit his influence. But since he is a forward man for the incubating state government to come, he is not an insignificant factor in Al's calculations of his chances for unfettered operations.

After Al's recovery his control of the town increasingly falters, however much his verbal wit and his carnal purgations may recover their vivacity and regularity. When Hearst arrives on the scene, Al's days will be numbered. His bout with the kidney stone prefigures the obstacles that will paralyze and then release his sphincter of control over the society of Deadwood.

When Victims Are Not Enough

The images of bodily catharsis have taken up the foreground of the reading so far, but we should not allow this exposure of the conventionally hidden to confuse issues of priority in catharsis. Burke cautions us not to invert the origins of such repressed imagery:

> Please note that in pursuing such a line of thought we should *not* be deriving tragic catharsis from bodily processes. Our theory would be turned in exactly the opposite direction. We should be saying simply that, when catharsis attains its full poetic statement (as it must if it is to be thorough), its terminology may also be expected to re-enact some or other of these bodily analogues. ("On Catharsis" 355)

As the imagery of the human body has unspooled, the social implications have worked their way into the picture. It is time to give the body politic its due. Social catharsis requires the cleansing of this body politic, a marking out of some humans as sacrifices to the generalized guilt of the society. "Trying to be cheerful as possible, one might say that victimage is *not inevitable*," Burke consoles. "But the *temptation* to victimage is ever born anew" (*Dramatism and Development* 29). Social catharsis in *Deadwood* needs victims.

While a complete and thoroughgoing victimology of *Deadwood* is beyond the scope of this analysis, we should not be surprised if even a glancing review reveals that with the passing of each of the three seasons of the series, violence will be a less efficacious resolution to the pollutants that clog Deadwood. But surprises do happen. Seven victims, including four members of one family, are murdered in the first episode of the first season of *Deadwood*. Later episodes will more than double that body count, but at least one killing will be part of the recipe for every episode. Nearly half the victims are killed at the behest of or by Al Swearengen, whose rate is little diminished in the culminating season, but who is increasingly outpaced by Hearst's cold-blooded dispatch in manufacturing victims. Although the lion's share of violence committed in *Deadwood* proves to be minimal or temporary in its promotion of catharsis for Swearengen or for Deadwood, some significant exceptions may command our attention.

First, for efficiency's sake, let us take advantage of Burke's taxonomy of victims. He lists the following types: "(1) There is the victim chosen because he is most blameless (the Christ-principle of victimage); (2) the victim chosen because most blamable (the villainy principle); (3) the victim as the result of a tragic flaw; (4) supernumerary victims, 'expendable' for the good of the plot as a whole" ("On Catharsis" 361). I will take up each of these (scapegoat, villain, tragic hero, fragmentary victim) in turn, if not in the identical order.

Deadwood is replete with villains, but rare is the one who becomes a deserving victim. Jack McCall would seem to be the mythic villain, the assassin of the crowned hero. But like the historical McCall, the killer of Hickok lacks the stature of his victim and ranks as a petty villain of the series. Swearengen suffers but is in far too much control to be a victim within the parameters of the series—at least until the historical Swearengen left Deadwood to become a victim in Denver.[6] The real villains of the series, Hearst and then a long step down to Cy Tolliver, are seldom victimized. Wolcott and the Pinkertons we meet commit some villainous acts, but their evil lies within their status as tools of evil people. If they are villains by virtue of their mercenary bent, then so is Dirty Dan. For all that, Wolcott and the Pinkertons who die are the closest thing to villainous victims in *Deadwood.* Their deaths carry away a paltry bit of pollution.

Contrary to villains, scapegoats are fitting victims to promote catharsis because they are the least deserving victims. Scapegoats are scarce in Deadwood—nearly every character deserves to die for one reason or another—but the instances are striking. The murder of the Metz family gives Al the chance to offer a fifty-dollar reward for the head of any Indian presumably involved in the slaughter. By the time someone presents a prize, the massacre has been forgotten, but Swearengen quietly pays the bounty, no questions asked. The head he purchases he installs in a wooden box, which he keeps in his office from then on. Periodically, he opens the box for a talk, until the head becomes a sort of orphic confidante. The magical power of the head may partly proceed from the innocence of the victim, who surely had no part in the Metz killings. Al knows because he helped arrange the attack.

Hostetler is the scapegoat of the second season. The horse that kills William Bullock was a mustang brought in by Fields; when Hostetler was about to geld the horse, Fields let the legs free; the whole incident was accidental. As Hostetler observes, "Every day since I been in this camp white folks shooting and stabbing each other, still walking around to do their business. . . . The only violence we meant was to that stallion's prick, and then to turn an honest dollar." But he assumes almost immediately that he will pay for the killing of young Bullock:

> A man that did go back to tell his part, that brought the horse that he set loose to them that he caused to suffer, paid respect for the pain that he couldn't fix—now if'n, if'n it happened that they forgave him, so that he didn't have to do to hisself what he wouldn't let be done to him, well then, by God, that man might think of setting forth with whatever loudmouth went along with him, that if he made it to Oregon alive . . . the two of them might open a livery. (2.10)

The return to Deadwood does not make Hostetler feel sufficiently forgiven, especially with the persistent aggravation of Steve the Drunk. Hostetler hangs himself for a crime that he did not commit, that was in essence an accident.

The scapegoat who most plays on the heart is Jen, the fledgling prostitute who is sacrificed for Trixie's attack on Hearst. She is chosen purely for the similarity of her dimensions to Trixie's, for her demeanor could not be less like Trixie's. "Unlucky fuckin' mutt" is Al's appellation for her in an aside (3.12). Her childlike innocence leads to Johnny's inability and refusal to kill her. Al steps in to cut her throat but must steel himself first with a long talk with the head in the box, the first scapegoat of the series being asked to advise on the sacrificing of the last. "I should've learned to use a gun; I'm too fuckin' entrenched in my ways," he complains. The blood sacrifice of the substitute was signaled, too, by Trixie crying over Jen's blood on the floor after she has dressed her in her own clothes, and later by Hearst's tracking her blood across Al's office with his boot prints. Jen's faultless death is set aside from all of Al's other murders by the fact that he excuses Jewel and insists that he will clean his "own fuckin' mess up. . . . I'll take that fuckin' scrub brush" (3.12).

These three scapegoats, the Chief, Hostetler, and Jen, are all distinctive in their destinies: the Chief and Jen are stashed away in boxes and Hostetler dies the lonely and hidden death of the suicide in a barn stall. Their sacrifices as scapegoats are less purgative for being so secretive. None of them is decisive in his or her contribution to social catharsis in Deadwood.

Supernumerary victims individually contribute a negligible pittance to social catharsis. Their accumulation delivers a certain amount of release, enough to contribute to a regular program of cathartic hygiene. *Deadwood* and Deadwood are partly driven by a steady diet of minor victims who are beheaded, clubbed with a two-by-four, drowned in tubs, smothered in mud, impaled on antlers, hanged from a porch, pushed from a cliff, sliced from ear to ear, stabbed in the groin and bled out, and shot, and shot, and shot. The sheer number of deaths and regularity of violence from episode to episode must provide some release to audiences, as they do in a spaghetti Western. Yet such sheer numbers and redundancy also are a confession that "fragmentary victimage" fails to achieve the grand catharsis of the redemptive sacrifice.

The tragedy of *Deadwood* is that even the villains and scapegoats turn out to have so little impact on social catharsis that they, too, are "supernumerary" in effect. Thus far our analysis of victims would seem to be consonant with the pattern of frustrated erotic and excretory catharsis of the body. No sacrifice is significant enough to free these characters more than briefly, especially Swearengen, whose ambitions are stalled and then blocked.

Consideration of Burke's other category of victims does not seem to follow suit. Here we find victims who die not for Al or Tolliver or Hearst or Trixie or any individual's freedom. The tragic hero's sacrifice is motivated by a key flaw in his or her character, but its significance is rooted in the culture for which the hero is an exemplar. "Fate" may be a good name for this relationship between the character of the tragic hero and the hero's society. The tragic victims of *Deadwood* die for the sake of Deadwood.

Three grand *katharoi* are sacrificed for the survival and growth of Deadwood, one per season. Hickok, William Bullock, and Ellsworth correspond to the Holy Trinity of the Father, the Son, and the Holy Ghost, so they need not resort to the tactics of repressed victims to achieve redemption. Their virtues promote the social values of power, domestication, and commerce, in turn. Wild Bill and Ellsworth are both shot in chairs when taken by surprise. William is crushed in the mud of the street and dies in Doc Cochran's office.

Wild Bill Hickok appears in Deadwood when the town is lawless and in search of someone who will fairly exert (patriarchal) power. As Bill well knows, he is not up to the job. But his timely sacrifice sets in motion the series of events that will bring law to Deadwood in the person of Seth Bullock. Seth had arrived in Deadwood with a distaste for the badge after his experiences in Montana, but Wild Bill convinces Seth that he is called, by his example as a hero above all else. From their encounter with Persimmon Pete, Seth had learned from Wild Bill that the law in a mining camp may work differently than law in civilization. The death of Wild Bill changes more than Seth; Bill's spirit passes into the town of Deadwood and becomes part and parcel of its culture forever after. A visit to the contemporary Deadwood will confirm Wild Bill's haunting of the place.

William Bullock may seem a less than plausible hero because of his immaturity, but he must be at least as good a son as Wild Bill was a father. William's character is about the frontier transition from wilderness to civilization, so the theme of his actions while alive is domestication. The morning of the day he dies, William is planting sunflower seeds that he had brought with him from North Dakota. He helps Seth salvage something of his dead father by calling ducks in over the ponds of Belle Fourche. William's presence in Deadwood, added to that of Sofia Metz, will lead to their two mothers planting the seeds of the first school. When William is killed, his mother, Martha, dedicates herself completely to the school's development. Her care for her son is sublimated into her care for all the children of the camp. William is cut off before he is mature by a wild mustang panicked by his unpleasant first experience of town life. His sacrifice will promote the advance of domestication in Deadwood in the form of education.

The third tragic victim brings the selfless sort of love known as agape to Deadwood. In the first two seasons, love was a commodity sold in the brothels. Ellsworth introduces a new relationship between love and commerce in his courting and marrying of Alma Garret. When he first conceives of proposing to Alma, at the instigation of Trixie, he wonders if God will allow him to marry her in order to help with Sofia and her child on the way. "When a boulder needs hauling, I will haul the boulder," vows Ellsworth (2.8). He is an unexpected helpmeet to Alma as she raises Sofia and institutes Deadwood's first bank. When Hearst wants to stop Alma's project, he fires threatening shots at her, but he has Ellsworth killed outright, figuring that will turn Alma away. Her widowing fails to discourage Alma, but we cannot say how her venture will turn out. Ellsworth's final words before he is shot demonstrate his selfless concern for his wife and daughter, as he talks with his dog about whether he should eat dinner with his family after the attempt on Alma's life:

> Would my conversation with her, in lingering after supper, have disrupted the little one's routine on a day that had been disrupted previous? Yes. Already she had seen a series of people taking a watch to protect that schoolhouse. And how many questions must have occurred to her? Cuz that is a bright child. "What is transpiring that we need guarding from?" And what memories must that have brought back, of her own dear family murdered in a sudden fake Indian depredation by shithead fuckin' road

agents? Not solely how would I like to be passing the evening, the like. When I've left, have I given the mother more calming down to do, before she gets the child to sleep? Them sorts of things is what you have to consider. (3.11)

By focusing completely on his mate and child, Ellsworth sets an example we have seen only in brief glimpses previously, as when Jane had nursed smallpox patients. Will his selflessness allow Alma's bank to succeed? Will love and commerce find a model to compete with Al and Trixie, Tolliver and Joanie, or Sol and Trixie? At the conclusion of the series, these remain open questions.

These three tragic victims show the right ways to apply power, domestication, and commerce to life in their society. In so doing they are culture heroes, quite apart from their personal failings. Note that Swearengen has endeavored to dominate Deadwood in the arenas of power, domestication, and commerce. He ultimately falls short of the accomplishments of the three tragic heroes, in that Wild Bill, William Bullock, and Ellsworth each inspire an institution that will persist in the culture in a way no petty ambitions of Al's ever could. The sheriff's office, the school, and the bank will continue to improve Deadwood even as Al's fortunes and those of other individuals continue to be frustrated. Perhaps we have a double plot in which the society of Deadwood rises as others—in this case Swearengen—decline.

But a third force may in time prove too much to resist for either Al or the culture of the town. Seth once caged Hearst for a day, under suspicion in the investigation of a labor organizer's murder. But as Hearst warned, Seth could not hold him. Trixie waylaid Hearst and shot him, but he survived the attempt and arose from the bed to walk the streets of Deadwood once more. Can Hearst undo the blockage and find a way to realize his vision of Deadwood? Can Hearst bull his way past the obstacles that Seth and Al insinuate into his path, in the same impulsive way he fashioned a door to the balcony by crashing through the wall of his room and onto the porch roof? Is this a purgation worth yearning for? Those who have peeked at the history books will discern the ending of this drama.

A Final Passage

When Al deputizes Johnny, who is the closest to Jen, to cut her throat, Johnny is inspired to prepare her for the act by apostrophizing her part in Deadwood society, if not in the world as a whole. The allegory he poses is a reinvocation of Preacher Smith's eulogy for Wild Bill, in which St. Paul reminds us that all the members of the body, even those feeble or less honorable ones, are equally necessary:

JOHNNY: What is this, Jen?
JEN: A wall?
JOHNNY: On the surface, yes. But inside, many creatures go about their lives such as ants. They got a whole operation going. They got worker ants and soldier ants and whore ants, to fuck the soldiers and the workers. Right inside that wall, baby ants. Everyone's got a task to hew to, Jen. You understand me? (3.12)

Preacher Smith's analogy to the human body here is transformed into an ant colony, a body politic. Jen's part in that world behind the wall is not just to be a whore, or even a baby, but to be a scapegoat, a replacement in Trixie's redemption ritual. When we first meet Jen, she is excited about the opportunity to learn new languages in Deadwood; in order for Al to kill her, Johnny must be gagged and bound. Silence and secrecy descend upon her victimage.

At least Jen remains a member of the social body—by fulfilling her role as a successful scapegoat. Al may not even have a real role. He appears at first to be the crassest of villains, but Milch encourages us to read him as heroic. We have already seen that Al falls short of tragic heroism, as he tries to achieve control of power, domestic order, and commercial prerogative, and fails. He fails in all these roles not because of his crassness but because he tries to achieve power, domesticity, and commerce *without* instituting a sheriff, a school, or a bank. In each cause he is obstructed.

As viewers we experience Deadwood through Al's body, and as our analysis of plot and imagery has abundantly demonstrated, his body is seriously blocked up in his episode of uremic poisoning. Although it recovers, his will to power does not recover the inertial flow that he enjoyed during the first season. Within a few episodes after recovering, Al counsels Bullock, "Our cause is surviving—not being allied with Yankton, or cogs in the Hearst machine" (2.8). Al is the apostle of free flow in the mining camp. But it is already apparent that Al will fail against both opponents, each of whom wishes to channel the flow to his own benefit. Later in the same episode, Al takes the box with the decapitated head out to his balcony and lets slip his own doubts: "Don't the decapitated deserve recreation, Chief? As much if not more than those of us not yet dismembered?" (2.8). Al can already foresee being cut off from the body politic of Deadwood as surely as he has overseen the removal of so many other pollutants from the camp.

Others will prosper after Al's washout. The culture of Deadwood can only flourish once the established institutions productively channel the flow of money, love, and information. Certainly Alma Garret would have to say that the flow of mining claims, of money, of gold, and of husbands through Deadwood Gulch has been good for her, so long as she has Sofia as her unchanging pivot. Certainly flow was good for Tom Nuttall's bicycle feat:

BYSTANDER: Do you suppose if the inventor had moved among us, he'd have made a model more suitable for sinkholes?
TOM NUTTALL: Guided and pedaled to rights, she'll roll as smooth as a ball on a green. . . . My bicycle masters boardwalk and quagmire with aplomb. . . .
BYSTANDER: Eight-to-one odds on the quagmire.
TOM: I shall swoop across it. Eight-to-one taken at a hundred.
BYSTANDER: Even money on the boardwalk.
TOM: Done! Taken to a hundred. Loose boards to be nailed. Commerce suspended. Animals, drunks, and sundries cleared from my lane of passage.
BYSTANDER: Done. (2.8)

Nuttall on his bicycle achieves flow through the heart of Deadwood's main street and wins his bet in the doing. When a roustabout mutters a bribe to throw the race, Nuttall explodes at him, "That is a laydown you propose! Corruption won't never breathe stinky on my bicycle!" (2.8). Of course, Nuttall is tragically wrong, as his ride will eventually precipitate the incident that kills young William Bullock and will transform the magnificent bicycle into something too corrupt for him to contemplate against the wall of Saloon no. 10, where Wild Bill has already been a victim; he has an employee remove it to the alley. But Nuttall has proven that free flow through the streets can be accomplished, with civic cooperation and planning. The boardwalk will get better odds than the quagmire.

Boardwalk culture will open Deadwood up to well-heeled outsiders, who will find their own ways of channeling flow to their own purposes. Hearst will harness the flow of gold out of the camp, but that is in the indefinite future of the series. So, too, in that indefinite future will come the bricking of the streets, another victory over the quagmire that will appeal to the Edwardian burghers of 1907. Mastering the quagmire with aplomb will be what Deadwood's Historical Preservation Commission of 1991 will surely have in mind when it will rebrick the streets to improve the flow of well-heeled outsiders into and through Deadwood Gulch. Promoting flow, Burke would say, is "the constant temptation of human societies, whose orders are built by a kind of animal exceptionally adept in the ways of symbolic action" ("Dramatism" 451).

Notes

1. Wolfe 9. In a review of *Deadwood*, amateur Black Hills historians Bill Swanson and Marty Krause assess the program's street realism with tempered praise: "The place was a tad too clean, too. We have early reports of mud in Deadwood streets that was two to three feet deep. It was always muddy and well-mixed with animal and human waste." See "Show Gets Two Thumbs Up" 17.
2. Kenneth Burke, "Rhetoric and Poetic," in *Language as Symbolic Action*, 296–99. My essay is in some ways modeled on Burke's five exemplary critiques of the workings of catharsis; see "The Thinking of the Body," in *Language as Symbolic Action*, 308–43. See also Burke, *Essays toward a Symbolic of Motives* 149.

3. For a discussion of the range of associations with the money/excrement equation, see Norman O. Brown, "Filthy Lucre," as well as "The Excremental Vision," in *Life against Death*, 234–304, 179–201.
4. The stifling, secreting, or "pinching off" of words is a recurrent theme in *Deadwood*, from the first actions of the first episode right through the last one. When Trixie shoots a customer in the head, Doc Cochran is curious about how the victim lives twenty minutes with a bullet in his forebrain, "the center of speech and thought" (1.1). The shooting victim's words slowly run down and when they stop, he dies. The use of secrecy in communication begins in the first episode and is endemic throughout the final episode. The many strategic uses of secrecy and the unspoken in *Deadwood* would be a study in itself.
5. Kenneth Burke, "*Somnia ad Urinandum*," in *Language as Symbolic Action* 344–58. See also Burke's comments on power as expressed through bodily catharsis in the characters of St. Anthony and Prometheus, in "Thinking of the Body," 314–22.
6. According to research by Mary Kopco, the director of Deadwood's Adams Museum, and Jerry Bryant, the Adams Museum's historical archaeologist, the historical Al Swearengen left Deadwood in 1899 and, after a stay with family in Iowa, was found dead on a Denver street on November 15, 1904: "He had suffered a massive head wound after being struck with a heavy, blunt object, according to reports of the time." Revenge for any of Swearengen's many crimes is presumed to be the motive, but the murder went unsolved. Based on his reading, Bryant felt the television series was quite generous to the historical Swearengen and called him "a real vicious bastard." See Lawrence 2.

4 "Land of Oblivion"
Abjection, Broken Bodies, and the Western Narrative in *Deadwood*

John Dudley

Like Tim Steckline, John Dudley examines Deadwood*'s "penchant for the macabre," its treatment of "corpses, bodily fluids, filth," focusing in particular on its treatment of female bodies and sexual violence. Dudley turns to Julia Kristeva's conception of "abjection," arguing that "like Trixie's battered body, images of abjection haunt the streets of Deadwood, inviting our fascination and repulsion." Abjection inevitably leads many of* Deadwood*'s female characters back to childhood traumas, explaining their apparent inability to break away from those who seek to control their bodies. Kristeva's connection of "colloquial speech and emotional violence" helps Dudley consider* Deadwood*'s concern with the "obsessive violence and power of language." Ultimately he suggests that the traumas are both "personal and historical," evident not only in a contemporary television production but in the very narratives that emerged from events such as the forced removal of the Cherokees, the California gold rush, and Custer's defeat at the Little Big Horn. The "theory of abjection," Dudley concludes, "provides a vital context through which to reexamine the dynamics of the frontier thesis, its ongoing fascination for audiences, and its representation in the seemingly mindless pandemic of violence that erupts in* Deadwood*."*

Since its debut in March 2004, *Deadwood* has attracted as much attention for the rawness of its language as for its claims to be yet another in a long line of "revisionist" Westerns. According to the show's creator, David Milch, what drew him to this subject matter is the central question: How can a society without laws maintain order? The answer, it would seem, is violence—or more precisely, the threat of violence—as conveyed through language. For Milch this function has everything to do with the nature of speech itself. In the commentary track that accompanies the first episode of the

DVD edition of the series, Milch establishes a relationship between the show's language and what he has frequently identified as its major thematic concern, the "discovery of the various principles by which a society ordered itself":

> If the theme you're working with is the negation of law, how do you make a viewer experience what it's like to be in an environment without law? Because obviously the viewer's experiencing in a passive way an entertainment, and the assault of the language, the sense that there is no protection for the viewer's own sensibilities, I think, begins to establish that kind of lawless atmosphere, emotionally, where . . . it's a kind of battering that I think ultimately brings the viewer to some sort of felt, emotional participation in the environment.[1]

The connection between verbal and physical violence is reinforced by the context in which these remarks are presented. Milch speaks over the miner Ellsworth's memorably profane oration, with which viewers discover the unique mix of vulgarity and syntactical density that defines the show's rhetorical style, and Milch's comments continue into the next scene—one featuring a more literal "battering."[2] Trixie, the lead "whore" at the Gem Saloon, is found to have shot an abusive customer in the head. When her boss and lover, Al Swearengen, hears the gunshot, he says to his henchman Dan Dority, "That's her derringer. I warned you about that loopy cunt!" (1.1). Upon entering the room, Swearengen and Dan find Trixie, her face bloody, desperately repeating her explanation, "I said not to beat on me! I told him!" Swearengen angrily silences Trixie, telling her pointedly, "No one asked for your version!" (1.1). The john, a gaping wound open on either side of his head, has remained inexplicably and grotesquely alive while the doctor is summoned; the small group that has gathered watches him die. This image helps establish the show's penchant for the macabre, when a curious Doc Cochran passes his medical instrument completely through the dead customer's skull. In conjunction with the horror of its imagery, this scene also introduces a crucial thematic concern, played out through the entire series, which involves the struggles

"Land of Oblivion" 73

11. Trixie. "Deadwood" (*Deadwood* 1.1).

of women to achieve subjectivity within a violent patriarchal society, the boundaries of which are defined and maintained by the unique characteristics of a sensational, stylized, and violent language. Trixie enters the narrative as both victim and aggressor, a strong and potentially dangerous woman whose independence poses a threat to Swearengen's business and indeed to his very identity as a dominant patriarchal figure. Swearengen's silencing of her "version" of events is accompanied by the beating she receives later in his office. Trixie's face, scarred and swollen for much of the first season, serves as a literal text upon which Swearengen announces his power to the camp.

As this early sequence suggests, *Deadwood* demonstrates the desperation with which women strive to gain subjectivity and power, as well as the mechanisms by which patriarchy denies, destroys, or usurps this subjectivity in fulfilling the national narrative of American expansion. In her reading of *Deadwood* as a "postfemininst undoing" of female subjectivity, Anne Helen Petersen claims,

> With time, the women of *Deadwood* consistently (and successfully) resist the strictures of patriarchy that surround them, achieving autonomy, self-expression, even, in all its complexity, happiness.

Yet their advances teeter in the balance as George Hearst (and the modernity and civilization he embodies) takes root in Deadwood.... It seems the lesson is, while much has been gained, much may equally be lost. (268)

Deadwood is, more than nearly any other Western, a story *about* women. Despite the remarkable limitations placed on them by law, custom, and circumstance, the primary women characters in *Deadwood*—Trixie, Alma, Joanie, and Jane—while initially defined by the men with whom they are associated, defy their status as women and emerge as potentially powerful figures in the narrative, even as men act to silence their voices.

In this essay I argue that Julia Kristeva's notion of abjection provides the necessary context through which to understand the extraordinary pairing of violence and language in *Deadwood* as a response to women's emerging subjectivity. Moreover, the increasing significance of the female characters and the interwoven narratives of gender, sexuality, brutality, and loss within Milch's "anti-Western Western" (as one HBO executive has described it) illuminate the recurring struggle of language to complete the conquest of the West as gendered space within the American imagination (qtd. in Wolk). As a genre that has undergone continuous and often violent revision since its origins in the early nineteenth century, the Western might be described as always, to some degree, "anti-Western" in its tendency to reimagine the foundational ideas and images that provide its identity. Always beginning anew, returning to its archaic and turbulent origins, the narrative of the American West can never fully contain the threat of the abject in its midst. Like Trixie's battered body, images of abjection haunt the streets of Deadwood, inviting our fascination and repulsion. Similarly, the feminized, abject West simultaneously calls forth and resists the narrative tradition upon which *Deadwood* comments and to which it ultimately belongs.

Both Milch's defense of the series' use of obscenity and the linkage of verbal and physical "battering" in these adjacent scenes suggest the relationship between colloquial speech and emotional violence provided by Kristeva in *Powers of Horror*. Kristeva claims that "the vocabulary of slang, because of its strangeness, its very violence, and especially because the reader does not always understand it, is of course a radical instrument of separation, of rejection, and, at the limit, of hatred" (191). This observation occurs within the context of Kristeva's larger argument about abjection in literature and culture. Associated with corpses, bodily fluids, filth, and—through its connection with childbirth—the maternal body, the abject is something that both repels and fascinates by reminding us of two things: the material condition of human existence and this condition's resistance to language. Abjection, therefore, forces the individual subject to confront that which defies acceptance into the symbolic order—something too awful for words. Kristeva writes,

> There looms, within abjection, one of those violent, dark revolts of being, directed against a threat that seems to emanate from an exorbitant outside or inside, ejected beyond the scope of the possible, the tolerable, the thinkable. It lies there, quite close, but it cannot be assimilated. It beseeches, worries, and fascinates desire, which, nevertheless, does not let itself be seduced. Apprehensive, desire turns aside; sickened, it rejects. (3)

In order to achieve or maintain our status as subjects, Kristeva argues, we must discard that which is abject, but we can never fully escape its hold on our imagination.

Like many canonical Westerns *Deadwood*'s obsessive depictions of broken and battered human bodies, often linked either linguistically or literally with sexual violence, call attention to the always unfulfilled promise of the frontier and the thwarted development of the iconic Western hero, who is denied the home and identity that would fill the psychological holes left by traumas both personal and historical. Through scenes of violence the audience of the Western finds the pain and the pleasure—the "felt, emotional participation," to use Milch's terms—inherent in narratives of abjection. Death exists in the narrative not as an abstraction or a philosophical problem, but in the form of dead bodies, as an immanent presence, needing constant disposal. Kristeva writes,

> The corpse (or cadaver: *cadere*, to fall), that which has irremediably come a cropper, is cesspool, and death; it upsets even more violently the one who confronts it as fragile and fallacious chance. A wound with blood and pus, or the sickly, acrid smell of sweat, of decay, does not *signify* death. In the presence of signified death—a flat encephalograph, for instance—I would understand, react, or accept. No, as in true theater, without makeup or masks, refuse and corpses *show me* what I permanently thrust aside in order to live. (*Powers* 3)

Kristeva identifies abjection as a critical component of much twentieth-century literature in which "the writer, fascinated by the abject, imagines its logic, projects himself into it, introjects it, and as a consequence perverts language—style and content" (16).[3] Such introjection—a complete immersion in the darkest corners of human behavior—might well describe the aesthetic and thematic power of *Deadwood*. What has been described as the "surface realism" of *Deadwood*, its commitment to re-create, as accurately as possible, the buildings, the clothing, the "muck," of an 1876 frontier settlement, also includes the painstaking exhibition of dead and dying bodies and their remnants, from the corpses that fill the "pest tent" or fall victim to Dan Dority's knife, Francis Wolcott's razor, or George Hearst's greed, to the ubiquitous blood stains that resist incessant scrubbing.

Indeed, the milieu of the American West, as depicted in *Deadwood*, provides the ideal setting for a condition described by Kristeva as inherently unformed and provisional. Presented as missing, failed, or incomplete parents and children, the characters in *Deadwood* seek, both consciously and unconsciously, entrance into a recognizable family structure, whether literal or figurative—a most basic ordering of consciousness into categories of "subject" and "object." For Kristeva, however, the presence of the abject inevitably undermines the acquisition of identity through *desire*, through the acknowledgement of the categories of self/other, subject/object, or inside/outside, and accommodates only rejection, expulsion, and denial. It is a "border that has encroached on everything" (*Pow-*

ers 3). The "exile" or "straying" that results from contact with the abject further resonates with the American frontier narrative, as well as the peculiar enjoyment, or "jouissance," that it provides:

> The one by whom the abject exists is thus a *deject* who places (himself), *separates* (himself), situates (himself), and therefore *strays* instead of getting his bearings, desiring, belonging or refusing. . . . For it is out of such straying on excluded ground that he draws his jouissance. The abject from which he does not cease separating is for him, in short, a *land of oblivion* that is constantly remembered. (*Powers* 8)

The particular "land of oblivion" that provides the setting for *Deadwood* is as noteworthy for what it lacks (law) as for what it possesses (gold). This lawless setting, a borderland representing neither wilderness nor civilization, draws such disparate—and desperate—figures as Swearengen, Wild Bill Hickok, and Seth Bullock, each a version of the archetypal frontiersman whose encounters with desire are frequently confounded by more primitive, inexplicable drives. As Kelly Oliver explains, "Even jettisoned, the abject can still threaten the social, the Symbolic order. The Symbolic can maintain itself only by maintaining its borders; and the abject points to the fragility of those borders" (*Reading Kristeva* 56). This theory of abjection, therefore, provides a vital context through which to reexamine the dynamics of the frontier thesis, its ongoing fascination for audiences, and its representation in the seemingly mindless pandemic of violence that erupts in *Deadwood*.

"The Body Is Not One Member": The Failure of Sacrifice

The story of Hickok's arrival and murder in Deadwood, which serves as the focal point of the first five episodes of the series, suggests the possibility of a ritualized sacrifice, of what Richard Slotkin identifies, in his series of books on the mythology of the American West, as "regeneration through violence." The violence in *Deadwood*, however, is remarkably atypical for the Western genre. There are few, if any, "gunfights"; instead, the most memorably violent scenes involve hand-to-hand combat, from Bullock's literal de-facing of an

Indian in season 1 to Dan Dority's eye-gouging of Captain Turner in season 3. Far from the ritualized shoot-outs of *High Noon* (1952) or *My Darling Clementine* (1946) or the macabre choreography of *The Wild Bunch* (1969), the ubiquitous depictions of death in the series—ugly, filthy, and awkward—allude to, but ultimately undermine, the plot of sacrifice, regeneration, and rebirth so closely associated with the "frontier" narrative. If the Western, as Lee Clark Mitchell persuasively argues, "has always celebrated a certain necrological impulse," frequently employing the beaten male body as "a self-contained, animated (if finally inanimate) object," *Deadwood* dwells on the body (significantly, both male and female) as abject, something repulsive and unable to be contained, resisting symbolization and integration into the discourse by which we make sense of the world (*Westerns* 172). In his study of the violence done to men's bodies in traditional Westerns, Mitchell argues that "Western heroes are knocked down, made supine, then variously tortured simply so that they can recover in order to rise again. Or rather, the process of beating occurs so that we can *see* men recover, regaining their strength and resources in the process of once again making themselves into men" (174). This motif is certainly operative in *Deadwood*, as Bullock's nearly continuous state of recuperation from various shootings and beatings reminds us—in the series' very first scene, set in Montana, his arm is bandaged from a recent gunshot.[4] What Deadwood so often lacks, however, are the regenerative rituals by which violence and death are purged from society.

In what has become a key text in the contemporary critical understanding of ritual, *Violence and the Sacred* (1977), René Girard argues that narratives of sacrifice, as well as the funeral rites that are essential to the maintenance of civil society, serve to establish clear boundaries between the living and the dead and to purify the community:

> Death is the ultimate violence that can be inflicted on a living being. It is therefore the extreme of maleficence. With death a contagious sort of violence is let loose on a community, and the living must take steps to protect themselves against it. So they quaran-

tine death, creating a *cordon sanitaire* all around it. Above all, they have recourse to funeral rites, which (like all other rites) are dedicated to the purgation and expulsion of maleficent violence.

Whatever the cause and circumstances of his death, the dying man finds himself in a situation similar to that of the surrogate victim vis-à-vis the community. The grief of the mourner is a curious mixture of terror and hope — a mixture conducive to resolutions of good conduct in the future. The death of the individual has something of the quality of a tribute levied for the continued existence of the collectivity. A human being dies, and the solidarity of the survivors is enhanced by his death.

The surrogate victim dies so that the entire community, threatened by the same fate, can be reborn in a new or renewed cultural order. Having sown the seeds of death, the god ancestor, or mythic hero then dies himself or selects a victim to die in his stead. In so doing he bestows a new life on men. Understanding this process, we can also understand why death should be regarded as the elder sister, not to say the mother and ultimate source, of life itself. (255)

Girard's paradigm aptly describes a central motif in the canonical frontier narrative, from Cooper's Leatherstocking novels to contemporary revisions of the myth, such as Clint Eastwood's *Unforgiven* (1992). In these stories the hero experiences terrible loss and builds hope for the community through the sacrificial death of a close companion, whether friend, family member, or love object. In *Deadwood*, however, the promise of a "renewed cultural order" is never fulfilled, despite the fleeting moment of possibility that Hickok's death and burial provides.

The viewing of Hickok's corpse and his subsequent funeral provide a bitter commentary on the frequent use of such scenes of ritual, particularly within cinematic Westerns. The fifth episode of season 1 opens with a close-up of flies crawling on the dead Hickok's face. As the camera pans out to reveal a crowd filing past the body, lying in state in the thoroughfare, the voice of a street peddler cries out, "Tuft of a recently decapitated Indian . . . 25 cents. . . . Authentic heathen hair tufts. . . . Head brought to camp same day as Wild Bill Hickok was killed" (1.5). The scene immediately suggests grotesque spectacle and prurient curiosity, rather than the "curious mixture of terror and hope" called for by Girard's funeral rites.[5] Bullock, surveying the carnivalesque atmosphere with disgust, orders the hawker to "cut that shit out" and is told, "No law against me selling these, mister." Bullock responds, "No law either against me breaking your fucking jaw, you don't quit it!" before grabbing the man's gruesome wares and throwing them into a nearby fire (1.5). While the desire to establish ritual suggests the camp's passage into the "civilized" social realm, reality instead consists of Hickok's body on display, in Bullock's words, "like a goddamned circus freak."

The failure of ritual as provider of order and meaning continues in the wake of Hickok's death. As a hastily arranged tribunal gathers in Swearengen's saloon to put Hickok's murderer on trial, Bullock and his partner, Sol Star, join the crowd gathered for Hickok's funeral at the site of his grave—a notably smaller group than the throng assembled earlier to see his dead body. Here the saintly but somewhat clownish Reverend Smith refers to Paul's First Letter to the Corinthians, verse 12, a passage that makes explicit the metaphorical relationship between the body and the community:

> St. Paul tells us, by one's spirit are we all baptized in the one body. Whether we be Jew or gentile, bond or free. And have all been made to drink into one spirit. For the body is not one member, but many. He tells us, "The eye cannot say unto the hand, I have no need of thee. Nor again, the head to the feet, I have no need of thee. They much more those members of the body which seem to be more feeble, and those members of the body which we think of as less honorable, all are necessary." He—he says that there should be no schism in the body, but that the members should have the same care, one to another. And where the one member suffer, all the members suffer with it. (1.5)

The integrity of the body politic that this scene seems to predict is quickly broken by the news, delivered as the dirt is shoveled onto

Hickok's casket, that Hickok's killer, Jack McCall, has been "turned loose" by a jury resolute in rejecting the rule of law.[6] An angry Bullock rebuffs what he sees as Reverend Smith's sentimental appeal to friendship and common purpose and watches McCall ride away on horseback, unscathed and unrepentant. Anything but a unified body, the camp resists the traditional consequences provided by ritual and remains a violent, turbulent space, even as elements of "civilization" begin to accrue.[7]

Significantly, Hickok's funeral rites occur *outside* Deadwood, in the graveyard on the hillside above the camp. Indeed, William Bullock's funeral in season 2, an even more traumatic moment of collective grief, occurs in the sheriff's front yard, across the creek from the town itself. Whatever catharsis these rituals offer has no claim within the dirty streets of Deadwood proper. In Girard's terms the community suffers from a sacrificial crisis in which the surrogate victim no longer functions as an outlet for society's aggressive impulses. Girard claims that "ritual in general, and sacrificial rites in particular, assume essential roles in societies that lack a firm judicial system" (18). In the absence of law, however, waves of violence continue to sweep over Deadwood, like the smallpox "plague" that consumes much of the first season's narrative. Young Bullock and Hickok notwithstanding, the majority of characters who leave the town (and the series) of Deadwood generally do so via Mr. Wu's pigsty, where their bones are picked clean by beasts whose own bodies will soon feed the surviving residents. The corpses that haunt *Deadwood* are the epitome of Kristeva's abject: "death infecting life" (*Powers* 4). Their presence serves to disrupt the ability of the characters to pass through the archaic, precivilized state—the "land of oblivion"—into which they have strayed. As William Handley notes, the Western narrative is frequently characterized by "intra-family violence," as the aggression of national expansion, far from being contained by violence against the Indian occupants of the land, instead spreads like a disease within the frontier community.[8] In *Deadwood* this internal violence is nowhere demonstrated more clearly than within the confines of the Gem and the Bella Union Saloons and the problematic "families" contained within.

"You Keep Drawing Breath": Man as Rule-Giver

Particularly in the paired relationships between the two saloon owners Swearengen and Cy Tolliver, and their chief prostitutes, Trixie and Joanie, *Deadwood*'s first season establishes the dynamics of abjection and its complex interplay of gender, violence, and language, which will unfold throughout the show's subsequent seasons. The series introduces Tolliver's somewhat upscale Bella Union as a mirror, an uncanny double, for the world of the Gem and its proprietor, Swearengen. Seemingly superior to the Gem in its more luxurious appointments, sophisticated games of chance, and highbrow aspirations, the Bella Union ultimately proves a darker place, its dysfunctional family of card dealers, bartenders, and prostitutes placed at even greater risk by the murderous whims of their sinister "father," Tolliver, than are the members of Swearengen's "flock" at the Gem.[9] The doubling motif is reinforced by the outward parallels between two men and by the complex relationship each man has with the woman who has served, at various times, as his lover, protégé, and most prized whore. Just as Al must assert his dominance over Trixie after she kills the abusive john, Cy is compelled to remind Joanie of his absolute power over her. Where Al's cruelty toward Trixie, however, is mitigated by some kind of genuine affection, Cy strikes an even more frightening and merciless figure, his life unredeemed by any meaningful intersubjective relationship with others.[10]

The disastrous episode involving the young con artists Miles and Flora highlights Tolliver's cruelty and demonstrates a striking intrusion of the abject into the superficially orderly and reasonable world of the Bella Union. When Cy captures and tortures Miles and Flora, two young thieves posing as innocents in search of their missing father, he does so for the benefit of his primary lieutenants, Joanie and Eddie Sawyer, after he senses their imminent betrayal of him. As the young siblings' names, borrowed from Henry James's *The Turn of the Screw* (1898), indicate, they are an uncanny and mysterious pair, and their episode, like James's tale, is both terrifying and fraught with psychological implications. In the previous scene

Joanie, upon catching Flora rifling through her jewelry, offers to let her escape from Cy's wrath: "Put down my things and I'll let you get out without raising hell." Flora replies, "Why don't you let me go *with* your things and shut your fucking mouth? Because I remind you of whoever the fuck I remind you of." Before leaving, Flora asks Joanie contemptuously, "Who am I? Your little baby? Your little sister? You?" (1.8). In fact, Joanie's embrace of Flora's sleeping body the night before has established her attraction to the younger girl as erotic object. Later Joanie pleads with Cy to let Flora go, something he is unwilling to do, despite the fact that Flora has stolen nothing of material value from him. Instead, it is clear that Tolliver wants to use Flora as a means through which to affirm his power over Joanie.

The ensuing scene involving Miles's and Flora's deaths reinforces Cy's role as a corrupt paternal figure for Joanie. After an implied passage of time, the camera focuses on Joanie's troubled face as she stands before the Bella Union's winding staircase. From the upper stairs Eddie appears, telling her, "Cy wants you up there, honey" (1.8). Eddie and Joanie are ushered into a bedroom and are ordered by Cy to stand directly opposite Miles and Flora, whose now-disfigured faces serve as younger selves and monstrous mirrors in which Cy's employees simultaneously see their own youthful past and ominous future.[11] Cy has evidently continued the beating of Miles and Flora in private, and they are slumped before him in chairs, their bodies caked with dried blood and dirt. Cy stands between Eddie and Joanie in the center of the room, and his own commanding image is shown reflected in the mirror on the dresser. In Lacanian terms this scene affirms Cy's position as logos and lawgiver, what Lacan calls "the name of the father."[12] After hitting Flora several times, Cy turns to Miles, calling attention to the violent dismantling of his body that has taken place: "Next fucking breath you draw, the smell of fucking sulfur's liable to be strong in your nose. Where is your fucking nose, anyway?" (1.8). Cy's indictment of Miles explicitly demonstrates his own notion of the mastery required of men over women, with clear implications for Eddie's alliance with Joanie, and their joint attempt to operate beyond Cy's reach: "You're found fucking guilty of being a cunt. I'm hereby passing judgment for you letting this little bitch push you around and tell you what to do when you were supposed to be a man and showing her the fucking rules!" (1.8). For Cy, to be a man is to be a rule-giver, and to fail at this task is to be robbed of one's manhood entirely. Cy asserts his own role as judge and executioner by shooting Miles in the head. Thereafter, he begins to torment Flora, and after Joanie asks him not to hurt her—"you mean before I kill her?"—he forces Joanie to shoot the abject figure of Flora, the budding flower who attracts both Joanie's sexual desire and her longing to rewrite her own traumatic past. "Why don't you put that out of its misery?" Cy asks as he hands Joanie the gun (1.8). The pretty young girl with whom Joanie has so strongly identified is reduced to an "it," a grotesque thing requiring disposal.

Not surprisingly the specter of childhood trauma fuels Joanie's response to Cy's ongoing cruelty. Not until episode 1.12 does the story reveal that Joanie was sold to Cy years earlier by her widowed father, who raped her and forced her into prostitution as a young girl. In a conversation with Alma Garret about her own contemptible father, whom Bullock has recently beaten in the Bella Union, Joanie confides the following:

> On our way from Syracuse to Indiana so my daddy could try farming, my mama got cholera and died. He didn't make any better a farmer than millinery clerk, but he had a way enough with words to get me believing that my mama in heaven wanted me to see to his needs. And then to add to the egg money by seeing to the men he brought, and he wanted me talking my sisters into seeing to his needs, and then to the men, 'til he sold me to Cy Tolliver. If he was here, I'd wish a beating mornings and evenings on my daddy, like your Pa took today. (1.12)

In fact, Joanie and Alma share much in common as traumatized daughters. Alma has been married off to a wealthy fool in order to pay her widower father's gambling debts, and when he appears in Deadwood after Swearengen orders the murder of her husband, it is only to enrich himself with the profits from her mining venture.

While any physical or sexual abuse on her father's part is never explicitly stated, Alma stiffens at the touch of his hand and remains wary of his behavior with her young ward, Sophia, finally demanding, "Get away from her!" and pulling Sophia away when his intentions toward Alma's money become clear (1.12). His pet name for Alma, "Button," evokes something small and insignificant, but useful—something that reacts to his touch—and, in the context of their uneasy relationship, the word carries distinct sexual connotations. Alma publicly displays guarded affection for her father, but when Bullock beats him senseless in her presence, her expression reveals not horror but relief. The brief scene between her and Joanie is a moment of acknowledged kinship, as she receives from Joanie her father's teeth, found on the floor of the Bella Union.[13] Both women, struggling with their fathers or the memory of them, continue to find themselves immobilized, Alma by her addiction to laudanum, Joanie by Cy Tolliver.

The presence of the abject serves as a weapon through which Cy—indeed the repressive patriarchy of Deadwood itself—consolidates and maintains power over women. After ordering Joanie to kill Flora, Cy prevents her from putting the gun to her own head. "Don't do nothing. Whatever you want to do will be a mistake," Cy quietly commands, gritting his teeth. "You keep drawing breath" (1.8). By directing her to shoot Flora rather than perform the act himself (as he does with Miles), Cy forces Joanie to simultaneously remove the object of her desire and erase her own desiring subjectivity. Cy, however, retains Joanie as the valuable commodity he has purchased, perpetuating her status as an instrument of his own desperate drive for power. In the following episode, while she looks for a location for her own brothel, now with Cy's imprimatur and financing, Joanie shudders at the abject image of Flora's empty dress lying in Mr. Wu's pigsty. The young con artist Flora, once the *ob*ject of Joanie's desire, has been rendered *ab*ject. Indeed, the ghostly presence of Flora's remains and its impact on Joanie exemplify Kristeva's description of the abject as something "quite close" but which "cannot be assimilated" (1). Repeatedly thrown back into the primal trauma she has sought to escape, Joanie remains trapped, revisiting and discarding the thwarted desire that ensued from the loss of her mother and the violence of her father.

A Mouth Filled with Words: Narrative as Sexual Violence

More than anything else, it is this motif of loss that binds the narrative threads of *Deadwood*, and the recurring confrontations with the abject provide the mechanism through which the key figures revisit and relive the traumatic losses that have driven them to this isolated and dangerous frontier settlement. One of season 1's most remarkable moments, a veritable soliloquy that includes Al's stunning revelation of his childhood trauma, occurs at the end of episode 11, as Al is being fellated by Dolly, the young whore who replaces Trixie as his evening companion.[14] This scene underscores the show's deployment of abjection to explain the mingled desire, loss, and violence that have always defined the frontier narrative.

The scene comes at the end of an episode that reveals much of the loss behind Al's monstrous behavior, an episode that opens with a friendly bedroom conversation between Al and Trixie—one quite different from the guarded sparring that marks even the most agreeable of Cy's dialogues with Joanie. Trixie reports on her observations from the thoroughfare below, and Al offers her a half-day off, before pulling aside the sheets and inviting her to join him, in a tone that beseeches rather than commands. The scene establishes an easy familiarity between the two characters that evokes the bonds of marriage, rather than those of slavery, which more accurately describe the extralegal relationship between pimp and prostitute. The rapport between Al and Trixie collapses later that day, however, when he learns that she has had a sexual encounter with Sol Star outside the boundaries of her professional responsibilities. Al humiliates Trixie by demanding payment from Sol in front of her. Sol insists, "I'm not paying you. It wasn't to do with you; it wasn't business" (1.11). But for Al it has everything to do with him precisely *because* "it wasn't business." Swearengen calls Trixie to his side and, addressing Sol, demands payment for Trixie's services.[15] As Trixie walks away humiliated, Al pockets Sol's coins and asks for a whiskey bottle, while a close-up shows his pain and anger. His reluctance to look Trixie in the eyes, to confront her directly—let alone to terrorize her—makes it clear that, unlike Cy, Al reserves his harshest criticism for himself, in allowing Trixie's companionship to become, as his language suggests, so "precious" to him.

The narrative reveals that the emotional vulnerability behind Al's bond with Trixie stems from her abjected state, and the uncanny fascination she holds for him is something that he fights off with language. "Throughout *Deadwood*," Petersen points out, "subjectivity is suggested through language" (276). In this context Al is quickly established as the series' dominant figure through his relentless penchant for violence and control, but more significantly through his mastery of language, his ability to impose *his* narratives on others. This episode's final scene provides a window into Al's unconscious and encapsulates the dynamics of abjection that fuel his compulsive drives. At the end of the evening, a somewhat unsteady Al, now well into that whiskey bottle, addresses Dolly, who is shown from a distance, seated quietly on his bed. "Now, I see what the fuck's in front of me, and I don't pretend it's something else. I was fucking her but now I'm gonna fuck you," Al begins, as if to affirm his commitment to the cold pragmatism his relationship with Trixie has threatened to undermine, "if you don't piss me off or open your yap at the wrong fucking time." "The only time you're supposed to open your yap," he continues, "is so I can put my fucking prick in it. Otherwise, you shut the fuck up" (1.11). Here Al makes explicit his need to deliver a monologue rather than engage in the kind of dialogue he had shared with Trixie that very morning.

The alternating waves of terror, pain, and affection elicited by Swearengen's interactions with Trixie inevitably lead back to childhood trauma. Kristeva claims, "The abject confronts us . . . with our earliest attempts to release the hold of *maternal* entity even before existing outside of her, thanks to the autonomy of language. It is a violent, clumsy breaking away, with the constant risk of falling back under the sway of a power as securing as it is stifling" (13). When Al commands Dolly to "suck my dick and shut the fuck up," she obliges, and the camera focuses closely on Al's face while he unearths a memory that explains a great deal about his character. Al returns to the story of an arrest warrant he has discussed earlier with Trixie: "The place where I found you, huh, is where this warrant's from. Could you believe that I may have stuck a knife in someone's guts twelve hours before you got on the wagon we headed out for fucking Laramie in? No! Because I don't look fucking backwards. I do what I have to do and go on" (1.11). Al's breathlessness implies the vigor of Dolly's performance, and he interrupts himself: "Whoa, whoa, whoa . . . what? You got a stagecoach to catch or something, huh? Slow the fuck up." Here the scene makes a humorous, and yet meaningful, parallel between Al's recounting of "seminal" moments in the past and his desire to defer ejaculation: he wants both "narratives" to proceed concurrently. At this point Al connects his career as a pimp, purchasing his girls at a Chicago orphanage, to his own abandonment as a child:

> Did you know the orphanage part of the building you lived in, behind it she ran a whorehouse, huh? Oh, so you knew? So, so what are you fucking looking at then, huh? God. Now, I'll tell you something you don't know. Before she ran a girls' orphanage, fat Mrs. fucking Anderson ran the boys' orphanage on fucking Euclid Avenue, as I would see her fat ass waddling out the boys' dormitory at 5 o'clock in the fucking morning, every fucking morning she blew her stupid fucking cowbell and woke us all the fuck up. And my fucking mother dropped me the fuck off there with seven dollars and sixty some-odd fucking cents on her way to sucking cock in . . . in Georgia. And I didn't get to count the fucking cents before the fucking door opened, and there, Mrs. fat-ass fucking Anderson, who sold you to me. I had to give her seven dollars and sixty-odd fucking cents that my mother shoved in my fucking hand before she hammered one, two, three, four times on the fucking door and scurried off down fucking Euclid Avenue, probably thirty fucking years before you were fucking born. Then around Cape Horn and up to San Francisco, where she probably became mayor or some other type of success story, unless by some fucking chance she wound up as a ditch for fucking come. Now, fucking go faster, hmm? Okay, go

ahead and spit it out. You don't need to swallow. Just spit it out. Anyways . . . (1.11)

Although the girls that Al has brought to Deadwood, then, have at least some value as commodities, Al's mother paid money to *dispose* of him, leaving him on the doorstep of Mrs. Anderson's orphanage, before selling her own body for the promise of wealth. Not coincidentally, the places Al mentions, Georgia and San Francisco, draw parallels between the story of Deadwood and earlier mining communities. San Francisco's emergence in the wake of the forty-niners, who followed the discovery of gold at Sutter's Mill is well known, but the first American "gold rush" in Indian territory took place on Cherokee land in north Georgia in 1828, prompting the Indian Removal Act of 1830 and the subsequent Trail of Tears. Just as this story is being replayed in the Black Hills, so is Al revisiting his own narrative of loss and displaced violence and, as the scene all too vividly suggests, figuratively forcing his version of the truth on his captive audience.

This scene also highlights one of the show's most widely discussed words, *cocksucker*, perhaps the most obvious example of the kind of linguistic "battering" that Milch describes as central to *Deadwood*'s aesthetic strategy.[16] Among the many, often comical, uses to which this word is put, one cannot ignore its resonance as a profane allusion to phallogocentrism and the privileging of a normative, masculinist narrative within language itself. To be called a cocksucker is to be robbed of the power to speak, to be denied a voice, and this epithet reaffirms an individual's status as something less than a man.[17] In modern usage and certainly within *Deadwood*, it is a term normally reserved for men, because to use it in reference to a woman would be redundant: the very definition of *woman* relies on the notion of an essential lack, of a missing phallus. For a prostitute such as Dolly or Trixie, to be a cocksucker is to get back to work, to perform one's essential function. As Luce Irigaray writes, "Woman, in the sexual imaginary, is only a more or less obliging prop for the enactment of men's fantasies," and among the women of Deadwood, the compliant, laconic Dolly proves a more obliging prop than Trixie, as evidenced by the body of the dead john in episode 1 (364).

Also casting light on Al's response to abjection is his involvement with Reverend Smith, who has been afflicted with seizures and demented ravings and whom Al has watched from his balcony with what seems like inexplicable curiosity and revulsion. Al explains his fascination with the debilitated minister when he tells Smith about his own brother, who also suffered from such seizures. During the scene with Dolly, Al remarks that "the minister's gotta fucking die. . . . You just gotta kill it and put an end to it. You don't linger on about it, you don't fucking go around weeping about it, and you don't, you know, behave like a kid with a sore fucking thumb, loco sucking it" (1.11). Al's sudden digression regarding the abject figure of the minister and the contrast between the oral fixation of a child and the proper actions of a man highlight the manner in which he has repressed the central traumas of his childhood: "I mean, you gotta behave like a grown fucking man. You gotta shut the fuck up, don't be sorry, don't look fucking back." This language mirrors Al's description of his own philosophy—a philosophy from which he certainly deviates, most notably in this very scene. In the following episode, Al in essence euthanizes the minister, suffocating him in a deadly embrace, and whispering to him as he stops breathing, "You go now, brother."[18] Like a "sore thumb" the minister is an afflicted member of the "body" of the camp, and Al ultimately chooses to eradicate his abject form. He cannot, however, so easily remove or erase the childhood memories that threaten his sense of identity; in his discussion of the minister's suffering, he uses the word *it*, not *he*, leaving unclear the referent. For Al *it* suggests the dehumanized body of the minister as well as his own troubled past. It is the presence of the abject, like the form of the stricken minister, that Al must continually revisit and reject. "You don't need to swallow," Al insists to Dolly. "Just spit it out" (1.11).

The Threat of the Maternal and the Language of War

Kristeva locates the origins of abjection in the period of ego formation she calls the *chora*, from the Greek for "region, country"—and which she defines as "the receptacle for narcissism" (*Powers* 13). Her formulation is crudely echoed in Al's reference to his mother as "a ditch for fucking come." Indeed, according to Kristeva, the *chora* is a temporal state embodied in the nursing child's relationship to the mother's body, something that is not yet conceived as "other" and is, paradoxically, both the focus of unquenchable self-gratification *and* a prohibited space. Before the Lacanian "mirror stage" allows the child to perceive the workings of the symbolic order, to define its own image as "other" and therefore construct a stable idea of itself as subject, as "I," the *chora* constitutes a condition in which the boundaries of the self are uncertain and undefined. According to Kristeva, "The mother's body is therefore what mediates the symbolic law organizing social relations and becomes the ordering principle of the semiotic *chora*, which is on the path of destruction, aggressivity, and death" (*Revolution* 27–28).[19] In other words the dangerous and self-destructive impulses of the *chora* are contained by the introduction of language. The symbolic order establishes the law, beginning with prohibitions surrounding the maternal body, most notably the incest taboo. It is, at the least, a dangerously narrow evasion of this taboo when Al invokes his mother performing the same act as Dolly while he ejaculates into Dolly's mouth, then urges her to "spit it out." Swearengen's actions, here as elsewhere, reveal his narcissistic fascination with the abject, as well as his strategic deployment of language in response to its recurring presence.

Al's command of language, his storytelling, simultaneously repress the painful memory of his mother and keep it alive in his troubled mind. "The sign," Kristeva argues, "represses the *chora* and its eternal return" (*Powers* 4). Stung by what he sees as Trixie's unfaithfulness and a betrayal like his mother's, Al offers a retelling of his formative childhood trauma in the scene with Dolly. Pawned off by his mother, delivered to the woman from whom he would buy his own prostitutes, Al makes clear that it is this loss, which can never be regained or filled, that incites his rage, his lust for wealth and power, and his violence. He can never leave behind the memories of his mother's recurring absence but is condemned to reenact this scene over and over, in his relationship with Trixie and in his obsessive retelling of the narrative itself. Indeed, the exchange of coins between Al and Sol Star over Trixie serve as a concrete reminder of Al's formative memories. In order to contain the unknowable threat that the abject presents, he struggles to transform it from abject to phobic object: something "other" that he can control or keep at bay. Kristeva describes the way a child learns to dismiss or conceal the phobic object through language: "Through the mouth that I fill with words instead of my mother whom I miss from now on more than ever, I elaborate that want, and the aggressivity that accompanies it by *saying*" (*Powers* 41). Al's profane soliloquy, accompanied by frequent reminders to Dolly, Trixie's replacement, to "shut the fuck up," represents the ongoing attempt to repress the eternal return of the confused and traumatic "want" that has defined his life. Moreover, this scene reveals the "absent cause" of Al's fury: the knowledge that his mother abandoned him. When confronted by instances of "the abject" later in life, the subject is thus thrown back into an archaic, presymbolic state, reduced, in Al's words, to a "kid with a sore fucking thumb," and as Kristeva claims, "It is no longer I who expel. 'I' is expelled" (*Powers* 3). Al's immersion in and contribution to the abject milieu of Deadwood produce a constant threat to his subjectivity, one that he fends off with his mastery of the coarse, violent idiom that is the lingua franca of this place.

According to Kristeva the male, in the process of acquiring and asserting subjectivity, responds to abjection by splitting the mother into both *abject* and *object* of desire, a split reflected in the grotesque parallels between Al's bitter story of his mother and his instructions to Dolly. The female child, however, in order to establish the normative boundaries of heterosexual identity, must abandon the mother in favor of the will of the father. Joanie's homosexual desire—an element of the story that figures prominently in the third season, in Joanie's emerging relationship with Jane—signals her rebellion against these boundaries, but her ongoing struggle against the patriarchal will of Cy can only be fulfilled with her own death. "The semiotic *chora*," Kristeva argues, "is no more than the place where the subject is both generated and negated, the place where his unity succumbs before the process of charges and states that produce him" (*Revolution* 28). In the case of Joanie, Al, Trixie, and indeed many of the primary characters in *Deadwood*, the apparent "death drive" that sets in motion so much of the story and that ultimately threatens to engulf them all can be attributed to the power of abjection, "a border that has encroached on everything," and through which they cannot pass.

If Kristeva's theory helps account for the motivations and actions of these characters, the parallels between personal and historical memory also inform the larger problem of abjection in the so-called frontier narrative. *Deadwood*, we are frequently reminded, begins only months after Custer's Last Stand at Little Bighorn—for Euro-Americans, the September 11 of the nineteenth century—and the show reminds us of the connections between personal and historical loss within the stories of the American West. In *The Fatal Environment* (1985), Richard Slotkin evokes Girard's notion of sacrifice: "Custer's defeat became a kind of atoning sacrifice, almost Christlike; the representative of American youth, courage, and soldierly virtue violently perishes, but leaves behind a redeeming example that summons his fellow citizens to the purgation of evil, the regeneration of virtue and vigor, and a renewed pursuit of our 'ancient struggle' against the forces of darkness" (10). This is clearly *not* the story, however, behind *Deadwood*. Against this historical backdrop, the show's principal figures, defined by the trauma of lost or inadequate parents, siblings, spouses, and children, are repeatedly confronted with instances of the abject—thrown back, against their will, to their own painful past. "Don't be sorry," Al tells Dolly. "Don't look fucking back" (1.11). As the appeal of *Deadwood* suggests, however, American culture, like Al, compulsively looks back, with a mix of nostalgia and horror, to its past, to the narrative of western expansion.

This narrative, moreover, cannot be separated from the gendered violence that forms a central motif in so many classic Westerns, as in *Deadwood*. In an interview Milch connects *Deadwood*'s use of language, sexual violence, and the embodied narrative of the West:

> It's very well documented that the obscenity of the West was striking, but the obscenity of mining camps was unbelievable.... They were raping the land. They weren't growing anything; they weren't respecting the cycles of nature. They were taking. And, in order to muscle up for that enterprise in an environment where there are no laws ... the relentless obscenity of the miner was a way of announcing the compatibility of his spirit with the world in which he found himself. (Milch and Carradine)

The geography of Deadwood Gulch itself constitutes an abject feminized zone, a narrow chasm carved into the Black Hills, its thoroughfare an open wound running with the bodily fluids of human and beast alike—a "ditch for come," in Al's monstrous words. It is a foul, yet captivating, vaginal space, a site of creation and destruction, luring men and destroying them without apparent reason or the restraint of patriarchal laws. The world that Milch describes and depicts is nothing less than Kristeva's notion of the abject, the "land of oblivion that is constantly remembered" and that exerts its pull on both its fictional participants and its captivated audience.

Within the American imagination the frontier landscape itself becomes a succubus, a dangerous temptress, promising regeneration but offering only death. In his study of the impact of Custer's Last Stand, Slotkin traces the ways in which the "virgin land" of the New World becomes, in a phrase borrowed from Whitman, a "fatal environment." Narratives of conquest, therefore, must overcome and contain this feminized landscape, whose fecundity is a double-edged sword. Susan Rosowski, in her examination of the mastery of language by the archetypal Western hero as depicted in *The Virginian* (1902), *Riders of the Purple Sage* (1912), and *Shane* (1949), notes, "Whereas the Logos of Greek philosophy and the Bible gives rise to generativity and creativity, the Western's Logos restricts meaning, denies generativity, and excludes procreativity" (173). This tension between restrictive patriarchal language and the fertile maternal body is demonstrated in *Deadwood*, not only through the recurring trope of men silencing women but also in the ongoing anxieties surrounding both the threat and the promise of motherhood.

Sovereignty over the female body is a central thematic motif in the series. Despite the many afflictions and mishaps that require his attention, Doc Cochran's primary professional responsibilities in Deadwood revolve around the hygiene of the prostitutes at the Gem and the Bella Union, including the distribution of abortifacients. When Alma Garret becomes pregnant with Seth Bullock's child, she consults with Trixie, who advises her bluntly, "If you take the tea, lay plenty of dope in. 'Cause I've killed seven, and every bleeding out I laced on good and tight and for a long fucking while after" (2.5). Indeed, despite the figurative depiction of Deadwood as a vaginal space, literal motherhood is a rarity, due in large part to the primary occupation of most women present. Just as the smallpox epidemic in season 1 and Al's kidney stones in season 2 serve as literal manifestations of collective anxieties, so does Alma's troubled pregnancy unsettle the town and haunt the third season of the series. To be sure, Deadwood is no place for children. Young Sofia Metz is orphaned by road agents who have slaughtered her family in the first episode of season 1, and she remains under almost constant supervision, before and after her adoption by Alma. William Bullock, despite his hardier appearance, is trampled to death in a freak accident in season 2, leaving the only prominent biological mother in the show childless. (This pattern is repeated when Hearst's cook, Aunt Lou, loses her son, Odell, to the whims of Hearst.) Women's creativity and procreativity alike are consistently stifled or disrupted by the violent world of Deadwood.

It is not uncommon to link the discourse of war with that of childbirth and maternity. "Within popular discourse," Kelly Oliver notes, "women's bodies, menstrual blood, and female sexuality can be used as tactics of war because of the potency of their association with the danger of nature, of Mother Nature, if you will" (*Reading Kristeva* 6). In "The Mother of All Things: War, Reason, and the Gendering of Pain," Vaheed Ramazani claims, "War, it seems, is the male's way of giving birth" (26). Ramazani argues that "gender and sexuality have been linked to war, historically, just as war has been linked to the concept of the nation—by an idealist assumption of teleological necessity that is based on a myth of bodily unity" (26).

However revisionist his methods, Milch's object of study in *Deadwood*—"how does chaos evolve into order?" (qtd. in Barra, "Man Who Made Deadwood")—revisits what Turner refers to as "perennial rebirth," "a return to primitive conditions on a continually advancing frontier line" in his foundational text, "The Significance of the Frontier in American History" (1893; chap. 1 in Turner, *Frontier*). Childbirth has historically been employed, of course, as a metaphor for the act of artistic creation, and this usurpation of female generative power in the service of patriarchal authority is not unique to *Deadwood*. According to Mark Singer's 2005 profile of Milch, while directing the scene in season 2 in which Doc Cochran and Al's underlings join forces to help Al pass his kidney stones, Milch encouraged the actors to approach the scene as they would a medical birthing procedure, and his analysis of the creative process draws some distinct parallels between the medical procedure of childbirth and his own concerns as a vivisectionist of the human condition. If, furthermore, birth is a fundamental trope for storytelling, its repeated denial and termination in *Deadwood* points to a troubling paralysis that impedes the characters' ability to transcend or travel beyond their circumstances and raises doubts about the possibility of any formal resolution to the overall narrative.

The threat posed by the maternal body, in fact, emerges as a crucial plot element that drives the series to its conclusion. In episode 11 of season 3, Hearst orders the murder of Ellsworth, and his disfigured corpse is paraded slowly through town in the back of a cart. Trixie, distraught over learning of Ellsworth's murder, impulsively marches to Hearst's room at the hotel and shoots him when he answers the door. Before doing so, however, she rips open her shirt, baring her breasts, and lifts her skirt as Hearst appears in the doorway. Her exposed body serves to distract Hearst from her true purpose, but it also evokes the dangerous power of the bare-breasted Amazon as an emblem of warfare. Trixie flees the scene, her shirt still open, while E. B. Farnum growls from behind his desk at the hotel, "Cover those things!" (3.11) As Ramazani notes, the image of "Liberty's bared breasts" adopted as a symbol of official power represents "purified impurity . . . carnality and instinct transvalued as Reason" (50). By co-opting the image of the Amazon, Ramazani continues, "a threatening feminine sexuality—its effluent, mutable, and reproductive aspects—is displaced toward an abstract, virilized ideal, a static and sanitized image of strength" (50). Indeed, the forces unleashed by Trixie's unsuccessful assassination attempt threaten to destroy the entire town, before Swearengen calls upon the other leaders of Deadwood to capitulate to Hearst's will and "clean up" the mess left by Trixie.[20]

The conclusion of the series mirrors its opening: Al feels compelled to contain the damage done by Trixie's decisive and violent actions in a way that confirms his brutality, his need for paternal control, and his ambivalent attachment to Trixie. "Loopy fucking cunt," he mutters, repeating his earlier utterance to descry Trixie's reckless behavior (3.12). In response to Hearst's call for retribution, Al cuts the throat of another prostitute who resembles Trixie and places her body on display for Hearst's inspection. Forced to put her own dress on the other girl's body in order to carry out the deception, Trixie must participate in the destruction and degradation of her own abject double, much as Joanie has done with Flora. Al's story "works"; Hearst is convinced, and he leaves town, his conquest of its assets complete. The establishment of patriarchal order contains—or at least defers—the threat of the feminine, even if it ultimately leaves Al under Hearst's thumb.

As Al's obsessive need for rhetorical and physical mastery demonstrates, power in *Deadwood* always involves the ability to control the story. The symbolic order, in Lacanian terms, is reserved for subjects; mere objects like Dolly must simply "shut the fuck up" and listen. To paraphrase Al's early warning to Trixie, no one ever asks for a woman's version. In his self-appointed role as omniscient narrator, Al's favored location is on the balcony outside his office, where he is able to survey the entire camp and collect intelligence. Indeed, the ability to establish visual surveillance is a crucial marker of power in *Deadwood.* Cy, too, takes in the view from his balcony, although, as his authority wanes, he spends more time in his first-floor office. As he consolidates his own standing, Hearst impatiently erects a rickety balcony of his own after acquiring the Grand Ho-

12. Al and Cy on the watch. "The Trial of Jack McCall" (*Deadwood* 1.5).

tel. According to *Deadwood*'s set designer, Maria Caso, the architectural features of Bullock and Star Hardware also reflect the importance of surveillance: "To me Bullock's character is all about control. He is the overseer of the town; he is always watching. That's why there is glass all around the store. Usually, a store owner wouldn't have big glass doors like that, but Bullock wants to see everything" (Caso, "Deadwood"). For each of these men, essential to maintaining his status as dominant subject, as rule-giver, is the ability to gather and command information.[21] Once gathered, this knowledge can then be translated into narrative, as happens with the rumors Cy helps spread about invalid claims; the newspaper stories Al dictates to Merrick, editor of the *Pioneer*; or the mysterious messages that arrive via Blazanov's telegraph. *Deadwood* is finally a story, like so many others, *about* storytelling—a text that highlights the obsessive violence and power of language but also its *limits*, its inability to completely represent, define, or contain the abject, the recurring confrontation with the material facts of human existence. Always in jeopardy, patriarchal oppression, whether on the blood-stained floor of the Gem or across the wider backdrop of the contested western landscape, requires constant maintenance. The abject frontier of *Deadwood* is a reminder of the repressed violence at the heart of the American experience, our own "land of oblivion that is constantly remembered."

My colleagues Amanda Emerson, Laura Furlan, Emily Haddad, and Skip Willman provided valuable suggestions on an earlier version of this essay.

Notes

1. Milch has presented this as the theme of the series in several interviews, including one incorporated into a 2005 article from *Entertainment Weekly*: "Milch's 25 years of writing such cop shows as *Hill Street Blues* and *NYPD Blue* (which he cocreated) have bred a healthy obsession with law and order. So he found the history of Deadwood—a Dakota territory gold-rush camp settled on land ripped from the Native Americans—to be a fascinating case study for a show: Not yet part of the United States, the renegade community had no law. 'It's about the discovery of the various principles by which a society ordered itself,' he says. 'Everything was accelerated there. Two years before [the show starts] there was literally not a white person, and in two years they had telephones. You watched American society going on at warp speed'" (qtd. in Wolk). See also Barra, "Man Who Made Deadwood." For examinations of the relationship between the show's profanity and its thematic unity, see Benz and O'Sullivan. In "No Law: *Deadwood* and the State," Mark Berrettini offers a compelling application of Althusser's notion of Ideological State Apparatuses to the show's narrative of emerging law and order.
2. Ellsworth's speech is a veritable sermon on the ideology of individualism, capitalism, and exceptionalism, which dominates the traditional Western narrative: "I'll tell you what. I may have fucked my life up flatter than hammered shit, but I stand here before you today beholden to no human cocksucker. And working a paying fucking gold claim. And not the U.S. government saying I'm trespassing or the savage fucking red man himself or any of these limber dick cocksuckers passing themselves off as prospectors had better try and stop me" (1.1).
3. In *Powers of Horror*, Kristeva examines the role of abjection in works by several authors, including Proust, Kafka, and Joyce, but her primary literary focus is on the works of Céline.
4. Of less frequency in Westerns, and of equal prominence in *Deadwood*, is the spectacle of disfigured or bloodied women's bodies, as demonstrated by Trixie's beaten face in the opening episode.

5. The ongoing presence of the Indian head, which Al keeps in a box and treats as a sort of analyst/confidante, represents, among other things, the persistence of the abject in the series.
6. In fact, the jurors reflect the community's wish to present itself as an unformed space inviting eventual incorporation into the United States. To enforce any law would be to assert a treasonous independence from the federal government, whose "courtship" Al and the other power brokers seek to encourage in the long term.
7. Subsequent scenes of ritual in the series likewise coincide with a continuation, if not an escalation, of violence. William Bullock's funeral and Ellsworth's marriage to Alma Garret in the final episodes of season 2 coincide with the grisly assassination of the rival Chinese gang by Wu and Al's men and Wolcott's suicide, respectively.
8. Citing Girard's notion of "impure" violence, Handley writes, "The destruction of native peoples served not nearly so much to bind whites as a community, since there was nothing purifying or sacrificial in the violence committed against Native Americans, as it served to spread aggression through the nation in the name not just of insatiable greed but of bloodlust" (19–20). As in so many canonical Westerns, Indians are frequently referenced but rarely present; in *Deadwood*—the genocidal conquest of their land is the clearly established backdrop for the story, but their appearance in the series is limited. The most prominent Indians, indeed, are dead: specifically, the head that Al pays a bounty for and later addresses with his confessional soliloquies and the "Sioux" warrior who ambushes Bullock on his way to find Jack McCall and bring him to justice in Yankton. Bullock, after smashing the man's face with a rock, decides to give his body an appropriate burial in the traditional Lakota manner. In a plot development that (ironically or otherwise) reiterates the nostalgic embrace of the "vanishing" Native American that has been central to the frontier narrative, Bullock pays respect to the honor of the individual and his culture, even as he chooses to illegally occupy land granted to the Indians by treaty.
9. The word *flock*, suggestive of a family as well as a spiritual congregation, is used by Johnny Burns in an exchange with Dan Dority, explaining why Al had initiated the confrontation with Bullock at the beginning of the second season. Dority: "Al's calling Bullock to the fold"; Burns: "Bullock ain't even of Al's flock"; Dority: "Al's gonna be calling numbers to the fold now that he can't trust like us. Some he don't even like. We're joining America. And it's full of lying, thieving cocksuckers that you can't trust at all—governors, commissioners and whatnot. By God, that's just the new way of things. And you just gonna have to get used to it, Johnny" (2.2). This connection between the familial dynamics of the Gem and

the struggle for communal and national identity reinforces the connection between the personal narratives of loss that haunt these characters and the broader narrative of western expansion that provides the show's historical context.

10. It is worth noting that the series provides almost nothing in the way of backstory for Cy's character, in significant contrast to the intriguing morsels of information about Al's childhood that are revealed.
11. In the subsequent episode Cy suggests that Eddie's distress over the murder of Miles and Flora is related to a sexual desire for Miles, a notion that disturbs Eddie and hints at some doubt or anxiety about his sexual history. Eddie angrily rejects Cy's insinuations about Miles, saying, "I never did that and you know it." Later Eddie demands that Cy "take it back" before he returns to work as a croupier in the Bella Union (1.9).
12. The establishment of the self as subject, the "I," is based, in Lacan's work, on the "mirror stage," the moment in which the child sees his own image in a mirror and conceives of himself as apart from the mother (and, of course, as Kristeva and other feminist critics discuss, it is a male child's experience that informs Lacan's understanding of this moment). In this scene one sees Cy's narcissism linked to his paternal self-image, in relation to Eddie and Joanie. Lacan writes, "It is in the name of the father that we must recognize the basis of the symbolic function which, since the dawn of historical time, has identified his person with the figure of the law. This conception allows us to clearly distinguish, in the analysis of a case, the unconscious effects of this function from the narcissistic relations, or even real relations, that the subject has with the image and actions of the person who embodies this function" (*Ecrits* 66–67).
13. In Freudian terms, of course, this moment suggests Alma's triumph—however fleeting—over her father's narcissistic drive for consumption and self-gratification, as his teeth, the markers of his compulsive and childish orality, are presented to Alma as a kind of trophy.
14. Mark Singer claims, "Perhaps the most disturbing scene during the first season is a four-minute soliloquy by Swearengen at the conclusion of episode eleven" (3).
15. In his conversation with Sol, Al reveals the sense of betrayal he feels and alludes to the bedroom scene with Trixie earlier that day:

> Don't you think I don't understand. I mean, what can anyone of us ever really fucking hope for, huh? Except for a moment here and there with a person who doesn't want to rob, steal or murder us? At night it may happen. Sun up, one person against the fucking wall, the other may hop on the fucking bed, trusted each other enough to tell half the fucking truth. Everybody needs that. Becomes precious to 'em. They don't want to see it fucked with. (1.11)

16. The aforementioned *Entertainment Weekly* article begins, "Much like the myth that Eskimos have hundreds of words for snow, *Deadwood* creator David Milch has hundreds of meanings for the word c——sucker" (66).
17. The interplay between logos and the phallus, as allied instruments of power, is evident in Al's extended illness in season 2, when his blocked urethra and his inability to speak both prevent him from asserting his authority over the camp.
18. In a later, parallel scene from episode 11 of season 2, Al reveals more about his own brother and his psychic wounds when he tells Dolly, after William Bullock's funeral,

    Fucking caskets . . . bring out the dunce in the entire fucking community. I took some fucking beating after my brother's fucking funeral. Smacks coming from every fucking angle. Still dizzy from the smack from the left, here comes a smack from the right. Brain can't bounce around fast enough. Headache I fucking had for three fucking weeks. The fuck fault is it of mine if my fucking brother croaks? Ain't even my fucking brother. Fucking people take me in, I didn't ask them to fucking take me in. Huh. Fucking flopping like a fish on the dock, my brother the perch. Huh. Fucking falling sickness. Let the old man beat you because he's sad and he has his load on. I did better in the orphanage, if that fat-ass Mrs. Anderson hadn't turned out a fucking pimp. Anyways . . . (2.11)

19. Kristeva distinguishes between the semiotic and the symbolic and the two conditions that help frame the child's relationship to language. The semiotic refers to the pre-Oedipal system of the *chora*, while the symbolic represents the patriarchal system of signification that governs the fully constituted subject. See *Revolution* 26–28.
20. The threat posed by Trixie's usurpation of the male prerogative of violent action offers an alternative to the model for female subversion described by Tania Modleski. In her study of female cross-dressing in director Maggie Greenwald's 1993 film, *The Ballad of Little Jo*, Modleski argues, the presence of a woman engaged in a veiled performance of masculinity allows us "to see how the very border between male and female worlds of popular culture shifts when a woman is working on what has hitherto been exclusively masculine territory" (151).
21. In the end the most powerful figure in *Deadwood* is, of course, Milch himself. It is he who controls the verbal and cinematic discourse, who puts the audience through the "battering" of the show's language. Though seldom credited as writer of an episode and never as director, he is, rather, the "creator," continually referred to with almost reverential awe by those involved with the series. In Lacanian terms he is the "subject supposed to know" (*Four Fundamental Concepts* 230–43).

5 The Final Stamp
Deadwood and the Gothic American Frontier

Wendy Witherspoon

Pointing out Deadwood*'s "generic cross-fertilization," Wendy Witherspoon initiates in her essay on Milch's use of the gothic a group of essays in this volume exploring how the series exploits generic conventions. Some of the "macabre" elements that Tim Steckline and John Dudley explore from theoretical perspectives Witherspoon recognizes as situating* Deadwood *at the intersection of two traditions, gothic and frontier literature. She outlines a long tradition of gothic frontier literature, which has "undermine[d] mythological constructions of the United States frontier as a site of rational progress." The gothic concern with "contamination" expresses a fear of interaction with "other" cultures, such as the Chinese or the Indians who "haunt" the series. The "gothic threat of sexual violation" is made all too manifest in the series, while the gothic's concern with the intrinsic violence of law and order's inability to control human behavior is one of* Deadwood*'s major themes.* Deadwood*'s two leads are types of gothic heroes: Bullock the ambiguous and tormented "romantic hero," Swearengen the "avenger" and the "interpreter."*

In exploring Swearengen as an interpreter who prefers to be behind his desk, Witherspoon offers another look at some of the issues discussed by Brian McCuskey. "It is not just the Indian killers who are guilty of genocide but also every person sitting at a desk, participating (however blindly) in the brutal forces of capitalism." The writing and interpreting done by Deadwood *characters signifies not only the coming of civilization but also connections between the brutal acts of the past and the future. Eventually Witherspoon uses* Deadwood *to define a "postmodern frontier gothic" in which "gothic threats . . . express communal guilt, suppression of secrets and the innate violence of society."*

In voice-over audio commentary for *Deadwood*'s pilot episode, creator David Milch jokes that he would have liked to return Wild Bill Hickok to the show as a ghost after Hickok's ignominious murder in the fourth episode so that actor Keith Carradine, who portrayed Hickok, could have had another crack at an Emmy nomination. Perhaps, Milch muses, Hickok could appear to Calamity Jane in a delirium-induced vision and upbraid her for excessive drinking (1.1). Milch's comment was made in jest, of course, as the series' gritty realism would seem to allow little room for supernatural moments—even if hallucinated. As it turns out, however, Milch's ghostly imaginings for Carradine's character are not merely specious; *Deadwood* is a show that evinces its creator's proclivity for generic cross-fertilization. For Milch generic hybridity is part and parcel of the show's theme: what it's like to live in a community without laws.[1] Much in the same way that the cinematic violence of the show gives the viewer the vicarious experience of living unprotected and vulnerable in a community without regulation, generic instability leaves the viewer without familiar signposts for navigating the stories' terrain. As Milch explains, "There aren't the conventions of storytelling to protect your expectations" (audio commentary 1.1). Although Milch's nearly naturalistic vision seems a far cry from the drippy sentimentality of the classic, eighteenth- and nineteenth-century gothic or from the overdetermined darkness of the contemporary gothic, the richness of *Deadwood* is certainly due, at least in some measure, to Milch's informed and adept ability to marshal seemingly disparate generic conventions.

One does not typically think of the gothic genre when considering the cinematic Western. In the first place the expansive, bright landscapes of iconic Western cinematography seem to foreclose the gloomy, tenebrous castles and foggy moors of most gothic settings.[2] Familiar literary and cinematic constructions of the U.S. West as a space symbolically linked to hegemonic conceptions of American exceptionalism seem to militate against the kind of transgressive desires suggested by gothic plots, replete with their haunted houses, mad doppelgängers, stupefying terror, and incestuous entanglements. The surface opposition of the cinematic Western and the gothic genre is stark: the former is conventionally linked with notions of the frontier as a site of positive rational progress, the latter with all that is regressive, repressed, and irrational. And yet as a liminal space that tests the boundaries of personal and national identity, the frontier is very much a gothic locale. Because of the surreptitious ability of the genre to challenge monolithic cultural discourse, gothic conventions have always been important devices for conceptualizations of the contested space of the American West.

Deadwood participates in a tradition of generic amalgamation by which Western writers (both strategically and inadvertently) invoke gothic motifs in order to undermine mythological constructions of the United States frontier as a site of rational progress. In the nineteenth century the American gothic genre turned away from its European counterpart by locating its terror in frontier spaces; as Leslie Fielder notes: "In the American gothic . . . the heathen, unredeemed wilderness and not the decaying monuments of a dying class, nature and not society becomes the symbol of evil" (160). While narratives of Western conquest became marked in the twentieth century—especially vis-à-vis Frederick Jackson Turner's famous "frontier thesis"—as narratives of "Americanization" and advancement, the trope of the frontier could never elide its gothic implications. Critics have begun the work of extrapolating the complex interplay of frontier and gothic modes in Western works. In "Race, Labor, and the Gothic Western," for example, Susan Kollin argues that Dorothy Scarborough's *The Wind* "employs gothic tropes in order to dismantle myths of the West, especially myths of western exceptionalism" (85). In *Frontier Gothic: Terror and Wonder at the Frontier in American Literature* (1992), contributors adumbrate the contours of a frontier gothic genre, exploring the works of authors such as Charles Brockden Brown, Charlotte Perkins Gilman, and Gerald Vizenor. In the introduction to *Frontier Gothic*, editors David Mogen, Scott P. Sanders, and Joanne B. Karpinski argue that American frontier gothic literature "expresses how alienation and fear both subvert and continually redefine the American ideal of the future as a frontier leading each of us and our nation to ever more positive cultural and psychological transformations" (26).

Consider the juxtaposition of frontier and gothic motifs in *Deadwood*'s opening moments in and around Bullock's Montana jail: images of the prefatory horse on a desolate frontier street at night, the frontier jailor and his inmate, and the threat of vigilante justice seem to fit squarely within the cinematic Western tradition. But we could just as easily note the scene's gothic connotations: the dim, flickering candlelight suggesting obfuscated visibility as a metaphor for murky understanding, the taciturnity of the marshal and the foregrounding of writing (Bullock is scribbling noisily in his journal) intimating the difficulty of communication, and the threatening mob violence expressing the failure of all that is rational, orderly, and civilized. The characterizations of the principle hero and villain, Seth Bullock and Al Swearengen, also borrow from the gothic genre. Brooding and violent, Bullock is a gothic hero in the mold of *Jane Eyre*'s Rochester (1847), offering both redemption and ruination for the women who love him and the community that needs him. And the particular monstrosity of Swearengen, whose brutality and exploitation are coterminus with the forces of civilization, recalls the Kurtzian "horror" of Joseph Conrad's *Heart of Darkness* (1899).[3] Another commonplace of the gothic, the threat of sexual violation, which stood in the nineteenth century as a metaphor for threats against the purity of national identity, is transformed in Milch's version: the Deadwood settlers are as contaminated and broken as the prostitutes who service them, and the violence and baseness of depictions of sex in the show remind us of the originary acts of brutishness — the displacement and murder of Native Americans — that form the haunted heritage of the United States.

As David Drysdale argues, *Deadwood* interrogates the notion of authority and critiques the U.S. role in contemporary politics (139). Even more radically, gothic motifs in *Deadwood* indicate that the very conventions of law and society are intrinsically corrupt. Much as in Dickens's *Bleak House* (1853), in which the Court of Chancery has its gothic "worn-out lunatic in every madhouse, . . . its dead in every churchyard," the establishment of law in *Deadwood* is very much a gothic ordeal (15). I argue that *Deadwood* should be considered a frontier gothic narrative because the particular amalgamations of this complex genre help explain the show's worldview: that the sociopolitical realm is marked by inherent violence and contamination; furthermore, the myriad ways in which Milch's characters navigate this gothic frontier setting reveal both the dehumanizing strategies some adopt for survival as well as—more frequently—the failures of adaptation that cause many to perish.

While there are many violent mutilations and murders in the show, only a few become hauntings that linger as markers of the foundational violence at the heart of the community. Most notable is the Metz family massacre, after which Sofia Metz survives as a ghostly reminder of the horrific event throughout the series. In the pilot's opening moments, Sofia is an effigy of whiteness and purity as her face pokes out of the covered wagon in broad daylight; however, the discovery later that night of her family's gruesome massacre on a dark forest trail stands in stark contrast. As Hickok and Bullock lead a horseback posse by torchlight into the massacre site and (significantly) fend off white wolves preying on the mutilated bodies, the scene is more than merely horrific; it adumbrates the gothic mode when Sofia, symbol of the virgin American wilderness, is pulled unconscious from under a bush and returned to camp, where she will function as a totem of communal guilt, of the endemic violence of the community, and of the paradoxical survival mechanism of "silence" on the gothic frontier. For Milch Bullock's rescue of Sofia represents "the best tendencies of the camp," but the massacre, of course, represents the worst—a hack job by Swearengen-associated road agents attempting to make their robbery look like the work of Indians (audio commentary 1.1). After she is rescued, Sofia begins to bear the burden of a classic gothic heroine, whose secret identity is often a metonym for a larger crime against the social order—most often a rape, a murder, or a stolen inheritance.[4] Sofia's story is meant to be taken as a symbol of the endemic violence of this community: throughout the series threats developing within the borders of the Deadwood community are always much greater than threats emanating from the "unsettled" frontier.

Even after her rescue Sofia remains a ghostly, freighted figure. Lying supposedly comatose in Doc Cochran's cabin, where she is inadequately protected from the threat of Swearengen, Sofia's body is corpse-like. When Swearengen's cruel pinch forces her bright

13. Sofia. "Tell Him Something Pretty" (*Deadwood* 3.12).

blue eyes to shoot open, the effect is startling and suggestive, for a brief moment, of a return from the grave. Sofia-as-possessed imbues a symbol of American innocence with gothic dimensions, and with her transformation she symbolically adumbrates communal and national culpability for the genocidal crime at the heart of the settlement: the extermination and displacement of the Sioux. Although Sofia sheds some of her ghostly bearing when she recovers from her wounds, the contours of her ability to haunt the show don't disappear but merely evolve.

Sofia rarely speaks throughout the series, and her speechlessness is crucial to her function within the show's gothic structure as a reminder of the genocidal crime at the heart of the settlement. The inability to speak, or what Eve Kosofsky Sedgwick calls "unspeakability," is a key motif of the gothic genre because it is part of an important structure in which characters find themselves both metaphorically and physically "blocked off" from one another. In psychological terms gothic stories such as Edgar Allen Poe's "Fall of the House of Usher" (1839) often center on a subject or "self" that must locate some crucial (often repressed) bit of information regarding its own history, and the story becomes a metaphor for an individual's struggle for a "complete" identity. The structure of "unspeakability" occurs whenever characters withhold information from one another or when characters are physically divided from one another—imprisoned, for instance, like *The Monk*'s Antonia (1796), in subterranean vaults. The central tension of the gothic mode concerns the threat that one of these physical, psychological, or oral divisions will be breached.[5] In the instance of Sofia and *Deadwood*, speechlessness aligns the orphan symbolically with all who have been brutalized and disenfranchised in the process of western expansion. Doc Cochran's injunction to Sofia, "Don't never say nothing to no one" (1.1), articulates the condition of her gothic function: her unspoken knowledge about the massacre becomes a secret that everyone knows but no one discusses. Gothic tension is produced each time the threat arises that this "secret" knowledge will be shared or made public; thus Sofia becomes emblematic of communal collusion in suppressing crimes, an act that binds the community in conspiracy and threatens to sunder it under the pressure of this conspiracy. Her speechlessness reminds us of the volatile partitions that form both inter- and intracommunity barriers and of the high stakes of breaching those partitions or knowing too much.

Unlike some other children in the series, especially the significantly named Miles and Flora Anderson, Sofia is almost stunningly passive. Miles and Flora, whose names allude to the child characters in Henry James's *The Turn of the Screw* (1898), prove to be no match for the adult villains they attempt to swindle, and they are finally brutalized and murdered by Cy Tolliver (1.8). Despite the realism with which Miles and Flora are portrayed, Milch's invocation of James's tale surely invites a bit of gothic speculation. In James's story it's unclear if Miles and Flora are manipulating the governess, whether the Bly house is truly haunted, and how Miles dies. Although Milch's Miles and Flora are clearly manipulators, and there is no uncertainty about their murders, Milch cannot exorcise the ghostly demons and interpretive plurality he conjures with his allusion to James's tale, even if he would like to do so. His Miles and Flora represent a paradox: one way to survive in his version of the U.S. frontier is "Sofia style"—doing nothing at all. Like succumbing to rapids and allowing the rushing water to propel one's body to the surface, passivity and inaction prove to be vital skills in Milch's world. Unlike Miles and Flora, who fail fatally in their attempt to imitate the adult doublespeak and duplicity they find in Deadwood, Sofia's gothic muteness preserves her in the community without laws. Satisfied that Sofia can't speak, Swearengen finally leaves her alone and blots out the crime's trail by murdering his agents himself.

If Sofia survives because unspeakability, passivity, and muteness are useful skills in Milch's representation of the nineteenth-century frontier, certain other characters will perish for lack of such traits. Wild Bill Hickok, for example, had to die not only for the sake of historical accuracy but also because the gunfighter figure is anathema to the postmodern gothic frontier in which there is no divine justice or unproblematic social order. As critics such as Douglas L. Howard have noted, Milch's preservation of Hickok's self-willed aura of spectrality in this historical moment is suggested by his arrival in camp lying prone in a covered wagon like "a corpse in state" (51). Rejecting Utter's respectable job offer in the fourth episode, Hickok asks his friend, "Can you let me go to hell the way I want to?" (1.4). Furthermore, Milch's portrayal of Jack McCall as dim-witted, grimy, and sadistically star-struck is fitting because the man who beats the drum of Hickok's march toward an ignominious death is also the man who marks the approach of a new representation of the frontier as a place of fragmentation and hopelessness.

Hickok must die because his figuration as a gunman/lawman is no longer viable in Milch's postmodern version of the frontier. Established as a nostalgic figure in such films as *The Gunfighter* (1950), *High Noon* (1952), and *Shane* (1953), as Richard Slotkin notes, the morally righteous and often aristocratic gunfighter is suggestive of a (mythical) historical moment of social stability (*Gunfighter Nation* 401). Milch endows his Hickok (to delicious effect) with an innate understanding of the criminal mind; Hickok sniffs out Ned Mason as the Metz family murderer because he empathizes with Mason's pathological desire to socialize after the murder: "I felt that way sometimes after a kill," he mumbles (1.1). And yet the gunfighter

14. Charlie at Hickok's grave. "Childish Things" (*Deadwood* 2.8).

is a figure who can't survive in a world of unspeakability; when what binds the community is its many suppressed secrets, and when there is no longer a single "truth" but only a "lie agreed upon," the community can no longer be held together by the might and simplicity of a gunfighter hero. The gothic mode provides the means by which the community mourns the loss of an era; even after Hickok's death, his presence will continue to haunt the series. In the second season Utter visits his grave, despairing about Jane, who seems to have "lost wanting to keep on" (2.8). As an evening breeze blows through the cemetery on a hill overlooking the town, Utter throws his hands in the air and twice pronounces disconsolately to Hickok's grave, "I don't know what . . . to do!" His words echo the sentiments of a community that pines for a simpler time, which, of course, never existed.

Confused mourning at the grave of the gunman/lawman is a fitting emblem for communal perplexity over the inability of the law to provide social stability. If there is a pervasive theme in *Deadwood*, it is that the law is a complicated institution. This is a recurrent concern in the gothic, dating to Ann Radcliffe's *The Mysteries of Udolpho* (1794).[6] When Emily inquires by what right Montoni is enforcing her marriage to Count Morano, for example, Montoni replies, "By the right of my will" (216). In an example from another eighteenth-century gothic novel, Caleb Williams's physical and mental imprisonments at the hands of Falkland in William Godwin's *Caleb Williams* (1794) illustrates the Godwinian principal that positive laws are always perverted in comparison to individual reason. Gothic imagery surrounding the law continues into the twentieth century, when, for example, Franz Kafka's "Before the Law" (1908) represents the law as even more cryptic and destructive.

In the cinematic Western motifs of law and lawlessness have similarly pointed to a range of issues, including the battle over the land, fears about urbanization and modernization, and anxieties about social transformation. The Western's conception of the subject in relation to notions of justice is ever-shifting. For André Bazin the Western is essentially a cultural commentary on "the relation between law and morality" (145). In John Ford's *The Man Who Shot Liberty Valance* (1962), Ransom Stoddard refuses to yield to force or reason, and "it is his faith in the triumph of law that makes him noble, rather than a fool" (D. Williams 95). More recently Clint Eastwood's William Munny in *Unforgiven* (1992) seems to long for vigilante vengeance in the face of what Orit Kamir characterizes as "positive law's unsatisfactory formalism," the law's inability to redress sufferings inflicted by crimes (215). In *Deadwood* those who bring "law and order" to the frontier also wreak havoc and violence in the process. As the prostitute-murdering character Francis Wolcott remarks, "I am a sinner who does not expect forgiveness, but I am not a government official" (2.12).

Wolcott's statement that political authority is a kind of irredeemable evil confirms the subtler imbrication of gothic motifs around the establishment of law in the show, which indicate that the law itself is intrinsically corrupted. The pilot's first scene, based on a story related in Kenneth Kellar's biography of Bullock, illustrates the complications that the establishment of law creates. As the jailed Clell Watson muses about the absence of law in Deadwood, Byron Sampson and a torch-wielding mob gather outside the jailhouse to inflict vigilante justice on the convicted horse thief. Bullock decides to hang Watson immediately rather than wait until the scheduled execution time the next morning because he wants to hang Sampson "under the color of law" rather than capitulate to vigilantism. Watson initially objects but quickly sees that the alternative to hanging is the mob's vengeance. Stepping on the little stool Bullock has set out, Watson places his head in a makeshift noose, and admonishes the marshal, "You help me with my . . . fall!" Watson jumps into the noose, but Bullock must yank his dangling legs to help break his neck, and a sober silence falls over the mob as Watson's suspended legs continue to twitch. Bullock's execution of Watson seems to be in the name of holding the law above vigilantism—"You call the law in, you don't get to call it off just because you're liquored up and popular on payday," Bullock tells Sampson (1.1).

On the other hand, Bullock's decision to make an exception of Watson and to dispatch him before his scheduled execution time makes Watson a (perhaps crude) example of what Giorgio Agamben would call the "bare life." For Agamben a bare life is the by-product of the establishment of a sovereign, an establishment that constructs the political status of all its subjects as a state of exception. As Nasser Hussain explains, "Bare life is produced in and through this fundamental act of sovereignty in the sense of being included in the political realm precisely by virtue of being excluded" (495).[7] Because Bullock makes an exception of Watson in the name of the law—executing him before his scheduled time in order to resist vigilantism—Watson becomes an example of the bare life, an exception to the law in the name of the law, underscoring the notion that the establishment of law only inscribes the subject in a system in which civil rights and protections are an illusion. Watson's execution marks the first of many *Deadwood* moments in which the establishment of a "lawful" society reveals, as Agamben predicts, that "every attempt to found political liberties in the rights of the citizen is . . . in vain" (181). The paradox Agamben deduces from the figure of the bare life has gothic implications: transgression is part and parcel of establishing the political-legal realm, and the threat of violence to the subject comes from within the system rather than outside it.

Bullock's resistance to serving as an officer of the law repeatedly reminds us of the insanity of working within the legal institution.[8] He is reluctantly drawn into the legal realm at the behest of Hickok before Swearengen finally (and ominously) calls him the "perfect . . . front man" for the settlement (1.8). It takes another lawman, General George Crook, to recognize the crux of Bullock's inner conflict: "a man—a former marshal—who understands the danger of his own temperament, might consider serving his fellows" (1.12). Bullock finally agrees with a typically terse and clench-jawed, "I'll be the fucking sheriff"—and in the next two seasons he time and again fails to control his temper in accordance with his official position (1.12). In the first episode of season 3, he savagely beats E. B. Farnum with little provocation. His violent and maniacal tendencies make him, as Swearengen so aptly says, the "perfect" sheriff for Milch's gothic frontier. Bullock's overwhelming anxiety (Olyphant seems always to be grimacing) comes from trying to stand for the *presence* of the law, an institution that threatens to tear the subject and the state asunder. No sane person, after all, would take a position as a protector of an institution that, as Agamben theorizes, perpetually inscribes the subject in a position of subjugation. In becoming synonymous with the law, Bullock enacts the violence that the law inflicts.

If Bullock's position as a lawman rips his psyche asunder, his position as a romantic hero is no less fraught. Such heroes of the tormented Rochester variety are plentiful in classic gothic fiction, as Eugenia DeLamotte explains: "If women's Gothic romance before Charlotte Brontë suspected that the hero who offered rescue and marriage was in some way the same villain who threatened to trap the heroine in his house forever, Charlotte Brontë's representation of Rochester as both hero and villain, egress and entrapment, brings that hidden identity to the surface" (211). Both sinning and sinned-against, Bullock is indeed a gothic hero of Rochesterian proportions. His affair with widow Alma Garret even triangulates a "madwoman in the attic" pattern, including Bullock's wife and his brother's widow, Martha Bullock. But the terms of the *Jane Eyre* motif are reversed in the *Deadwood* triangle: Alma is a drug addict while

Martha is virtuous and intellectual, and the "egress" Bullock offers Alma is a fleeting, bed-rocking "escape" from the domestic confines of her dreary and loveless marriage. In contrast to *Jane Eyre*, in which Jane and Rochester each suffer greatly before finding a secluded haven of mutual respect, there can be no such haven in Milch's frontier. While Brontë's Jane, like many nineteenth-century frontier heroines, serves as a "civilizing" force on her man, Milch's figuration of Alma ridicules the antiquated notion of the "Angel in the House."[9] Neither a feminist paragon of intellect and fortitude (despite her position at the bank) nor a "cultivating" force of selflessness and virtue, Alma, unlike Jane Eyre, cannot produce in her man the kind of magical and soothing transformation that signifies "civilization."

In nineteenth-century literature an Alma-like figure would have functioned as a white female exemplar of national virtue, and the threat of her sexual violation within the context of a gothic novel would have stood metaphorically for all the forces that threatened to violate the purity of national identity. A primary concern of the gothic has always been the delineation of borders, which is most often effected by establishing a binary between contaminated "other" and pure "self." *Jane Eyre*'s Bertha Mason is one example of a fictional British colonial subject whose dark skin and insanity mark her as "other" in relation to the protagonist, a doppelgänger relationship intended to reify the purity and virtue of the ruling class. With respect to sex and sexuality, the formula of the nineteenth-century gothic placed virtue in distress and threatened to "contaminate" it via rape or violation—the threat of Jane Eyre's moral violation by entering into a bigamous marriage, for example. The role of the gothic heroine was to successfully fend off the monster or villain and to preserve her virtue and her "pure" self. In the postmodern frontier gothic, however, all is already contaminated, and there is no feminine virtue as a figure for national righteousness to be protected. Instead, gothic threats, including monsters, ghosts, insanity, and secrecy or "unspeakability," express communal guilt, suppression of secrets, and the innate violence of society.

While the upper-class Alma doesn't function as a gothic heroine, neither do the prostitutes at the Bella Union or the Gem, in and of themselves at least. Whether it's the dirty and destitute Trixie or the spiffy and well-appointed Joanie Stubbs, the show's white prostitutes are portrayed largely without gothic effect. Openly and repeatedly violated and harboring no modesty or secrecy, they stand as reminders of the "contaminated" bodies that populate the frontier and the body politic. One notable exception to the absence of gothic motifs surrounding the town's prostitutes occurs in the second season and is embodied in the figures of Chinese prostitutes brought to town by George Hearst and his henchman, Mr. Lee. When Mr. Wu angrily knifes open the canvas covering of the Chinese prostitutes' cages in "Something Very Expensive," for example, Wolcott calmly explains to Tolliver that the rivalry between Wu and Lee is equal to that between the Sioux and the whites (2.6). With Wu apparently outraged at the mistreatment of the Chinese prostitutes, the Wu-Lee rivalry forms a shadow story to the main plot: ostensibly about moral righteousness and "civilization," men's appetites boil down to the desire for sex and money. In Wolcott's version there is no moral center; all parties are equally land grubbing and corrupt, which obscures the historical reality of Chinese oppression in the West, and the gothic motifs that surround Wolcott's interactions with both Chinese and white prostitutes reveal the fissures in his story and in his psyche.

The common element in the gothic depiction of prostitution in the show is Wolcott. The traditional gothic threat of sexual violation as a metaphor for the risk of a "contaminated" national identity is void in *Deadwood*'s world because individuals and the body politic are all contaminated; instead, the tension that creates gothic drama in the show surrounds the question of how long individuals will be able to "bear up" under the burden of their own violent secrets. Standing next to the cages of the Chinese prostitutes in "Childish Things" (2.8), Wolcott tries to assuage the guilt of the fratricidal Mose Manuel with a sinister, "Money has significant properties in this regard." In the next moment, however, the staring eyes of the Chinese prostitutes provide a perfectly gothic and unsettling moment of live haunting: corpse-like, violated, and seemingly possessed of the knowledge of Wolcott's sins, the Chinese prostitutes' gazes unravel him. Screaming at the caged prostitutes to close their eyes, Wolcott stumbles to Chez Ami, where his intended "release" of violence is disrupted for the time being. Wolcott's sadistic and insane (gothic) tendency to brutalize prostitutes is, after all, a re-enactment of whatever violent secrets he harbors in his soul, and it is fitting that he and the Chinese prostitutes meet gothic ends: Wolcott's hanging body and the smoke and ashes that remain after the dead Chinese prostitutes are unceremoniously burned linger as gothic reminders of the horrors that the U.S. heritage produces within the U.S. psyche.

Whereas Wolcott perished under the pressure of his own violent secrets, Swearengen is the show's principal villain because of his remarkable capacity to contain the world's brutality within his soul. Like a two-headed Janus figure, he reminds us that civilization and barbarity are twins. He exhibits gruesome physical cruelty in the opening episodes—strangling the battered Trixie with his foot, reducing Calamity Jane to tears with a menacing look, and stabbing Persimmon Phil. However, as Heather Havrilesky writes, Swearengen also has a very "civilized" sense of pragmatism, "a very practical belief in rules and order, an eye-rolling tolerance for slackers and miscreants, and a firm grasp of the value of incentives" (*Salon.com*). The unpredictability of Swearengen's character is what lends him a sense of gothic monstrosity, the most telling and terrifying attribute of which is uncertainty or indeterminacy. As Kim Michasiw writes, such indeterminacy is key to gothic fear: "Not: the cannibal monster is in the nursery snacking on the soft skulls of the infant twins. Rather: the cannibal monster may be in the nursery, or he may be somewhere else, or she may be in the nursery disguised as one of the twins. Or: there may be no cannibal at all, though this would be a fine place for one" (237–38). One never knows which Swearengen will show up: the criminal who tries to slip the addicted widow more opium, the compassionate man who gently suffocates the Reverend Smith in an act of compassion, or the murderer who violently drowns his own employee in a tub of water in order to protect a business relationship.

In the pantheon of Western cinematic and literary character types, Swearengen is an "avenger," a frontier settler who has been transformed into a monster but whose evil services the advance of civilization. In the original form of the avenger myth, as Doug Williams explains, "Indians murder a young man's family. Spiritually, the civilized boy/man dies in that instant; all that is left is a murderous rage against Indians, and indeed, wilderness itself" (108). The Indian-killing Quaker trapper, Nathan Slaughter, of Robert Montgomery Bird's *Nick of the Woods* (1837) is one example of this archetype; John Wayne's Ethan Edwards in Ford's *The Searchers* (1956) is another. Ethan hates Indians because "their presence reminds him of the mythical Indian within him, of the human monster without God or community" (D. Williams 109). In the postmodern world the human monster has become the norm rather than the exception, and although Swearengen refers to Indians as "dirt worshippers" (1.1) and orders bounties on their heads, Indians as a metaphor for savagery no longer suffice. Instead, Swearengen wreaks his havoc on the camp's Anglo settlers, preying on their own base desires.[10] Milch's spin on the avenger myth, in the character of Swearengen, is that his violent facade belies a man whose rampages stem from deeper psychological hurts and betrayals sustained in the "civilized" East.[11] Fittingly, while classic "avengers" are excellent frontiersman like Edwards of *The Searchers* or even Munny of *Unforgiven*—men who seem more comfortable in the wilderness than in the confines of society—Swearengen is much more comfortable behind his desk. In this way Swearengen's function as an emblem of the dark forces of civilization is even more striking: it is not just the Indian killers who are guilty of genocide but also every person sitting at a desk, participating (however blindly) in the brutal forces of capitalism.

Swearengen's ironic role as the principle "civilizer" is reinforced by his gothic role as "interpreter" of the "foreign" landscape. The task of interpreting positions the gothic hero or heroine in a moment of what DeLamotte would call "negative capability" or not knowing, which creates gothic suspense (48). Interpretation was such a commonplace of the classic, nineteenth-century gothic that

Jane Austen mocks the convention in *Northanger Abbey* (1818), when the avid gothic reader Catherine Morland has her curiosity piqued by an old chest she discovers: "What can it hold?—Why should it be placed here?" (143). Disappointingly, for Catherine, the chest turns out to be simply an innocuous antique. In gothic novels that take their own gothic conventions more seriously, however, such artifacts often harbor skeletons, lost manuscripts, and other ghostly relics of secret violence, the interpretation of which is key to the hero's identity.

One of the earliest instances of Swearengen's interpretive powers is humorous: Mr. Wu tries to communicate with Swearengen about the robbery and murder of his opium couriers by drawing a map of the robbery scene. Furious that his own opium supply has been cut off with the crime, Swearengen demands to know who the murderers were, "Who?!" Swearengen shouts. "Wu!" Mr. Wu rejoins, in a who's-on-first-style misunderstanding (1.10). Swearengen quickly discovers the robbers' identity and murders one of them as a token of justice for Mr. Wu. As the series escalates, Swearengen's interpretative skills evolve. Moments after Swearengen recovers from an episode of kidney stones and a stroke, Dan Dority wants to update him on the confusing events in the camp: "You got to bring all your ... wiles to bear, Al, 'cause developments need *interpreting* on every ... front" (2.5). Later in the series Swearengen correctly decodes a cryptic note from rival George Hearst and avoids an ambush. The primary reason Hearst would bother to send Swearengen the note in advance is to test Swearengen's interpretive powers, to see who can "read" the frontier better and who will be the ascendant gothic villain. When Swearengen fails to interpret the next Hearst missive correctly, however, he pays dearly—with his finger.

Swearengen's calm exterior belies the fact that he struggles in his position as interpreter. Often he's left in (gothic) darkness. When Hearst's top thug, Captain Turner, sends his own coded note to Dority, inviting him to fight to the death, Swearengen delays until he can "decipher his reason" (3.5). He mulls the meaning of the proposed fight for the entire episode until finally, sitting alone at his desk, he downs a shot of whiskey, wheels his chair around, and begins to speak to the decapitated head of a Sioux chief that he keeps locked in his armoire: "Watching us advance on your stupid teepee, Chief, knowing you had to make your move, did you not just want first to fucking understand?" (3.5). Swearengen's question is met, of course, with silence, and he finally shrugs, closes the armoire door, and tells Dority to fight. Swearengen's secret communion about interpretation and understanding with the severed head of a Sioux chief perfectly encodes the terms of the gothic frontier. The Indian head represents the crime against the social order—Native American genocide—that is at the heart of the horror of *Deadwood*, and the gothic implication in this scene is that the only way one can interpret the "civilizing" forces of the frontier landscape is via death. The Native American watches the encroachment of Western civilization on his tepee and is finally able to interpret white motivations when he is no longer able to articulate or speak of them. Although Swearengen both perpetuates and laments the brutish forces that are conquering and bringing so-called law to the frontier, even he is unable to fully comprehend the degree of horror that such "civilization" implies; *only* a figure like Swearengen (or like Kurtz in *Heart of Darkness*) is able to live with the extent of the knowledge he does possess without being torn asunder.

Just as interpretation is a never-ending horrific quest for Swearengen, so it is for Milch, who has had his own demons to tame.[12] Swearengen finally becomes a figure for the filmmaker who wants to reimagine the frontier with a postmodern sensibility and who struggles to find his way. Fred Botting explains that in the postmodern gothic, the landscape is characterized by void and annihilation, transgression has become the norm, and the center and the periphery have exchanged places in disorienting fashion.[13] The postmodern frontier gothic is expressed via generic boundary crossing, in images of unspeakability and uninterpretable actions. Such is Milch's representation of the frontier in this particular historical moment, but as he noted in a promotional video for another of his HBO television shows, *John from Cincinnati*, quoting Henry James, of course: "The question of the final stamp, the pressure which fixes the mark, is yet to be determined."

I wish to thank University of Southern California Department of English chair, Margaret Russett, and Professor William Handley for their guidance on this essay.

Notes

1. As Milch explains, the possibilities of writing about a space where people lived outside the protection of laws are what attracted him to the historical town of Deadwood, South Dakota, as a setting for a television show: "I had been writing shows, mostly cop shows, which had to do with the intersection of law and order, or the failure to intersect, and I was interested in what it would be like to examine a society where there was order more or less but no law whatsoever" (audio commentary 1.1).
2. André Bazin writes that the classical Western "has virtually no use for the close-up, even for the medium shot, preferring by contrast the traveling shot and the pan which refuse to be limited by the frame line and which restore to space its fullness" (147).
3. Frances B. Singh argues that *Heart of Darkness* is an example of the gothic at work in modernism: "In *Heart of Darkness*, we see a representation of state-sponsored terrorism and political horror being born from the conventions of the literary Gothic" (214).
4. See DeLamotte.
5. In other words, as Sedgwick has outlined, gothic horror sometimes occurs in vaults, such as the rape of Antonia in a subterranean passage in *The Monk*, but more often gothic violence occurs at the threshold of a barrier, as the rioters in *The Monk* are burned to death trying to escape the convent they have just set afire, and Ambrosio, in the same novel, stabs Antonia only after he realizes the vault is being invaded. As Sedgwick explains, "The worst violence, the most potent magic, and the most paralyzing instances of the uncanny in these novels do not occur in, for example, the catacombs of the Inquisition or the stultification of nightmares. Instead, they are evoked in the very breach of the imprisoning wall" (*Coherence* 13). For Sedgwick the fear evoked in these breaches usually served as a metaphor for a linguistic despair over the use of direct language; however, her theoretical point can be extended such that in this gothic structure, "unspeakability," can be seen both to emphasize and to complicate a text's ideological intent.
6. As Leslie Moran suggests, the law in gothic novels is represented as "an archaic past that haunts, corrupts and renders labyrinthine the straight path of rule and reason" (87). Further, the law in gothic texts is often

associated with "the ad hoc, unreason, the outmoded, with the judicial in contrast to the Parliamentary, unwritten law in contrast to the written law" (87).

7. Agamben deduces the aporia of the "bare life" through the obscure figure of the "homo sacer," the man/criminal in ancient Roman law who could be killed but not sacrificed (8). The "homo sacer" embodies the state of exception in which, for Agamben, every political being exists. This condition makes every individual into a "bare life," living outside the protection of the very law it tries to establish: "At once excluding bare life from and capturing it within the political order, the state of exception actually constituted, in its very separateness, the hidden foundation on which the entire political system rested" (9).

8. Bullock's resistance to serving as marshal recalls Ford's portrayal of Wyatt Earp (Henry Fonda) in *My Darling Clementine* (1946). Ford's Earp repeatedly declines the Tombstone mayor's offer of the marshal job with a terse "not interested," until the discovery of his brother's murder and the rustling of the family's cattle prompts Earp to pin on the badge.

9. The ascension of the British gothic novel in the eighteenth century coincided with the growth of the ideology of "separate spheres," which valorized the proper female role as domestic and distinct from the public world of economics and politics.

10. As Jason Jacobs notes: "At first sight, Al appears the opposite of a civilizer but he provides the essential means by which the miners slake their fatigue and anxiety: the provision of sex, drugs, and gambling; these services offer the transient pleasures of losing the self in acts that, ultimately, destroy the self. Al's insight is into the darkness of men's appetites rather than their aspiration for joy; into the primitive, sometimes brutal, urges of men rather than their hopes for a better life" (13).

11. As Swearengen recounts the story of his abandonment while Dolly performs oral sex on him, his attempt to emphasize his lack of self-pity—"Don't be sorry, don't look back because, believe me, no one gives a fuck"—only emphasizes the degree of his anger (1.11).

12. In "The Misfit: How David Milch Got from *NYPD Blue* to *Deadwood* by Way of an Epistle of St. Paul," Mark Singer documents Milch's storied personal life.

13. Botting explains that "Gothic figures and fictions now circulate with greater visibility to manifest the absence of strict, prohibitive mechanisms or a strong, exclusionary force" (285–86).

6 "Down These Mean Streets"
Film Noir, *Deadwood*, Cinematic Space, and the Irruption of Genre Codes

Nicolas S. Witschi

While Wendy Witherspoon explores Deadwood*'s "generic cross-fertilization" from gothic and frontier traditions, Nicolas Witschi uses a similar term, "cross-genre borrowings and adaptation," to argue that "for all its distinctive Western features,* Deadwood *connects itself just as emphatically to the conventions of the hard-boiled tradition of film noir [as to the Western], with the two aesthetic and formal traditions coming together specifically in the context of a story about a city's urban built environment." He offers a brief history of the intersecting developments of the Western and the detective novel, demonstrating how they both influenced film noir, which has been described as an urban Western with a cowboy-turned-detective hero. He particularly focuses on Bullock, Witherspoon's "romantic hero," whom he describes as "the camp's beat-walking, tough-talking, hard-boiled cop," a figure he claims connects writing with walking, both of which make him, "in action as well as in words . . . the figurative binding agent of the community."*

Like others in this volume, Witschi looks at Deadwood*'s language, arguing that "dialogue serves throughout* Deadwood *as a site of genre complication and mixing." He identifies how a number of elements, thematic and stylistic, associated with film noir are used in* Deadwood*, then focuses on how the series "deals with narrative point of view and how it represents the built environment" to expose "the extent to which the series engages in the noir genre at the expense of the Western." Witschi's focus on the "spaces" of the urban noir in* Deadwood *links the series to the contemporary critical interest in post-Western urban life, revisiting the question of how Westerns compel viewers to see the West as a terrain made up of very specific elements and conventions. Later in the volume, Michael Johnson examines* Deadwood*'s spaces from a quite different perspective.*

My Mom was so excited when I got this job, that I was gonna play the hero in a Western. And I came home at the holidays and I showed her the first episode. We weren't ten minutes into it, and she said, "I thought you were gonna be in a Western." And I said, "I am in a Western." She said, "Not the ones I grew up watching. I told all the ladies at church that you were finally gonna be in something they could watch. And now I've got to call them all back."

Timothy Olyphant, on being cast as Seth Bullock

But down these means streets a man must go who is himself not mean, who is neither tarnished nor afraid. The detective in this kind of story must be such a man. He is the hero; he is everything. He must be a complete man and a common man and yet an unusual man. He must be, to use a rather weathered phrase, a man of honor—by instinct, by inevitability, without thought of it, and certainly without saying it. He must be the best man in his world and a good enough man for any world.

Raymond Chandler, "The Simple Art of Murder"

Just about every one of *Deadwood*'s thirty-six episodes features a significant arrival in or departure from the camp. Indeed, the importance of these comings and goings is signaled in part by the daily position that Al Swearengen is shown taking up on his balcony, from which perch he carefully notes any changes in the town's rapidly growing population. In "Leviathan Smiles" (3.8), a particularly noteworthy pair of arrivals bookend the drama of the day. Soon after the episode begins, Wyatt Earp and his brother Morgan rush into camp with all the whooping and shooting that one might consider typical of a genre Western. And more ominously, at the very end of the episode a mob of torch-carrying Pinkerton "detectives" rides in under cover of darkness (both of these arrivals are duly observed and noted by Al). To the characters in the drama, the first of these two arrivals presents, briefly, the possibility of shrewd and skilled gunmen who might eventually set themselves up in competition with Al and Seth Bullock, while the latter demonstrates George Hearst's investment in brute strength. Aside from their significance within the story, these two arrivals also neatly demonstrate the genre-challenging aspects of the series as a whole. As familiar character types the Earp brothers and the Pinkertons stand as quintessential figures from two distinct, related, but often separate genre traditions: the Western and the detective story.[1] Their parallel arrivals in camp certainly hint at the extent to which the series as a whole explores the intersections of these two traditions. Moreover, the overarching context of the story, namely, the growth of a mining camp into a bona fide city with a diverse population and complex political and economic structures, indicates that these two genres have proven essential to telling the story of urban development in the American West.

In the study of adventure narratives and their various subgenres, it has become an all-too familiar observation that the detective story, particularly in its noir or hard-boiled incarnation, is by and large a Western transposed into an urban environment. Leslie Fiedler, for one, echoed a well-established critical position when he observed that "the private eye is not the dandy turned sleuth; he is the cowboy adapted to life on the city streets" (476). But as more-recent work by David Hamilton Murdoch, Marcus Klein, and Cynthia Hamilton has affirmed, detective fiction was a common feature of the popular literary marketplace well before the ascent of the mythic cowboy figure; the two literary genres in large part evolved coevally and in often overlapping ways.[2] Moreover, as printed text gives way to cinema as the primary means by which the public experiences and consumes these parallel modes, the sense of interdependent reciprocity continues. As Rick Altman has observed, within this history hybrid genre productions have often proliferated; at one time it was easily possible to see "such things as Western chase films, Western scenics, Western melodrama, Western romances, Western adventure films, and even Western comedies, Western dramas, and Western epics" (52). Thus, while an ostensible noir thriller like *High Sierra* (1941) may usefully be read as emerging out of the Western tradition, so can a Western like *My Darling Clementine* (1946) be seen, as Scott Simmon amply demonstrates, as both negatively reacting against and, in many respects, embracing the aesthetics and ethos of urban noir (193–294). Similarly, other Golden Era productions such as *Pursued* (1947) and *Station West* (1948) have their hybrid elements, as do (as Simmon hints) the spaghetti Westerns inspired by Sergio Leone's films. And in a more recent cyclical return to genre hybridity, Clint Eastwood's *Unforgiven* (1992) may also quite plausibly be understood to feature both Western and noir genre elements.[3]

Into this history steps David Milch's *Deadwood*, the latest exemplar of cross-genre borrowings and adaptation. On one hand, as a drama located in a semirural location in the United States' intermountain West during the latter half of the nineteenth-century, the show certainly bears the familiar markings of a Western: guns, cowboy hats, horses, saloons and stagecoaches, a few Indians, bad men and loose women, and even a schoolmarm or two—and plenty has been written about the series along these very lines.[4] However, for a variety of reasons, most of them concerning heightened levels of violence and language that are, to some at least, offensive, the show presents a challenge to genre-bound ways of thinking.[5] Timothy Olyphant's mother, for one, was sufficiently disenchanted by the first episode that she declared that it was not a Western, at least not of the sort she had grown up with and could share with her friends from church. And Milch himself has said on more than one occasion, "I did want to do a show on the American West, but I didn't want to do a Western. I've never really understood or cared for the conventions of the Western" (qtd. in Barra, "Goodbye Deadwood?" 20).

Rather, the conventions that Milch apparently does care for are those of the urban crime drama. Starting as a writer for *Hill Street Blues* in the 1980s and moving on to become the creator and producer behind the iconoclastic NYPD *Blue*, Milch was instrumental in creating for television shows that were often referred to as "hard-edged programming" that "made use of deeply flawed characters whose lives were as bleak as the deteriorating urban landscapes where they lived and worked" (Snauffer 182). That these "deeply flawed characters" on whose difficulties these shows concentrated were chiefly male further aligns these productions with the "male melodrama" of film noir, as Janet Staiger has described the form. As someone whose television career has been founded on the production of gritty police procedurals, Milch brings a sensibility to the show that allows him to acknowledge and exploit several multigenre features. Thus, for all its distinctive Western features, *Deadwood* connects itself just as emphatically to the conventions of the hard-boiled tradition of film noir, with the two aesthetic and formal traditions coming together specifically in the context of a story about a city's urban built environment. Which is to say, given the current West's predominantly urbanized population, *Deadwood*'s genre hybridity thus speaks directly to the story about the American West perhaps most in need of telling: the rise of the city.[6]

Of course, the attribution of genre classification occurs more often than not after the fact, with stylistic and even ideological characteristics being retroactively read into or applied on top of an existing form or production. For example, it may very well be that only in the wake of a film such as John Sturgis's *The Magnificent Seven* (1960) can the influence of Western genre cinema on Kurosawa's *Seven Samurai* (1954) and other films be fully appreciated—Sturgis's remake actually makes possible a reading of Kurosawa's films as having "Western" elements. It is thus worth heeding James Naremore's cautionary note about not being too quick to consign to any one genre a text that may have multiple systems of reference at work within and around it (5–6). That is, we run the risk of missing much of what a series such as *Deadwood* accomplishes or has to offer by defining it by one or another set of conventions, stylistic elements, themes, and so forth. However, as Naremore also argues, film noir in particular has become a historically powerful idea, an organizing principle that has of late been invoked by filmmakers from Clint Eastwood to Quentin Tarantino as a legitimizing category not only in critical terms but also for both aesthetic and marketing purposes (10–11). It is in this regard that *Deadwood* functions, its numerous references to the hard-boiled tradition working to engage a television audience that is no longer very interested in the Western as a form. For one, the show embraces such elements as noir's "cynical treatment of the American Dream, [its] complicated play with gender and sexuality, and [its] foregrounding of cinematic style" (Naremore 2). And at the level of style, Milch's series very much relies on the "formal and narrative conventions of film noir" as Edward Dimendberg enumerates them: "'low-key' lighting rich in shadows, voice-over narrators, crime story narratives, violent protagonists, and femmes fatales," all coordinated through a visual style dominated by "aerial or long-shot skyline views of the metropolis, [and] crowd sequences filmed from ground level" (5, 7). The two elements in this last catalog that perhaps least describe *Deadwood*, voice-over narration and the predominance of "skyline views" and crowds, nevertheless do exist in abundance throughout the series. How it deals with narrative point of view and how it represents the built environment, two formal elements that are more central to the aesthetic of the hard-boiled detective story than to that of the Western, most clearly demonstrate how *Deadwood* exploits genre in telling a Western tale.

One tried-and-true staple of Westerns is the quick-draw gunfight, and in this respect *Deadwood* begins with what would appear to be a genre-satisfying example. In the pilot episode Bullock and Wild Bill Hickok together challenge a man who appears connected to the slaughter of an immigrant family, and the confrontation leads directly to a gunfight. However, the uncertainty over which man's bullet, Bullock's or Hickok's, kills the bad guy is never resolved. The point of this lack of resolution seems to be to frustrate any attempt to brand a hero out of this particularly clichéd type of confrontation, and the series largely eschews such showdowns after this opening teaser. The *possibility* of another gunfight, however, is raised with the arrival of Wyatt Earp in town, though here too the expected genre event is averted, this time in a very telling conversation. Having just witnessed a tense encounter between Bullock and the newly arrived Morgan Earp, Cy Tolliver explains to Hearst the potential for goading the situation further to their mutual advantage:

TOLLIVER: There is no losing in a match like that, Mr. Hearst.
HEARST: Never been much for draws.
TOLLIVER: Well, I—I—I meant to say, let the matter be joined aright, whether Bullock or this gunsel stood at the finish, there's no losing in it for you.
HEARST: What does "joined aright" mean?

TOLLIVER: Say Bullock was first provoked out the public eye, so his throwing down in public seemed . . . overquick. There's all kinds of implications to that, legal and political too.

HEARST: Have you taken steps to join this matter aright?

TOLLIVER: Only steps I took so far, Mr. Hearst, was to bring me into your presence. As to what steps will be required if you give the go-ahead, easy as the sheriff sparks, and cocky look as his kid wears, the number should be few. (3.8)

As they are shown debating the prospect of provoking a showdown, Tolliver and Hearst in fact represent different assumptions about the supposed genre each character inhabits. Tolliver relishes the idea of a duel in the street between two gunfighters, while Hearst (who has hired the Pinkertons scheduled to arrive later in the episode) declares that he cares not for "draws." And after Tolliver sputters out a backtracking explanation, Hearst rather sarcastically echoes Tolliver's diction. Which is to say, they differ even in their approaches to language, with Tolliver's more abstruse and arcane-seeming syntax providing a further point of difference between them.

This is not to say, however, that this brief exchange reveals Tolliver to be a "Western" figure while Hearst stands as the "hard-boiled" character. Rather, the manner in which these two characters are represented demonstrates the extent to which the series engages in the noir genre at the expense of the Western. The key genre moment in this exchange, in fact, may be pinned on one word: *gunsel.* Derived from the Yiddish *genzel,* which is a gosling or little goose, this word first appeared in early twentieth-century books on criminal slang in reference to "a (naïve) youth; a tramp's companion, male lover" (OED). The *Random House Historical Dictionary of American Slang* (ed. Lighter) identifies the word's early usage as "derisive" and adds that its appearance in Dashiell Hammett's 1930 hard-boiled novel, *The Maltese Falcon,* may in fact be the source of a key shift in the word's meaning. Hammett has become quite well known for confounding his editors with slang. As the story goes, in his original draft he had the character of Sam Spade refer to

Wilmer, the gun-toting thug who accompanies Casper Gutman everywhere he goes, as a "catamite," which was plainly understood slang for "a boy kept for homosexual practices; the passive partner in anal intercourse" (OED). When his editor objected, Hammett simply substituted another word meaning the same thing. However, its use in describing a gun-wielding henchman has led to an understandable misinterpretation of the term as slang for gunslinger. This word's appearance in John Huston's film version of the novel further cemented its new meaning (though here too the implied definition is ambiguous), and thus did a largely desexualized "gunsel" become part of the detective noir vocabulary.[7] So when a television audience hears Tolliver refer to Morgan Earp derisively as a "gunsel," it may very well think that he is simply referring to the young man's self-styled status as a hired gun; those with a little more knowledge of noir slang might just as easily detect the sexual implication that Tolliver might be making as he looks at a handsome "proper hero" (as Al calls Wyatt after assessing his physical attributes) and his traveling companion. Or both. The point is that by having the character who advocates for a Western-style gunfight do so by calling, in part, on a vocabulary with a very specifically ambiguous history in the noir tradition, the writers of this particular exchange have thoroughly conflated genre types and expectations. Which is to say, the ambiguity of definition that characterizes the history of *gunsel* is an excellent analog for the ambiguity of genre codes at work in both this brief conversation and in the series as a whole.

Considered more broadly, dialogue serves throughout *Deadwood* as a site of genre complication and mixing, and critical questions about the show's language are usually framed if not on historical or taste-related grounds then within a discussion of its adherence to or departure from the conventions of the Western. Brad Benz, for instance, in an essay that quite neatly encapsulates the ongoing critical discussion about language in *Deadwood*, concludes with the observation that "*Deadwood*'s discourse creates a distinct new vernacular for the Western genre, one that, like tall talk, blurs fact and fiction, as it liberally mixes language both historic and contemporary" (249).[8] As Benz explains, the writing on the show employs a wide vocabulary, some of it demonstrably connected to the Deadwood of 1876 and some of it not, but all of it fundamentally geared toward "transgress[ing] the generic boundaries for discourse in Westerns" (249). Certainly the sensibilities that Milch brings from his experience with *Hill Street Blues* and NYPD *Blue* have much to do with this. However, there are even more specific ties to the hard-boiled school of writing at work. In a profile for the *New Yorker*, Mark Singer reports that Milch's "teacher and avatar [at Yale] Robert Penn Warren . . . favorably compared his dialogue-writing skills with Hemingway's" (194); and Hemingway, as Leonard Cassuto and John T. Irwin, among many others, have noted, was unmistakably an influence on hard-boiled fiction writers such as Hammett (Hemingway himself jokes about it in *The Sun Also Rises* [1926]).[9] But even without considering this chain of influence in the writing of hard-boiled dialogue, the roots of *Deadwood*'s dialogue are clearly affirmed when Milch offers, "I'd say there's a lot of the spirit of Hammett, particularly the Hammett of *Red Harvest*, in 'Deadwood'" (Barra, "Man Who Made Deadwood" 53). It is thus not unreasonable to read classic hard-boiled fiction as being an influence on the series.

More to the point, it is an influence that imbues each of the characters in the show, including those who say "gunsel," with the qualities of a narrator. The power of words, of dialogue, to shape and present a story is certainly a central theme throughout *Deadwood*.[10] Consequently, although the series does not share noir's explicit use of the first-person voice-over narrator, the *idea* of a narrator is either represented or hinted at throughout. In the first episode alone, the miner Ellsworth offers to pay Trixie one dollar per minute for the privilege of listening to her recount her difficulties; Alma Garret briefly mentions that she might find the local curiosities useful in an article she is purportedly writing; and while Bullock and Star unload their wagon into their newly pitched hardware tent, Bullock notes that his partner might do well to write a book with all his (Star's) grandfather's clever aphorisms. In subsequent episodes historical events that contextualize the events in camp, things ranging from Custer's defeat at the Little Big Horn to General Crook's campaign of vengeance to the extensive politics surrounding South Dakota's incorporation as a territory, are rendered through extended dialogue narrations. And throughout, dramatic monologues bring to light the troubled histories of characters such as Doc Cochran, Calamity Jane, E. B. Farnum, Joanie Stubbs, and Al Swearengen, just to name a few.

Far and away the most prominent narrational voice in *Deadwood*, however, belongs to the camp's beat-walking, tough-talking hard-boiled cop, Seth Bullock. Once again the opening of the series, this time the very first sequence of the first episode, proves instructive. After a brief, establishing shot of a jailhouse and other buildings encircling an open space containing a gallows, the show cuts inside the jail to reveal a man behind bars, Clell Watson, and a second character sitting at a desk writing, Bullock. In the very first exchange of dialogue in the entire series, Clell asks, " Is that some sort of a letter, Marshal?" The one-word response, "Journal," prompts an equally brief, "Journal. Good" (1.1). What exactly Watson means by "Journal. Good" is unclear; their conversation does not explicitly come back to the question of Bullock's writing (nor does the matter of Bullock's keeping a record of his thoughts and actions come up again in the rest of the series). A few minutes later, though, as Bullock is about to hang the prisoner "under color of law" rather than hand him over to a lynch mob, he takes a moment to write down the prisoner's last communiqué to his sister. The unconventional nature of this act is indicated by the warning given by Bullock's friend, Sol Star, who says, with a measure of confused hesitation, "Move the fuck back, while my partner . . . while my partner's takin' his sweet-ass time writing whatever the fuck he's writing over there." Bullock then asks who among the would-be lynchers will "give his last words to the sister," a request that becomes a litmus test for sensible behavior in the face of mob loyalty (1.1). Taken together these two text-based events in the middle of the opening sequence firmly establish Seth Bullock as a literate man, a principled and compassionate man, and above all a man interested in preserving and passing along the stories of individuals. Although he will in short order reveal a number of character flaws, he has already been established as what Raymond Chandler once identified as the quintessential hard-boiled hero: "the best man in his world and a good enough man for any world" (59).

Bullock's function as the narrator of the community's conscience is most directly dramatized in the middle of the third season, in the episodes titled "Unauthorized Cinnamon" and "Leviathan Smiles." In response to Hearst's orchestrating the grisly murder of a Cornish mine worker who "talked union" (3.3), Bullock writes a letter of condolence to the dead man's family. This letter is then read aloud at a gathering of the town's "elders," who decide to publish it in Merrick's newspaper. Although it does not impugn Hearst directly, it unambiguously asserts an ethical principle by which a community should live, a statement that effectively embarrasses Hearst. Jack Langrishe summarizes the letter's import by wondering aloud whether it may be interpreted as "proclaiming a law beyond law to a man who's beyond law himself? It's publication invoking a decency whose scrutiny applies to him as to all his fellows" (3.7). As if to underscore the community-wide significance of this letter, "Leviathan Smiles" opens with Bullock's text, figuratively speaking, going for a walk. After the opening credits and before the arrival of Wyatt Earp already discussed, Bullock's letter is shown being delivered by Merrick and Blazanov, the town's telegraph operator. Without a word of dialogue, the two are seen picking their way across a muddy street early in the morning. They stop first at the Grand Hotel and then make their way to the Gem Saloon, distributing freshly printed newspapers along the way and, implicitly, bringing Bullock's articulation of a community ethos out to the people.

The act of walking through a cityscape has, in fact, been described as a distinctive visual feature of film noir. Dimendberg describes the trope of the walk as a stylistic element that is alternately nostalgic, fragmentary, and "healing." Indeed, walks through an urban environment usually serve to establish the space and, at the same time, develop a character's or a set of characters' responses to that space (136). These responses can augur both unifying and alienating forces. And while it is certainly strange to consider a letter's figurative walk through the space as typical of the show's noir element, it is less so to observe that if any one aspect describes Seth Bullock's physical presence, it is the sight of him walking. Dressed stiffly in an armor-like waistcoat, morning coat, and hat, and moving forward with a gait perhaps slightly reminiscent of John Wayne's, Bullock moves through the town much more broadly than any other character, perhaps even Doc Cochran. More to the point, Bullock is shown again and again walking toward something or some place. In this manner, in action as well as in words, he again is represented as the figurative binding agent of the community.

But he is not alone in this trope either. A particularly significant walk occurs in "True Colors" (3.3), a walk in which Al Swearengen gives a tour of the camp to his newly arrived old friend, Jack Langrishe. The final stage of their tour takes them to a section of the town where Al observes, "This is new. This entire area is recent." He gestures to the various hulking edifices around them, noting who lives where. In front of one house he confesses, "This—I can't remember who this fucking belongs to." When Langrishe asks who owns the central square, a small grassy mound with benches where people sit and mill about, Al responds with: "Well, I guess this belongs to fucking everybody" (3.3). In his "study of spatiality in film noir," Dimendberg works quite compellingly to move beyond an ultimately tautological taxonomic discussion of film noir. Instead, he offers a reading of the *spaces* of film noir—both those represented in film and those postwar community loci out of which the films grow and which themselves grow out of a culture fascinated by the films—to highlight "the construction of common spatial fantasies and anxieties" wherein "film noir can be both a symptom and a catalyst of spatial transformation" (12). Referring to the so-called mean streets of the inner city that were being abandoned in favor of a decentered, suburban mode of community, Dimendberg concludes that "the representations of the built environment in the film noir cycle reintroduce forgotten fragments of the city into consciousness" (10). *Deadwood*, it can easily be argued, participates in a very similar project of representing the built environment. Al and Jack's walk thus reveals a city both beginning to organize as a community ("I guess this belongs to fucking everybody") and growing beyond the ability of any one person to know it fully ("I can't remember who this fucking belongs to"). Indeed, this phenomenon is attested to in the sequence not only by the seemingly improvised springing up of a park but also by the purpose of Al and Jack's stroll in the first place: to locate a spot suitable for the building of a public playhouse, a theater.

The building of a city is a theme explicitly introduced in the opening credits of the series. As Milch explains, "The horse is the electricity, is the life, is the beating heart, and then the horse looks into the mud, and up comes Deadwood" (*Deadwood* 137). Starting with the image of fire reflected in the water of a muddy puddle, perhaps as concisely elemental an image as you could possibly muster for the beginnings of something out of nothing, the opening credits sequence moves, via the horse, through images of mud, fire, a forest, blood, ice, mining, a camp, just the hint of sex, bathing, gambling, whiskey, commerce, and, finally, the image of a building that ultimately resolves itself once the shimmer in the puddle comes to a rest. Amanda Ann Klein argues that this sequence invokes the bipolar "syntax" of the Western genre, "the archetypal struggle between nature and civilization," doing so "in order to prepare the viewer for a series that complicates and questions an often-romanticized period of American history" (95). It certainly does all this; however, if the image in the puddle is considered or, more precisely, if the idea of the image in the puddle is considered, then the opening sequence also serves to deromanticize the idea of the city. That is, with respect to the idea of the town of Deadwood rising out of the muck, it is not an image of "Deadwood" but rather the *reflection* of an image, another image altogether and one that has the ultimate effect of flattening the perspective, of compressing the scene spatially to suggest a more crowded and compressed built environment.

This sense of crowding is repeated throughout the show in the many telephoto-compressed long shots of the main thoroughfare through the camp. Unlike the documentary photographs of historical sites that potentially offer sightlines to an endlessly receding horizon, Hollywood back-lot productions of urban environments

15. Bullock with his stepson's casket. "The Whores Can Come" (*Deadwood* 2.11).

must deal with the problem of limited space by representing a city's endlessly straight thoroughfares with slight turns or kinks in the road, so that, from the perspective of the camera, a block of apartments or a large house often closes off the frame (consider the various prospects down the main streets in *Back to the Future* [1985]—here they almost all end in a building rather than in a straight road heading out of town, or the majority of exterior shots in *Seinfeld*, for that matter). Similarly, *Deadwood* also must rely on limited production space for construction—the hulking masses of the square in which Al and Jack find themselves are as much a consequence of production necessity as they are tied to the theme of the show. But tied to the theme they nevertheless are. *Deadwood* emphasizes these very spaces, as well as dozens of images that place characters in a physical squeeze between deep background and an extreme foreground. One example of this sort of image is the sight of Bullock walking toward his house with a casket for his son on his shoulders (2.11); another is a shot of Alma Garret right after she has offered to sell part of her claim to Hearst (3.3). In both cases the characters are compressed visually against massive and crowded spaces that allow for very little of the Western's traditional open spaces to intrude.

David Milch has acknowledged Dashiell Hammett's *Red Harvest* as an influence on *Deadwood*. As William Marling explains, Hammett's novel is less about the Montana mining camp it purports to depict ("Poisonville") than it is a thinly veiled depiction of the much more urbanized spaces of San Francisco (108). In similar fashion, although *Deadwood* may be set in a distant frontier mining camp, its concern is ultimately with urban space. And it is in this respect that *Deadwood* may most confidently be referred to as hard-boiled or noir. The narrator and the walk are, to be sure, two very different elements of film noir. The first is chiefly a matter of form, which the series skillfully hints at but does not really exploit; the latter is more a matter of content, though it offers a set of representations that arise from the ideological framework of the show, namely, the concern with the alienating and potentially overwhelming elements of the built environment. Taken together, though, they offer the possibility of judging the extent to which *Deadwood*, in Naremore's terms, invokes noir as a self-legitimating set of practices. Thus, *Deadwood* is ultimately of a piece with films like *The Big Lebowski* (1998) and *Down in the Valley* (2005). The former is adapted from a Raymond Chandler novel and recovers the "Western" aspect of the noir genre by introducing a cowboy voice-over narrator/chorus figure; the latter follows its characters through the contemporary suburban spaces of the San Fernando Valley and passes through a movie set where the church-building celebration from *My Darling Clementine* is being restaged before devolving into a shootout in an empty tract-home garage. In both of these films the characters, on a thematic level, deal with the difficulties encountered while trying to embrace a Western ethos of individual heroism in the context of an alienating urban or built environment. The signature moment in *Deadwood* of this mode comes in Al's walk with Langrishe, when he simply doesn't know whom a particular house belongs to; the city is beginning to grow beyond his knowledge. In thus positioning itself most fundamentally as a tale about a western city, in addressing fundamental questions about the nature of community and the potential for alienation within the context of a built environment, *Deadwood* aligns itself as much with the noir tradition as it does with that of the Western. More to the point and perhaps a bit paradoxically, it thus renders itself more immediately relevant to today's increasingly urbanized West than it does to the mythic West of the familiar genre tale.

Notes

1. According to the index entries in Ramon F. Adams's *Six-Guns and Saddle Leather*, Wyatt Earp ranks second behind only Billy the Kid in the number of references to the person found in western (and Western) texts. See Barra, *Inventing*, for an exploration of Earp's popular image; on the representation of Pinkerton detectives in popular culture, see Marcus Klein 133–94; Denning 118–48; Panek 5, 132–35.
2. Among the critics who have articulated positions similar to Fiedler's are Henry Nash Smith and John Cawelti. For a more detailed rundown of this critical history, see Witschi 382.
3. On *High Sierra* as a "crucial transitional work" between genres, see Irwin 209–19; see Simmon 197–208 for an analysis of John Ford's 1946 version of the OK Corral story that demonstrates how, generically speaking, "the classic Western invents itself through the encounter with film noir" (207). Of course, to move from hard-boiled fiction to film noir is not a move one makes without some qualification. See esp. Irwin, Marling 237–69, and Naremore 48–63 for useful discussions of the various ideological, narrative, and historical frameworks shared by detective fiction and noir cinema. On Eastwood's film, see Naremore, who concludes his study by noting that the impressive staying power of noir as a discourse may in part be seen in the fact that "the last important western was Clint Eastwood's distinctly noirlike *Unforgiven*" (277). For an aesthetics-based reading of noir elements in classic Westerns, see Ursini.
4. A good place to begin is with the essays collected in David Lavery's *Reading Deadwood*; of particular note is the contribution by Amanda Ann Klein.
5. On objections to the show's language, see Millichap 186–87; Benz 239–40; Oldenburg.
6. On the American West as a population space that is much more fundamentally urban than the East or the Midwest, see Riebsame et al. 55; Abbott. On the literary exemplars of this "new" western landscape, see Comer.
7. Studlar 125. In 1965 the mystery writer Erle Stanley Gardner, perhaps hoping to set the record straight about the kinds of liberties with vocab-

ulary generally taken by his colleagues, first recounted the anecdote about Hammett's mischievous wordplay in an essay for the *Atlantic* titled "Getting Away with Murder."

8. See also Oldenburg, which presents opinions on the matter from former Western TV actors such as Dennis Weaver and *Bonanza*'s David Canary. The latter opines, "I have a prejudice against the *Deadwood* thing because, to make it that real, and bring in the swearing, I think that's really messing with the genre."

9. Cassuto 41–46; Irwin 189–92. See Millichap on David Milch's indebtedness to Warren. See Cassuto 45 for a brief mention of Hemingway's self-aware joke about hard-boiled writing.

10. See McCuskey, elsewhere in this volume.

7 "Right or Wrong, You Side with Your Feelings"

Jennilyn Merten

"Violence," says David Milch, "like any other human activity has the capability to evolve in all kinds of complicated ways, to have all kinds of accidental outcomes associated with it, including kindness and generosity" (Deadwood 153). Describing Deadwood as "a Western about being a Western," Jennilyn Merten argues that the series self-consciously and often playfully explores — and extends — themes that have always been significant in Westerns though sometimes overlooked by critics and popular conceptions of the genre. In her view Westerns have always already been about feelings, language (not silence), and community. "The series does not so much revise and critique as reveal, often in the genre's most stereotypical and weakest moments, its deeply rooted feeling" and "the feeling that accompanies its restraint." Her exploration of the connections between violence and emotions, sometimes even tenderness, addresses the disruptive feeling of some viewers: how have I come to care so deeply about characters who so often behave so reprehensively? Working with the insights of Lee Clark Mitchell, she argues that violence reveals the emergence of the emotional self and of intimacy with others. The paradoxical intimacy of the Deadwood community, rendered in the framing of the cinematography as well as in speech, is at the heart of the series. Ultimately the series presents a provocatively new rendition of language and community that, while adding something new to the genre, simultaneously borrows from it.

Toward the end of *Deadwood's* first season, the town's preacher is convinced that his flesh is rotting. He lurches into the Gem Saloon like a wayward drunk, stopping to sing with the whores at the Gem's new piano, attracting the attention of the camp patriarch, Al Swearengen. The addled preacher is bad for business, and Swearengen swiftly evicts him, though he nurtures a quiet sympathy for the man. Like many of his sympathies, Swearengen's concern for the

16. Al taking care of the preacher. "Sold under Sin" (*Deadwood* 1.12).

preacher evokes a loss in his own ledger, in this case, a disquieting reminder of his dead brother. And when the preacher finally loses all sanity and bodily control, due, Swearengen learns, to a brain lesion, the saloon keeper offers to care for him—though not in the way we might expect or, perhaps, precisely in the way the series has taught us to expect. The scene that follows is signature *Deadwood*. Swearengen puts a pillow over the preacher's face and directs the timid Johnny through the labor of suffocating a man: "Make a proper seal. Stop up the breath. Apply pressure even and firm like packing a snowball" (1.12). Al's demonstration for Johnny is at once a bold prescription for murder and a tender lesson in alleviating suffering. As he cradles the preacher's body in his arms and covers his mouth, Al offers him a sure way out: "You can go now, brother" (1.12). Before leaving, Swearengen strokes the dead man's face, clearly letting go of another man and another memory as well.

This scene is a startling example of the marriage between violence and intimacy that makes *Deadwood* a provocative example of the contemporary Western. Indeed, the series is a blunt, daring, and achingly curious exploration of the genre's preoccupation with violence from an endless and overlapping set of lenses: abuse, brutality, venality, revenge, bigotry, mud, shit, disease, plague and injury, modernity and annihilation, human traffic and human desire, inarticulate profanity and rapid-fire eloquence, self-recrimination, self-loathing, and sheer loneliness. What results is noteworthy for the genre—and for the genre's long-standing role in our cultural imagination. HBO's primetime show is not a revisionist history, a morality play, or a critique of the genre that ends, as a few notable and popular contemporary Westerns arguably have, by unconsciously recapitulating the very nostalgia and hero worship of the old West's imagined halcyon days, filled not with gentle weather but with wall-to-wall shoot-outs. Both critics and viewers of Clint Eastwood's *Unforgiven* (1992), for example, continue to argue about whether the film is a pioneering erasure of the genre's romantic veneer or, when the sun has set, just another pretty veil over an already artificial sunset. *Deadwood* avoids both extremes, in simple terms, through unexpectedly good storytelling. It is neither in love with the Western nor out to teach it a lesson. It is a Western about being a Western.

Such narrative self-examination can be a bore or devolve into self-congratulatory caricature. Yet this cable television show is remarkably and successfully earnest, in large part to a cast of characters whose sophistication has become a welcome staple of contemporary television shows like *The Sopranos, The Wire, Mad Men,* and others. *Deadwood* goes straight to the heart of our preoccupation with the Western and reveals a complex structure of feeling inseparable from the genre's familiar prerogatives of violence. The notable emphasis on community further stresses the interconnectivity between intimacy and violence. Rather than sever intimacy, the varied forms of violence regularly become catalysts or disguises for kindness, empathy, and a developing solidarity between *Deadwood*'s independent and opinionated personalities.

This does not mean that *Deadwood*'s narrative structure directly redeems violence. When its characters do glimpse redemption, they do so by negotiating the costs, failures, and desires of violence that draw them into intimacy with others. However, *Deadwood* does not apologize for or excuse its characters for the sheer quantity of this violence or its putative casualness. *Deadwood* is less interested in the genre's explicit or implicit justifications of violence that have provided, through the Western's iconic narrative architecture—gun battles, Indian wars, and vigilante justice—a form of moral expediency for national allegories and agendas.[1] Swearengen offers his own take on morality: "I got a healthy operation, and I didn't build it brooding on the right and wrong of things" (1.4). "Violence poses less a social or moral dilemma than an emotional one," as Lee Clark Mitchell observes in his comprehensive reading of Westerns (*Westerns* 169). Indeed, *Deadwood* is more interested in the genre's emotional life of violence and the desire that prompts violence in the service of justice, revenge, ambition, madness—and desire. "Right or wrong," Dan tells Johnny, "you side with your feelings" (3.12).

Not surprisingly, the series employs great creativity and depth exploring the feelings of its motley crew and the tender and tortured effort they make to articulate them. In this way *Deadwood* departs from a class of Westerns, not limited to but including many B Westerns and the ironically vacant spaghetti Westerns of Sergio Leone, that has stereotyped the genre as emotionally impenetrable and left it open to attacks by critics like Jane Tompkins, who has argued that Westerns encourage its heroes to a "suppression of the inner life" (66).[2] For Tompkins, in particular, the Western becomes an object lesson in avoiding the display of emotion while erasing those "feminine" attributes that tempt display: "For to show that your heart is not hard, to cry when you feel pain, your own or someone else's, is . . . soft, womanish, emotional, the very qualities the Western hero must get rid of to be a man" (121).

However, as others have asserted, and as *Deadwood* reveals, the Western displays significantly more feeling than it appears to, by consistently placing at the root of its lawlessness and entrepreneurial justice, its pinched-lipped stoicism and handsome style. Indeed, it is the presence of violence in the Western that often signals feeling. Similarly, the struggle for language, or even its suppression, is not necessarily a suppression of feeling; the very restraint native to the Western reveals, not an eventual elimination of feeling as Tompkins suggests, but a negotiation of its delivery. Mitchell observes:

"The point of violence directed at a physical body is to arouse a tension that allows an emotional self to exhibit its capacity for restraint" (*Westerns* 183). Besides, the Western's iconic silences are just as often broken by cocksure and talkative heroes from the Virginian to Butch Cassidy. Mitchell continues, "We come to realize how fully silence is a sovereign condition not simply and passively assumed but arduously achieved—or likewise, how restraint is a chosen mode of behavior rather than simply an automatic response, a mere psychological tic or symptom of warped, antisocial tendencies" (186). *Deadwood*'s particular interest in this emotional self and its sophisticated exploration of the genre's relationship to feeling thus allows it to approach the genre's iconic characters, themes, and criticisms with self-consciousness and playfulness. In a manner consistent with recent trends in characterization found in literature about the West, *Deadwood*'s reliance on unforgettable characters living in close proximity to one another, along with revelatory examinations of emotion and its often botched expression, provides a timely reminder of the Western's flexibility and depth.

David Milch has indeed created an extraordinary ensemble cast, and the series' violence acquires its emotional life through these protean characters. Remarkably, *Deadwood*'s depth of character extends to its female cast. In *Deadwood* women get emotional lives, not simply emotional disavowals of violence. With the strategic development of all its characters, *Deadwood* displays scenes of sexual intimacy (with or without men) not often privileged in the Western.[3] However, Milch does not entirely depart from the genre's familiar faces of B Western fame: the feisty whore, the reluctant marshal, the legendary gunman, the gun-slinging cronies, the racial other, and the naive easterner, or in other words, the good, the bad, and the ugly. In *Deadwood* the outlines of these stock characters fade into the contradictions illustrative of good storytelling. Where the sketch remains, it serves to bolster the genre by combining familiarity with unexpected complexity.

Certainly, the series' broader exploration of intimacy would not be possible without this adept rendering of *Deadwood*'s players. Al Swearengen might have easily remained nothing but the caricature of a Wild West villain whose vacuous turpitude invites audiences to despise him unthinkingly—or simply a more nuanced "good badman."[4] He is thankfully neither. Swearengen is a striking, contradictory man whose unpredictable gestures of kindness frequently accompany his calculated violence. He displays ruthlessness and vulnerability, elicits sympathy and disgust, and reminds viewers how intellectually satisfying the discomfort of moral ambivalence can be. Swearengen's rich personality becomes *Deadwood*'s paradigmatic source for exploring the coupling between violence and intimacy, as well as exemplifying one of the series' underlying claims: feeling will always trump morality and law if these abstractions are understood only as codes of action meant to supersede emotion.

Swearengen is a richly developed Western character, based in part on a historical figure, as are Bullock and others, such as the more legendary Wild Bill and Calamity Jane. Many historical details about Wild Bill are self-consciously accurate: the red sash and the ivory-handled guns, his final letter, and his final day, for instance. Yet the emphasis is not on historical accuracy, except perhaps to suggest that while Hickok will be presented in his own clothes, he will not be fashioned into another legend. And in this gesture we begin to see the series' playfulness with the genre's narrative structure. When Wild Bill Hickok arrives laden with the well-turned pages of legend, it is the production of legends, as it is in Ford's landmark film *The Man Who Shot Liberty Valance* (1962), not the legend itself that is the center of the story.[5] As the reenactment of Hickok's last days unfolds, Milch makes a clear effort to flesh out a man from the myth, not for historical accuracy but for emotional accuracy.

In a wry and sympathetic commentary on celebrity, a couple of drunks harass Hickok as he tries to keep a low profile helping Bullock and Star frame their hardware store. Fighting the lucrative potential of his own billing to the local bars, Hickok implores Utter: "Don't shop me to those places, Charlie" (1.4). *Deadwood* presents a man exhausted by his mythic immortality and mortal foibles, who pleads again with Charlie: "Can't you let me go to Hell the way I want to?" (1.4). Heroism (or notoriety) is only one portion of Hickok's heavy burdens. Milch's disaffected Hickok is quite human, his self-consciousness about his status mirroring Milch's self-consciousness about staging one more rendition of the legendary man's last days, which he ironically parlays into an actual offer of reenactment for Charlie Utter by a self-important witness. The cardplayer demonstrates for Charlie:

> Of a sudden, McCall produced a revolver, and shouting "Take that, damn you!" he fired. Muzzle couldn't've been three inches from Wild Bill's head, and I'm told that Hickok fell dead immediately, but I won't testify to it, because the bullet, after it passed through Wild Bill's brain, struck me in my right wrist, and I lost several seconds to pain before regaining my senses. (1.7)

Hickok's murder and celebrity funeral proceedings reveal some of the series' early and tentative moments of intimacy. For his companions Charlie and Jane, that intimacy is expressed, as it is in other moments with other characters, in the middle of verbal assaults. When Jane returns to camp after the murder, her drunken belligerence is in full force. Charlie cares for her, and we see as she is yelling the next morning that he has covered her tenderly with Bill's buffalo coat.

JANE: Oh, Christ, are we arrested?
CHARLIE: I explained all this to you, Jane, that I'm the fucking deputy, and I fixed the overflow cell in case you come back.
JANE: Shut up then.
CHARLIE: And you replied I was boring the shit out of you 'cause Doc already told you all about it.
JANE: Well, evidently I don't remember fuck-all.
CHARLIE: No, 'cause after every other fucking thing we went through last night, you got to make us stop at that new joint across from Nuttall's.
JANE: Would you kindly shut your fucking mouth? Hey, what the fuck's Bill's coat doing here?
CHARLIE: Well, he wouldn't have seen it useless or a souvenir. I figured I'd give it work keeping the bed warm.
JANE: Uh, where is it headed now I'm the occupant?

CHARLIE: It ain't going anywheres.
JANE: Thank you, Charlie. (2.3)

As in many conversations in *Deadwood*, the verbal violence shifts flexibly—and as quickly as a drawn gun or knife—from abuse to kindness. Later, as Charlie stands at Bill's grave, he continues to express his concern for Jane and his loyalty to both Bill and her: "As far as Jane, as drunk as you've seen her, you've never seen her this worse. Between us, maybe havin' lost wantin' to keep on. So I ... I don't know what the fuck to do! But you know I'll ... I'll keep tryin'" (2.8).

Deadwood's characters reach out tentatively toward one another in spite of or through the psychological and physical violence they inflict on one another. Yet their emotional development as characters evolves from the emphasis the series places on community and collective survival, which Milch examines using the Wild West's mythically atavistic conditions. Violence is the process by which the intimacy and proximity of community are worked out; Milch's directorial approach to his cast parallels his construction of his characters' paradigms:

> What I am trying to suggest to the actors is that the modern situation is predicated upon the illusion of the self's isolation—that business of I'm alone, you're alone, we can bullshit each other when we're fucking or whatever else, but the truth is that we're alone. Right? Well, I believe that that is fundamentally an illusion. (qtd. in Singer 192).

Deadwood's prolific violence can be read in the service of negotiating a fragile albeit reluctant deconstruction of this illusion. As Swearengen remarks to Trixie, "Trust. Hell of a way to operate, huh?" (1.3). Over the series' three seasons, the numerous acts of violence point increasingly away from individual opportunism and toward shared vulnerability. The very premise of the Wild West town, including Deadwood, relies on the conceit of self-determination in the absence of government, but the replacement of the Western's open range with the bustling, close quarters of *Deadwood*'s mining town stresses the interdependence of others in the context of painfully relative impunity. In *Deadwood* the community does not receive the shallow or nonexistent depiction it often gets in Westerns. The townspeople's vulnerability to violence or their disavowal of it typically exists only as an inciting incident for the hero's story, as Will Kane's final gunfight exemplifies in the classic *High Noon* (1952). Matthew R. Turner suggests one need simply look at a genre's parodies to find its most typified conventions, including the reductive characterization of the Western community. In the Western parody *Rustlers' Rhapsody* (1985), the film's singing cowboy Rex "states that each Western town is identical, and to prove his point he tells the town drunk that they have 'a very pretty, but somehow asexual schoolmarm'" (Turner 50).

Deadwood dramatically expands the Western's portrayal of its townspeople through the regular inclusion of other forms of (non-homicidal) violence. Smallpox, pregnancy, wounds, accidents, and Al's kidney stone all extend the characterization of violence and draw attention to the body's vulnerability and the need for community. More than two episodes are devoted to the drama of Al's illness and convalescence, rendered evocatively in "Requiem for a Gleet" (2.4). As Swearengen reminds Doc Cochran later, "No one gets out alive" (3.7). Al's illness brings into sharp relief Johnny's, Dan's, and Trixie's affections for Al and their reliance on him for strength. Likewise Al's incapacitated state emphasizes his own dependence on their and Doc Cochran's ministrations. But it is the Doc who thanks Al for not dying under his hands: "Thank you for saving me" (2.4). Their shared vulnerability and intimacy are poignantly portrayed: the four of them help Al pass his stones in a scene deliberately reminiscent of birthing. The shot ends from above, and from this vantage point we can see the exhausted bodies slump together on Al's bed in a naked display of affection and unity. The Western hero's moment of convalescence and recovery, usually but not always aided by a woman, is replaced here by a communal intimacy.

Slowly the characters caught in the sump of *Deadwood*'s thoroughfare begin to resemble a nascent community whose shared history of abuse creates tentative networks of empathy. Indeed, *Deadwood* is a strange family of "abused abusers." Almost everyone has been sold, violated, or abandoned, or all three, regardless of their sex, their skin color, or the color of their money. In season 1 when the widow Garret's father attempts to take her new wealth, he does so as a "father's liberty" that he has presumably taken before. The conflation of her body with her material wealth is certainly no accident when her father explains coyly, "I'm not victimizing my daughter but merely asking for a small portion of the ample proceeds from her veins" (1.12). Swearengen himself was abandoned and used, as his narrative hints, in much the same way as his whores were, and he finds both the cynicism to coldly recapitulate the cycle and brief but critical moments of empathy. Al's relationship to his prostitutes is certainly one of dominance. Yet when Dolly responds to Al's story of his childhood abuse with "they hit us too," another of Al's reveries (and his blow job) is interrupted. He chooses this time to shift from himself toward another, bringing his eyes to face Dolly: "They hit you too, huh?" (3.4). The unacknowledged similarity in their lives is mirrored in Al's echo.

Much of Swearengen and others' childhood abuse is familial, and it is no surprise that most of *Deadwood*'s characters no longer have family; they are in Deadwood precisely because they've been abandoned or lost loved ones, some, like Bullock and the Doc, in the national family drama of the Civil War. *Deadwood*'s residents have also deliberately abandoned the civilization and jurisprudence of the United States and its parental influence. An exasperated Swearengen queries Wu, "When did you start thinking every wrong had a remedy, Wu? Did you come to camp for justice or to make your fuckin' way?" (1.12). But by the end of the second season, it is Hearst and the U.S. government—as fathers of another sort—that try to extract every vein of gold from *Deadwood* and ultimately transform a group of self-serving individuals into a fragile family of their own.

Through the depiction of this transformation, Milch is able to explore how seemingly atomized individuals broker, through a negotiation of the uses of violence, the intimacy that proves his point:

that they were never alone in the first place. For the Western this is an important exercise. The preservation of the community is at once a foil for the hero's inward struggle to act (and be a hero) and the reason the successful hero often feels incapable of remaining there. Many a ride into the sunset—or through John Ford's iconic doorway in *The Searchers* (1956)—involved a man at odds with his own violence, but in *Deadwood* nobody leaves. The community and its developing intimacy are themselves a negotiation of violence, a point shared by most Westerns but writ large in *Deadwood*.

Initially the series' negotiation of community suggests that like family, one's enemy is of a more intimate variety. *Deadwood*'s emphasis on the internal drama of violence in community diverts the Western's narrative of violence away from an outward or national contest of domination often emblematized by the subjugation of American Indians. Although Deadwood lies in the middle of the conflict between the Lakota Sioux and the federal government, and the community's existence is made possible by this conflict, the government's agents are portrayed as a source of more conflict and violence than the Sioux. Here too the drama remains a familial one: Deadwood must fight off the county commissioners and the representatives of the Hearst monopoly, all of whom are eager to take advantage of its wealth. In an odd way *Deadwood*'s inhabitants seem a little like the Sioux, whom the government patronizes like a bastard relative and whose putative savagery requires either formal domination or extermination. It is not surprising, then, that Swearengen talks to the severed head of the Lakota Sioux Indian, whose bounty he has paid, finding himself in a position of similar, if not equal vulnerability, with a bounty given to the neighboring territory to annex and tame Deadwood. Deadwood's counterattacks on Hearst and the murder of the county commissioners become the self-defense of a beleaguered child.

As Dan explains to Johnny:

> Al's gonna be calling numbers to the fold now that he can't trust like us. Some he don't even like. We're joining America. And it's full of lying, thieving cocksuckers that you can't trust at all—gov-

ernors, commissioners, and whatnot. By God, that's just the new way of things. And you just gonna have to get used to it, Johnny. (2.13)

Yet by working together, Swearengen, Bullock, Wu, Merrick, and others outwit the abusive parent when they can. Sometimes they use violence, and at other times they take strategic nonviolent approaches through subterfuge or even letter writing, as Bullock ingeniously does when Hearst has had another Cornish miner murdered.

The trajectory of *Deadwood*'s violence often depends, then, on the internal emotional narrative of revenge and self-preservation (both as an individual and as a community). In broad terms the violence that the series explores is sanctioned by law but also transcends the emotional limitations of law. In other words the goal is not simply to be "lawless" but to find "laws" that reflect the emotional drive to satisfy an individual definition of justice or survival. Institutional punishment fails, as Robert Solomon suggests, "if punishment no longer satisfies vengeance, if it ignores not only the rights but the emotional needs of the victims of crime" (308). When law is absent or corrupt, as it is in *Deadwood* and many Westerns, violence seeks emotional redress where the law is insufficient to placate feeling, as in the case of Hickok's murder. It could be put this way: the state administers justice, and the people seek revenge. But in *Deadwood*, as in many Westerns, revenge *feels* more like justice. For example, it is the moment of murderous revenge in Sam Peckinpah's *Pat Garrett and Billy the Kid* (1973) that, Hubert Cohen argues, finally reveals the enigmatic Billy's capacity for feeling: "After Billy has killed the perpetrators and listened to Paco's dying words, we discover a profound sense of justice and an intense anger hidden behind's Billy's easygoing expression" (71). This is perhaps because, as Solomon argues, "justice is not, first of all, a set of principles or policies; it is, first of all, a set of personal feelings, a way of participating in the world" (293). Though Solomon does not deny the troubling consequences possible in vengeance, he goes on to suggest that our larger concept of justice develops from our feeling of personal injustice, and subsequently "that our sense of justice cannot ignore and to some extent even develops out of these rather vile emotions" (293–94).

In *Deadwood*'s third season, when Hearst orders the murder of Ellsworth, he sets off a series of retaliatory acts by Trixie and finally Swearengen that attempt to satisfy revenge and, in so doing, exact some form of justice. Both Trixie's attempted murder of Hearst and Swearengen's actual murder of the prostitute Jenny (whom he delivers to Hearst as Trixie) are guided by a desire to satisfy feeling. Al explains the dilemma to the dead chief's head:

> This fucking place is gonna be a fucking misery. Every fucking one of them, every fucking time I walk by, "Ooh, how could you? How could you?" With their big fucking cow eyes. The entire fucking gaggle of 'em is gonna have to bleed and quit before we can even hope for peace. What's the fucking alternative? I ain't fuckin' killing her that sat nights with me sick and taking slaps to her mug that were some less than fucking fair. (3.12)

Jenny pays for Al's feelings for Trixie. When Johnny balks at her killing and Dan's explanation that Al had no choice, Dan echoes Al: "Feeling how he feels about Trixie, is what I'm saying. Come on, Johnny, you side with your feelings. Right or wrong, you side with your feelings. Now can you come to yourself in time to be of some fucking use?" (3.12). Interestingly, it is only during Al's reverie on his feelings that we hear him take an interest in the word *fair* and, consequently, an interest in offering Trixie, if not Jenny, a form of personal justice.[6]

In this instance, as in most, *Deadwood* refuses to offer up cold morality and settles on the need for satisfaction instead. The community's major players share this need and are willing to back it by protecting Trixie through Al's subterfuge. At this point the audience is most likely to squirm at Jenny's murder but nevertheless finds its feelings aligned with the camp's. And this is where *Deadwood* succeeds at exposing the heart of the Western: how to satisfy justice (feeling) when the law is nonexistent, corrupt, or unequal to the crime.

This satisfaction is not a wholly irrational project but relies on the *reason of feeling* and the removal of contradiction implicit in that phrase. In "The Romance of Competence," Wendy Chapman Peek suggests this paradox is a particularly Aristotelian one. Arguing that competence is more important for the Western hero than the display of masculinity, she suggests that the hero can use strategies inscribed as both masculine and feminine and still remain a man if he succeeds in his goal. (This strategy is readily apparent in the example of letter writing above.) This emotional flexibility "accords with Aristotle's 'intermediate man,' the person who must decide for himself what the appropriate action is in any given situation" (218). Aristotle writes:

> It is hard work to be excellent, since in each case it is hard work to find what is intermediate; e.g., not everyone, but only one who knows, finds the midpoint in any circle. So also getting angry, or giving and spending money, is easy and anyone can do it; but doing it to the right person, in the right amount, at the right time, for the right end, and in the right way is no longer easy, nor can everyone do it. Hence [doing these things] well is rare, praiseworthy and fine. (qtd. in Peek 219)

Peek points out, for example, that anger for Aristotle is not a vice but part of his "'virtues concerned with social life.'" "He recognizes that anger is in some situations an appropriate response to the circumstances. For example, the proper response to something outrageous is outrage. The intermediate position of 'mildness' does not mean 'without anger'; rather, it means neither prone to nor incapable of anger" (219–20). Managing anger and violence successfully demands emotional flexibility, something Swearengen realizes when it becomes clear Hearst cannot be beaten with more violence. However, he must convince his own men, as well as Bullock, not to simply strike back.

Bullock's hot temper and well-tuned sense of justice create for him a constant struggle between obeying his emotional impulses and trusting the law to mediate what might otherwise be punished by quick, sure violence. Taking the law into his own hands allows him to satisfy his feelings on his own terms. When Jack McCall kills

Wild Bill and escapes after a bogus trial, Bullock seeks Old Testament retribution where the law has failed. And though his own killing of a Sioux prevents him from murdering McCall, Bullock makes sure to find a judge and jury who will hang him. But to refer to Solomon once more, revenge is not simply a form of retribution but "a matter of emotion, often delayed, protracted or frustrated emotion, and like punishment, it is always for some offense, not just hurting for its own sake (even if, in some other sense, it is deserved)" (305). Yet these emotions can be difficult to mediate on one's own. Bullock is unable to trust his own emotions and finds it difficult to mete out appropriate justice; sometimes, as in the case of Alma Garret's lecherous father, he abdicates his desire for punishment to others (but only after he has viciously beaten him). But when he asks the general to look after her father, the general finds Bullock's inner struggle appropriate sentiment for Deadwood: "I would add, in a camp where the marshal can be bought for bacon grease, a man, a former marshal, who understands the danger of his own temperament, he might consider serving his fellows." He concludes, "We all have bloody thoughts" (1.12). Not surprisingly, Swearengen and others recognize that Bullock is a good candidate for sheriff precisely because he has the right *feeling*; they see his honest sense of justice *and* his emotional temper as the right qualities for the demands of the camp—though they often regret both.

But when justice is not at stake, Bullock finds that killing without any feeling or rather any motive but self-preservation has other emotional consequences. When he comes upon a sacred Indian burial ground, a Lakota Sioux warrior attacks him without warning. A distraught Bullock explains the fight to his partner, Sol, on his return to camp: "We fought like fucking hell. He's just trying to live same as me, do honor to his friend, trying to make sense out of things and we wind up that way and I wind up after, beating him 'til I couldn't recognize his face" (1.7). The fight is a fair fight; Bullock has no purpose beyond self-defense, and once the Lakota is dead, no purpose at all. The battle between the Sioux man and Bullock is not a recapitulation of the master narrative of racial subjugation or of Slotkin's epic account of "regeneration through violence" in which redemption or progress is achieved through killing—often the very thing one purports to love. Here again the narrative drama is personal, internal, and emotional rather than epic. Without anger or revenge to motivate his unnecessary brutality, Bullock is faced with nothing but an unnamable impulse within himself and death.

In a parallel incident, when Dan Dority is called out by Hearst's man, he meets the challenge aware that the fight is a contest meant to demonstrate the larger battle for dominance between Hearst and Deadwood's citizenry led by Swearengen. In a gruesome act of preservation, Dan pulls out the captain's eye and ultimately beats him to death. Like Bullock Dan struggles to overcome his pain at killing a man in a fair fight, where the captain's loyalty to Hearst parallels his own to Swearengen. Johnny, who knows Dan has killed numerous other times at Al's behest, cannot understand the shift obvious in Dan's sullen reaction. Swearengen explains to Johnny (and the audience): "A fair fight, something Dan and I have always struggled to avoid, is different. You see the light go out of their eyes . . . it's just you left, and death" (3.5). While it seems that a fair fight ought to absolve the combatants of such strong emotions, these two scenes suggest that it is precisely the fairness, its empathy and intimacy with another individual, that accentuate one's own vulnerability and proximity to death. By contrast murder has a way of producing a feeling of immortality, of reenacting one's own survival in the termination of another. In other words, for Bullock and Dan it is a fight (a killing), not a murder.

These scenes are classic Western moments in many ways, among them in the way they deliberately highlight another preoccupation of the Western, particularly the post–World War II Westerns: how it feels to kill a man. This sentiment is aptly delivered by William Munny (Eastwood) in *Unforgiven*: "It's a hell of a thing killing a man. You take all he's got and all he's ever going to have." As Dan cries in the Gem's back room, *Deadwood* reminds viewers (and critics) of the tenderness and violence inseparable in so many Western leading men: Marlon Brando as Rio in *One-Eyed Jacks* (1960), John Wayne as Tom Doniphon in *The Man Who Shot Liberty Valance*

(1962), and among many others, Chris Cooper as July Johnson in the television version of Larry McMurtry's *Lonesome Dove* (1988), whose own scene of crying provokes the response, "Men have tears in them same as you."[7]

Few other genres have been as occupied with the ethics and sentiments of violence as the Western, although a fuller study of the explosion of graphic novels and comics turned big-budget celluloid—their digital landscapes broad and vivid as any Western—would be critical work for the genre. Mitchell argues, "Scenes of violence are highlighted in other genres fully as much as in Westerns, but not primarily to provide the hero with conditions for self-definition" (*Westerns* 169). Discussing historian Robert Warshow's work, Mitchell notes that he initially conceives of violence as a legitimate guide for a moral justification of force but takes a contradictory turn when concluding: "It is not violence at all which is the 'point' of the Western movie, but a certain image of a man, a style, which expresses itself most clearly in violence" (169).[8] Mitchell explains, "Violence in the Western, in other words, is less a means than an end in itself—less a matter of violating another than of constituting one's physical self as a male" (169). Though Mitchell's central point here concerns the display of masculinity, it argues for investigating the emotional desire behind that self-definition.

Deadwood's exploration of violence moves far beyond the visceral display or style Mitchell discusses by marshaling an arresting use of language. However, *Deadwood*'s language does not merely put into words what has sometimes been kept silent or displayed through masculine posturing and dress. In that sense *Deadwood*'s profusion of language does not substitute for violence but becomes another form of violence, as readily as it reflects moments of intimacy. And its own silences and moments of reserve provide a running commentary on the Western's relationship to language that has been misread and hijacked for an enormous commercial campaign based on the premise of masculine silence.

Because violence is seemingly portrayed as the antithesis of speech, it is easy to conclude that violence lacks any language or feeling. Of course *Deadwood*, or most Westerns for that matter, can hardly be accused of being "anti-language," as Jane Tompkins asserts in a sweeping generalization of the genre. "The Western's attack on language is wholesale and unrelenting, as if language were somehow tainted in its very being," she writes (52). Although violence will for some critics of the Western simply remain a poor substitute for language, *Deadwood* suggests an aesthetic or extension of language full of its own signs, gestures, and style that exceeds that of most Westerns but nevertheless recapitulates the genre's unique linguistic concerns.

Certainly the most notorious and remarkable aspect of *Deadwood*'s storytelling is its language; when *Deadwood* speaks, the language is as gorgeous as it is obscene. The series' pervasive and deliberate use of profanity unites the Western's emphasis on gesture with speech. Profanity invokes speech even as it stresses gesture, and its endless possibility for meaning increases both its linguistic power and its potential ineffectualness. The most often used expletive, "cocksucker," actually evacuates its literal meaning (if not its negativity) by the plurality of its usage: a cocksucker is a government whore but not a woman, a thief, a liar, a shit-heel, a hypocrite, a failure—the word's meaning is cut from the context and intensity of delivery. Profanity gains meaning through its specific performance and evokes the visceral component key to its delivery. As a narrative or aesthetic strategy, profanity emphasizes the series' constant proximity of intimacy to violence.

Notably *Deadwood* does offer acts of unabashed kindness relatively free of profanity: Charlie comforts Joanie as she sells the Chez Ami and struggles to find her place in the world. Mrs. Bullock carefully suggests to Jane that she might share some of her scouting experiences with the school children, whose lessons Jane has been watching with great interest. The Nigger General cares for Steve, and Doc Cochran fashions a boot for Jewel, among other examples. However, just as often, *Deadwood*'s residents shout, scream, and profanely threaten their kindness in acts of violence that offset vulnerability. Words have not exactly failed to express emotion, but they present an apparent contradiction: violence expressed verbally (even when it involves more spit than speech) can reveal an inarticulate affection and trust. Utter helps Bullock recover from his emotional account of his brother's death by loudly chattering about bodily functions. "My bowels are in an upheaval. I'll walk off to pass wind. Don't ever say I'm not a fucking gentleman" (2.2). Likewise Swearengen acknowledges the Doc's illness and their mutual vulnerability by yelling at him: "I ain't learning a new doc's quirks" (3.7).

While Al suffers under Doc's ministrations to remove his kidney stones, Dan expresses some of his worry to Trixie. Her dismissive response reminds him to keep his feeling in check: "We'll bang the pipe and play the fiddle and we'll rend our fucking garments." But she is quickly subdued by her own grief and implores him in a softer tone to destroy the Gem Saloon if Al dies: "Say you'll burn it down for me Dan" (2.4). In the preceding episode Trixie coldly articulates her blunt reality to the affectionate Star—"A man can get me in his life for five bucks, two if he just wants a handshake"—but she cannot make him agree with her relationship to the term *whore* (2.3). In her frustration to control her own meaning, she tries to disavow speech altogether: "I wish I were a fucking tree" (2.3). Star's challenge to her self-definition forces Trixie to a point of vulnerability and selfhood she cannot hide in profanity. And as she continues to yell at Star all through season 3, we know that her anger arises in the service of avoiding the vulnerability she feels at being offered a more human status when Star and Swearengen refuse to let her remain a whore.

In these moments *Deadwood* acts self-consciously toward the genre, acknowledging its reticence while calling attention to the emotional subplots and gestures beneath its characters' initial shows of invulnerability. But this effort is not a simple unmasking or forced emotionalism; it is better storytelling. And when *Deadwood*'s characters find they cannot comfort one another directly, a moment of soliloquy meant for their own comfort substitutes instead. After Trixie's suicide attempt, Al channels his worries into a regard for her own:

> How hard is the legislature gonna squeeze our balls with regard to our title and properties, huh? I don't want to talk to these cocksuckers, but you have to, in life, you have to do a lot of things

you don't fuckin' want to do. Many times, that's what the fuck life is, one vile fucking task after another. But don't get aggravated. Then the enemy has you by the short hair. It'll be different after the annexation. That's all. There's nothin' to be afraid of. Everything changes. Don't be afraid. (2.2)

Milch is not afraid to be playful with the genre's quieter heroes as well, a type best embodied by Bullock. After telling Mrs. Bullock that he does not like the strength of her tea (something he has not mentioned before), she replies with tense courtesy, "I am not a mind reader, Seth" (3.2). And although the speeches for public office hold important consequences for the town, Milch makes quite a show of the men's discomfort with words when forced to write and deliver speeches. As Mrs. Bullock presides over these men turned schoolboys, she is clearly another of the genre's familiar faces—the eastern-bred schoolteacher come to the dirty thoroughfares (and language) of the West. And Bullock turns to her for help with words as the Virginian and many Western heroes have:

SETH: Will you look this over?
MARTHA: Certainly.
SETH: Words that doing the wrong jobs, piling on too heavy, or at odds over meaning—
MARTHA: I'll mark my suggestions.
SETH: Nothing showy is the main thing.
MARTHA: I understand. Shall I gather my school supplies?
SETH: I'm much obliged. (3.1)

Deadwood's evocative use of speech—and speeches—also reveals the hegemony and elasticity of language within the boundary of community. Those with the most elaborate speech have the upper hand and can more easily negotiate their place in the social strata; they are poised, like Swearengen, Tolliver, and others, to interpret change, to make plans, and they adapt to the necessities of annexation. And though they do not eschew physical violence themselves, they recognize its limitations when facing the abstract power of language. Swearengen says to Dan Dority, "You can't murder an order or the telegraph that sent it" (2.1). Yet Swearengen, Bullock, and others also guess that language might be used cunningly when they are physically outflanked; without guns they opt for words. When Dan asks how he will handle Hearst without violence, Al explains: "Don't I yearn for the days a draw across the throat made fucking resolution? Why, Dan, by composing my thoughts, tropes, and gambits for the talk between us that is yet to come. Will you excuse me?" (3.1).

Though restraint and even silence have their place in *Deadwood*, not surprisingly one's ability to communicate effectively determines one's power. For many of the show's prostitutes, a quick retort is the only advance against being perpetually silenced. For a woman like Alma Garret, whose education and financial success ensure her ability to articulate well, high speech mitigates some gender limitations. Her success also allows her to indulge in cruder speech when advantageous, as she does when confronting Farnum about the camp's peril by offering to buy his hotel: "Name your price. How do you males put it . . . Shit or get off the chamber pot?" (2.4).

What results is a blurred scale of high and low speech, where for those with the least ability to articulate or read others language becomes a form of assault. Indeed, the miners feel assaulted when the county commissioner and the Hearst interests spread rumors and deliberately obscure the meaning of their language regarding the legitimacy of the gold claims. The miners respond as though assaulted and return the violence, if not in kind, then in force. The commissioner tries to hide behind his words (and the cashier's cage), declaring his position of power through the abstract statement: "You cannot fuck the future; the future fucks you!" (2.5). But if the miners have lost their chance to alter the future regarding their claims, they haven't lost the ability to make the commissioner pay for his role in determining the future. The commissioner quickly finds the verbal architecture he is hiding behind no match for the immediacy of his physical peril.

Yet sometimes it is precisely when words fail that the failure reveals a moment of intimacy between two differently advantaged residents of the camp. Kindness does not resolve the injuries or

17. Jane and the General. "Complications (Formerly 'Difficulties')" (*Deadwood* 2.5).

upset inequities, but it collapses, for a moment, the division between individuals and allows them to read each other more fully. One of the more transgressive acts of intimacy occurs between Jane and the Nigger General when she invites him to share her whiskey in public. Though the camp relegates them both to the periphery, the Nigger General for his race and Jane for her disregard of gender codes, they enact their rebellion through physical camaraderie.

Hearst is perhaps the most averse to language of any of the camp's residents. Not surprisingly, he finds himself isolated from the affections of men; he is "the boy the earth talks to"—but men do not: "The only conversation I want to hear is the earth telling me where to dig into her" (3.3). He does not struggle to articulate himself or to maintain emotional reserve and has no care where others might struggle. Rather, he hires the excoriating and verbally manipulative Mr. Wolcott to be his voice. Consequently, though, he does not participate in the moments of intimacy and community shared by others that are born out of the difficulty of language. He continually delegates his voice to others, either literally through Wolcott or through the acts of violence committed by his men. Although he does have several talks with Swearengen and Tolliver, he still opts to send his message as a series of *X* marks on a scrap of paper and, finally, with an axe to Al's fingers and the body of the even less verbal captain. Deadwood's residents may embody a spectrum of articulateness, but their participation in the community, as opposed to Hearst's, results from the intimacy created through the struggle with language, as Swearengen's and Wu's literal struggle with language displays through their developing friendship and loyalty. And though Hearst weeps for his own losses, he does so with no one to cover, in kindness, for his display. Paradoxically the naked emotion is weaker than the emotional restraint negotiated by the camp's members' acting together.

Ultimately *Deadwood*'s varied scenes of intimacy temper the assault of its brutality. The series labors hard to suggest that while violence may aspire to power, it reveals more vulnerability than invincibility. (Even Al scrubs the blood off his floors.) The suggestion remains that it is emotional indifference or a continued belief in the mutual exclusion of rationality (as law) and emotion that is most troubling in justifications of violence, and, finally, that the genre's preoccupation with justice is in actuality a preoccupation with feeling. Arguably *Deadwood*'s self-conscious and evocative approach to engaging violence became a significant and pleasurable part of the Western (re)imagination, not long after Mitchell precipitately suggested that "there seems little room for either customary violence or landscape to be revised" (*Westerns* 259). Of course, Mitchell could not have known that the first decade of the twenty-first century would see nearly one hundred new Westerns, many critical and popular successes not shy on feeling, language, or violence. Certainly *Deadwood* occupies an important place in the postmodern life of the genre and does not so much revise and critique as reveal, often in the genre's most stereotypical and weakest moments, its deeply rooted feeling. And the feeling that accompanies the Western's restraint is simply the root of a story whose longing we ignore at our own peril. In the end *Deadwood's* elaboration of its emotional motives, consequences, and intersections with intimacy suggests a way of understanding violence that disrupts the seeming inviolateness of the Western's myths, and it reveals a more complex and therefore more helpful story of its desires.

Notes

1. See Richard Slotkin's chapter "Myth and Historical Memory," in *Fatal Environment*. Also Stanley Corkin, "Cowboys and Free Markets: Post–World War II Westerns and U.S. Hegemony," *Cinema Journal* 39.3:66–91.
2. In "'Men Have Tears in Them,'" Hubert Cohen looks closely at the display of emotion between A and B Westerns and the postwar transformation of the Western's presentation of feeling. He argues that despite a handful of deliberately emotionless and stylized films, most of which he attributes to Leone, both postwar and prewar Westerns offer numerous (and often overlooked) examples of emotional display and tenderness.
3. Certainly many Westerns before the 1970s and 1980s contain peripheral romances, and some the intimation of sex (or rape) like *High Plains Drifter* (1973), but even when broadcasting standards allowed increasing amounts of violence, a proportional amount of sex—and emotional intimacy—did not in general exist. Revisionist Westerns of the last two decades such as *Dances with Wolves* (1990), *The Ballad of Little Jo* (1993), and *Brokeback Mountain* (2005), among others, allow intimacy a greater portion of the narrative structure; indeed, the social restriction on intimacy due to race or gender becomes a central theme in the Western's preoccupation with justice.
4. For a basic overview of the "good badman," see Steckmesser and Prassel.
5. Like Stephen Crane, John Ford, and many others, Milch knows that when it comes to the Western, history and myth, fact and fiction are particularly hard to unravel. In his self-consciously ironic film *The Man Who Shot Liberty Valence* (1962), Ford "insists upon both the 'fact' *and* the 'legend,' viewing them as mutually sustaining interpretive gestures rather than as a misreading of the other" (Mitchell, *Westerns* 23–24).
6. When "fair" comes up again in relation to Dan's reaction to a "fair fight," the word is couched in an explanation of feeling.
7. All the Westerns cited here are mentioned in Cohen's comprehensive article, "'Men Have Tears in Them,'" which takes particular issue with Tompkins's reading of the Western's display of emotion, as well as other critics' assertions of the genre's dispassionate approach to language and feeling.
8. Warshow continues, "Watch a child with his toy guns and you will see: what most interests him is not (as we so much fear) the fantasy of hurting other, but to work out how a man might look when he shoots or is shot. A hero is one who looks like a hero" (qtd. in Mitchell, *Westerns* 169).

8 "A Brooding and Dangerous Soul"
Deadwood's Imperfect Music

David Fenimore

David Fenimore provocatively explores how another kind of "generic cross-fertilization" impacts the "feeling" and meaning of Deadwood: *music and especially the music that accompanies the closing credits. Unconventional choices yet thematically evocative, the songs originate in and evoke the U.S. folk traditions, from bluegrass to spirituals, establishing "a badge of authenticity that goes beyond historical accuracy." He notes how the songs were chosen: "Much like the way the scripts were created, the process of picking* Deadwood's *closers was at once more collaborative and less deliberate than the dictatorial Ford's." As the previous quotation suggests, Fenimore compares* Deadwood's *music to songs in well-known but more conventional Westerns, finding neither the familiar strains of Ford's use of spirituals nor, by implication, the multigenre composition that characterized the use of Tex Ritter's traditional ballad as a leitmotif throughout* High Noon. *Rather, he argues that the music articulates and reinforces some of the series' post-Western themes: "Country blues easily generalizes into an evocation of folk experience running at an acute angle to the master narrative of Caucasian culture and commerce, transmitting a complex of ideas and historical associations relative to poverty, disenfranchisement, displacement, exploitation, and violence. It is musical shorthand for marginality." While he demonstrates how songs, "considered individually, . . . in some way provide commentary on the surface narrative of the episode they conclude," his most deft analysis is of the "collaborative effect" of the closing songs, which "function as a simulated resolution for [the] episode," fulfilling viewers' expectations with a "concluding aesthetic gesture, an open-ended and suggestive metanarrative, an intensification and rhythmic resolution of the show's themes and ideologies."*

If you're expecting to find a key to all *Deadwood* musicology, a detailed episode-by-episode analysis of the thirty-six closing songs, stop reading right here.

That's actually a loose paraphrase of a similar disclaimer by Jane Wallace, who served as music supervisor for *Deadwood*'s second and third seasons (and unofficially, it seems, for the first as well). In "Dear Lost Reader," her account of the selection process for the songs that accompany each episode's ending credit roll, she describes working with David Milch's wife, her college buddy Rita Stern, to "throw the bear some meat" (i.e., suggest to a tired, grumpy, and preoccupied series creator and executive producer some songs that might work with each episode).[1] She disavows any "rhyme or reason" for the selections, writing that, in search of likely songs,

> [I would] go mood or theme or character surfing.... Rita fields what I send her and finds her own songs too. David makes the final picks, but I keep bombarding them with choices until I think we really have it.... So our tunes were squeezed in at the end just before each episode was "locked" to broadcast.... Every song got chosen for different reasons. The only common ground was that David, Rita and I all seemed to go for imperfect music.

Imperfect much of the music may be, in the sense of not slick, not popular, and not highly produced. The tropes of "westernness" are not invoked. This is not your grandparents' television theme music. No singing cowboys, no Nashville "country and western," and no European classical Ennio Morriconish or Coplandesque Music of Wide Open Spaces—in other words, no triumphal French horn calls, wood block clip-clops, or orchestrated folksongs, what Wallace calls "the usual slick stupid 'faux' spaghetti western stuff." *Deadwood*'s closers are drawn instead from the spirit or the fact of genuine U.S. roots music, dominated by acoustic stringed instruments, genuinely or deliberately artless solo singing, and raw emotional immediacy.

I suggest that there is, in fact, some reason and a lot of rhyme to the selection of these thirty-six songs. Besides functioning as a predictable element in *Deadwood*'s grand design, the songs serve as a badge of authenticity that goes beyond historical accuracy. They operate at a number of levels to signal the show's complex and sometimes problematic attitudes toward class, community, and especially race. These patterns are worth discussing if only because the power of music, especially song, can be vast yet subliminal and thus easy to overlook. In several cases, as I try to show, a particularly apt choice reaches beyond its particular episode to intensify the meanings at play in the entire series.

The selected tunes play a prominent role in the show's musical landscape in large part because there is so little music during the episodes themselves. In his audio commentary on episode 4 from the first season, Keith Carradine notes that music is "sparingly used" in the series. In his commentary Ian McShane calls attention to the simplicity of the show's postproduction process, the late stage at which sounds recorded by the camera or generated elsewhere are mixed into the final soundtrack, for which *Deadwood*'s editors received an Emmy in 2004 and were repeatedly nominated in succeeding years. The audio dimension of *Deadwood* is dominated by its densely profane dialogue, of course, but running counterpoint to the script is the *musique concrète* of Main Street: the crack of rope, creak of leather, slap of flesh, and slop of muddy boot; whiskey gurgling into clinking shot glasses; and the sodden thump of body on floor. Very seldom is music used to program the audience's response to the story or characters. Scattered throughout the thirty-six episodes are a few seconds here and there of music by composers Johnny Klimek and Reinhold Heil focusing the tension of a climactic scene. But these are rare exceptions, almost always signaling an episode's imminent conclusion. Just as seldom, though more significantly as we shall see, the characters themselves break into ragged fragments of song.

Given the near-documentary texture of *Deadwood*'s audio design, then, you'd be forgiven at first for thinking that those quiet little songs at the end of each episode convey some clue, coded message, or other elliptical thematic reference. Their very positioning suggests that they play the role of musical denouement: as each frame snaps shut, its many plot threads a-dangling, a viewer's attention is abruptly concentrated on a usually unassuming voice, accompanied by a guitar and one or two other acoustic stringed instruments, most often singing a folksong or folk-influenced popular song. As episode follows episode, this modest device grows into a comforting ritual, a signature moment of sudden and enchanting unity in the wake of narrative complication and a jostling crowd of story lines to be continued. To be sure, it is a familiar production strategy on prime-time TV, if for nothing else to keep the viewer from heading to the refrigerator during the credit roll, but *Deadwood* was the first series to rely on the roots and branches of American folksong for this purpose.

Unlike the opening theme by David Schwartz and the occasional bits of programmatic music during the show, these songs are all previously copyrighted recordings, licensed from publishers for use in this specific context. If not historic or archival recordings of early to mid-twentieth century North American musicians working in the folk tradition such as Bukka White, Spider John Koerner, June Carter Cash, and Mississippi John Hurt, they are almost entirely by contemporary artists working in or influenced by that tradition. As Wallace describes them, "Folk music, blues, bluegrass, country, spirituals, hymns, and eccentrics were all game." Aside from *Austin City Limits* and the odd PBS special, this is the most sustained exposure of a national (and international) audience to U.S. roots music. You can hear Bessie Smith, Lightnin' Hopkins, and Bob Wills on local and national public radio programs such as *American Routes* and on some satellite channels, but not very often on prime-time television.

Why is authentic folk music considered "imperfect"? The esoteric limbo to which it is usually consigned is a more general case of the obscurity in which blues artists labored until recently, when, along with other roots music, blues became popular not just with folklorists and musicologists but among a growing middle-class audience seeking alternatives to heavily produced popular music. A point made repeatedly in blues scholarship is that today's blues audiences are mostly white—take a look around any B. B. King or Keb' Mo' concert—and the *Deadwood* closing playlist exploits this crossover phenomenon.

The marginality of most of these tunes in relation to mainstream commercial music can symbolize the camp's extralegal status on Indian lands outside the jurisdiction of Dakota Territory, and indeed the songs literally play out at the margin of the show, as the credits roll. But when music is played or sung by a character within the show's narrative frame, that person is always European, and the overtly marginalized groups within *Deadwood* are nonwhite: Indians (represented by Bullock's attacker in episode 6 of season 1, by rumors, and by a severed head in a box), blacks, and Chinese. Of these Milch and company seem to have picked an unusually high proportion of songs by black musicians, just over 33 percent by my calculation (some artists are of ambiguous or undeclared racial identity). Why so many, in a show with only four black characters, all of them minor and transitory? Wu is the only nonwhite leading character (and in the original scheme of things, wasn't he going to lead the army that rescues the camp from Hearst's hired gunmen?), and he is represented only by the Orientalist microtonal wail near the end of Schwartz's theme, meant to evoke the sound of a *jinghu* single-stringed fiddle and the sole sonic acknowledgment of hundreds of Chinese supposed to be inhabiting the town. Lamentably, none of the songs no doubt sung by Chinese miners or railroad workers seem to have survived, only songs written by whites about Chinese miners and railroad workers such as "John Chinaman's Appeal" and "John Chinaman, My Jo." Even contemporary cover versions of these are scarce, and, after all, Wallace, Stern, and Milch were confining themselves to commercially available recordings.

Furthermore, while token Chinese characters have always been a staple of film and TV Westerns, the number of African Americans in the nineteenth-century West has been vastly underrepresented in the genre. So a song by Memphis Slim or Bessie Smith efficiently anchors the show's politics to populations—whether Asian, African, or Native American, or "hooples"—excluded from power and visibility by virtue of race or class, victims of the Darwinian market forces taking over the town (or the recording industry). Country blues easily generalizes into an evocation of folk experience running at an acute angle to the master narrative of Caucasian culture and commerce, transmitting a complex of ideas and historical associations relative to poverty, disenfranchisement, displacement, exploitation, and violence. It is musical shorthand for marginality, whereas to modern television viewers, the presentation of Chinese music, in whatever form, might trigger a different set of associations—ancient, exotic, and trans-Pacific—outside the frame of U.S. ethnicity as it is traditionally constructed in Westerns. Mood and texture—and perhaps a residual adherence to generic conventions—thus take precedence over narrative logic and historical accuracy in the case of racial representation. "Wu" says this isn't 1876?

This leads to the question of how *Deadwood* constructs its own version of authenticity. Few critics or crew members, when discussing the show can avoid addressing the A-word. Much is made of the main characters' and locations' basis in historical fact, the enormous effort and expense of making the set look like the "real Deadwood," and the verisimilitude, or lack of it, of its gloriously ornate gutter speech. Was there really a place called the Gem? Did they actually talk like that? And did they all wear those hats? Such FAQs boil down to the basic issue of how an "anti-Western" distinguishes itself from that which it reacts against, including a decades-old obsession with looking "period," a tradition of artificiality that has over time solidified into its own set of generic expectations. The songs suggest a way to approach this question: in the same way that U.S. roots music achieved popularity as a *style* (as distinguished from a set of enthnomusicological archives), self-consciously distinct from corporate-dominated Tin Pan Alley and teenage pop, *Deadwood* sidesteps questions of verbatim authenticity to claim authority as an alternative to the traditional Western, a revision of both the commercial product and the system of signifiers associated with it.

Authenticity, after all, is a slippery and unstable construction, as William Handley and Nathaniel Lewis emphasize, and particularly hard to associate with any single representation (7). *Deadwood*'s closing music evades the problematic and reductive association with "Western" fiddles and banjos—which after all are rooted in British, Celtic, German, and even Eastern European and African musical modes—by frequently evoking one of the few musical genres that is unequivocally a product of the American landscape: blues. As Bill Handley and Nate Lewis write, "A national culture's sense of its historical distinction—its sense of its origin . . . determines or limits the meaning of authenticity" (7). The African American experience lends *Deadwood* a sense of historicity long missing from the hollowed-out clichés of the classic Western, connecting private anguish with larger issues of race, class, and gender.

An example: in episode 6 of season 1, "Plague," smallpox sweeps the camp, and in an early show of civic unity the town sets up a hospital tent and dispatches riders for vaccine. Shots of Jane, Doc, and others tending to the sick cut to the credits and the plaintive yet resolute voice of Booker T. Washington "Bukka" White singing "High Fever Blues," recorded shortly after the artist's release from Parchman Farm prison in 1940:

> I'm taken down with the fever, and it won't let me sleep (2x)
> It was about three o'clock before he could let me be. (Taft 674)

In "Going Down Slow," chapter 10 of his pioneering 1960 study *Blues Fell This Morning*, Paul Oliver surveys the frequent mention of sickness and death in rural blues lyrics as a reflection of early twentieth-century African Americans' limited access to medical care and their susceptibility to malnutrition and contagious disease (243–52). Figuratively speaking, it represents a sickness of the body politic, and like recognition and reversal in a classic tragic plot, White's musical "fever" crests with each stanza's repeated second line and breaks in the third.

> I wish somebody would come and drive my fever away (2x)
> This fever I'm having sure is in my way.
>
> This fever I'm having sure is hard on a man (2x)
> They don't allow my lover come and shake my hand.
>
> What's the matter with the fever sure is hard on a man (2x)
> They say it ain't the fever, your lover has another man.
>
> Doctor get your fever gauge and put it under my tongue (2x)
> The doctor says all you need your lover in your arms. (Taft 674)

Sam Charters notes the "sense of deprivation" in White's song that transcends its literal meaning (104), and it is not hard to understand illness in the blues as a coded lament for social confinement and economic oppression. Furthermore, the separation from the lover doubly signifies the pathology of a racist, segregated society. Deadwood is suffering from more than a biological epidemic; it is full of young single men, prone to violence, socially isolated, and enslaved to the quest for easy riches. The smallpox epidemic reifies their situation, and like White being driven back into the arms of his beloved, precipitates a new political order.

Considered individually, many of the other songs in some way provide commentary on the surface narrative of the episode they conclude, and Wallace makes a few of the more obvious connections explicit in her letter:

> "Twisted Little Man" [1.1] just plain suited Swearingen, "God and Man" [1.5] rode in on a larger theme about God hiding when Man goes looking for him. My favorite part of that song is the last line about God—"How big is his teeth?" Jelly Roll Morton foreshadowed government imposing itself as an unwanted intrusion in Deadwood's future. June Carter Cash's voice is just raw and moving, she slid in the episode [1.8] where Trixie tried suicide and "Will the Circle be Unbroken" just matched her character's resigned deadened face.

Any moderately attentive viewer could add to her list. Two more prominent examples are Mark Lee Scott's modern version of A. P. Carter's thirties hymn "Fallen from Grace" following Hickok's murder in episode 3 of season 1 ("Reconnoitering the Rim") and Bob Wills and the Texas Playboys singing "Stay a Little Longer" at the end of season 2, after Martha Bullock decides to remain in Deadwood following her son's death and Wu, in the same episode, declares himself an American (2.12). Presumably the viewer is also being addressed here, in hopes of our returning for a third season (alas, for only a "little longer").

For that matter Wallace's comments, written while season 2 was shooting, don't plumb all the possibilities. Following "The Trial of Jack McCall," in which Bullock pursues Hickok's murderer and Jane nurses Andy Cramed, "God and Man" also invites a meditation on Bullock's mission of vengeance and perhaps on divine justice and human mercy as well.

However, the relationship between most episodes and their closing songs is more obscure, even to the point of opacity. You could tie yourself up in scholastic knots disputing the relationship of Lyle Lovett's bittersweet "Old Friends," at the end of episode 7 of season 1, "Bullock Returns to the Camp," with any of its new plot points and continuing threads: Bullock sparing a drunken McCall? Brom's funeral? The appearance of Flora and Miles? Doc, Jane, and the Reverend tending to the sick? Trixie's betrayal of Al? All of them finally converge on Lovett's melancholic Hill Country croak, as distinctive in its own way as any of *Deadwood*'s characters, transcending linear speculation and comforting the afflicted viewer with its rural intonation, traditional musical structure, and sentimental yet eccentric lyrics. Like most of the closing songs, Lovett's serves a purpose beyond commentary on the plot. It functions as a simulated resolution for its episode, a two- or three-minute transitional metanarrative between the show's sixty minutes and whatever comes next. However, unlike the pulsing and distinctive electric hoedown that consistently opens every show's narrative frame, it is not the individual closing tune but the accumulating weight of all these variegated choices that adds to the show's aura of authenticity. Sort of like the hats.

Unnoticeable because it is so conventional, and solely instrumental, the (slightly anachronistic) ragtime piano music in the Gem that soothes Reverend Smith in season 1, episode 10, is a familiar trope of the Western saloon scene. Nor does *Deadwood* abandon a related convention: incorporating vocal music within the story frame. This is as old as Wister's Virginian singing a minstrel song, a device codified by the singing cowboys yet given deeper resonance by more historically accurate choices of song. This isn't Gene Autry breaking frame to strum a guitar and croon "Uncle Noah's Ark" or Dean

18. Wild Bill Hickok's funeral. "The Trial of Jack McCall" (*Deadwood* 1.5).

Martin and Ricky Nelson in *Rio Bravo* (1950) singing "My Rifle, My Pony, and Me." Instead, folk songs and other decidedly non-Hollywood U.S. music from both sides of the sacred-secular divide pop up regularly within the narrative of *Deadwood*, as they might have in 1876. More interesting is the eighteenth-century Protestant hymn "How Firm a Foundation," led by the preacher at Wild Bill's funeral. This is as authentic a period piece of music as *Deadwood* could ever find:

> How firm a foundation, ye saints of the Lord,
> Is laid for your faith in His excellent Word!
> What more can He say than to you He hath said,
> To you that for refuge to Jesus have fled?
>
> When through the deep waters I call thee to go,
> The rivers of woe shall not thee overflow;
> . . . .
> Thy soul, though all hell shall endeavor to shake,
> I'll never, no never, no never forsake. (1.5)

When Jane hums it an episode later while tending to Andy Cramed in "Plague," we are reminded of the first tentative coming together of the camp's inhabitants at the funeral and of this civic spirit's flickering spark borne and protected by unlikely characters like Jane (1.6). As the first northern European music brought to the North American continent, hymnody carries particularly heavy cultural and ideological baggage and has gradually become a trope of Western film, as common as the tinkling barroom piano. John Ford, one of the first directors to explicitly interrogate the Western genre, recognized the power of a familiar hymn when he incorporated some of his favorites, notably "Shall We Gather at the River," in film after film (postmodernly commented on by Sam Peckinpaugh in *The Wild Bunch* [1969]). In *Deadwood* the hymn can signify a number of often contradictory ideas: sacrifice, martyrdom, and hope, as well as European hegemony, militant Christianity, manifest destiny, and struggling communities in the wilderness.

Song, after all, functions in a different and more complex fashion than instrumental music. "Song," writes Kathryn Kalinak in *How the West Was Sung* (2007), "creates meaning through its simultaneous construction as music and text" (3). It is tempting to seek significance in the text of the hymn, indeed in all the lyrics of *Deadwood*'s motley collection of folk, blues, ballads, and alternative country songs, as if in a gnostic text. In fact, as Wallace makes clear, the songs were chosen in an often last-minute three-way collaboration between Milch, Stern, and Wallace. The cultural connotations of this layered system of word and wordlessness bear far more strongly on the narrative than any close reading of the words alone.

Deadwood was not shot with the same obsessive attention to every element as a full-length motion picture, each second of which exists at the nexus of converging and sometimes conflicting artistic, commercial, and cultural forces. Kalinak has examined the play of these forces on the folksongs woven into Ford's films, which the director took a personal interest in seeking and selecting, often directing the musicians and exercising a great deal of control over their arrangements and performances. Much like the way the scripts were created, the process of picking *Deadwood*'s closers was at once more collaborative and less deliberate than the dictatorial Ford's. Yet they work, like Ford's famous choices, as hyperlinks or what Kalinak calls "access points" to the episodes' deeper levels of meaning, and more so because the motives for choosing them may have been more instinctive than deliberate (3).

However they were made, a few of the *Deadwood* team's song choices achieve something more than mere thematic reference, however gnomic that reference might be. Beyond their function as structural element and generalized trope of authenticity, certain particularly inspired selections work in concert with the script to make artful transitions across the frame from the narrative to the extranarrative space of the credit roll. In classical terms they bridge the "diegesis" by combining the episode's diegetic music—the music or other sounds within the frame of the narrative, audible to the characters—with the nondiegetic soundtrack or "commentary sound" only heard by viewers outside the frame. This connection can be made on several levels, even the relatively abstract level of sonic texture. Jane's drunken singing segues into "God and Man," a tonally perfect transition between her voice and those of Sonny Terry and Brownie McGhee, echoing the same whimsical and loose spoken-and-sung dialogic structure.

As another example of this timbral reinforcement, take Michael Hurley's "Hog of the Forsaken." Of this wonderfully eccentric and appropriate song, Wallace writes,

> All three of us ended up with the same favorite, Michael Hurley's "Hog of the Forsaken," that one was a lucky find after David rejected the first round. It fit the episode where yet another body is thrown to Wu's pig, and the last sound is that of the contented pig chomping [1.1]. I looked for Biblical references after I found the song, and realized this wonderful nut-bag guy had just made it up himself . . . a *Deadwood* kind of guy.

It begins with a raggedly sawed fiddle emanating directly from the snuffling grunts of Wu's pigs tearing into the corpse, referencing at a distance, in a more restrained and perhaps parodic way, the ferocious fiddle playing of the opening theme. Hurley's deliberately amateurish singing, voice cracking into an almost painful de facto yodel on the high notes, could likewise echo the camp's motley throngs—the "hooples"—adding a note of grim humor to the macabre deed just done. Hard to believe Hurley didn't compose his song for the occasion, but the recording was released in 1976, over a quarter-century before the first *Deadwood* was locked for broadcast.

> an' The Hog of the Forsaken
> got no reason to cry
> he got to chew the angels
> fallen from on high. (1.1)

Ideally this kind of profound transdiegetic connection is achieved on multiple levels in addition to tone and theme. One of the earliest and best occurs at the end of "Deep Water" (1.2), when Charlie and Jane take Sophia out of town to protect her from Dan Dority. A complex musical conversation is initiated when they try to calm her—and themselves—by singing "Row, Row, Row, Your Boat," a U.S. setting of a British nursery rhyme that was not published until 1881, yet another anachronism to bedevil the literalists. Their clumsy round, punctuated by Jane's cursing, segues into the credits and a piece of music stunning in its sophistication and appropriateness: an a cappella Native American field recording from 1943, "Creek Lullaby." It was collected in Lawrence, Kansas, by Willard Rhodes of Columbia University, a music professor paid by the Bureau of Indian Affairs to hunt down Native songs for a recorded catalog, just as Al has offered a bounty for the "heathen savages" who he claimed have perpetrated the Metz family massacre. So with one song lasting less than a minute, as Edward Buscombe puts it, "the voice of the Other forces its way through" (54). Milch and his collaborators have quietly ruptured the surface narrative with an ancient voice carrying the genetic and cultural memory of other such pursuits and massacres. Much lies buried here, waiting to be excavated. The identity of "Margaret" is never explicitly revealed to be a young Haskell Institute student at the other end of an ethnographer's microphone, so the deeper layers of meaning—broken treaties, genocide, cultural colonialism, as well as the twin ironies of

Native American music in effect soothing the sole survivor of a purported Indian attack, and the presence of all three characters as usurpers on Indian Territory—are accessible only to dedicated *Deadwood* research dogs and those familiar with relatively obscure rereleases of archival recordings. Nevertheless, even for the uninitiated the emotional charge of Sofia's plight is amplified by this plaintive and unaccompanied female voice crying across eras, oceans, and ethnicities:

> Baby, sleep, sleep, sleep.
> Father has gone to find turtle shells.
> He said he will return tomorrow.
> Baby, sleep, sleep, sleep. (trans. Barbara Hall)

"The . . . Western," writes Armando Prats, "would keep the Indian all but invisible, yet it must still 'present' him somehow" (2). Swearingen's Indian is a voiceless, faceless head; Margaret's Indian is a headless, faceless voice. Hers is the only Indian voice in the series, singing, not speaking, and riding high above the diegetic voices of the Anglo characters. If as Prats says "the Indian's *silence* becomes . . . the central fact of his *story*," it is significant that as Sofia is threatened by unnamed forces masquerading as Indians, Margaret's anonymous voice ruptures the episodic frame (150–51, emphasis in original).

Kalinak argues that the focus on American folksong in Westerns and its deliberate or unconscious use to encode ideology, ethnicity, and cultural associations culminate in the distinctive sensibility she is soon unapologetically calling "Fordian" (101). Ford used music both within and without the diegesis as a symbolic system working in concert with his script and mise-en-scène to intensify the composition. "In Ford films, group singing symbolizes the power of community and signals acceptance," observes Kalinak, summing up the moral terrain of Ford's musical program. "Villains don't sing" (83). Most of *Deadwood*'s closing songs are by solo singers or at best raggedy duos, suggesting a fragmented society seeking some sense of community and finding only temporary and shaky alliances, improvised for the moment. When choral music does appear within the diegesis, it invariably marks a spike in the town's civic spirit. And when Al Swearingen sings, you'd better pay attention.

Al's solo number is part of a grander transdiegetic scheme, crosscut with the most public musical ritual in the entire series. This outstanding and seamless combination of musical genre, narrative logic, and ideological intensification is the tour de force that brings "Amateur Night" to a close (3.9). Although it isn't singing per se, a bacchanalian event fuses the camp into tentative community, and like the graveside scene cited earlier and the wedding festival concluding season 2, represents another temporary compromise between social contract and Hobbesian individualism. Appropriately then, faced with Hearst's Leviathan, the town rallies to a song with a very complicated and portentous lineage. "Garryowen" or "Garry Owen" was a seventeenth-century drinking ditty used as a British march during the Napoleonic Wars. General George Custer adopted it for the same purpose, and since then it has seen much use by the modern military and also as both diegetic and nondiegetic music to accompany the depiction of troops in war films as well as in Westerns, including *Little Big Man* (1970) and *The Searchers* (1956). It emblemizes the European American origin of most of the camp's main characters, and its specific allusion to Custer may foreshadow the expected but never realized massacre by Hearst's hired riflemen, who arrived at the beginning of the episode. Its role in this episode of *Deadwood* is further complicated by a parallel and contrasting scene: while most of the citizens are dancing to a Welsh drinking-song-turned-military-march, Al stands alone, wiping his bar and wistfully singing a British folksong, "The Unfortunate Rake." Also known as "Pills of White Mercury" (because the singer is dying of syphilis), this graphic broadside ballad is the grandfather of the southwestern cowboy song "Streets of Laredo," which inherited its familiar tune:

> It's all on account of some handsome young woman,
> 'Tis she that has caused me to weep and lament....
>
> So blaze your bright muskets all over my coffin,
> saying there goes an unfortunate lad to his home. (3.9)

Ah, it must be so lonely at the top! Al, performing this song in what approximates its original style, never comes closer to winning our sympathies. Immediately following this tender moment, the credits roll, set to the virtuosic banjo duo of Tony Trischka and Bela Fleck playing their version of "Garry Owen" called "Did You Ever Meet Gary [*sic*] Owen, Uncle Joe," a surrealistic medley of classical and traditional melodies gathered under the single title. Al, the hooples, and an entire web of historical allusions both evident and buried—all wrapped up in five minutes of music with a boot planted on either side of the diegesis.

Speaking about British ballads, one of the best-known and widespread examples of this cultural immigrant to the United States is used to close the episodic frame at the exact midpoint of the series, "Something Very Expensive" (2.6). Of all thirty-six song selections, this one stands out as an exemplar of all the others. You could call it the *Deadwood* anthem.

Variously classified as a "murder ballad" or "outlaw ballad" (though not so typical of the latter), "Pretty Polly" is described by alternative-country musician Rennie Sparks as "a ritual . . . a secret opening, a knife slashed in the veil of experience through which deep knowledge may seep" (48). The concentrated essence of what David Thomas calls folk music's "brooding and dangerous soul," it narrates the savage misogyny and psychotic individualism of George Hearst's agent Francis Wolcott, who has just gone on his bloody rampage in Joanie's brothel (162). The scene immediately before Wolcott kills his third victim, as Maddie realizes what is about to be done to her, is scripted nearly in lockstep with a common variant of the old ballad:

> Willie O Willie, I'm afraid of your ways. (2x)
> The way you've been acting, you'll lead me astray.
>
> They went a little farther and what did they spy, (2x)
> A newly dug grave, and a spade lying by.
>
> Polly, Pretty Polly, your guess is about right. (2x)
> I dug on your grave the best part of last night. (2.6)

The distant ancestor of "Pretty Polly" is "The Demon Lover," whose many British variants were collected over a century ago by Francis Child. In one version an aristocratic female protagonist is about to be murdered for her ample dowry when she distracts the man—or demon—by baring her breasts (shades of Trixie shooting Hearst!) and pushes him off a cliff. But this is a different Polly. Her U.S. experience has changed her from the clever rich girl who outwits a serial killer into his helpless victim. As collected in early twentieth-century Appalachia by Cecil Sharp and Maud Karpeles, some of whose informants called it "The Cruel Ship's Carpenter," the Americanized "Pretty Polly" suggests that the unmarried protagonist is pregnant, and that her lover does away with her in order to remain unattached:

> She knelt down before him pleading for her life. (2x)
> Let me be single if I can't be your wife.
>
> He stabbed her in the heart and her heart's blood did flow. (2x)
> And into the grave poor Polly he did throw.[2]

Sparks explains the ballad's transatlantic metamorphosis by noting the change in what each character represents:

> A new kind of person stalked the New World. This "New American" was a lone hunter, a self-reliant killer. He found freedom in movement and isolation. He was Wild Bill Hickok. . . . [He] attacked the wilds . . . with a fury that defied rational explanation. (45)

Sparks suggests that the female (elsewhere she uses the term *goddesses*) represents the wilderness. In *Deadwood* it is the rupture of the earth that is the miners' single-minded mission. The song conveys meaning on a number of levels beyond an explicit reference to Wolcott's deed: the overarching theme of violence against women that begins with Trixie's beating and the Metz massacre and culminates in Jen's sacrificial slaughter in the final episode, the exploitation of the town's prostitutes, and the "rape" of Indian Territory and of nature itself.

Besides being collected by two generations of ethnomusicologists, "Pretty Polly" has been widely recorded in its adopted home. Its first commercial appearance was at the height of the first American "country and western" music craze, in a 1938 recording by the Coon Creek Girls. A year later they played it at the White House as part of a command performance for King George VI and Queen Elizabeth of England, who presumably took its newly enhanced misogyny with a stiff upper lip. Although they could have selected a more traditionalist 1995 recording by the New Coon Creek Girls, the version selected by Wallace, Stern, and Milch was recorded in 2003 by Ohio musician Hilarie Burhans, who sings the six central stanzas accompanying herself on the clawhammer banjo. As in many modern recreations of traditional folk music, Burhans's banjo is recorded in the studio at a higher level relative to the vocal track than is customary on archival recordings, such that it transcends mere accompaniment and claims equal partnership in the composition. It is characteristic of the evolution of orally transmitted ballads to have their stories gradually stripped away to leave only an allusive minimum, thereby intensifying the lyricism of the original narrative almost to the edge of surrealism. Burhans takes this one step further by pitting her instrument against her voice, as if the story were contained as much in the tone of the vocal as in the lyrics. Further advancing this process of lyrical abstraction is a keening background chorus, overdubbed in the recording studio. Thus the song is not a traditionalist performance per se. Neither is it an archival recording or even a re-creation of one; the rawness and imperfection of the earliest recordings tend to appeal only to dyed-in-the-wool folkies and audio connoisseurs. But what remains of the lyrics carries associations with a millennium's worth of medieval carnage and carnality, hybridized with twenty-first-century technology to make it sound old to modern ears. From its minor-key drone to the amoral and brutal world it evokes, the song sums up the episode, and the entire series, at every level. "Pretty Polly" models the transformation of the traditional ballad into a modern musical composition—and the construction of authenticity in *Deadwood* as a whole.

As I hope this essay has made clear, the collaborative effect of *Deadwood*'s thirty-six closing songs exceeds the sum of its parts in the same way that an ideal cast works together as a cohesive ensemble, rather than as a pack of separate characters. The songs perform like a parallel cast, with a new character joining the community after each episode. Like the characters, sets, and dialogue, most of the songs are carefully constructed simulacra that construct the show's authenticity by meeting our expectations of imperfection and thereby exploiting the cultural attitudes and conditioned responses constellated around the genre. Their very imperfection makes them perfect.

Nancy Cook suggests that "it may be easier to construct a singular, albeit fictitious identity than it is to write the complexity of identity as we currently configure it" (143). We grew to expect, had we been allowed to follow the story to its intended conclusion, that the town's inhabitants, including Wu's Chinese and an African American or two, would have prevailed in an epic battle against Hearst's pistoleros. To a greater or lesser extent, expectations like these are met at the end of each hour by a concluding aesthetic gesture, an open-ended and suggestive metanarrative, an intensification and rhythmic resolution of the show's themes and ideologies. Most consistently, like the ragtime piano in the Gem Saloon, the closing songs one by one serve to soothe the stunned viewer, settling accounts before the next episode of *Deadwood*'s dangerous world begins.

Notes

A mostly accurate episode-by-episode listing of the thirty-six songs may be found at http://tinyurl.com/cf2ztaj. One exception: in episode 5 of season 2, the title "Life Is Like That," attributed to Big Bill Broonzy, is actually performed and sung by Memphis Slim, accompanied by Broonzy on guitar.

1. The "lost reader" addressed in the salutation of this open letter refers to Lost Highway Records, which issued the soundtrack CD and on whose website the letter was originally posted.
2. The lyrics of "The Cruel Ship's Carpenter" as transcribed here are essentially identical to most American versions of "Pretty Polly" and were the basis for the writer's re-oralization of the tune.

9 Calamity Jane and Female Masculinity in *Deadwood*

Linda Mizejewski

*While Linda Mizejewski, like other essayists in this collection, considers genre, using revisionist critics of the Western who read "this genre as a space where masculinity, far from being bulletproof and monolithic, has always been unsettled and conflicted," she also initiates a series of essays that use recent methodologies — the construction and performance of gender, queer studies, spatial geography, disability studies — to examine the spaces and characters of the series. Assuming the concepts about the performance of gender put forth by Judith Butler, she turns to Judith Halberstam's definition of "female masculinity" to explore "*Deadwood*'s dismantling of essentialist masculinity in the Western." However, rather than revisit the familiar figures wrought by John Wayne, Gary Cooper, and Clint Eastwood, Mizejewski focuses on the representation of a woman. Offering her own revisionist reading of the genre, she argues that the figure of Calamity Jane points to "the presence of diverse bodies and sexualities within the histories and legends of the West." Ultimately the representation of Jane serves "as a register of contemporary cultural contentions about gender and sexuality, a dynamic that began in the earliest fictionalizations of this figure."*

Mizejewski contrasts Milch's portrayal of Jane with earlier, more sanitized versions such as Doris Day's "heterosexual" glamorized Calamity, suggesting that the "first few episodes of Deadwood *parody and replay stereotypes of Jane from earlier representations." She situates* Deadwood*'s Jane in a long line of masculine women in the Western, women who "made masculinity both visible and highly privileged but also highly unstable — a description that also fits Milch's* Deadwood, *where the violent crises of masculinity are unresolved." While Tolliver, Bullock, and others might still be struggling with their masculinity, Mizejewski sees Jane's "narrative trajectory" from "abjection" to her partnership with Joanie Stubbs and "her membership in the community" as opening up a new reading of "frontier history" by dislodging "heterosexuality as the only legitimate sexual relationship."*

Early in the 1953 musical film *Calamity Jane*, Doris Day as Jane sings and dances her way from a stagecoach to a Deadwood saloon, where she shoots her gun to clear a path to the bar. When the survivors of an Indian attack stumble in, she angrily rebukes them as "white-bellied coyotes" because they didn't stop to see if one of their party had survived. Jane stomps out and mounts her horse to undertake the rescue herself. The first episode of David Milch's *Deadwood* makes a telling homage to the 1953 film when a tipsy and infuriated Jane, played by Robin Weigert, similarly berates a saloon full of men who balk at riding out to find a possible survivor of a road massacre. Heading out to join the rescue party, she yells, "I don't drink where I'm the only fucking one with balls!" (1.1).

In contrast to earlier fictionalizations of this figure, *Deadwood* is fearless in citing the famously obscene language and debilitating alcoholism of Jane's historical counterpart, Jane Canary (1856–1903). Both the 1953 musical and the series introduce Jane as a scruffy, cross-dressed figure, but whereas the Doris Day character is headed for a makeover and heterosexual romance, Jane remains filthy and masculinized throughout the Milch series. In its third season, *Deadwood* was also fearless in following the implications of Jane's butch dress and demeanor by having her become involved with the show's femme lesbian character, the former prostitute Joanie Stubbs.

Unlike the heavy drinking and the salty language, the lesbian attachment departs from historical documentation about Jane Canary and follows instead the path of imagination that has animated a vibrant cultural life for Calamity Jane beginning with fictionalizations in dime novels of the 1870s. Biographer James D. McLaird points out that Canary's celebrity waned in the last years of her life, so she was largely forgotten when she died of complications from alcoholism in 1903. But the legend of Calamity Jane enjoyed a huge comeback in the 1920s as the vanishing frontier became an object of nostalgia (221–22). Since then the Jane character has been cleaned up, glamorized, or sentimentalized by a variety of actresses, including Jean Arthur, Ellen Barkin, and Angelica Huston.[1] However, no mainstream popular representation has, until *Deadwood*, scripted the possibility that this butch, cross-dressing figure may have been attracted to women. This has not precluded a queer cultural life for Calamity Jane. The Doris Day musical has long had a gay cult following because of its butch-femme mise-en-scène and over-the-top performances. Also lesbian playwright Carolyn Gage wrote a one-woman one-act play about Calamity Jane in 1989 as "a celebration of the survival of the masculine woman . . . in an era when there was no lesbian or transgendered movement or culture" (vii).[2]

Milch's *Deadwood* plays this card and raises the stakes by entailing the larger cultural picture of sexuality and gender in the legendary West. Critics have pointed out that Jane's gender transgressions occur within *Deadwood*'s ongoing critique of the Western's phallic masculinity. My argument here is that the female masculinity of Jane's character in this series pushes that critique by insisting on the presence of diverse bodies and sexualities within the histories and legends of the West. The first few episodes of *Deadwood* parody and replay stereotypes of Jane from earlier representations, showing her in an adolescent crush on Hickok, fluttering her eyelids at him like a Victorian coquette. But although Jane's story begins with her attachment to the legendary gunfighter, it ends with her attachment to a fictional lesbian femme. In her final appearance in season 3, Jane and her lover, Joanie, have been given Hickok's buffalo robe, and we see the women joyfully wrapping themselves in its warmth, embracing the genre's legends and extending the embrace to include bodies and desires not visible in traditional versions of the West. *Deadwood* gives Jane an additional story arc as well, from dissolute outsider to tentative citizen of the fledgling town, so we can see how Calamity Jane continues to work as a register of contemporary cultural contentions about gender and sexuality, a dynamic that began in the earliest fictionalizations of this figure. In fact, the Calamity Jane figure comes full circle in Milch's *Deadwood*; her female masculinity both delineates and destabilizes masculinities as it had done in the 1870s dime novels in which she first appeared as a fictional character.

The 2005 McLaird biography painstakingly sorts out the facts and fictions that had been liberally mixed in histories of Calamity

Jane, including her own, for more than a century. McLaird reveals Jane Canary as a flamboyant, hard-drinking frontierswoman who often adopted men's attire. However, through most of her life, Canary was likely to wear women's clothing and engage in traditionally feminine occupations, although not always reputable ones, as a prostitute, waitress, dance-hall girl, wife, and mother. Nevertheless, she vigorously promoted and exploited her celebrity persona, embellishing or creating stories about her frontier adventures as a bull whacker and an Army scout and posing for studio photographs in her buckskin trousers, rifle in hand, her hair tucked into her hat.

Popular culture has both celebrated and rehabilitated this transgressive figure. As McLaird explains, Calamity Jane was characterized as "primarily masculine" in the nineteenth-century legends, but twentieth-century lore recast her into more-palatable gender roles by emphasizing select biographical details such as her famous nursing skills (252). Writing of this character's history, Janet McCabe points out that the foregrounding of Jane's role as a nurse during the Deadwood smallpox epidemic allowed her to conform to Victorian ideals of feminine nurturing and charity (67–68). Also, because Canary made a deathbed wish to be buried next to Bill Hickok—perhaps as a bid for attention and fame—she is often cast as the romantic partner of the famous gunfighter, despite historical evidence they were never intimate and may not even have been friends. Similarly, the 1940s claim by a Montana woman to be Jane's long-lost daughter by Hickok received warm popular response. The claim was discredited, but the false documentation quickly became the basis for the "real" Calamity Jane (McLaird 252). Jane Canary did have two children, but the story of a lost lovechild provided a way to popularize the Jane figure through the traditionally feminine narrative of maternal melodrama, as seen in Larry McMurtry's 1990 novel *Buffalo Girls* and its 1995 television adaptation. Unlike the television version the McMurtry novel reveals at the end that the lost daughter never existed except as Jane's sad fantasy, so the mother-daughter relationship is all the more melancholy as a structuring device.

Milch's *Deadwood* is distinctive not only in resisting heterosexual romance and maternal melodrama as narratives for Jane but also in using both Hickok and the presence of children as strategies to tell alternative stories about the masculine woman in the West. *Deadwood* also resists the romanticization of Jane's dress and behavior into tomboy cuteness, camped-up sexiness, or even attractive androgyny, as seen in other film portrayals.[3] Milch's Jane is a crass and unkempt figure, usually drunk, her obscene language linking her to Deadwood's foul-mouthed men and to the town prostitutes. But unlike the prostitutes she is indifferent to male opinion and desire because of her status outside the economies of both gold and heterosexuality. The narrative implies that Jane has money from her previous work as an Army scout, but until she moves in with Joanie in season 3, she lives on the streets. Jane is in fact a figure of abjection through most of the series; unwashed and ungroomed, she vomits on the sidewalks and speaks openly of wetting herself and passing gas.[4] Jane's nursing skills during the smallpox epidemic and afterward are never sentimentalized, nor do they transform her into a Victorian ideal of nurturing womanhood. Seeing the stirring of a patient she's nursed through a surgery, she yells, "Hey, you fat fuck, you're alive!" (2.11).

As this suggests, *Deadwood*'s Jane is often a comic figure, as in a few of the earlier representations (*Calamity Jane, The Paleface* [1948]), but the humor is darker and edgier, often pointing to her abjection, defiance, and social awkwardness with both men and women. Waking up on the floor in a puddle of her own urine, Jane abashedly tells Joanie, "Yo, a piss puddle. Must not have seen that when seating myself" (3.1). When Joanie insists Jane wear a dress and underwear for the Garret-Ellsworth wedding, Jane squirms in her finery like Huck Finn in drag, and when she spots a man who seems to be looking at her, she punches him in the face and knocks him flat (2.12). For her physical portrayal of this character, Robin Weigert said she imitated the body language of the cowboys on the set (audio commentary 1.6), stomping and swaggering, ungainly even in her gestures of affection toward Joanie. The clumsiness of her body language also conveys her marginalization, her literal discomfort with both feminine and masculine society.

Female Masculinity and the Western

The Jane of *Deadwood* is faithful to the "primarily masculine" Calamity Jane of nineteenth-century legends, raising a key question about McLaird's summary of Jane's changing cultural configurations. If Calamity Jane's popularity in the twentieth century depended on her rehabilitation into femininity, what had been her appeal and function as a masculinized figure in nineteenth-century Western lore? Milch's Jane, as an unreconstructed figure from those early legends, closely corresponds to Judith Halberstam's description of female masculinity: "a biological female who presents as butch, passes as male in some circumstances and reads as butch in others, and considers herself not to be a woman but maintains difference from the category 'man'" (*Female* 21). Halberstam takes great pains to emphasize that female masculinity is not the same as lesbianism, though the two histories have often overlapped, and she calls for the historicization of specific kinds of masculinities, male and female, that have been produced in various eras. Most of all, she underscores the importance of female masculinity in the development of modern masculinities in the late nineteenth and early twentieth centuries (*Female* 46–47). Although the Western is not one of the sites Halberstam explores, recent scholarship on that genre suggests its salience in the production of modern United States masculinities as well as the importance of female masculinities in that development. Calamity Jane emerges very early in this genre, and the Milch version of her character captures the instability of gender identity evident in those early texts.

While scholars such as Jane Tompkins and Richard Slotkin have focused on the conservative nature of gender roles in the Western, recent studies have reconsidered this genre as a space where masculinity, far from being bulletproof and monolithic, has always been unsettled and conflicted, beginning with its founding texts.[5] Daniel Worden's work on the nineteenth-century dime novel, for example, argues that masculinities in these texts more often evade rather than embody patriarchal politics, especially by featuring masculinity "unhinged from the demands of heterosexual coupling and reproduction" (38). Along the same lines, discussing the gender dynamics of Owen Wister's *The Virginian* (1902) and the Zane Grey novels, Lee Clark Mitchell frames these novels in the context of the cultural crisis precipitated by the first wave of feminism (*Westerns* 139). Masculinity in the Western, he argues, is most often not an assertion but rather a question of "how to be a man." The genre's essentialism about gender is thus often poised in tension against a "constructivism that grants manhood to men not by virtue of their bodies but of their behavior" (153–55) — a description that fits Jane's unruly call to action, in the Milch text, through a citation of her own phantasmatic male anatomy.[6]

Halberstam's line of inquiry about female masculinity illustrates how Milch's *Deadwood* returns to the gender instabilities on which the Western was founded. The Calamity Jane legend developed in the context of the 1870s dime novels that lionized a number of tough, cross-dressing women characters, as described by Janet Dean in her work on these pulp Westerns. Figures such as "Mustang Madge," "Hurricane Nell," "Backwoods Belle," and others who dressed, worked, and fought like men led Dean to argue that masculinity in these texts was a practical quality not necessarily attached to male bodies but rather "available to anyone in the West" (37–38). Analyzing the Calamity Jane character in Edward Wheeler's 1878 *Deadwood Dick on Deck; or, Calamity Jane, the Heroine of Whoop-Up*, Dean demonstrates how identities and genders shift not just for Jane but for other key characters through the use of constant disguises that elude a "true" self. This playful experimentation with gender identities suggests, for Dean, that the Western genre began as "a space where conventional identity categories are tested and contested" (48). In Halberstam's terms the masculine women of the Western made masculinity both visible and highly privileged but also highly unstable — a description that also fits Milch's *Deadwood*, where the violent crises of masculinity are unresolved.

The gender instabilities of these fictions emerged from certain real-life conditions in the West, as Susan Lee Johnson's extensive study of gender in the mid-nineteenth-century California mining camps makes clear. In these all-male communities homosocial relations included homoerotic ones, often documented by descriptions of "boys" who may or may not have been cross-dressed women (170–75). The presence of both feminized men and cross-dressed women provided heightened anxieties about "real" masculinity. It also provided the rich line of ambiguous female characters that continue to populate Westerns, from the tough pioneer women portrayed by Barbara Stanwyck and Joan Crawford to the explicit cross-dressing tale conveyed in *The Ballad of Little Jo* (1993).[7] Writing of the latter, Tania Modleski remarks that the "proliferation of masquerades" beginning with the Deadwood Dick stories "verges on exposing the Western as primarily about costumes, poses, and theater" (162).

In *Deadwood* Jane's relationships to those crises of masculinity are both structural and semiotic. Jane is not a part of any of the major plot lines; she prowls the margins of the narrative just as she prowls the streets, as McCabe puts it (65). However, her narrative trajectory, from Bill Hickok to Joanie Stubbs, delineates *Deadwood*'s narrative arc from traditional ideas and stories of the West, in which power resided in the body of the gunfighter, to the modern West, where power is decentralized, no longer phallic nor exclusively tied to the gun, the most obvious symbol of masculine power. In one of the few generic Western gunfight scenes in *Deadwood*, Bill Hickok and Seth Bullock together pull their guns on a road agent who had killed a family and made it look like an Indian massacre (1.1). But as critics have emphasized, *Deadwood* begins with Hickok's death and the end of that era of the classic gunfighter-hero (Howard 46–47; McCabe 64–65). Jack McCall, the killer of Bill Hickok, is a sociopath and a miserable coward, illustrating that the use of a gun requires neither bravery nor masculinity.

Deadwood traces the decline of the traditional West to the rise of technology and corporations. But the Joanie Stubbs character exemplifies this movement toward modernity in other ways. Joanie is introduced as a prostitute, her work and identity tied to her body and gender. But she becomes a businesswoman, opening up her own whorehouse. When male violence shuts it down, she still has enough money to live independently, neither wife nor prostitute and thus not defined by a relationship to men. This figuration looks toward the New Woman of the latter part of the nineteenth century and imagines her sources in the primitive communities of the West. Joanie's progress is also, in Foucauldian terms, an illustration of how resistance to power reconfigures the economy in which that power presides. Refusing masculine authority, she and Jane together produce masculinity as the butch component within a butch-femme couple, furthering *Deadwood*'s dismantling of essentialist masculinity in the Western.

When *Deadwood* opens, economic and political power in the Deadwood camp is not only phallic but specific to the patriarchal power of brutal saloon keeper and entrepreneur Al Swearengen, whose dominance seems absolute. As G. Christopher Williams puts it, "Swearengen divides the world into two groups—his own cock and those who suck it" (148). But Swearengen's patriarchal supremacy is slowly eroded through the course of the series, most graphically through a bloody fistfight and a kidney stone procedure early in season 2 that shockingly demystify the all-powerful male body and especially the penis. David Scott Diffrient links these episodes to the sight of a naked penis in the second episode of the series, a move that both exposes and undermines the phallic power of the Western through "various forms of troubled corporeality" (193).

In season 3 phallic masculinity is even more radically displaced with the arrival of mining tycoon George Hearst, who has the capacity to buy out and destroy the entire town. Hearst understands the symbolic effects of physical power; demonstrating his ruthless authority, he cuts off Swearengen's middle finger, a humiliation with specifically phallic significance (3.2). Hearst's clout is masculine and patriarchal, as evidenced in his bullying of the wealthy mine owner Alma Garret, but this is not the phallic masculinity usually associated with the Western. Hearst is an older man with a bad back, incapable of the physical combat that Swearengen undertakes with Bullock, for example. But Hearst's power is far more ranging than brute violence; his is corporate power, institutional and economic, buoyed by the forces of industrial capitalism that presage the end of the frontier, first glimpsed in the telegraph lines that Swearengen recognizes as the end of his omnipotence.[8]

So as the series progresses, masculinity in *Deadwood* is detached not only from specific bodies but also from a privileged relationship to physical force and violence. As Diffrient points out, Swearengen and his men are "increasingly willing to put down their weapons long enough to talk" (196). This is the context for a major strand of the Calamity Jane narrative in *Deadwood*. In an incident that haunts her throughout the series, Jane fails to stand up to Swearengen in a suspenseful encounter involving Sofia Metz, the little girl who survives the road massacre by Swearengen's agents. Jane is standing guard at Sofia's bedside when Swearengen menacingly appears to find out for himself if the child will survive to tell the truth about what happened to her family. Instead of confronting him, Jane collapses in terror and is unable to act. Diffrient sees this as Jane's lack of "phallic drive necessary to stand up against Al Swearengen," an act of "feminine subordination" (195). But in *Deadwood*'s gender/power structure, the feminine/masculine divide is not so neatly parceled out. If subordination to Swearengen is "feminine," then Swearengen's cohort of thugs could be considered feminine, too. Conversely, Sofia's would-be killer, dispatched by Swearengen, is stopped by Doc Cochran not through the use of force but through the doctor's ability to shame him about such a low deed. *Deadwood* gives us no evidence that Jane's cowardice is due to an essential femininity or a lack of phallic power, but it gives us ample evidence that her cowardice is related to the self-destructive fear that keeps her drunk most of the time.[9]

This is not to suggest that violent masculinity, misogyny, and patriarchy are dispelled in *Deadwood*. Its major dynamic remains the Oedipal story of fathers and sons: Bullock versus Swearengen, then Swearengen and Bullock versus Hearst. Bad and abusive fathers haunt the backstories of Bullock, Alma, and Joanie. But this series is more self-conscious about its masculinist dynamic than most Westerns. When the town leaders meet in Swearengen's saloon to strategize about Hearst in season 3, one of the prostitutes in the back room notes that Alma Garret, founder of the town's bank, was not invited. "Guess if you got a pussy, even owning a bank don't get you to that table," she remarks to her fellow whores (3.7).

In this milieu Jane's butch presence is unsettling as someone who has "got a pussy" but has rejected its conventional meanings, revealing the arbitrary status of those meanings and in turn the arbitrary nature of sex and gender categories. The hotelier E. B. Farnum refers to her as "Hickok's half-woman friend." This ambiguity about her body is encapsulated by an anecdote she tells after returning from a journey at the beginning of season 2. Jane talks about an "immigrant fella" who "went sweet on [her]." He brought her flowers and gifts and eventually told her, "I wanna suck your cock" (2.2), a punch line that she singularly enjoys but which reduces her listeners—Bullock and Hickok's friend Charlie Utter—to uncomfortable silence. Given that "cocksucker" is the most widely used epithet of contempt in *Deadwood*, Jane's story resounds with unnerving resonances. Was Jane passing as male and being courted as a "boy" who would receive flowers—like the "boys" Johnson documents in the mining camps? Or was her admirer expressing a fetishized desire, both knowledge and denial of Jane's female body?

The anecdote foregrounds what it means to "pass" as male and thus what masculinity entails in the Western, as seen in the capitulation of the macho Swearengen to the elderly Hearst. It also raises the question of male desire in Westerns, a site of intensive male bonding.[10] Homophobic anxiety permeates the dialogue in *Deadwood*, reflecting the homosocial/homoerotic culture that Johnson describes in the mining camps. The men's language in particular resounds with threats and disavowals of male homosexuality, as would be expected in frontier mining communities, where women were not always available. The most common denigration is "cocksucking," and the metaphors for political, territorial, economic, and physical threats or submission focus on sodomy: "ass fucking," "bending over," "taking it up the ass," "grabbing ankle." At one point Hearst calls attention to his own inviolate power by taunting Commissioner Hugo Jarry, who proposes a Socrates-like relationship with him. Hearst pretends to take the Greek reference literally, demanding, "Are you saying you want to fuck me?" The commissioner meekly admits he "forgot that part of the story" (3.10).

What *Deadwood* never forgets is the fluidity of homosociality and its exposure of the range of affections entailed in male bonding in the Western. While homophobic language dominates the dialogue, actual male homosexuals in *Deadwood* are scarce. In season 1 Cy Tolliver makes an accusation of his employee Eddie, but the text never verifies it. In season 3 the proclivities of the flamboyant Jack Langrishe and Gustave the tailor are suggested without visible follow-up. But emotional male responses to other men often challenge conventional notions of a monolithic cowboy masculinity in *Deadwood*. We see Swearengen cry at the sight of Reverend Smith, the minister dying of a brain tumor, and we see Bullock's grief at the death of Hickok. Hickok's killer, McCall, taunts Bullock when he sees tears in Bullock's eyes: "Are you crying?" he sneers. "Did he [Hickok] stick his dick up your ass?" (1.5). Jack McCall is one of the show's most contemptible villains, so his snickering questions about men weeping and loving other men only reinforces the way *Deadwood* valorizes those emotions as part of its challenges to the stoic, monolithic masculinity of the traditional Western.

Jane's inclusion in this proliferation of masculinities in *Deadwood* calls to mind Halberstam's claim for the role of female masculinity in the articulation of male masculinities. Jane's anecdote about her suitor is positioned in the same episode as a revealing incident concerning Dan Dority, Swearengen's hulking lieutenant, a massive brute who regularly carries out Al's orders for murder. We see the depth of Dority's emotional attachment to the saloon owner when Dority pouts and weeps because Swearengen publicly sided with another man, Silas Adams, against Dority in a dispute, indicating Adams to be his new lieutenant. When Swearengen soothes Dority's hurt feelings, the latter's joy is so overwhelming he reaches out for an embrace, which his boss deftly avoids. A few episodes later, when Swearengen regains consciousness after the kidney stone incident, Dority is beaming at him with so much affection that Swearengen says, "Did you fuck me while I was out? Then quit lookin' at me like that" (2.5). This is similar to Jane's line, in the last episode of that season, when she slugs the man she thinks is eyeing her in her female clothes at the Garret-Ellsworth wedding: "What the fuck you lookin' at?" she hollers. The incorporation of Jane in these challenges to gender norms in the Western serves to widen the spectrum of what masculinity can entail.

Citizenship and the Butch-Femme Couple

Jane's relationship to Joanie in *Deadwood* contests the monolithic heterosexuality of the frontier West and adds another dimension to McCabe's argument that Jane is positioned as the "formal nexus point" of competing histories, legends, and myths about the frontier (61). Discarding the heteronormative version of the legend that would make Bill Hickok her lover, the Milch series treats the relationship as a friendship based on Hickok's kindness and ability to see past her awkwardness to her core decency and generosity. McCabe emphasizes that in the first two seasons the Hickok-Jane story in *Deadwood* focuses on her grief at his loss (74–75). In the third season this grief becomes the connection to Joanie, linking "official" stories of the West, such as the Hickok legend, to illicit or submerged histories.

We learn about Joanie's sexuality in the first season, when she is introduced as the head prostitute at the upscale saloon run by the malicious Cy Toller. Refusing Tolliver's attentions, Joanie stares back at him defiantly while she bathes and kisses a young woman who works for him (1.5). The three seasons of *Deadwood* reveal the gradual liberation of Joanie from Tolliver's grip. He both supports and subverts her independence when she opens up her own bordello. But when her fellow businesswoman and two prostitutes are murdered, Joanie sinks into a despair so profound she contemplates suicide at the beginning of season 3 (3.1).

Jane, too, has despaired after Hickok's death, leaving Deadwood for a while but returning to die there, she tells Doc Cochran, apparently through alcoholism (2.2). Bill's friend Charlie Utter, alarmed to see Jane "a drunken, fuckin' mess," as he says at Bill's graveside, urges her to befriend Joanie because she has also suffered the loss of friends (2.8). Clearly, these women save each other's lives. By the end of season 3, Joanie is no longer a prostitute and has begun a more respectable life—which ironically, includes loving and living with Jane. "Some happiness has come into my life now," she tells Tolliver in the final episode (3.12).

To represent this outlaw sexual history, *Deadwood* draws Joanie as an amalgam of various historical and fictional figures. McCabe identifies her as a version of the feminine character who befriends Jane in the Doris Day movie and undertakes her makeover (76). In that film their friendship creates, wittingly or not, the butch-femme couple celebrated in gay culture. Joanie is also certainly an allusion to the Black Hills brothel madam Dora DuFran, for whom Jane Canary worked at various times in her life. After Jane's death DuFran wrote a short book claiming she plucked a dead-drunk Jane from the streets in 1886, an event that was "the beginning of [their] friendship, which lasted until death came to her" (8).[11] In McMurtry's *Buffalo Girls* Dora is portrayed as the only person whom Jane loved. "I loved her the minute I saw her," Jane says of Dora. "We're buffalo girls, we'll always be friends, [Dora] said. Many a time we danced together, I'd pretend to be a cowboy in those dances" (114). Later separated from her friend, Jane reports, "I have been crying for her almost every night" (157), and dreams of growing old with her "in a snug house" (289). In the HBO adaptation of this novel, the friendship is heavily sentimentalized, with Dora dying in childbirth and Jane ending up as the foster mother of Dora's child. Alluding to this textual history, *Deadwood* cast Kim Darby as Joanie; Darby bears a strong resemblance, in face and voice, to Melanie Griffith, who played Dora in *Buffalo Girls*. By rereading the Dora DuFran figure as a femme lesbian who would be attracted to a butch Jane, *Deadwood* also draws on the traditional connection of the prostitute and the lesbian, often conflated in nineteenth-century culture as women outside reputable heterosexuality (Halberstam, *Female* 51).

While male homosexuality is thoroughly abjected in *Deadwood*, the status of lesbianism, until season 3, had been more liminal. Until her sexual connection to Joanie, Jane's obviously butch character was not easily categorized; her attachment to Hickok could be read as a queer boy-to-man attraction, and there was no indication that she was attracted to women. Lesbianism, on the other hand, was legible through the femme body of Joanie, a sympathetically drawn character who could "pass" as straight and who resembled the glamorous femmes on *The L Word* (Showtime 2004–9), which was launched the same year as *Deadwood*. Joanie embodied the ready-for-prime-time lesbian, feminine and attractive, with typically limited representations of her sexual life. Aside from her kiss of the prostitute to signify her orientation, the only other indication of her lesbianism is her wary relationship with the young con woman Flora, who unsuccessfully attempts to seduce her (1.7–1.8). So Joanie's lesbianism could be read as a titillating backstory for an attractive character.[12] But when the Joanie-Jane relationship is eroticized, lesbianism becomes legible through the more recognizable sign of the butch-femme couple and is validated through the narrative as part of Joanie's gradual liberation from male-defined roles. In this narrative turn Jane's butch presentation comes into focus as not just queer but specifically lesbian. As a critic for *AfterEllen* pointed out at the time, this was a radical departure from lesbian representation on television, where butch characters are rarely seen (Helberg).

Certainly lesbian sex on *Deadwood* is never visible in the way that heterosexual acts are regularly and graphically represented. Nevertheless, the emergence of Jane and Joanie as a couple pulls homosexuality, or at least lesbianism, from its marginal status to make it visible as a dynamic in this series. The crossover occurs in a scene of Jane bathing, suggesting the movement of both Jane and homosexuality from abjection. This scene parallels the one in which Joanie bathes and caresses the prostitute in season 1, which established bathing as a site of lesbian eroticism. It also parallels two other scenes of Jane bathing, which are significant because a major element in Jane's characterization is filth, physical and linguistic. In fact we see no other *Deadwood* character so often in a bath. The implication is that because Jane bathes so rarely, the occasions are notable, but these scenes also mark Jane's passage from alienation to participation in the community. Both baths are precipitated by events involving children, a motif that is also important in Jane's movement toward citizenship: she bathes in order to attend the funeral of little William Bullock (2.11) and again when Martha Bullock asks her to speak to the schoolchildren about General

Custer (3.2). Also, by exposing Jane's nude body—her breasts and buttocks—these scenes both sexualize this character and reveal how a female body can, even in the nude, maintain its masculinity; pouting, yelling, and scowling in the water, Jane remains butch in these bath scenes.

When Joanie insists on Jane bathing in preparation for the William Bullock funeral, the atmosphere of the scene is tense, with Jane irritably ordering Joanie to turn away as she undresses and plunges into a tub of hot water, loudly complaining that it "burned [her] fuckin' snatch" (2.11). The camera emphasizes the distance between the two women in the room, just as their bickering reveals their frustrated inability to express their sorrow about the death of the child. In contrast the bath scene that changes their relationship is set in a much more intimate atmosphere, framed in close-up as Joanie gives Jane a sponge bath by lamplight (3.7). The scene takes place in Joanie's boardinghouse room, where she has taken Jane after finding her intoxicated and vomiting in the street. Sitting by the washbasin, Jane at first protests when she thinks Joanie's hand has gone too far up her sleeve, but then she expansively and drunkenly takes off her shirt, proclaiming that she can't put on "airs" of modesty because she's "been disrobed in front of every barnyard creature that hunts, pecks, or rolls in the fuckin' mud"—a comic reference to her own status as a creature skulking the streets of Deadwood. But Joanie's gentle soaping of her neck and shoulders immediately changes the tone of the scene, and it becomes clear that Jane knows that Joanie is a lover of women, just as Joanie knows of Jane's emotional vulnerability. "I would never hurt you, Jane, or touch you if you didn't want," Joanie tells her. Jane awkwardly indicates that she indeed wants to be touched and specifically wants her breasts to be touched. Eyes clenched tight, she says, "I won't open my eyes, but you can go ahead and kiss me if that's what you fuckin' do." As the women draw closer for the kiss, we can see Jane trembling with emotion.

Their relationship becomes public almost immediately, as indicated in the follow-up incident when, as Jane and Joanie leave the boardinghouse the next morning, they are rebuked by the angry landlord with a protest sign quoting the biblical book of Romans to condemn their "vile affections": "'For this cause God gave them into vile affections: for their women did change the natural use into that which is against nature.' Romans 1" (3.8). The incident is delivered as dark humor. "Fuck yourself up your ass," Jane shouts angrily, as she pretends to write that directive over the protest sign. The irony is that in *Deadwood* moments of genuine affection are rare, while much of life is vile. Murder victims are fed to the pigs; mine laborers are abused; Chinese prostitutes are kept in cages; road agents are hired to massacre a family and make it look like the work of Indians. "Vile affection" is the attitude of this series toward the entire genre of the Western.

However, the protest indicates that, in a town as small as Deadwood, portrayed as buzzing with spies, gossips, and informants, Jane and Joanie's relationship is no secret. The public nature and function of their relationship are revealed in the following episode (3.9) when, as a couple, they lead the schoolchildren through the town, an act that both asserts their membership in the community and dislodges heterosexuality as the only legitimate sexual relationship in frontier history. Joanie and Jane become involved with the children because Joanie's former bordello was being used as the schoolhouse, but she has sold the building and made certain a new building would be designated as the permanent school. The town's schoolchildren need to be walked to their new schoolhouse, a trek through the muddy and often dangerous main thoroughfare, full of bucking horses, whores, drunks, and gold miners lining up for whiskey shots sold at wooden stands. Also, as Robin Weigert points out in her audio commentary on this episode, the town is "in grave danger" because of the increasingly menacing presence of Hearst's men. The children act as a "lens," she says, through which we see the town's vulnerability (audio commentary 3.9). The safe passage of the children also signifies a major theme in *Deadwood*: the messy emergence of community and order out of vice and violence. So the town's—and the show's—most prominent couple, Sheriff Bullock and his schoolteacher wife, protectively follow the procession to the new school. However, the group is led by Jane and Joanie,

19. Jane and Joanie. "Amateur Night" (*Deadwood* 3.9).

holding hands, Jane intoxicated and holding onto Joanie for support, but clearly walking in public as a couple. Bookending the procession, the two couples become the public signifiers of community-building and the future of the West. While these two pairs, heterosexual and homosexual, are traditionally designated as legitimate/illegitimate, this is a binary dynamic of the Western that *Deadwood* continually exposes and erodes.[13] The breakdown of this particular binary begins in season 3, episode 4, which concludes with the parallel scenes of three couples: Jane and Joanie awkwardly shaking hands as they agree to live together; the Bullocks holding hands and conversing in bed; and Swearengen getting fellated by the young prostitute Dolly, whose humanity he suddenly realizes through a touching conversation about his childhood memory of being forcibly restrained.

The procession with the schoolchildren is not the first occasion in which Jane functions as part of a public stand. After her return to Deadwood at the beginning of season 2, she joins Bullock, Utter, and Sol Star when they band together, guns at the ready, to demand Bullock's badge and gun back from Swearengen, crucial items left behind after the Bullock-Swearengen fistfight (2.2). This stand allies Jane with the group that *Deadwood* positions as its moral center, an alliance emphatically associated with Bill Hickok, who had brought them together before he died. In contrast the third-season alliance with the common good is associated not with Hickok but with Joanie, because of the latter's key role in securing the schoolhouse.

The use of children to signal citizenship for Jane and Joanie is a remix of the maternal melodrama narrative, which in earlier fictionalizations serves to draw Calamity Jane into the normative gender role of motherhood. *Deadwood* steers away from this narrative altogether and instead posits Jane's maternal instincts as part of her fierce protectiveness. We see this in her attitude toward Joanie, too: "Who will look out for you?" she demands as she realizes Joanie's demoralized state at the beginning of season 3 (3.1). *Deadwood* also associates Jane with children to invoke her own childlike nature, seen when she entertains the schoolchildren with stories and later plays with them as if she were among her peers (3.11). In Jane's introductory scene, in fact, she both curses the travelers who are blocking the trail ("Ignorant fucking cunts!") and peeps playfully at a little girl with her family in a wagon (1.1).

This turns out to be Sofia, the child who survives the road massacre of her family and who is the center of Jane's crisis when she cowers in front of Swearengen, allowing him to approach Sofia to check her condition. Despite this failure Jane participates in a second rescue of Sofia later in the same episode, when she and Charlie sneak the child off to their wagon outside town to make certain she's safe. Trying to soothe the child to sleep, she and Utter are comically inept parent figures, arguing and swearing about the right way to sing "Row, Row, Row Your Boat" (1.2). Generally, *Deadwood* deploys Jane's maternal instincts not to assert a traditional gender role but rather to align her with the forces that eventually form a community out of the unruliness of Deadwood: Bullock and Utter, who symbolize the stability of both law and enterprise; Doc Cochran, whose compassion is matched by his considerable knowledge; Martha Bullock, who organizes a school; and Joanie, who establishes a permanent schoolhouse.

Deadwood ended after three seasons, before it could resolve any of its story lines. However, Jane sums up the trajectory of her narrative in a monologue late in season 3, when she tells Joanie about a dream that poignantly weaves together her anxieties about loss and shame as well as the possibilities of healing and redemption. The two women are undressing for bed, and Joanie responds emotionally as she listens and understands the importance of what Jane is saying. The dream reveals that for Jane the trauma of losing Bill Hickok is conflated with her shame in not defending Sofia from Swearengen. Charlie is the messenger in this dream, who tells her they're in the place and time where Hickok will be murdered: "Don't you know this is the night you couldn't look out for that little girl, when you was at Cochran's and Swearengen come in and scared you and you went down to the creek to weep." But in the dream Charlie also reminds her that together, she and he "spirited that child from Cochran's to where [their] stock was outside of camp and [they] watched out on that little girl and sung to her." He instructs her to remember, during the times when she is "most ashamed," that "the middle of the dream"—her act of cowardice—is not the whole story (3.10).

In a moment of self-reflection not often seen in Jane, she then interprets the dream's origins. If she wondered why she dreamed that dream, she tells Joanie, it's because she had been in a similar shameful situation on the day she was supposed to help lead the children to the school. She was drunk in the street and had to be roused to help Joanie make that march; later that night, she says, she also ran to get help when Joanie was threatened by Tolliver. "And you and me walked those kids to school, and before I went to sleep, you kissed me," Jane concludes. "And Charlie helped me find that little girl, the very night I got scared and run, and the both of us sung a round to her, and then you went ahead and kissed me" (3.10). In response Joanie gently takes Jane's face in her hands for a kiss.

Jane realizes that the dream is an instruction to push past her shame by remembering the moments of redemption. She also realizes that she can do this because of Joanie's love. This is a significant turn for Jane as a character whose self-contempt has kept her in an abject state for most of the series. Also, because this redemptive memory is enabled by a lesbian relationship, Jane's status as "nexus" of contested frontier histories takes on additional meanings. Jane's character in *Deadwood*, McCabe reminds us, is "involved in contested debates over what is remembered and forgotten in the tangled memories of frontier history and legend" (68). Lesbian history on the frontier, which may or may not have included Jane Canary's own experience, is imagined in *Deadwood* as one more enrichment and complication of what we think of as "the West."

This updating of the Calamity Jane legend is as much about contemporary politics as about possible alternative histories of the West. McCabe points out that Jane's story is "a changeable script" that "resurfaces within our cultural imagination every now and then" with different meanings (76).[14] These meanings are often tied to changing ideas and contentions about gender. Jean Arthur, who played Jane in the 1937 DeMille film *The Plainsman*, cited her as an American woman "who blazed the trail toward emancipation" because she took up male privileges such as smoking, drinking, and wearing trousers (McLaird 231). Similarly reading Jane as a register of social concerns, Tamar McDonald notes that the Doris Day version of Calamity Jane is not about nineteenth-century Deadwood but about "1953 Everywhere USA: the pressure to comply with mid-twentieth-century gender norms" (180). In *Deadwood* the story line that positions Jane and Joanie as citizens emerges in the decade when contentions about gay rights and gay citizenship came to the forefront because of debates about marriage. Many states passed marriage laws to prevent same-sex marriage, while other states passed legislation allowing it. The first state to approve same-sex marriage was Massachusetts, which made this move in 2004, the year *Deadwood* debuted. The objectionable nature of the butch-femme couple is suggested in the final episode of season 3, when Joanie goes to Cy Tolliver to make amends and wish him well. His reaction to her announcement about her "happiness" is bitter and homophobic. "Does a girl have to drive cattle for you to eat her pussy?" he snarls (3.12). Tolliver is one of *Deadwood*'s least sympathetic characters, but his vicious remark reminds us that this version of Calamity Jane is a deeply contentious one.

However, the last episode of the series also gives Jane and Joanie a final scene affirming the power of both legend and a new kind of story. Jane gets drunk because she's upset over a miscommunication with Joanie, who finds her sulking and petulant in bed. In his audio commentary on this episode, Milch remarks that Jane has never been in love before and is puzzled that lovers can misunderstand each other (3.12). To draw Jane out of her bad mood, Joanie announces that Charlie has sent them Hickok's buffalo robe, and when Jane happily snuggles into it, Joanie embraces her in the robe. "Warm," Jane murmurs contentedly, in a comment that seems to describe the embrace of Joanie as well as the robe and memory of Hickok. The iconography of this final embrace—Bill's robe around Jane, Joanie's arms around the robe—includes the traditional, legendary past but frames it differently with the suggestion that the West included stories of women loving women.

Significantly, the Jane-Joanie narrative is entirely separate from the Hearst narrative; they are the only characters who do not seem threatened by the changes that are sweeping through Deadwood, perhaps because they are imagined as part of a different fiction and history, one that is primarily about women and intersects with, but is not the same as, Milch's story of fathers and sons.

Notes

1. McLaird describes and analyzes these popular representations in detail, mapping out how the treatments of this legend have varied through media conventions and changing attitudes toward the frontier and the Western (221–36).
2. Taking another approach to Jane's sexuality, Larry McMurtry suggests at the end of his 1990 novel *Buffalo Girls* that Jane was a hermaphrodite: "It was a disappointment, the Docs didn't really know what to make of me either, they used names that I won't repeat—I can't spell them anyway—to refer to my condition" (342).
3. Jane is cute and perky in the Doris Day film and is tomboyish but attractive as played by Ellen Barkin in *Wild Bill* (1995). Jane Russell plays the character for over-the-top laughs in *The Paleface* (1948). The only film version that visualizes Jane as a homely, ungainly figure is *Buffalo Girls*,

although Angelica Huston's portrayal of Jane is far more restrained and even more respectable than the Jane of *Deadwood*.

4. Jane's abject status gives her racial mobility as someone who identifies with the "low other." She has no qualms about sharing a bottle with Nigger General Samuel Fields, despite his own uneasiness about this (2.5). When she offers to help him bury his black friend Hostetler, she mocks his caution to her about how this will affect her "popularity with [her] fellow white people" (3.6).

5. Tompkins, for example, sees masculinity and femininity as the distinct poles across which Westerns structure their anxieties and their stories (40–41), as does Slotkin. See Slotkin on the ideology of "virility" and the vigilante in *The Virginian*, for instance (*Gunfighter Nation* 156–83), compared to Mitchell's take on that novel (*Westerns* 95–119), which emphasizes its context of the turn-of-the-century women's movement. Also see Michael Johnson (98–146) on the performance of gender in early Western novels and the "uncertainty about gender roles, sparked in part by women's activism in the public sphere" (129).

6. I am drawing here on Judith Butler's concept of sexual identities as phantasmatic (93–119). Especially useful in regard to female masculinity is her insight that the stories we tell about bodies are "necessary fictions" (98) or "spectres" produced by the symbolic order "to safeguard its continuing hegemony" (104).

7. In her essay on the generic contexts of *Brokeback Mountain* (2005), Halberstam comments on the film history that delivered the tough cowgirls played by Stanwyck, Crawford, and Mercedes McCambridge, among others ("Not So Lonesome" 198–200).

8. O'Sullivan describes the threat to Swearingen's power made by the new telegraph lines (122–23).

9. Jane shows a similar terror when Cy Tolliver makes a threatening appearance at Joanie's place one night, and Jane runs for help rather than confront him (3.9). In her audio commentary on that episode, Robin Weigert remarks that Jane seems to have an "instinctive terror" about confrontations with evil, an instinct "beyond the rational" (audio commentary 3.9).

10. See Halberstam's description of this tradition in "Not So Lonesome."

11. DuFran emphasizes Jane's charity and generosity. "The only way to sober her up," she writes, "was to tell her someone was sick and needed her services" (7). In *Deadwood* Joanie first appears to fall in love with Jane when she sees Jane nursing back to life a man she does not even like (2.11).

12. The representation of lesbian characters as femmes who can "pass" is discussed by Holmlund as part of the larger problem of lesbian representation in mainstream visual culture.

13. In his widely cited text on Hollywood genres, Schatz describes the traditional Western as structured by the basic conflict of "civilization vs. savagery," expressed in a variety of sets of oppositions: "East versus West, garden versus desert, America versus Europe, social order versus anarchy, individual versus community, town versus wilderness, cowboy versus Indian" and so on (48). An example of *Deadwood*'s erosion of those binaries is the character of the sheriff, Seth Bullock, who struggles to maintain moral and civic order but also struggles with his own inclination for violence and his illicit passion for the town's wealthy widow.
14. McCabe's own interpretation of Jane in *Deadwood* posits that in the first two seasons, Jane is specifically a configuration of post-9/11 America; she locates Jane at the nexus of contested memories and histories revolving around her traumatic loss of Hickok.

10 Queer Spaces and Emotional Couplings in *Deadwood*

Michael K. Johnson

Building on the way Linda Mizejewski closes her essay by exploring the significance of the lesbian relationship between Jane and Joanie, Michael Johnson argues that "theories of queer space and postmodern theories of sociology, each of which is concerned with the relationship between public space and private space and with movements between the two," offer particularly fruitful approaches to Deadwood. *In an analysis of the series' homophobic language, he points out that* Deadwood *persistently calls viewers' attention to sexual practices generally invisible until the end of the third season. Invoking "queer theory's multivalent understanding of the word's usage and meanings" and its interest in the dialectic of public/private and its relationship to space and drawing on Mimi Sheller and John Urry's "sociology of mobilities (and the recognition of associated immobilities)," he focuses primarily on "the way* Deadwood *uses and represents space" and the ways in which what is designated public and private is "undermined by characters' movements back and forth between them," noting in particular the homelessness and constant movements of Joanie and Jane. Mobility allows characters such as Trixie and Jewel, whose stories are "juxtaposed" at the end of season 1, to "explore the possibility of a new self." Like Jennilyn Merten, Johnson argues that emotion is important to* Deadwood, *suggesting that "emotional experience . . . may be a more transgressive form of queer experience than sexuality in* Deadwood." *The series' "'emotional couplings,' which may or may not involve physical sexuality, and which may involve same-sex couplings as well as opposite-sex ones," originate in private spaces but "ultimately affect the public world of Deadwood" and thus are central to the series' major theme: the evolution of a society in a frontier town. Johnson concludes that "the alliances forged in this newly formed society sometimes make possible the realization of private desires heretofore deemed impossible."*

Deriving its sense from post-structuralism rather than empirical history, queer space demarcates a practice, production, and performance of space beyond just the mere habitation of built and fixed structures. Against the domination of space by abstract constructs of urban planning and the implantation of technologies of social surveillance, queer space designates an appropriation of space for bodily, especially sexual, pleasure.

>   DIANNE CHISHOLM, *Queer Constellations*

Spatial models of civil society do not attend to how people (and objects) *move*, or desire to move, between the supposedly private and public domains. Indeed, it is often argued that the very freedom of mobility holds the potential to disrupt public space, to interfere with more stable associational life and to undermine proper politics. But focusing on movements within and across public space brings into view subaltern publics that have potentially disruptive politics.... We suggest that public and private life have always been mobile, situational, flickering and fragmented.

>   MIMI SHELLER and JOHN URRY, "Mobile Transformations of 'Public' and 'Private' Life"

A queer space is an activated zone made proprietary by the occupant or *flâneur*, the wanderer. It is at once private and public.

>   JEAN-ULRICK DÉSERT, "Queer Space"

For a television series that has very few gay or lesbian characters, *Deadwood* contains an astonishing number of references to homosexuality and homosexual practices. Male characters consistently and constantly refer to one another as "cocksuckers." "Yeah," Al Swearengen comments to Mr. Wu about one of the two men who have stolen a heroin shipment. "Cocksucker. Swe'gen bring you cocksucker" (1.10). One of the aforementioned dope-stealing cocksuckers, Leon, comments to Al while shooting up in a bathhouse, "I'll apologize. Bring that slant-eyed bastard over here. He can get in the fucking tub with me. I'll apologize and then I'll kiss him. And then I'll tie him off and I'll shoot him up and then I'll blow him ... with fucking soap" (1.10).

Arrested for the murder of Wild Bill Hickok, Jack McCall taunts

Seth Bullock, "Did you love Hickok so much? Was you sweethearts? Did he stick his dick up your ass?" (1.5). Al, holding up a list of names of officials in Yankton to be bribed, comments, "First notice of our cost to avoid getting fucked in the ass by those legislative cocksuckers" (1.9). Although Al waxes poetic about the possibility of opening a house that caters exclusively to what he calls "specialists," we see only women as prostitutes in the Gem. When Cy Tolliver comments to Flora about her brother, Miles: "My first take was that they were fucking your brother for money over there like they were doing you over here," it's not entirely clear whether the comment is only to goad her or a reference to some of the actual sexual practices available that make the Gem's "atmosphere" so different from that of the Bella Union (1.8). We might ask: is there a "queer space" in the Gem, unseen and unmentioned except for the occasional inconclusive comment?

Deadwood is particularly open to queer reading, as it constantly draws our attention to sexual practices that are(n't) there, repeatedly evoking homosexuality (e.g., through character dialogue) while simultaneously keeping queerness invisible, even more hidden than the activities of the show's notorious "tit licker," a character whose nonnormative sexual desires can only be realized in a special "closet" that hides those activities from public view (but not public awareness). However, the screens that hide that sexual activity also demarcate a space for it, and "degenerate" (to use E. B. Farnum's designation) as that activity may be, the "tit licker" is accorded a space to realize his desire (1.10). Such "queer spaces," spaces appropriated "for [nonnormative] bodily, especially sexual, pleasure," when understood as specifically homosexual pleasure, are not even demarcated by being visibly hidden. In such a context it is not surprising that the show's most clearly identifiable homosexual character, Joanie Stubbs, is also one of the most migratory, moving from one room and one building to another, trying to escape the male violence that follows her and that makes each space seem more inhospitable than the last; or that the show's "queerest" character, the cross-dressing (Calamity) Jane Canary, whose nonnormative gender and social behaviors would require several pages to enumerate, is even more migratory, a homeless wanderer whom it takes three seasons to bring from lurking in the woods outside the camp into the "pest tent" on the edge of the camp to wandering the streets of Deadwood, her "home" marked only by the places she stashes her bottles of liquor. Eventually she is lured inside the Chez Ami (converted from whorehouse to schoolhouse) to tell of her experiences as a scout for General Custer and then, near the end of season 3, onto the floor of Joanie's room and finally into Joanie's bed to form *Deadwood*'s only "out" homosexual couple.

A fictional enactment of how a society is formed in the frontier town of Deadwood, South Dakota, *Deadwood* conceptualizes that formation in a way consistent with theories of queer space and postmodern theories of sociology, each of which is concerned with the relationship between public space and private space and with movements between the two. Central characters in queer theory's conceptualization of queer space are cruisers and flâneurs (wanderers), understood "as figures of a counterdisciplinary, antidiscursive practice whose wayward and wanton flâneries permeate, traverse, and transgress the boundaries and grids of urban architex/cture" (Chisholm 26). In drawing on queer theory and postmodern theories of space, I suggest a broad understanding of what constitutes—or *what might become*—queer space. From the perspective of queer theory, normative space and queer space are unstable terms, and the difference between the normative and the queer is situational and subject to change. Any normative space, even such a sacrosanct space of heterosexual normativity as the wedding altar, is *potentially* queer.

A point of contact between *Deadwood*, queer theory, and postmodern sociological theories is the shared interest in "wayward and wanton" movements that "permeate, traverse, and transgress" official boundaries. Critical of traditional sociological models of the relationship between public and private, Mimi Sheller and John Urry argue that conceptualizing that relationship in terms of separate and distinct "spheres" and "spaces" fails "to capture the multiple mobile relationships between them, relationships that involve the complex and fluid hybridizing of public-and-private life" (108). They suggest instead a "sociology of mobilities (and the recognition of associated immobilities)" that is attentive to "flows and networks that enable mobility between and across publics and privates" (108). The extended story arc of *Deadwood* illustrates just such a "sociology" of mobilities and immobilities in a frontier context where identities and social relations are in flux, and where characters find themselves torn between the possibilities of something new and compelling allegiances to older ways of being and doing.[1]

The "flows" in season 1 of *Deadwood* involve individual characters on the move—from one side of Deadwood's main street to the other, from the Gem Saloon up the stairs to Al Swearengen's office and back again, from various places of business and residence to Farnum's hotel for breakfast. Even Al's oddest customer, "the tit licker," is a man on the move ("He lines 'em up at two-foot intervals, smock tops down, and all but sprints past 'em" [1.7]). Mobility is also economic (Mrs. Garret striking it rich), psychological (as various characters shift from one sense of identity or social role to another), and social/political (the ever-shifting alliances, allegiances, and animosities between individuals and groups of characters). The emphasis on flows and networks is reflected stylistically by a frequently moving camera: pans, zooms, tracking shots, handheld cameras, moving crane shots. In a typical sequence (from the episode "Mr. Wu" [1.10]), we follow Sol Star, Seth Bullock, A. W. Merrick, and Charlie Utter as they walk down the sidewalk after a crowded breakfast at Farnum's, enjoying a continuation of what Merrick calls their pleasurably "meandering conversation," a sequence filmed in a long tracking shot, the camera moving backward in front of the men as they walk, talk, stop to converse, step over passed-out bodies, and negotiate the flow of traffic in the opposite direction as well as the crisscrossing flow of workers carrying bales of wool and such from the street to the buildings that line the sidewalk. Even character dialogue connotes motion. At the Bella Union the common greeting for old colleagues is "Let's get something going" (1.4).

Focusing primarily on season 1, my essay explores the way *Deadwood* uses and represents space, especially in terms of clearly designated public and private spaces, and the way those designations are undermined by characters' movements back and forth between them. As Jean-Ulrick Désert suggests, "Queer space crosses, engages, and transgresses social, spiritual, and aesthetic locations, all of which is articulated in the realm of the public/private, the built/unbuilt environments"; my essay examines the moments in *Deadwood* when public space is appropriated for private purposes, or to articulate private desires that contradict the public roles the characters play and, conversely, those moments when private space is colonized for public purposes (20). Private interests and public interests in *Deadwood* sometimes collide, sometimes converge, and public and private spaces sometimes double one another; individual desires are sometimes curbed for the sake of the social good, but the alliances forged in this newly formed society sometimes make possible the realization of private desires heretofore deemed impossible—and those private desires represent the possibility of a "potentially disruptive politics," of making alliances that subvert Deadwood's developing hierarchy of social relations (Sheller and Urry 114). Space in Deadwood that is put to double use—particularly when that usage combines public and private—I designate as queer space.

In speaking of queer spaces and sometimes of queer couples, I draw on queer theory's multivalent understanding of the word's usage and meanings. Queer designates the odd and the uncanny. Queer is also used to designate homosexuality and homosexuals and is often more broadly applied to nonnormative sexuality generally. Even more broadly, Michael Warner suggests that queer "represents, among other things, an aggressive impulse of generalization" as a means of favoring "a more thorough resistance to regimes of the normal. . . . [Queer] gets its critical edge by defining itself against the normal rather than the heterosexual" (qtd. in Hall 15). As Donald Hall comments, Warner's "use of the term 'regimes of the normal' points to the ways that notions of normality—of proper place and role—represent a mode of government, a form of management of peoples, their activities, and expressions of selfhood" (15). Drawing on queer theory's broadening of the term *queer* to include multiple forms of sexuality and affiliation that differ from the norm (and its understanding that "normal" depends on context), I suggest that space is sometimes made "queer" in *Deadwood* when it is appropriated as a stage for the performance of individual acts of resistance against the various legal and illegal efforts to regulate and control the "lawless" town and the behavior—particularly individual expressions of selfhood that depart from "proper place and role"—of its inhabitants. Such regulation may appear in the form of establishing an ad hoc government, or it may appear, for example, in the form of the control exerted by Al Swearengen over the town's criminal activities and over the identities and activities of the women he employs as sex workers.

Histories and theories of queer space are predominantly concerned with gay and lesbian activity and activism, in the transformation of public spaces (such as parks) into meeting grounds and sites of sexual activity, in the establishment of "gay neighborhoods," in making visible the history and presence of homosexuals in specific locations, such as in articulating the hidden history of place-based institutions (e.g., bathhouses). However, as Désert notes, "Though the erotic nature of space is, by itself, difficult to categorize, the act of sex . . . need not be what defines queer space. The definition of queer space by erotic program would be as limiting as the word *homosexual*" (20). Although I *am* interested in identifiable homosexual characters in *Deadwood*, and although part of my essay is devoted to a reading of the character Joanie Stubbs as a lesbian, I also follow Désert by not limiting my understanding of queerness to specific types of sexual activities. Queer space represents "an appropriation of space [not only] for bodily, especially sexual, pleasure" but also for emotional experience, which may be a more transgressive form of queer experience than sexuality in *Deadwood*, and I suggest that emotion is often the determining factor, or at least the catalyst, for the shifting of public and private spaces. As distinct from the terms *gay* or *lesbian*, "'queer,'" Eve Kosofsky Sedgwick writes, "seems to hinge much more radically and explicitly on a person's undertaking particular, performative acts of experimental self-perception and filiation" (*Tendencies* 9). Emotional experiences in Deadwood often result in (or are the result of) just such experimental and performative acts—in moments when identities and social relations are in flux, when individuals become "queer subjects."

In a context where sexual activity is carefully regulated and commodified, most significant are the show's "emotional couplings," which may or may not involve physical sexuality, and which may involve same-sex couplings as well as opposite-sex ones. For example, the private heterosexual relationship that develops between Trixie and Sol is, in a sense, a queer coupling, as their initial sexual encounter transforms a public space, the hardware store ("She come looking for goods and things took a turn"), into a private one and at the same time subverts what passes as "normal" sexuality in Deadwood (which is a commodity to be sold) (1.11). Thus Swearengen's vulgar insistence during a public meeting in the Gem that Sol pay him ("You owe me five dollars. If you ass-fucked her, you owe me seven.") for a private sexual activity demonstrates how threatening and potentially disruptive emotional relationships are to the town's developing social structure, which rests on a hierarchy of power in which men like Swearengen and Cy Tolliver regulate desire by commodifying it (1.11). Excessive emotional attachments threaten the public world of business, profit, and economic exchange. More often than not those emotional attachments that begin in private spaces ultimately affect the public world of Deadwood.

Queer Couples

SWEARENGEN: I'll tell you the truth. I begin to wonder if I mightn't be fucking queer. (3.3)

SWEARENGEN: You want a blow job while I talk to you?
CLAGETT: [with a look] No.
SWEARENGEN: I wasn't offering it personally. (1.5)

Queer theory offers several potentially fruitful avenues for approaching *Deadwood*. Henry Benshoff suggests that "the most important way that homosexuality enters" into the productions of popular culture "is through subtextual or connotative avenues. For the better part of cinema's history, homosexuality on screen has been more or less allusive: it lurks around the edges of texts and characters rather than announcing itself forthrightly" (13). Although Al Swearengen is an identifiably heterosexual character, much of *Deadwood*'s "allusive" and "connotative" homosexuality lurks around him.

Benshoff suggests that we might think of a queer interpretation in terms of queer readers as well as queer texts: "The queer spectator's 'gay-dar,' already attuned to the possible discovery of homosexuality within the culture-at-large, here functions in relation to specific cultural artifacts," working to produce "queer" interpretations of (seemingly) "straight" texts (15). As Linda Mizejewski observes elsewhere in this volume, *Deadwood* is "more self-conscious about its masculinist dynamic than most Westerns." Although, Mizejewski continues, "actual male homosexuals in *Deadwood* are scarce," and "homophobic language dominates the dialogue," I would suggest that *Deadwood*'s "self-conscious" approach to the dynamics of the Western help to facilitate queer readings. As Mizejewski notes, "What *Deadwood* never forgets is the fluidity of homosociality and its exposure of the range of affections entailed in male bonding in the Western." If the language of *Deadwood* suggests homophobic anxiety, "emotional male responses to other men often challenge conventional notions of a monolithic cowboy masculinity" in the series.

It is also not surprising to find homophobic language in a context of homosociality, and the presence of such language may facilitate rather than hinder a queer reading, for the language suggests the presence of desires that are otherwise not allowed to be spoken. In any male-dominated society, Sedgwick writes, "there is a special relationship between male homosocial (*including* homosexual) desire and the structures for maintaining and transmitting patriarchal power" (*Between Men* 25). The central contradictory element in a patriarchal society that depends on establishing homosocial bonds between men for its continuance is the asserted and overdetermined distinction between homosocial and homosexual desire. At the same time that men are told continually that the only relations that really matter in culture are those between men, they are also told that the greatest taboo is to cross the line between homosocial and homosexual desire. But as Sedgwick notes, "for a man to be a man's man is separated only by an invisible, carefully blurred, always-already-crossed line from being 'interested in men'" (*Between Men* 89). From the perspective of queer theory, one interpretive approach might be to see how a text negotiates that line by either sharpening or blurring it (or doing both at once).

In a scene that illustrates the dis-ease with which the men of Deadwood sometimes approach homosocial bonding, Charlie Utter, politely removing his hat, nervously asks Sol and Seth, "And I was half-wondering, too, if you'd want to join Bill and me for dinner. Tonight or some other time." As the actor's physical performance conveys the character's discomfort, so does Utter's comment following this speech: "I feel like I should've brung posies" (1.3). Al, on the other hand, seems equally at ease with the homosexual and the homosocial, his comments suggesting that he also takes pleasure in the discomfort he causes by crossing (or seeming to cross) the "always already crossed" line between the two. In "Mr. Wu," an episode that explores a variety of bonds between men, Al comments to Silas Adams, "Gotta go to the bathhouse. You want to accompany me?" When Silas gives him a look, Al responds, "No one's looking to fuck you up the ass. I gotta execute someone" (1.10). That Al's inclusion of Silas at the scene of this execution is part of his "seduction" of Silas away from his loyalty to Magistrate Clagett suggests that Silas was not completely inaccurate in his initial queer reading of Al's invitation. The bathhouse itself is already a queer space, a public place for private activity (bathing), and already established in the late nineteenth century as a meeting place for gay men, made queerer by Leon's rambling offers to "blow" Wu, and made particularly so by Al's decision to use the "privacy" of the bathhouse to stage an execution, one that has multiple public ramifications, not the least of which are the messages that act sends to his rival (Tolliver), his partner (Wu), and a potential partner (Silas).

It isn't surprising that some of the show's most interesting same-sex relationships involve Swearengen, the town's dominant homosocial player. The harrowing disintegration of Reverend Smith's health in the last half of season 1 is seen predominately from Al's perspective, who often watches Smith from the Gem's balcony, and it is his gaze from that balcony that in some ways delineates the public space of Deadwood. Al's control of that space is threatened as the series progresses by other men on balconies: Tolliver in seasons 1 and 2, and in one of the nicely symbolic moments from season 3, George Hearst announces himself as a major player in controlling the town's economy by smashing a hole in the wall of his hotel room and stepping out of that private space into his own commanding view of Deadwood's public space. The walls that divide public and private in Deadwood are decidedly porous, subject to change, whether through "smashing," through the revelation of connections hitherto unknown (a door and stairway leading from the Gem to Merrick's newspaper office, revealed in season 2), or newly installed (Trixie's secret entrance to Sol's house in season 3).

Reverend Smith's illness, his loss of physical and psychological control due, the Doc theorizes, to a growing brain tumor, transforms him into a public spectacle. And although Al publicly states that such activities as Smith showing up at the Gem to enjoy the piano playing is bad for business—no one wants to see a man of the cloth in a whorehouse—the driving emotions, whatever public face Al puts on it, seem to be pity and sympathy. If the Reverend is incapable of seeing to his own privacy, Al helps to remove him from the public eye. Oddly, the places where most of the Gem's business is transacted, the whores' rooms, are rarely seen on screen until the Reverend is moved into this private space, away from the public gathering area of the saloon. From the perspective of a queer reading, the final episode of season 1 brings us appropriately to a scene of two men in bed—in a room usually reserved for prostitution, an appropriation of a space normally devoted to (commodified) sexuality for another, more emotionally intimate, type of bodily experience. Although we have seen Al kill before, this scene is remarkable for his subdued dialogue and his tenderness. He embraces Smith, cradling his head in his hands, gently stroking his face as he prepares to suffocate him, which he does as he softly comments to

Johnny, "Make a proper seal, stop off the breath, apply pressure even and firm, like packing a snowball. . . . You can go now, brother" (1.12).

As a space reserved for sexual commerce doubles as a place for mercifully ending a life, Smith also doubles as Al's brother, who suffered from a similar malady, and enables an expression of familial affection for the orphaned Al. That this scene is also allusively sexual is suggested by the place itself (a room devoted to sex), by the physical action (the tenderness of Al's killing embrace), and by its juxtaposition with another scene of consummation that directly precedes it, of the Bullock-Garret romance (a private action that follows Bullock's very public beating of Alma's father). And both of these scenes resonate by being juxtaposed with the season's penultimate event, the murder of Clagett in Al's office (a clandestine killing for a public purpose). The juxtaposition of these three scenes suggests another element of *Deadwood*'s queerness; its continual blurring of the differences between sexuality and violence, intimacy and death—the lines between them are as "mobile, situational, flickering and fragmented" as those between public and private life.

There is no better subject for a subtextual queer reading than the relationship between Swearengen and Mr. Wu. After all, these are two men who share only one word in the English language: *cocksucker*. That their business dealings transgress racial boundaries and thus must remain invisible to the public sphere makes possible a number of textual moments that can be opened up to queer interpretations, particularly those moments when the two must meet secretly, in Mr. Wu's slaughterhouse, for example, in order to share the experience of pleasurable plotting behind closed doors. In the episode "Mr. Wu," juxtaposition (of Wu and the "tit licker") again facilitates a subtextual reading. From the street outside the Gem, Farnum anchors our viewpoint, voicing his mutual distaste for his social "inferiors," as they arrive simultaneously at the front door of the Gem, Wu hurriedly walking down the street from one direction ("What is this celestial doing approaching the Gem's front door?"), and, from the other direction, with the same purpose of motion but more surreptitiously, the man that the morally upright Farnum calls "a degenerate tit licker" (1.10).

Wu, who usually enters "the back way," comes in through the front, a transgression of appropriately "celestial" behavior. Wu's queer action evokes responses of disgust (from the women workers in the Gem) or outraged confusion (Johnny). His angry march into Al's office transforms that room into a queer space—unusual things happen when Wu and Al are together. As Johnny observes, his dialogue overlapping shots of the tit licker emerging from behind the screen, a handkerchief to his lips, "Those are the first 'cocksuckers' I have ever heard shouted from that room, Dan, that didn't come from Al's mouth and that wasn't followed by Al coming over that railing, pointing at you and beckoning you up them stairs with your fucking knife" (1.10). The juxtaposition of scenes involving the tit licker and Wu, the coincidence of their arrival at the Gem's front door—one for sex, the other for business—the cloaking of each activity from public view in different private spaces, the breaking of propriety that each character's actions represent, the evidently improper orality ("the first 'cocksuckers' . . . that didn't come from Al's mouth") involved in each clandestine meeting, the inappropriate public revelation of the private orality (the gesture of the handkerchief to the lips, Wu's raised voice shouting, "Cocksuckers!"), all facilitate a queer reading of Al and Wu's relationship, one that, by its interracial and extralegal nature, is already outside normal boundaries. Typical of many of Al's statements, his concluding comment to Wu to enter properly next time, "or we'll start getting people having the wrong idea of things around here," can easily be read as a double entendre referring to either homosocial or homosexual relations (1.10).

Deadwood is replete with same-sex couples and partners, Swearengen and Wu, Sol Star and Seth Bullock, Charlie Utter and Bill Hickok, Mrs. Garret and Trixie, Merrick and Blazanov. This interest in same-sex couples is an element of the Western that *Deadwood*, as it does with other genre conventions, self-consciously explores. For that matter, as Judith Halberstam observes about *Brokeback Mountain*, the film "simply suggests, proves, and confirms that the genre was always queer or at least always homo" ("Not So" 190). The queerness of *Deadwood*, or its amenability to queer readings, may result from its general self-consciousness about genre conventions. As Halberstam continues, "No Western is without its homoerotic inflections if only because the genre demands that men leave their women to become men and that they spend huge amounts of time with another man in a relationship of surrogate marriage" (195). In its interest in same-sex couples, *Deadwood* follows Western convention, although it differs in the nearly equal attention it gives to same-sex female couples.

In *Deadwood* it is the same-sex couple in particular that represents the possibility of transgressing other barriers, particularly barriers of class, caste, and race. In addition to the racially transgressive Swearengen-Wu partnership, this transgressing is perhaps best exemplified by the relationship that develops between Trixie and the upper-class Mrs. Garret. When Mrs. Garret adopts the orphan girl whose family was murdered, Al sends Trixie ostensibly to help care for the newly named Sofia but also to find out if the child remembers anything that could implicate him in the murders and to exploit Mrs. Garret's laudanum addiction as a way to further his plans to acquire her gold-rich property.

Rather than seducing Alma with dope, Trixie helps her kick the habit. Her first action in Alma's hotel room is to touch the child and then give her a bath. Individual bodies brought together threaten the systems that humans collectively create, whether the legal systems of established government or the systems operated by Al and Cy designed to alleviate hoople-heads of their money. The intimacy of bodies touching bodies, when not regulated by a system that reduces any such touching to a commodity status, as a means to an economic end, threatens the smooth operations, if not of the law, then certainly of the plotters and exploiters of desire. Al hopes to use Trixie to seduce Alma through her desire for dope, but instead of a seduction, the two women and the girl child form a temporary same-sex family. When Trixie first meets Sofia, she states, "I'm Trixie. Trixie," one of the first moments when Trixie asserts a sense of self separate from her role as "Al's whore" (1.5). Through Sofia, in whom she may see her younger, innocent self (after the bath, she brushes Sofia's hair and styles it like her own; Charlie comments to Trixie, "She favors you. She could be yours."), Trixie begins to imagine herself anew (1.7).

The emotional bond that develops between the two women and the child in the space of Alma's hotel room undermines Al's goals, but it also leaves Trixie unmoored, a "queer subject," a wanderer, her identity crisis visually represented by her constant crisscrossing of the Deadwood main street as she moves from Al's room to Alma's room, from one set of allegiances to another, from one identity firmly established—as Al's whore—to the possibility of becoming something and someone else. That crisis leads to Trixie's disappearance from public space and from Al's watchful eye, as she overdoses alone at Doc Cochran's and as the doctor later keeps her hidden there as she convalesces. The temporary resolution of the crisis comes when she once again enters the public space of the street, and we see her from several different vantage points: from the Bella Union balcony, from Alma's window, and from Doc's perspective, as she walks back to the Gem to place herself once more in a stabilizing identity. As Bullock comments to Sol regarding Trixie, "Big pull to that. Going back to what you know," a statement that could be applied to many of the characters (including Seth himself), who find themselves returning to the stable identity offered by roles (e.g., whore, sheriff, alcoholic, addict) that they know rather than the (frightening, disorienting) possibility of performing the self differently (1.9).[2]

That dilemma, the competing appeals of old identities and new possibilities, exemplifies *Deadwood*'s exploration of a "sociology of mobilities (and the recognition of associated immobilities)" (Sheller and Urry 108). Even a character such as Jewel, whose agency is limited (by physical disability, by age, by gender, by social status), can find a way to creatively reimagine herself, and her story arc mirrors the way other characters explore the possibility of a new self—particularly Trixie, whose story is juxtaposed with Jewel's quest for a leg brace that she hopes will literally improve her mobility. Initially reluctant to make the brace, Doc comments, "I will not have you lose the mobility that you do have for the sake of a few weeks' illusion," a comment that exemplifies the fears of many of the characters who contemplate performing the self differently (1.11). Is that newly imagined self just an illusion? Will the movement from one identity to another merely lead to greater immobility? Season 1 ends with Jewel's appropriation of the public space of the saloon to stage her own "performative act of experimental self-perception," becoming the center of attention, "as nimble as a forest creature" with her new brace, enjoying the bodily pleasure of dancing with Doc across the floor of the Gem (rather than, as is more usual, scrubbing it) as the stationary Al and Trixie watch from opposite sides of the room (1.12). Jewel's dance points the way for Trixie, whose own most important performative acts are yet to come.

At the end of season 3, Trixie, who has left prostitution behind to learn bookkeeping from Sol and who has earned a position at the bank established by Mrs. Garret, once more takes to the street—the only actor in a town full of Hamlets, each in his own way hesitating to act against Hearst—in the role of self-appointed assassin, her real identity and purpose concealed by taking on her former social role as whore, as she distracts Hearst with bared breasts and a lifted skirt long enough to shoot him (unfortunately, not fatally). Hearst identifies her only as a "bawd" (3.11). In response to Hearst's demand for the attacker's death, Al kills one of his prostitutes (Jen), who resembles Trixie, for Hearst to identify (3.12). Her twin/her double/the "bawd" dies, and Trixie lives on, her identity as a public citizen anchored by the secret murder of her former self. The cost of her continued agency as a participant in the public sphere is another woman's life.

Joanie Stubbs

I can move the dyke. Held me in her arms all night like I was a little fucking kid.

FLORA

I'll not have vile affections or uncleanness on these premises! Find my specific meaning at Romans 1:24–26.

SHAUGHNESSY, as Joanie and Jane leave the room he lets to Joanie

> Fuck yourself with a fist punch up your ass.
>
> JANE CANARY, responding to Shaughnessy

As the mirroring of the two names Al and Alma suggests, doubling is a theme that runs throughout *Deadwood*, emphasized by the way individual character arcs mirror one another, by the way particular spaces are put to double use (e.g., the Gem is both a bar and the stage for Jack McCall's trial), and, particularly in season 1, by the frequency with which we see the images of characters reflected in mirrors. There are multiple other examples of doubling and/or duplicity. Mrs. Garret fakes being high to conceal Trixie's duplicity in helping her break her addiction. In the Bella Union doubling is referenced through the establishment of duplicitous behavior from its earliest opening. Old friend Andy Cramed arrives and introduces himself as a new acquaintance, a charade revealed as false once he and Cy leave the public space of the main floor for the privacy of the safe room. Fearing that public knowledge of a smallpox case will be bad for business, Cy sends for the doc because "someone fell" rather than reveal Andy's illness (and eventually dumps Andy in the woods to keep that knowledge private) (1.4).

At the end of "Mr. Wu," Reverend Smith visits the hardware store to ask Seth and Sol, "Are you Messieurs Bullock and Star?" He knows them as having been "the kindest men of all in the camp to [him]," and although he acknowledges that Seth and Sol "are the absolute images of them," he fears they are really devils in disguise: "What makes me afraid is I do not recognize you as my friends. And naturally, I am afraid. . . . And if you are not devils, I—then I am—I am simply losing my mind" (1.10). The identity trouble that Smith professes here affects all the characters. Cy looks at Eddie, his demeanor altered by the murder he's witnessed, and wishes he could see instead "the old Eddie that knows the percentages and how to play 'em" (1.9). Charlie does not recognize himself in the newly tailored frock coat he wears for the opening of his business ("I'm one for a good appearance and all, but it's a little out of my path") (1.9). Seth fears he is an imposter who has "borrowed" his dead brother's life (and family) (1.10). And after suggesting to Dan the murder of Mrs. Garret's father, Seth asks, "What kind of man have I become, Sol?" (1.12).

The story of Trixie, the prostitute from the Gem, is mirrored by the story of Joanie Stubbs, the prostitute (and madam) of the Bella Union, as each one struggles to break away from an identity as someone else's whore over the three-season story arc. Trixie is also doubled by Mrs. Garret, who, like Trixie, is an addict who overcomes an addiction (and who similarly relapses), and who also enters into a sexual relationship with a hardware store owner. After the beating of Alma's father, Joanie comforts her by confessing to her that not only did her own father sexually abuse her, but he also coerced her into prostitution before selling her to Cy, and she comments, "If he was here, I'd wish a beating mornings and evenings on my daddy like your pa took today" (1.12). The nature of the exploitation of their daughters may differ, but the doubling of these two fathers provides a point of connection and affiliation between the two women.

Put into motion by Cy's business decision to evict the ailing Andy from the Bella Union to die in the woods, Joanie undergoes an identity crisis that stretches through all three seasons, one that is figured through a variety of visual images that suggest the splitting, doubling, and fragmentation of her sense of self. There are two key scenes involving Joanie that I would like to examine in more detail: the crucial scene in her character arc, from "Suffer the Little Children," in which two "children" (young con artists) are murdered in her hotel room (one, Flora, by her own hand); and an earlier scene from the same episode, also involving Flora, in which the girl appears at the door of Joanie's room after witnessing Dan kill a man to "protect" her. In the later scene Cy uses Joanie's private space to stage a mock trial (and real execution), a performance meant to display his business philosophy of punishing those who try to take advantage of him (1.8). The cinematic staging of these two scenes reflects the transformation of the room from a private space where physical and emotional intimacy takes place to a public stage where emotional attachments are derided, mocked, and violently severed for the purpose of furthering Cy's business interests.

The very architecture of Joanie's room at the Bella Union suggests a mirror—divided in two by twin support posts that frame an entry into either half of the room. Actual mirrors also figure prominently. When Cy enters the room to complain that Joanie's "sadness" is dampening the Bella Union's atmosphere, we first see him reflected in the mirror above Joanie's bed (1.6). While some characters may gaze into a mirror in a moment of private self-reflection, Cy is more concerned with his reflection in the mirror of public opinion. Explaining his reasons for murdering Miles and Flora (and for doing so in such brutal fashion), Cy comments to Joanie later on the Bella Union's balcony, "Certain things you have to do to impress upon people what you're willing to do. . . . Do you have to enjoy it? No. Do you have to look like you do? Yes." For the sake of business, Cy has divorced himself from emotion, and he consistently derides those who display emotional weakness. When Sol intervenes in the violent beating of Miles and Flora, commenting, "I guess they needn't get beat anymore out here," Cy responds, "You can help your delicate sensibilities by turning the fuck away." When Joanie implores Cy not to hurt Flora, he comments, "Listen to that, Flora, that's the person you robbed, who has those kind of 'feelings' for you." Cy has so invested himself in his public role, in what he has "to look like" to "impress upon people" what he is willing to do, he seems at times to be the only character in Deadwood without a split identity of some sort (1.8).

The mirroring of Flora and Joanie is clear from their first meeting in the public space of the Bella Union, as the two actresses share a resemblance, with Flora appearing as a younger, shorter version of Joanie, a resemblance made more pronounced when Joanie styles Flora's clothing and hair similarly to her own. Frequently seen reflected in mirrors, Flora's duality also involves the difference between the innocent role she plays and her larcenous intentions. When she is rifling through Joanie's jewelry box, Joanie comments, "Can you tell the stones from the paste?" Flora may be paste as well, but she plays her role with audacity. Flora's character is not only split between her public performance and her private intentions, but she also recognizes that Joanie sees in her someone else: "Who am I? Your little baby? Your sister? You?" Perhaps what Joanie sees in the mirror of Flora is an image of her own younger self, a self that she has figuratively murdered through her alliance with Cy and then literally murders through shooting Flora; her attempt to then turn the gun on herself at the end of that scene plays out a suicide she has already committed psychologically (1.8).

The scene in which Flora spends the night in Joanie's bed is the most explicit indication of homosexuality in season 1 (a same-sex kiss in an earlier episode seems more of a slap at Cy than an expression of Joanie's desire). Flora certainly identifies Joanie as lesbian, which, from her perspective, is a weakness to be exploited, and her assumed role of emotionally distraught innocent is also a calculatedly seductive persona, her verbally expressed need for protection and guidance neatly juxtaposed with body language that combines vulnerability and sexual accessibility. The camera during this scene often accommodates the actors' movements by slow pans and zooms rather than cuts, and we remain physically in the intimacy of the moment until the two women are reclining on the bed, with Joanie's arm protectively around Flora. Camera positioning also places us either to replicate Joanie's point of view or to focus our attention on Joanie's face as she looks—or tries not to look—at Flora. When Joanie brings Flora a soothing drink, the camera tilts down to show Flora the way Joanie sees her, her vulnerability emphasized by the height of the camera, by her upturned face, and by the long moment when she simply looks up into Joanie's eyes and then slowly removes the wrap over her shoulders. Shortly after Joanie sits beside her on the bed, Flora has her head in Joanie's lap and is asking, "Can I stay? Can I sleep here with you?" (1.8)

While there is a physical component to the coupling here, the scene emphasizes emotional intimacy over sexuality—which, in the larger context of Deadwood's economy, is a resource to be commodified. Thus Cy immediately reframes Joanie's developing emotional attachment to Flora in terms of a violent sexual metaphor: "Joanie Stubbs, is that a fresh scalp I see hanging from your belt?" (1.8). Private experience is articulated by Cy as a public act, imagining as he does Joanie displaying a trophy of her presumed conquest for all to see. His comment is also prophetic, as Joanie will soon have reason to claim Flora as a kill, or rather Cy makes it a self-fulfilling prophecy, as he will force her to sever her private emotional attachment to the girl by making her play the public role of Flora's executioner.

In the earlier scene the room serves as a queer space housing a same-sex couple who enjoy a few moments of emotional intimacy, even if Flora's duplicity makes that experience of intimacy the emotional equivalent of wearing costume jewelry. That space is constructed onscreen as queer space through staging, placing the bed at the center of action, and through camera placement, using close-ups that emphasize intimacy and establishing a point of view that suggests that we are looking through Joanie's desiring gaze. The onscreen depiction of this space differs quite sharply in the "trial scene" and might be described as queer in a different sense of the word—uncanny, odd—suggesting that in moving from one side of the room to the other (from where the bed is located to the dressing area) we have also gone "through the looking glass." Off-kilter camera positions, visually distorted or out-of-focus images, and unusually high and low angle shots make Joanie's room almost unrecognizable, an intimate space violated and transformed by the public violence that Cy stages there.

Several reverse shots show Cy reflected in a full-length mirror that stands to the right of Flora, and, in the scene's master shot, the support posts behind Cy similarly suggest mirror frames. In another example of doubling, the composition here also mirrors a scene that takes place after Hickok's funeral. Joanie makes her first entry alone into Deadwood's public space to attend the funeral, an act that angers Cy. After her return we see her helping two women with their baths. The arrangement of the actors into a bathing tableau, highlighted by a swath of golden light, suggests a painting, and the image may have been designed to allude to Jean-August-Dominique Ingres's *Le Bain Turc* (1862), especially to the bathing women in the foreground of that painting. When Cy enters the room, we see the three women from his point of view; one woman (to Joanie's right) has her back to the camera, but we see her face framed in a

20. Joanie helps with the bath. "The Trial of Jack McCall" (*Deadwood* 1.5).

mirror on the wall looking back at Cy. The face reflected in the mirror visually echoes Joanie's appearance, looking straight into the camera (and at Cy); a window behind Joanie frames her head and shoulders as the mirror frames the reflection of the bathing woman. The third woman, sitting upright in the tub and to Joanie's immediate left, likewise doubles Joanie in her position and pose, sitting upright rather than reclining, head turned to face Cy. The two bathing women are positioned to mirror each other as well, facing in opposite directions but seeming to emerge from the same body. The visual tangle of bodies makes it difficult, at first glance, to tell how many women are in the room, to discern between what is real and what is reflected, and even to tell where one body ends and another begins (1.5).

If we interpret this image expressionistically, the scene suggests the fracturing of Joanie's identity, as if the women and the reflections in this scene represent her internal conflict—her self not just doubled but fragmented here into multiple parts. The homoeroticism of the scene is obvious, made more so by a long kiss between Joanie and one of the women, but the queerness of the scene is in the way this physical space is transformed into psychological space, to reveal visually and concretely Joanie's developing identity crisis.

Emotional Couplings in *Deadwood* 229

In the trial scene the positioning of Joanie and Eddie inside the "mirror" frames made by the support posts may similarly suggest that Joanie and Eddie are refracted images of Cy, parts of himself trying to separate themselves from his actions, but the image may tell us more about Joanie and Eddie—their enclosure by the wooden posts indicating how trapped they feel in the public roles that Cy forces them to perform. That they are not completely enclosed, that parts of their bodies bleed outside those wooden frames, suggests as well their desire to escape from the roles Cy has assigned them—and which each in his or her own way tries to do throughout the remainder of the season and the series.

After the deaths of Flora and Miles, Cy tells Joanie, "Your happiness is important to me. Whatever I got to do, if you're too much in my shadow, things too tough on you, we're going to stop it, do something else," and we believe that Cy will relinquish his control over her identity about as much as Joanie does (1.8). Joanie is not so much in Cy's shadow as she *is* Cy's shadow, as he has shaped her identity to reflect his philosophies and to advance his interests. The conflict in the episode arises when Joanie speaks for herself, when she resists acting as Cy's double, when she places an emotional attachment before the Bella Union's business operations. For the most part, though, they are enough alike that they even speak the same lines of dialogue. "You're not going to get out of here alive," Joanie tells Flora, and in a last attempt to protect her and warn her away from continuing her actions, "You're going to die here," a line that Cy repeats after Flora stabs him as a promise that he intends to keep rather than a warning. Particularly in the advice that she offers Flora and other women working in the Bella Union, Joanie often echoes Cy. So much does Cy see her as a part of himself that he literally speaks her part in several conversations. During the trial scene he comments sarcastically, "See, that upsets Joanie," and then, in a mockery of Joanie's voice, comments, "Oh, Cy, do up the boy. My God, I can't stand to see the other," before shifting back to his part of the conversation, "You want me to see to the boy, Joanie? Because you know that I'm clay in your hands" (1.8). He does the same thing on the balcony, staging a conversation in which he speaks both parts.

When she first enters the room, Cy tells Joanie to come over "here on what the dagos' call [his] sinister side" (as if he has another), and he ultimately forces her to double his sinister killing of Miles. Seen through Flora's damaged vision, the two characters almost blur together. This is Joanie as Cy has made her, a distorted self nearly indistinguishable from him. Because of the positioning of the two actors, with Cy slightly behind Joanie, his arms down at his side, Joanie's extended arm seems to merge with Cy's body, creating the visual illusion that the hand that clutches the gun has indeed become Cy's left hand, as Joanie performs the role of the left hand matching the act of violence the right hand has already committed. On the balcony later Cy tells Joanie, "You bring . . . warmth into my life. I can't bear to see you unhappy like this" (1.8). With Cy Joanie is always forced to be his other side, whether that's his "sinister side" or the side that desires "warmth." He doesn't see the contradiction of making Joanie both the repository for the warm emotions he must repress in order to project the appropriate public image and forcing her to coldly murder someone for the sake of making a public statement. The impossibility of performing those opposing roles is suggested by Joanie's comment on the balcony that her only escape is to kill Cy, to have Cy kill her, or to kill herself.

At the end of the episode, it is appropriate that she is the first person to notice Trixie's reentry into public space and her return (after her own suicide attempt) to her public identity as Al's whore, and perhaps in Trixie we see a foreshadowing of Joanie's own future troubles, the difficulty inherent in breaking free from "regimes of the normal."

If we can identify Joanie as a lesbian, as if such identity categories would necessarily mean anything to her, she becomes here a queer subject, her identity troubled, expelled from her own room ("That ain't my room anymore") by the events that took place there, her first experimental and performative act taking to the streets of Deadwood in search of another space where she can be more than a shadow self, in search of somewhere safe perhaps from male violence and violation (1.9). Joanie's initial flânerie through Deadwood, searching for a place to purchase, is not so much the idle saunter of the traditional flâneur taking in the city's lesser-known sights, but rather a troubling experience that quickly brings her to reminders of the recent traumatic past: the sight of Flora's dress in Wu's pigpen, the only remaining trace of the girl's presence.

Her disorientation is presented to us visually through a moving subjective camera that captures the street scene with fast blurred pans, the public space of the street serving to externalize her queer state of mind. As Désert writes, "Our cities and landscapes double as queer spaces" in part because the "squares, the streets, the civic centers, the malls, the highways are the place of fortuitous encounters and juxtapositions" (21–22). Joanie's experimental act, going alone into Deadwood's public space in search of a new life and a new identity, leads to a surprising and fortuitous encounter with Charlie, the first meeting with a man whose friendship and loyalty provides the foundation for other alliances that will eventually help her break away from Cy's "sinister side." Seldom the most comfortable of speakers, Charlie is the camp's best listener, the jail cell inside his public freight office doubling as a therapeutic private confessional for many of the show's characters. Early even in this first conversation, Joanie observes, "I was out of breath, but now I'm better," their mutual insecurities about their latest endeavors providing a comfortable point of association between them. Although Joanie still refers to herself as "just a whore," by making a new affiliation in the public thoroughfare, she begins to experiment with a new identity (1.9).

Joanie's lesbianism is expressed most often not through sexuality but through taking care of other women, helping them to bathe, offering advice on how to play the role of prostitute effectively, but that desire to "take care" of women is undermined by the debilitating effects of the role she prepares them to play. Her entry into Deadwood's public sphere as a business owner results not in self-fulfillment but in the violent death at the Chez Amis of three women she loves, murdered by Francis Walcott, an event that uncannily repeats and expands the violence that drove her from the Bella Union and sets her identity crisis once more into motion. Joanie remains a queer subject for much of season 3, refusing to enter the building she owns, living in the temporary space of a rented room, drawn inexorably back to the Bella Union, a place where she can't stay, her visits there marked by a hurried, almost frantic, pace.

However, in the public/private space of a rented room, made queer space by the same-sex couple that takes up residence there, Joanie takes care of Jane, gently bathing her, even kissing her. Although confronted by Shaughnessy's homophobic disapproval the next day, a couple has been formed that may be a lesbian couple rather than a "queer" one, with each finding in the other a way to stabilize her identity, experimenting with the possibility of making a place for herself rather than wandering through space that belongs to others (3.8). In the episode "Amateur Night," Jane and Joanie help escort the children from the Chez Amis to the new school. Civic duty (protecting children) provides a cover for Jane and Joanie, hands joined, to come out as a couple into the public space of Deadwood's main street. They enter the street no longer as wanderers but as citizens with a public purpose. Their handholding in the streets represents an appropriation of space for an act that is both public and private—a model that the children (each paired with another) behind them imitate as well as a mutual expression of private affiliation. At the end of season 1, we see two men together in bed (Reverend Smith in Al's killing embrace), and season 3's conclusion mirrors that scene with another same-sex couple in bed—two women this time, Jane and Joanie—their bed the only place of calm in the storm of public turmoil that surrounds Hearst's departure from Deadwood, and their embrace one not of death but of a new life together, warmed both by each other and by Bill Hickok's robe—a gift from Charlie Utter. This private emotional attachment does not seem to affect Deadwood public space so much as represent an escape from it, a path that many of the characters will follow as Hearst's consolidation efforts leave less room for mobility.

The counterpoint to Al's killing of Smith in season 1 is his murder of Jen at the end of season 3, another "gentle" murder (or at least that's the "something pretty" Al tells Johnny) motivated by both private feeling and public need. As Dan observes, "Right or wrong, you side with your feelings," and the private emotion that determines Al's course is for Trixie, whose life he saves by murdering Jen. The public display of Jen's corpse contrasts with the privacy of Smith's death. And whereas season 1 ends with a series of events that play out in public or that foreshadow future public actions (the killing of Clagett, Jewel's dance, the Bullock-Garret affair), season 3's conclusion reverses that movement by having the characters (often literally) turn away from public space. After Hearst's exit Cy turns away from the street in disgust and goes inside the Bella Union, leaving Leon's corpse on the balcony. Trixie and Sol move quickly across the street toward the privacy of their house. A loser in the election ("How do you think you might enjoy the private life?" Al asks), Seth turns and walks slowly away, his back to the camera, toward an uneasy and restless privacy, acknowledging to Charlie that "laying head to pillow and not confusing [himself] with a sucker" is "going to be a project tonight" (3.12). Only Farnum turns toward Deadwood's public space, stepping out of the hole in the wall of Hearst's vacated room, perhaps the only remaining character who believes in the illusion that he commands the public space he sees. Even Al is reduced to near immobility, alone in his office, his only motion that of scrubbing Jen's blood from the floor. Hearst's monopoly suggests that Deadwood's period of mobility is coming to an end, that the movement between private and public will be much more difficult, and that "queer" spaces will be harder to find. Only the coupling of Joanie and Jane suggests that the possibility of transgressive usages of space remains, even in the dominated public space of Hearst's Deadwood.

Notes

1. Two recent articles, Mark L. Berrettini's "No Law: *Deadwood* and the State" and Anne Helen Petersen's "'Whores and Other Feminists': Recovering *Deadwood*'s Unlikely Feminisms," similarly respond to this central dynamic within the narrative of *Deadwood*, although each article examines that dynamic through different interpretive frameworks than my

own, with Berrettini, for example, looking at *Deadwood* through the lens of the Althusserian notion of interpellation and what Berrettini calls "anti-interpellation." Particularly useful is Berrettini's analysis of the role of George Hearst in season 3 as representative of the State and the conflict generated by his effort to consolidate power within the camp as an allegory for the exercise of and resistance to State power. He suggests, "We might view the attempted resistance to consolidation as an attempted resistance to interpellation and to the production of subjects" (254). In particular *Deadwood* "situates Swearengen's and Bullock's pioneering spirit in relation to ideologies of law and order and as anti-interpellation" (254). However, the Althusserian framework seems to lead to a concept of society that too neatly divides into categories of the State and the resistant (or, conversely, subjected) individual, repeating a model of society that posits the public and the private as separate and opposing spheres. Thus the article doesn't account for the way that characters such as Swearengen can be both resistant to interpellation and at the same time "recruit" other individuals in order to constitute them as subjects, transforming individual women, for example, into a particular type of subject—whores—who are as "replaceable as subjects" for Swearengen as mine workers are for Hearst (254).

2. Anne Helen Petersen looks from a feminist perspective at the way the female characters in particular respond to such opposing pulls, observing, "*Deadwood* permits celebration of feminist progress but highlights the very real regression that takes place when we succumb to the pressures of society and capital" (269). In addition to providing an interesting allegorical reading of the series in terms of the historical progress of feminism, Petersen usefully discusses *Deadwood* as a revisionist Western in terms of its more realistic and complex portrayals of the genre's dominant female character types, the prostitute and "the Victorian Woman," who, "like the whore, is consistently stereotyped" in the traditional Western (273). Whereas in the "fictitious land of screen and page, the Western prostitute is romanticized, renamed, and refigured," *Deadwood* alternately "presents the harsh reality of life as a prostitute [but also] opens the narrative to allow these women to explore their sexuality, the potential for love, and the perils of sudden emancipation, but never in a manner that unrealistically elides their past" (269, 275).

11 Who Put the Gun into the Whore's Hand?
Disability in *Deadwood*

Nicole Tonkovich

Like Michael K. Johnson, Nicole Tonkovich focuses on issues of mobility and imagines a "fuller life" for the character of Jewel, certainly one of the "diverse bodies" whom Linda Mizejewski mentions, but she does so through the lens of disability studies. What she calls "the sheer profusion of maladjusted, diseased, and wounded bodies in the series" confronts every viewer, and Tonkovich offers a more nuanced and compassionate way to make sense of them beyond Milch's obvious interest in the grotesque. She argues that Deadwood *develops its characters into complex subjects, "depend[ing] in large part on discourses of disability" to effect that transformation. As Tonkovich explores the "narrative arc of the three-season drama," she demonstrates how "learning to live with the presence of incurable disability coalesces otherwise self-regarding individuals into a community." As Johnson points out the parallels between Trixie's and Jewel's stories, Tonkovich notes that Tolliver's treatment of the plague-ridden Andy Cramed parallels the Reverend Smith's thematically crucial sermon about when one "member suffer[s], all the members suffer with it" (1.5). She concludes that "how the community ultimately deals with its suffering members is a measure of Deadwood's evolution," finding in many instances an "ethic of care" within* Deadwood.

From Gunsmoke *to both versions of* True Grit *to the more recent* 3:10 to Yuma, *from the arthritic retired marshal in* High Noon *to the legless beggar in* The Good, the Bad, and the Ugly *to the tin-nosed villain in* Cat Ballou, *physical disability has long been an underrecognized element of the Western. But instead of simply measuring the representation of Jewel against this history, Tonkovich undertakes a critically more illuminating task. Borrowing a term from disability studies but also elaborating on it, Tonkovich considers how a character can "serve as a narrative prosthesis," making the case most extensively about a critically overlooked character who is usually "part of a back-*

ground tableau," *Jewel.* Played by actress Geri Jewell, herself disabled, Jewel helps to recuperate other characters, but Tonkovich also forcefully argues that far from being "abject," she "enjoys a greater degree of health than almost any other woman in the series," that she is "active, self-directed, clear-sighted, not addicted to opium to dull her pain," that "she offers pointed ripostes that mark her as smart, sassy, and an efficacious speaker." Onscreen and off, Jewel asks "us to join her in the dance of an enlarged reality."

Disability is perhaps the essential characteristic of being human.
ROSEMARIE GARLAND-THOMSON, "Integrating Disability"

Al Swearengen is introduced to the viewers of *Deadwood* as he is in the process of fleecing Ellsworth, a prospector working a paying claim and drinking away his profits at the Gem Saloon. Their transaction is interrupted by a gunshot, and Swearengen shouts, "That's her derringer! I warned you about that loopy cunt!" Upstairs Swearengen's mistress, Trixie, has just shot an abusive trick through the head, and he lies dying, propped against the wall. The doctor arrives, the john dies, and Swearengen buys the doctor's complicity: "Doc, you drink free today. And I hope any word of this would keep the gun out of the whore's hand." As he storms out, dragging Trixie, Swearengen instructs, "Get the gimp to clean this place up" (1.1).

The scene that follows establishes that Swearengen is a "conniving, heavy-thumbed motherfucker," as Ellsworth has noted, and a vile and abusive pimp. "You don't shoot nobody, 'cause that's bad for my business and bad for the camp's reputation," he growls at Trixie. Then, tenderly, he takes her bruised face between his hands and croons, "He beat the living shit out of you, didn't he?" Knowing that his solicitude is merely a prelude to violence, Trixie pleads, "Do what you gotta do to me." Swearengen erupts, shouting, "Don't tell me what to do," and throws her against the wall. As she falls to the floor, he puts his boot to her throat, beginning to strangle her. Nearly voiceless, Trixie yields, gasping, "I'll be good" (1.1). This set of initial interconnected episodes introduces a set of themes—violence, greed, dishonesty, and sexual abuse—and a set of main characters who seem at first to be stereotypical: Ellsworth, the decent miner; Trixie, the vulnerable prostitute; Jewel, the as-yet-invisible "gimp" who mothers the prostitutes and their pimp; and Swearengen, whose implacable cruelty establishes his domain in this lawless territory. Acknowledging the stereotypes of Western storytelling, *Deadwood* then inverts them, fleshing out the two-dimensional image of the violent West by developing its characters into complex subjects. This transformation depends in large part on discourses of disability. A notable feature of *Deadwood* is the transformation of Swearengen from a violent, fearsome, and repulsive bully into a more complicated human being—still violent, to be sure, but also compassionate, flawed, and charismatically complex: "a very good man with none of the behaviors of goodness" (Milch, *Deadwood* 17). In this essay I explore the interrelationship of Swearengen's transformation, the narrative arc of the three-season drama, and the importance of the one minor character who is central to these developments: Jewel, the Gem's housekeeper.

After several intervening scenes we return to Trixie's story. This second scene opens with the juxtaposition of women's bodies. The viewer shares Jewel's point of view: Her back is toward the camera and her fully clothed right shoulder fills the left side of the screen. Following the line of her raised left arm, we see that she holds a feather duster that tickles the surface of a framed black-and-white photograph of a woman with her back to the camera, a reclining nude. Jewel is clothed and clearly at work; the woman in the photograph is preparing for work even in her apparent repose. Both seem oblivious to being watched. As the scene develops, a third working woman—Trixie—joins these two: partially clad and, seen in a tight close-up, bruised and battered. Together, Trixie and Jewel give the lie to the pornographic photograph, which depends on the fiction of the whole, desirable, sexualized, willing, and accessible womanly body.[1]

In a series where verbal mastery is a signifier of power, the constrained speech of these three women suggests the obstacles each faces in the outlaw spaces of Deadwood. In her silence the reclining nude offers no denial to the masculine fantasy that her photograph purveys. Below stands Trixie, who has just been beaten by a man who has refused to pay for her services; she has then been choked, muted, and nearly killed by the man who owns her. Opposite stands Jewel, whose hesitant and slurred speech echoes the physical limitations apparent upon her small and contorted body. Nevertheless, Trixie turns to Jewel for help, pressing a cameo brooch—another image of a silent and idealized woman—into her hand, urgently demanding, "I need another gun" (1.1).

Of these women Jewel is most powerful. Although limited in speech and in movement, she is not immobilized by fear of physical harm or fantasies of beauty like those represented in the photograph. She immediately fulfills Trixie's request, although such an act logically endangers them both, should Swearengen discover their collusion. Curiously, he does not. When Trixie later yields the second derringer to him, Swearengen does not ask her how she obtained it. Nor does he suspect Jewel's complicity, for to Swearengen, preoccupied with controlling the economic and political affairs of Deadwood, Jewel is a momentary annoyance with a dragging leg, a distraction, whose work is necessary but should be done, as he puts it, "somewhere where I can't see you" (1.5). Viewers and critics of the series seem to have agreed. For example, in David Lavery's collection of essays on *Deadwood*, Jewel is named just four times, each time dismissively: as "grotesque" by Joseph Millichap (110); as "the crippled barmaid" by G. Christopher Williams (149); as "the crippled cleaning woman" by Kathleen E. R. Smith (86); and as the "physically crippled broom-pusher Jewel" by David Scott Diffrient (188). David Milch also uses the dismissive adjective to describe Jewel, speaking of her as "this crippled girl" (87) and as "the cripple Jewel" (*Deadwood* 181).[2]

Over the trajectory of *Deadwood*'s three seasons, this initial interchange, involving Jewel, Trixie, the cameo, and the derringer, develops into a centrally important narrative thread.[3] Each season alludes to this opening scene or retells it with minor variations that build upon its meaning. It unites concepts that drive the series: sexuality, the exchange of women, power, violence, and—perhaps less obviously but equally central—disability. It is disability that interests me here, particularly as it is embodied by Jewel, whose understated character nevertheless plays a crucial role in the series. Unlike Trixie, whose character develops continually over the thirty-six episodes, Jewel is infrequently seen, usually forming part of a background tableau, delivering coffee to Al, emptying his commode, scrubbing bloodstains from the Gem's floor. She is nevertheless a node of great power. In a community marked by digressions from the norm, populated with "wily misfits, dim-witted misfits, bloody-minded opportunists, gamblers with nothing to lose, abused abusers," she becomes the touchstone against which we measure Deadwood's evolution from lawlessness and cruel self-interest into a community mindful of the rule of law (Singer 192). By the end of the first season, she has served as a means of redemption for the flawed and suffering Doc Cochran and has helped to demonstrate the complexity of Al Swearengen, both of whom extend themselves to her "as fully in compassion as one human being can to another" (Milch, qtd. in Singer 192).

In this line of thinking, I am indebted to the work of several scholars whose work has demonstrated how centrally the representation of disability functions as a narrative prosthesis, defined by David T. Mitchell and Sharon L. Snyder as "a crutch upon which literary narratives lean for their representational power, disruptive potentiality, and analytical insight" (*Narrative Prosthesis* 49).[4] Plots may trace how a particular character has become disabled; characters develop in response to threatened, transient, or permanent disabilities; a narrative may follow a community's efforts (and/or failures) to normalize a disabled character. Fans of *Deadwood* will anticipate how these lines of theoretical reasoning manifest themselves in the series. Extending Mitchell and Snyder's critique of the uses of narrative prosthesis, I also recognize the uses of prosthesis as "an extension, an augmentation, and an enhancement" (Smith and Morra 2). I do not wish here to be uncritically celebratory of prosthetic possibilities, and my analysis will mark their limits even as it points to the activism that Jewel's character suggests. I conclude by arguing that the character of Jewel functions as a prosthesis that amplifies our understandings of disability by asking us to imagine a fuller life for her character, one that is not directly narrated but rather hinted at as *Deadwood*'s plot develops. As embodied by activist actress Geri Jewell, who ironically calls herself "the C. P. [cerebral palsy] Comic," Jewel is not a role Jewell leaves behind at the end of her working day (qtd. in Haber). Rather, she challenges viewers to think productively about how disability functions, not only in film but also in historical narration and in the world.

"The Healing Powers of Obstinacy"

Within Deadwood, even God, if he exists, is disabled, as Doc Cochran makes clear as he attends to the mortally wounded William Bullock: "I doubt he's omnipotent; I know he's myopic" (2.9). The sheer profusion of maladjusted, diseased, and wounded bodies in the series demonstrates a central claim of disability studies, that eventually everyone will become disabled.[5] Within the filmic world of *Deadwood*, one of the narrative functions of disability is to present an obstacle against which the strength of a character "proves out." As Swearengen lectures A. W. Merrick, "Pain or damage or despair don't end the world. . . . Stand it like a man and give some back" (2.7). Erin Hill notes "the sheer number of bodies and ailments displayed in the series [and] the diversity of purpose for which these ailments are put on view," tracing the "affliction" of bodies in Deadwood to larger metaphorical issues such as crises in the body politic. Yet in Hill's essay, which catalogs ailments "ranging . . . from toothaches to brain tumors," Jewel, a permanently "afflicted" member of this community, receives no analytical consideration (171).[6]

Seeking to remedy this omission while advancing Hill's insights, I argue that Jewel's presence in the series reminds us that disability has a temporal dimension. In *Deadwood*, as in life, disabilities are of several varieties: temporary setbacks, such as illness or a wound, whose surmounting tests the strength or weakness of an individual character; more grievous terminal afflictions that result in meaning-laden deaths; and permanent disabilities that have no apparent cure. These temporal distinctions carry ideological meanings, as Robert McRuer establishes. He astutely identifies the "neoliberal logic" by which disability functions in apparently sympathetic societies, arguing that "all disabilities . . . are essentially temporary, appearing only when, and as long as, they are necessary" (29). Their cure drives the narrative, establishes ableism as the desirable state of existence, and allows viewers to ignore serious and enduring disabilities, excluding them from normalcy.

Deadwood's approach to disability, however, is more complex. Temporary disability indeed celebrates the strength of character demanded to transcend it and restores normalcy. Terminal and permanent disabilities, however, demand more than sheer obstinacy for their amelioration: Learning to live with the presence of incurable disability coalesces otherwise self-regarding individuals into a community. Moreover, permanent disabilities such as Jewel's have the potential—both in the filmic world of *Deadwood* and in the lived world of its viewers—to "[resist] the demands of compulsory able-bodiedness" and to "imagine" a "public sphere where full participation is not contingent on an able body" (McRuer 30).

In the early episodes of *Deadwood*, which draw on the commonplaces of the Western heroic myth of invincibility and silent stoicism, temporary disability serves to establish characters' strength and bravery. For example, in the opening scene of the series, Seth Bullock's right arm is in a sling, for he has been shot in the shoulder by a horse thief. The injury seems neither to interfere with Bullock's writing in his journal nor with his hastening the death by hanging of the thief, to whose weight he adds his own, encircling the man's torso with his wounded arm and jerking him downward. By the time Bullock hops onto the back of Sol Star's wagon, headed for Deadwood, the sling has disappeared and he is again a whole man. Even the most powerful man in Deadwood becomes severely—but temporarily—disabled. Swearengen suffers a near-fatal stroke while trying to pass a kidney stone. His recovery is largely the result of his focused will. Restless at his confinement in bed and tired of "hearing secondhand news from imbeciles," he barks, "I want use of my fucking limbs." The scene continues:

DOC: It strike you as overweening, Al, settin' nature to a schedule?
AL: I'm not settin' terms for nature. I'm settin' them for myself.

DOC: Who has dominion over nature? Al Swearengen, owner and proprietor.
AL: As to when he takes his leave, you're A-1 fucking right. (2.5)

By the next episode Swearengen is standing on his balcony overlooking Deadwood's main thoroughfare. Cochran, observing him, proclaims, "You, Al, are an object lesson in the healing powers of obstinacy and a hostile disposition" (2.6).

The women of Deadwood are doubly disabled, coping with their own afflictions and serving as the receptacles of men's frustrations with their own real and imagined failures. The prostitutes, who comprise most of the town's population of women, routinely suffer venereal diseases; endure verbal, physical, emotional, and sexual abuse; and are subject to accidental or intentional drug overdoses, pregnancies, and abortions. Alma Garret is addicted to laudanum, which she uses to escape the pain of being married to a cruel coward. Calamity Jane, the freest and bravest of this feminine company, draws most of her courage from the bottle. Left alone with Sofia, whom Doc Cochran has asked her to protect, Jane is faced down by a merciless and cruel Swearengen, who has come to assess whether the child can identify those who massacred her family. Jane challenges him when he enters the room without knocking, shouting, "I ain't scared of nobody." Yet she is almost immediately cowed by Swearengen's threat, "If I take a knife to ya, you'll be scared worse and a long time dyin'" (1.2). Thereafter, she is unable to do more than to make incoherent and ineffectual verbal threats as Swearengen advances menacingly toward Sofia, pinches her arm, and learns that she is alive and recovering. As Swearengen turns to exit, he is silhouetted against the backlit window in the door of Cochran's rooms: The window, draped with a soiled white curtain roughly torn vertically, suggests violent sexual penetration, and hints that Jane has been a victim of sexual violence. She later sobs in Utter's arms, "He scared me, Charlie! I ain't been scared like that since I was a little girl" (1.2).[7]

Like the men in the series, women develop complexity of character as they overcome disability. Trixie and Joanie find ways to survive without Swearengen and Tolliver; Alma Garret, with Trixie's assistance, weans herself from laudanum and begins to take control of her sexuality and her wealth. Their stories suggest that for women, the ideologically plausible route to healing lies in caring for others. As Rosemarie Garland-Thomson has written of nineteenth-century sentimental fictions, "disability is interpreted as a lack that must be compensated for by . . . the 'benevolent maternalism' of . . . middle-class women" (*Extraordinary Bodies* 17). Anne Helen Petersen, however, notes that in *Deadwood* women discover that caring for one another breaks down the barriers of class, "[turns] whores into affectionate caretakers, [and transforms] masculinized cowgirls into affectionate nursemaids" (278). Thus Joanie and Jane nurse the wounded Mose Manuel; Alma, Trixie, Jane, and Joanie all care for Sofia; and Jane finds psychic release from her grief at the death of Hickok by nursing the plague victims.

Yet this ethic of care is not distributed according to gender in *Deadwood*: the Reverend Smith also attends to the plague victims, Bullock and Star protect Smith, Doc Cochran is responsible for all the ill and stricken characters, and as I will argue in some detail later in this essay, even Swearengen proves to be a compassionate caregiver. Merciful behavior, then, is a striking example of how narrative prosthesis functions: the compassion demanded of violent and powerful men becomes a measure of their fitness to survive as a community.

"There Should Be No Schism in the Body"

As Mitchell and Snyder astutely observe, in many classic narratives "disability is a metaphor of personal and social ruin" (*Narrative Prosthesis* 10). In *Deadwood* disability's intimations of mortality signal major shifts in plot direction. Although Swearengen wills his physical body to recover, throughout the series' second season, as Tolliver increasingly challenges his economic and political dominance, Swearengen begins to manifest symptoms of decay: He first reads with a magnifying glass, for example, and then dons glasses, his waning vision signaling his diminishing power. Early in season 3 George Hearst amputates the middle finger of Swearengen's dominant left hand—the hand with which Al has heretofore wielded his deadly knife. His visible and permanent wound—a metaphoric castration—shows the limits of "obstinacy and a hostile disposition" in the face of advancing capitalist "amalgamation and capital."[8]

The death of Wild Bill Hickok is as surely the result of the terminal disability of old age as it is of McCall's murderous insanity. Hickok, *Deadwood*'s closest approximation to a mythic hero, enters the camp lying in a darkened wagon, nursing a migraine headache, a pose and occupation more suggestive of a neurasthenic woman than of the holy terror his name invokes.[9] He is losing his eyesight, and he seems to have lost his nerve as well. His debilities receive remarkably little direct narrative explication; viewers must fill in the reasons for Hickok's drinking, gambling, and self-destructive behavior. He meets his death without struggle or resistance, demonstrating that not all disability is temporary and that force of will is not a universal antidote.

Hickok's death is a watershed moment, allowing the rule of law to be ushered by Bullock and Swearengen.[10] This transition requires both the legal redress of Hickok's murder and the amelioration of fratricidal strife in the larger community, a plotline carried out with continual reference to the Civil War. Deadwood seems to be on the verge of deadly conflict: the Gem Saloon and the Bella Union, situated opposite each other on the muddy thoroughfare, represent an economic competition that threatens the ultimate unity of the camp, and Tolliver seems uninterested in Swearengen's attempts to negotiate their "areas of overlap so [they're] not at each other's throats" (1.3). Swearengen and Bullock are locked in an irresolvable standoff concerning the rule of law in Deadwood, while the never-distant and ongoing crisis over the annexation of the Black Hills threatens to pit the cavalry against the miners and settlers of Deadwood. The arrival of a cavalry troop led by General Crook is signaled visually as a return of the repressed: we first see the soldiers through the eyes of Doc Cochran, who has just nursed Reverend Smith through a cataleptic episode and has been reminded thereby of battlefield carnage. As Cochran stands at his door, his eyes shaded against the bright daylight, the sound of horses draws his attention. From the rising dust a spectral sight emerges: men wearing Civil War uniforms ride before his eyes. They are not a hallucination but real soldiers who had once served in the Civil War and are now fighting the Indian wars. Although the function of this armed force should be, by one logic, to protect citizens from murderous Indians, the soldiers have—perversely it seems to Swearengen and his cohort—been charged to remove *them* from Dakota Territory, "by force if necessary" (Grafe and Horsted 158). In the final episode of season 1, the cavalry threatens to garrison in the town rather than "leave the camp to find its own way" (1.12).

These schisms, real and potential, echo the ongoing struggle of the nation at large to reunite following a war of brothers. Season 1 focuses on how community emerges from self-interested and murderous strife, a progression led by the most selfish, strongest, and potentially most dangerous of them all, Al Swearengen. Initially he opposes even the most rudimentary social order, arguing against prosecuting the murder of Hickok:

> We're illegal. Our whole goal is to get annexed to the United fuckin' States. We start holdin' trials, what's to keep the United States fuckin' Congress from sayin', "Oh, excuse us, we didn't realize you were a fuckin' sovereign community and nation out there. Where's your cocksucker's flag? Where's your fuckin' navy or the like? Maybe when we make our treaty with the Sioux we should treat you people like renegade fuckin' Indians. Deny your fuckin' gold and property claims. And hand everything over instead to our ne'er-do-well cousins and brothers-in-law." (1.5)

If holding trials and establishing a public system of justice is something Swearengen cannot yet contemplate, and if he cannot imagine the settlement of property claims as anything more than a familial dispute among distant relatives, he must nevertheless figure out how to mitigate the indiscriminate cruelty and senseless violence that has led to Hickok's murder. The resolution to this conundrum is effected through the stories of characters who would appear to be most at risk in the face of implacable self-interest: those with permanent and/or fatal disabilities.

The consequences of fratricidal strife are laid out in the sermon delivered by Reverend Smith at Hickok's funeral. Like many others in the camp, Smith suffers a debility—several debilities, in fact. At first, he is presented simply as a naive oddity, a "holy fool"; the potential humanity of other characters is established by the degree of their tolerance and respect for him.[11] Smith, a former battlefield nurse at the war's bloodiest battles of Shiloh and Manassas, begins the service with a figurative and a literal allusion to the Civil War: "Mr. Hickok will lie beside two brothers. One he likely killed, the other he killed for certain, and he's been killed now in turn. So much blood. And on the battlefields of the brother's war, I saw more blood than this. And asked then, after the purpose, and did not know. But know now to testify that, not knowing, I believe" (1.5). The speech that follows has been understood as "emblematic" of *Deadwood*'s first season (Singer 19; Peterson 274). Smith continues, "The body is not one member but many. . . . [Even] those members of the body which we think of as less honorable—all are necessary. He—he says that, there should be no schism in the body, but that the members should have the same care, one to another. And whether one member suffer, all the members suffer with it" (1.5). How the community ultimately deals with its suffering members is a measure of Deadwood's evolution. The seriousness of this theme is emphasized by this episode's parallel narration of how Tolliver treats Andy Cramed, his old friend and one of the first in Deadwood to be stricken with smallpox. As soon as Tolliver understands the nature of his friend's illness, he orders that Cramed be taken into the woods and left to suffer and die alone. Tolliver's actions establish him as one who will never be absorbed into the emerging unified community, while an ad hoc coalition of others, led by Swearengen, unites to dispel the epidemic's threat by publicizing it, sending for medicine, and establishing a hospital for quarantine and treatment. Among those who seem to be immune to the disease are Cochran; Jane, who discovers the delirious Cramed; and the Reverend Smith.

Smith's own increasing affliction soon compromises his usefulness as a nurse. Like Swearengen, Bullock, Tolliver, and others, who overcome their disabilities through force of will, Smith initially seeks to deny his affliction, thinking it to be temporary, perhaps "some sort of convulsion or seizure . . . brought on by irregular hours" (1.6). He thinks he might need glasses to correct his failing eyesight. Although he tries literally to follow Swearengen's prescription to "stand it like a man and give some back," his affliction is progressive and terminal. He believes he can smell his flesh rotting; he loses control of one arm, and his eyes become uncoordinated. Worst of all, as he tells Cochran, "Formerly . . . when the word took me as I read scripture, people felt God's presence through me and that was a great gift that I could give to them. Now the word does not take me when I read nor do I feel Christ's love. Nor do those who listen hear it through me" (1.9). Soon, in a darkly comic scene, he is shown preaching a demented sermon, whose text, "Circumcision . . . is indeed profiteth if thou keepest the law, but if, uh . . . if thou are a transgressor of the law, thy circumcision become uncircumcision," is elicited by his inspection of the genitalia of a yoke of oxen in Deadwood's main thoroughfare (1.11). His painful and slow decline demonstrates that his self-characterization as a "frail and feeble vessel" is distressingly literal (1.5).

Unlike Cramed, who is contagious, Smith presents no clear and present danger to anyone else in Deadwood. Thus he elicits a disinterested compassion from the strongest members of this community. Bullock and Star, although initially amused and annoyed by his ravings, nevertheless trust him to watch over their goods while they are away. Smith, in his turn, renders them his thanks as he concludes his sermon, "You've been so kind to me, a stranger. Many of us have asked being broken, how are we to live? Well, you took me into the body of the camp. 'I'm from Etobicoke, Ontario.' 'I'm from Vienna, Austria'" (1.5). As Star and Bullock come to realize that Smith's illness is terminal, their compassion increases. Later, as his illness intensifies, he confesses: "You are the absolute images of [Bullock and Star]. But what makes me afraid is I do not recognize you as my friends." They remind him, using his own words: "I'm from Etobicoke, Ontario." "I'm from Vienna, Austria" (1.10). Bullock and Star, surely not candidates for Christian salvation, nevertheless form the nucleus of a community that arises from the grave of Hickok.

Caring for Smith in his terminal illness, then, signals the community's potential to transcend the dark legacies of fraternal strife. The logical man to care for Smith is Doc Cochran, whose work as a battlefield doctor in the Civil War was met with "futility." As Milch writes, "He hears the screaming all the time, and so he feels that he's a failure" (*Deadwood* 181). Smith's decline thus poses a threat to Cochran. Diagnosing a brain tumor, the doctor becomes increasingly despondent, slipping into dissolute drunkenness yet willing to fulfill what Milch calls medicine's "pastoral" imperative: "*I will walk with you into whatever darkness awaits*" (*Deadwood* 192). Despite his propensity for grave robbing and dissecting corpses, Cochran refuses to consider euthanizing Smith. Knowing that he cannot cure Smith, knowing that he cannot even ease his suffering, Cochran does not abandon him but transfers him to the ministrations of Swearengen.

Less apparently (and more amusingly), Smith presents a potent threat to Swearengen as well. As he descends into imbecility, he quite literally enters Swearengen's territory, drawn by the Gem's new piano, which, he says, "relieves [his] headache." Although Smith "ain't been tryin' to lead no lost souls to the Lord" inside the saloon, Al frames his disruptive presence as an economic issue: "A man of the cloth slows business down" (1.10). Yet, as is often the case with Swearengen, a blustering claim of economic self-interest masks his fraternal impulses. Observing Smith's difficulty rising from his chair, Swearengen asks, "How you dealin' with the fits, huh?" and offering further, "Used to have a fuckin' brother given to that. We'd make pennies off it when it'd come on him in the street" (1.10).

Smith soon returns to sit at the center of a merry circle of half-clothed whores, who are cavorting to the tinkling piano, watched by Cochran, Trixie, and Jewel. This time Swearengen is notably cooler. He declares to Cochran, in a moment of supreme dramatic irony, "Well, he ain't comin' back in my joint. He's a fuckin' man of the cloth in case he forgets. Kickin' up his legs like a four-bit strumpet." At the same time, Swearengen and Cochran begin to strike an unspoken bargain. The doctor offers a key piece of information: He is now certain that "it's a tumor" causing Smith's seizures, aphasia, and loss of memory. "Nothin' to be done, huh?" Swearengen asks. "No," Cochran confirms (1.10).

Swearengen's responses to Smith's peccadilloes have nothing to do with his concern about the behaviors appropriate to "a man of the cloth," little to do with the Gem's losing business, and everything to do with his biography. Smith is the embodiment of Swearengen's dead brother, a reminder to Al of his own mortality.[12] Once he knows that Cochran cannot heal or relieve Smith, he acts. His euthanasia of Smith is in every sense a fratricide, but it is a murder set in deliberate contrast to McCall's slaughter of Wild Bill. By killing Smith Swearengen exorcises his own familial demons and establishes himself as one who can wield power over life and death in a compassionate and rational way. His godly qualities are emphasized by Cochran, whose prayer is interrupted by Swearengen's knock at his door. "It's your—your competition," Cochran mumbles (1.12).

Cochran arranges for Smith to be returned to Swearengen's "joint," knowing full well that Al will take the necessary action, a sequence emphasized by the juxtaposition of three crucial scenes. Back in his rooms Cochran prays: "Admitting my understanding's imperfection, trusting that you have a purpose, praying that you consider it served, I beg you to relent. Thy will be done, amen." Cut to the whores' rooms at the Gem, where Swearengen instructs Johnny Burns in the finer points of merciful death-dealing. Notably Swearengen does not use his usual prostheses—dope or the knife—but takes an intensely personal approach. This is, after all, a family matter. He picks up the cloth with which Trixie has been sponging the Reverend's brow, saying to Johnny, "You want to be a road agent? *Deal out death when called upon?* Make a proper seal, stop up the breath, apply pressure even and firm, like packin' a snowball." "You go now, brother," Swearengen murmurs as he smothers Smith (with love?) (1.12, emphasis mine). He then strokes Smith's face, closes his eyes, and folds his hands across his chest. Wiping his own eyes, Swearengen then marches immediately upstairs, where he watches with approval as his surrogate, Silas Adams, slits the throat of an extortionate territorial official, Magistrate Clagett. The sequence of these scenes cleanses Smith's death from any tinge of sentiment and demonstrates that Swearengen, who understands the correct use of murderous force, might be the appropriate man to oversee Deadwood's political future.

Smith's euthanasia thus functions as a narrative prosthesis. Too holy to live in the corrupt world, he dies that the community may live. His fatal disability is the means by which Swearengen's character is explicated, softened, and deepened. Swearengen's act shows mercy not only for Smith but also for Cochran, who has in effect commissioned him to perform the act he cannot do. Thereby Swearengen is transformed from a villain who, at *Deadwood*'s inception, would conspire to murder an innocent child into a compassionate friend and brother who murders, with merciful intent, an innocent but terminally damaged man of God.

"I'm as Nimble as a Forest Creature"

If Swearengen's disposal of the Reverend Smith demonstrates that he has learned the appropriate uses of lethal force, it offers little indication that his compassion extends beyond the demands of the moment. Nor does it heal Cochran, serving only to confirm his knowledge that, if Swearengen has the power to deal death, he, a doctor, lacks the power to save lives. Thus to complete the compassionate and salutary development of these two powerful but wounded men, a second and supplementary story of disability is narratively intertwined with Smith's, written on a body that bears a striking resemblance to his. Like Smith's, Jewel's body is contorted. Her extremities seem beyond her control, and her face is twisted into a permanent smile. Like Smith Jewel cannot be cured by Cochran. Her permanent affliction cannot be overcome through "obstinacy," nor is it terminal. As Cochran learns to embrace his pastoral responsibilities toward Jewel, she becomes his salvation. And in the second season of *Deadwood*, as Jewel's relation to Swearengen is amplified, the series advances a narrative guarantee that the changes in Deadwood, initiated by Hickok's death and rehearsed in

Swearengen's measured and controlled application of homicidal force, will become permanent.

Season 1's final episode opens with the delirious Smith hallucinating on a pallet in Cochran's rooms. He seems to be dictating a letter: "My darling wife, I have sixty-eight dollars put by. [panting] Our belly cleaveth to the earth. [panting] I hope to be home soon, Amanda. I'll help with the cider pressing. [groaning, seizure] Our soul is bowed down to the dust." It is productively unclear whom he addresses: he might be dictating a letter to his own beloved, as did Hickok before his death; he might also be hallucinating, echoing the words of the suffering soldiers for whom he acted as scribe as they dictated their final thoughts to their loved ones. Cochran hunches in the background, manufacturing a prosthetic brace for Jewel. He has heard these ravings before, as he later reminds God: "What conceivable godly use is his protracted suffering to you? . . . What conceivable godly use was the screaming of all those men? Did you, did you need to hear their death agonies to know your—your omnipotence? Mama! Mother, find my arm! Mommy! Mommy! Mommy they—they shot my leg off. It hurts so bad. It hurts so bad" (1.12). Cochran's bowed posture in this scene, mirrored later as he fits the prosthesis to Jewel's leg, invokes Christ's washing the feet of his disciples, a salvific humiliation that invokes Smith's sermon about the oneness of the body, to be demonstrated in acts of intimate care, for when Peter objected to Christ's washing his feet, Jesus reproved him, saying, "If I wash thee not, thou hast no part with me" (John 13:8).[13]

Jewel has asked Cochran to manufacture a brace like that illustrated in a book containing drawings and a photograph of reconstructive prostheses. Such devices, as David D. Yuan has established, were perfected in the aftermath of the Civil War in an effort to transform wounded veterans into "rehabilitated . . . citizen[s]" whose bodies "properly emblematized the body politic" (72).[14] As Cochran realizes what the book is, he recoils, exclaiming, "I don't read goddamn books on the Civil War. No. . . . I don't need to look. I was goddamn there." At first he refuses to help Jewel, his refusal stemming at least as much from his own fear that he might "fuck

[her] up" as from his concern for her welfare (1.11). But he eventually consents to help her in an effort to compensate for his inability to ease Smith's suffering.

Having euthanized Smith, Swearengen loads his body onto the Gem's sled and drags the corpse to Cochran's rooms, egregiously and mercifully lying by telling Doc that Smith, that "wily cocksucker," "waited" to "pass" "'til [he] got him off the sled" (1.12).[15] Visibly relieved but aware that his medical arts have been useless to Smith, Cochran announces his intent "to drink in" for the remainder of the evening. This Swearengen does not allow, insisting that the doctor return with him to the Gem to do his drinking. Leading him by the hand through the back door, Swearengen delivers him to the ministrations of Dan Dority. It is not whiskey at Dority's hand that reclaims Cochran, however, but a beaming Jewel, whose name echoes that of the saloon. Demanding to know how the new boot has affected her, the doctor asks her to "move around a bit." The piano is playing a waltz, and Jewel jubilantly invites Doc to "give [her] a whirl." He first refuses, but she insists: "I'll teach you how." In her simple offer we are asked to realize that although she has limited control of her legs and feet, Jewel knows how to dance. Having found a way to use her impaired body to express joy, she is willing to share this skill with Cochran. He embraces her in a shuffling waltz, a physical collaboration whose outcomes are much more affirmative than the parallel cooperation of Cochran and Swearengen in attending to Smith. At the same time, in Swearengen's office above, two sworn enemies face off in another cooperative enterprise, as Bullock, ignoring Clagett's blood on the floor between them, agrees to "be the fuckin' Sheriff," an office that Swearengen now agrees is necessary—and that must be filled by his nemesis—in order to ensure the rule of law in Deadwood (1.12).

As the scene closes, Jewel and Doc dance to "Green Grow the Lilacs," a tune that recalls Walt Whitman's Civil War elegy, "When Lilacs Last in the Dooryard Bloomed."[16] In the final conversational interchange of these two damaged characters, Jewel offers Doc an instructive simile: "Say 'I'm nimble as a forest creature,'" she commands. Thinking she is speaking of herself, he replies, "You're nimble as a forest creature." She corrects him: "No, say it about yourself" (1.12). He complies, in the saying and in the act of dancing realizing that his salvation consists in "nimble" adjustments to the contingencies of mortality and in meaningful connections to damaged survivors in an emergent community. Above, from his balcony, Al looks on.

The "Loopy Cunt" and the "Nine-Cent Whore"

An enterprise that depends heavily on visual prosthesis, *Deadwood* both labors to approximate historical realism and warns its viewers against simple credulity. Two sets of contrasting tropes signal the oscillation: the juxtaposition of photographic and filmic realism and lived reality, and the contrast of characters played by actors whose disabilities are feigned and temporary and the character of Jewel, whose disability is permanent, and who is played by Geri Jewell, a disabled performer. This permeable boundary between dramatic artifice and lived reality suggests another, more productive dimension of prosthesis: as "an extension, an augmentation, and an enhancement" (Smith and Morra 2). The conflation of Jewel and Jewell thus may lead us to imagine productive dimensions of difference that extend beyond the imaginary world of Deadwood.

"Jewel's Boot Is Made for Walking" begins with the image of her feet struggling through Deadwood's infamously foul streets. She carries a book, and her labored journey mirrors an earlier scene in which Smith drags his paralyzed leg through these same streets, clutching his Bible. She loses her balance and falls into a particularly disgusting puddle; no one on the crowded street offers to help her stand. This scene is one of the few times we see Jewel outside the protective walls of the Gem Saloon, and thus marks the degree to which viewers may assume that her disability has limited her mobility. Cochran's reaction to seeing her at his door echoes that misprision. Seeing her in what seems to him to be a zone of danger, he offers her supportive pity. He assumes that Swearengen has sent her: "Who's sick? What's he doin' makin' you walk to tell me?" Jewel's answer makes it clear that she has not been sent; no one has helped her walk the muddy street, and no one has insisted that she rehabilitate herself. While it is never clear how much Jewel expects of the prosthetic brace she wants Cochran to make for her, it is apparent that she does not expect a miracle. She merely hopes that "it'll help [her] walk better" (1.11).

Cochran, anxious not to fail again, delivers a lecture that signals the limits of visual prosthesis: "For your information, Jewel, that boy in the drawing was goddamn able-bodied before he got his leg shot up, not born with difficulties and hardships that got no cure and took from you the coordination a brace like that would require." While the images in the book Jewel has found show braced legs, they do not show full bodies. Nor does the photograph provide the narrative content that Cochran supplies: the prosthesis offers a support, an extension, or a brace, but it is neither a cure nor a resolution. The outcomes of prosthesis depend on a fuller story—on context, cause and effect, resistant and productive imagination. Cochran's ultimate response is to use the images as a suggestion, not as a prescription, and to construct for Jewel a prosthesis that is adapted to her stature and needs. While it cannot cure her, it can increase her mobility.

In a later scene Cochran comes to show Jewel his drawings for the device. Their conversation takes place in the whores' quarters, where once again Jewel's body is presented in contrast to an idealized black-and-white photograph. In this image sits a woman with her skirt pulled above her waist. Her legs are crossed jauntily, and tight white bloomers emphasize the wholeness and beauty of her legs, hips, and buttocks. Cochran shows Jewel his drawings but warns her again that prosthetic devices have potentially dangerous effects: "To interfere, even with the best of intentions and have you misjudge your capacities 'cause you rely on some mechanical contraption and wind up hurting yourself, would be a poor use, indeed, of my very limited skills. . . . I do not want to fuck you up." With heavy irony Jewel replies: "No, we wouldn't want that." Notably, Cochran's plans are not prescriptive but cooperative. He says, "Different from the . . . harness-type attachments in that Civil War book, I thought *we* might try something like this." Jewel replies simply: "*Let's*" (1.11, emphases mine).

21. Jewel with Doc. "Jewel's Boot Is Made for Walking" (*Deadwood* 1.11).

In once again placing Jewel below an idealized photograph, this scene enjoins viewers imaginatively to expand the limits of her on-screen role. It asks us to read beyond the stereotypical and limited assumptions about disability: that disabled people are limited in mobility and imagination, that they are asexual, and that they must wait for help rather than act as collaborators. It turns our attention, as well, to Jewel's limited but resonant functions within the minor scenes in which she plays. Her work, although abjected, is not feminized, for every function Jewel performs is also done by male characters: She cooks (as does E. B. Farnum); she sweeps (as does Miles); she brings Al his coffee (as does Dority); she scrubs bloodstains (as does Swearengen). Like Johnny she serves peaches to visiting dignitaries, even adding "unauthorized cinnamon" (3.7). It could also be argued that Jewel enjoys a greater degree of health than almost any other woman in the series. Were she a woman of higher social class, supported by a wealthy family, she might take to her bed, perform neurasthenia, and write herself into subjectivity.[17] An orphan, lacking these supports, Jewel is nevertheless active, self-directed, clear-sighted, not addicted to opium to dull her pain. The prosthetic brace is her idea: "I came here on my own," she tells Cochran (1.11). Her choices resemble those taken by Alma, Joanie, and Trixie, whose characters develop as they claim agency over their own bodies.

Although Jewel's halting speech is the antithesis of the profane oratory Deadwood values, she offers pointed ripostes that mark her as smart, sassy, and an efficacious speaker. While Burns and Dority, two capable, armed men, hover in futile confusion about whether to allow Cochran to see the dangerously ill Swearengen, barricaded behind his locked office door, Jewel spurs them to action, shouting, "Dan! You need to fucking break the door down" (2.3). Lest the significance of this verbal performance be overlooked, Jewel recounts the incident to Al in a later moment, as all those who have cared for him hover over his recovering body (2.5). Soon Swearengen has regained enough strength slowly to descend the stairs and resume his position downstairs in the saloon. Jewel, sweeping nearby, snarkily remarks, "God, he's always draggin' that fuckin' leg." Her taunt emphasizes their mutual condition. Significantly, she does not make it in private but at a crucial moment for the recovering Swearengen and in the full hearing of Tolliver, who waits at the bar. Swearengen ignores Jewel, engaging Tolliver's less damaging observation that he is "movin' somewhat rheumatic," with the reply that it's the "early morning fuckin' chill" (2.7).

Swearengen's disregard of Jewel is perhaps to be expected of a man who must attend to larger concerns of money and power. In his preoccupation he quite literally does not see her as she leaves the Gem to visit Cochran. Jewel's movements are reported to him by Trixie, his spy, who is looking out the window one morning. Having learned that Jewel has left the Gem, he cannot imagine why and twice thereafter asks her where she has gone. The first time, when he asks, "Where the fuck were you?" she replies, "At the Doc." His only response is, "Fix me a cup of coffee." Later, however, he asks again, more pointedly: "What was your purpose at the Doc's?" She flippantly retorts, "I'm knocked up." While the rejoinder is clever and funny, it reminds us, as well, that a major and important function of Jewel's "gimp sense of humor" is to assert her sexuality (1.11).[18] Her retort challenges Swearengen and viewers alike to acknowledge their limited understanding of her character.

To come to a fuller understanding of Jewel, we must first identify her dual functions: in the classic mode of narrative prosthesis, she acts as a prop or crutch by which Swearengen's humanity is established. In an amplified sense of the term, she expands, augments, and enhances viewers' understanding of disability (Smith and Morra 2). Arguably, the degree of Swearengen's development—from despicable violence at the beginning of season 1 to a more humane subjectivity, established by the middle of the series—is due in large part to his relationship to Jewel. Swearengen has purchased most of the Gem's workers, including Jewel, from "Mrs. fat ass fuckin' Anderson," the owner of a Chicago orphanage where he was abandoned by his mother (1.11). Yet—and this is a centrally important point—Swearengen does not sell Jewel into prostitution, although she clearly would be a commodity in Deadwood, where "strange" is often the signal for illicit sex. For example, Joanie propositions the ailing Cramed, asking him, "You ready to meet some strange?" (1.4). "I'd go with the strangeness, boys," Tolliver advises Leon and Con Stapleton as they try to jumpstart their Chinese brothel. "Take it head on, turn it to your fuckin' advantage" (2.7).

Trixie correctly but incompletely reads Swearengen's relationship to Jewel. Defending him against Jane's charge that "he had a design to murder that little one," she counters, "Far as it fucking goes, he also brought the cripple from that orphanage," explaining that he does *not* keep Jewel "around against some hoople-head only having nine cents and wanting a piece of pussy. . . . Why she's around is . . . it's his sick fucking way of protectin' her." While this fact does indeed demonstrate the complexity of Al's character, balancing "entries on both sides of the fucking ledger," Trixie's account overlooks how necessary Jewel is to Al (2.3). And that necessity stems from the fact that Swearengen cannot—literally and figuratively—see Jewel as a sexual being. As he tells Cochran, "She told me she was knocked up, but I assumed that was her gimp sense of humor" (1.11).

If the seizures of Reverend Smith have conjured up Swearengen's repressed brother, it is an occasional memory, perhaps exorcized when Smith dies. Jewel, on the other hand, is a daily presence who reminds Swearengen of his past, an abject necessity whose presence he strives to overlook (McShane, audio commentary 1.12). His determination not to see her points specifically to details of his own history that he needs to repress. Jewel knows Swearengen even more intimately than does Trixie. She lives in the Gem, cooks and serves his food, and empties his piss pot; thus she is the first to suspect his kidney stones, and she, more than he, tracks the increasing severity of his illness. Swearengen, all the while, can imagine that he is protecting her because she is a "cripple." Needing his protection, she poses no threat of abandoning him to go elsewhere to "[suck] cock for a living," as did his mother on the way to the "first gold rush" in Georgia decades earlier (Milch, *Deadwood* 26; "Imaginative").[19]

Thus Swearengen does not consider prostituting Jewel and is incapable even of imagining her as a sexual being. The narrative line of season 2's final episode returns to the matter of the "gun in the whore's hand," in the process presenting viewers with a vision of Jewel that is more nuanced than Swearengen's oedipally limited understanding. In season 1, even before she dons her prosthetic brace, Jewel has somehow obtained a derringer for Trixie. Now Trixie prepares to attend the wedding of Alma and Ellsworth. Tugging at the bodice of her new pink dress, she frets, "Stick me one more fuckin' time, Jewel, I'll drop you in a pool of fuckin' blood!" Smiling in reply, Jewel hands her the cameo, instructing: "Wear this." Trixie is shocked and amazed: "Devious fuckin' cripple, you are." Jewel grins. "How'd you pay that time then for the gun I sent you to buy?" Jewel's reply is classic "gimp humor": "Sold a piece of pussy" (2.12). If we accept her statement as irony, we remain as uncomprehending of the complexity of her character as is Swearengen. If we take the assertion literally, we are faced with two possibilities, since it is unclear whether Jewel sold herself for sex or brokered the sale of someone else. In either case she asserts her own value: To have bought a derringer, the "pussy" she has sold—her own or someone else's—is clearly worth more than nine cents. Her retort establishes her as another broker of sex and of power in Deadwood. The homology of this episode with the first season is sealed with the concluding scene, in which Jewel and Doc Cochran once again dance in the Gem. The repetition asks for a further attention to Jewel's mobility, for we recall that it is Jewel who has taught Doc how to dance and how to be "nimble."

In the grim events of the third and final season of *Deadwood*, the protagonists who are our usual figures for power and violence become progressively weakened and emasculated. Seth Bullock is powerless to avenge the death of his stepson William. Cy Tolliver spends much of the season abed, recovering from a stab wound in his lower abdomen; George Hearst has arrived and symbolically castrated Swearengen; Bullock's attempts to use socially sanctioned democratic processes are subverted by Hearst's machinations. None of these strong and violent men seems able or willing to dispatch Hearst, knowing that he will only be replaced by a horde of others like him. Yet the season ends with violence to Hearst and his (likely temporary) expulsion from Deadwood. This violence comes at the hand of a woman, a "loopy cunt" armed with the very derringer for which Jewel has "sold a piece of pussy."[20] Present or absent, Jewel's off-screen actions thus prove central to the narrative arc of the series. Al's initial request to Doc, to "keep the gun out of the whore's hand," has been overruled, and Trixie does what no one else in Deadwood can: she confronts and tries to kill Hearst. Her act jolts the masculine community into unified action, this time in a scapegoating ritual wherein the prostitute Jen is substituted for Trixie to appease Hearst's wrath.

Once more, in the season's concluding episode, the initial cluster of symbols is invoked. Trixie has another abusive trick, this time one who has damaged the entire community. Al, still concerned for "the camp's reputation," must punish the deed (1.1). Exercising a rationalized control over life and death, he decides to spare Trixie, notably because she has shown compassion toward him in his disability: "What's the fucking alternative?" he soliloquizes. "I ain't fuckin' killing her that sat nights with me sick and taking slaps to her mug that were some less than fucking fair" (3.12). Al's sacrifice of Jen occurs off-screen, but it is important to probe beyond the

22. Al in his office. "Tell Him Something Pretty" (*Deadwood* 3.12).

televised narration to imagine the act. It happens in his office, under a black-and-white photograph of a woman clad in a low-cut evening gown, her skirt hiked above her knees, and her legs revealingly spread. Hung above Swearengen's desk, it is the visual equivalent of a thought balloon, spelling out what the man thinks about as he sits there. As I have suggested throughout this essay, the pornographic images that adorn the walls of the Gem and the Bella Union mark the distance between sexual fantasy and the grimmer realities of sex for hire. While the faux oil paintings of the Bella Union (most notably *The Naked Maja*) signal its higher class of fantasy in contrast to the grittier and more realistic black-and-white photographs that hang in the Gem, both highlight the disjunction between pictorial realism and the system of economic exchanges that such realism engenders.

Al reverts to his old methods, slitting Jen's throat. The act is a direct echo of his initial threat to silence Trixie, as he stands with his boot to her throat. To ensure that the prosthetic substitution of Jen for Trixie will convince Hearst that justice has been served, Jen must be dressed in Trixie's clothing. Trixie completes the task, dresses Jen's body, and, as a final act, pins the cameo brooch to Jen's bosom. The substitution of one whore for another depends on a kind of mascu-

23. Preparing Jen's body. "Tell Him Something Pretty" (*Deadwood* 3.12).

line blindness, a limited and stereotypical vision that does not look beyond setting and costume. This final episode is emblematic of *Deadwood*'s simultaneous skill at effecting these manipulations while directing its viewers to use their imaginations to probe its limits.

"Difficulties and Hardships That Got No Cure"

The final episodes of season 1 emphasize the functions and the limits of prostheses, small and large. The title of episode 11, "Jewel's Boot Is Made for Walking," suggests the expansive promise of prosthetic enhancements, setting the boot in contrast to Jewel's former prosthesis, a broom. "Set your broom to one side and sit down," Cochran commands her. "I said put your broom aside." She answers jokingly, "You have to remove it from my clutches" (1.12). The brief interchange emphasizes both the potential of mobility and the stubborn fact that the prosthesis does not "cure" her paralysis. Jewel's broom stands in ironic contrast to the cane carried by the fashionable and dandified Otis Russell, Alma's father. His prosthesis is apparently more for show than for function, since he appears to need it only as an external manifestation of a masculinity he fears he lacks. Other prostheses join the broom and the cane in these episodes, more pointedly critiquing the uses of the scopic and the visual, asking us to mark the artifices that produce the effect of realism (Russell's cane) and to supplement that artifact with our own resistant imaginings (of, say, Jewel's off-camera peregrinations).

For example, the telegraph arrives in Deadwood, speeding the arrival of legitimate news but also allowing gossip and disinformation to circulate indiscriminately. As Clagett reminds Swearengen, "You can't murder an order or the telegraph that transmitted it" (1.12). Merrick buys a camera, an "American Optical back-focus single swing with a Meyer-Gorlitz trio plan 210 millimeter lens. The finest photographic apparatus manufactured in this country." His bumbling attempts to manage the device humorously mark the limits of a technology that, like Merrick himself, is sterile and of limited effect. (He routinely sets off the flash powder before he opens the shutter.) He goes to great lengths to arrange his subjects to yield appropriately dignified versions of what he hopes will be remembered as authentic history. For example, as E. B. Farnum is sworn in as mayor and Tom Nuttall as sheriff, Merrick calls for a second version of the image, a less "candid moment" for which Nuttall should remove "that putrid apron around [his] midsection" (1.11). Likewise, Merrick arranges an image of General Crook and his staff to exclude Burns, whose presence in the image is not sufficiently heroic, "stern and resolute" (1.12).

Merrick's efforts to control the posing, composition, and expressions of the cavalry heroes in his photograph, coupled with Cochran's earlier warning to Jewel about the limits of the photographic illustrations published in her book, is reinforced again and again in these episodes. The corrupt Clagett, introducing Crook to Swearengen, speaks effusively, if ironically, of Crook's "bear[ing] victory's garland for having routed the Minneconjous at Slim Buttes." Crook offers a counternarrative, describing the engagement as "the first meeting out of recompense for the massacre at the Little Big Horn" (1.12). Neither calls it what it was: a massacre of Indian women and children, the implementation of the murderous scorched-earth policy that characterized Plains warfare. Here prior narratives of heroism and revenge determine the pose and framing of the photographically realistic image.

The emphasis on prosthetic enhancements in these episodes thus offers a cautionary tale about how literally we should take the truth of a television show dealing with mythic narratives—the gold rush, the settlement of the Black Hills, a gunfighter nation—a compelling drama whose care with "extremely accurate" props is intended to produce a "seamless melding" of fictional and historical worlds ("Making Deadwood"). *Deadwood*'s affiliated marketing products—DVDs, fan websites, and the accompanying book authored by Milch, all promote and exploit the series' authenticity. Black-and-white or sepia-toned photographs of its stars, blurred and damaged to approximate the appearance of nineteenth-century photographic portraits, share the pages of *Deadwood: Stories of the Black Hills* with nineteenth-century images provided by the Adams Museum and House in present-day Deadwood. "The Real Deadwood," a "bonus feature" repeated in all three DVD sets, narrates the factual history of the Deadwood gold rush, illustrating it with shots of *Deadwood*'s costumed and made-up series characters. Other such "bonus features" offer "behind the scenes" glimpses of the art of stagecraft, showing how T-shirt-clad twenty-first-century actors are transformed into nineteenth-century characters. ("Is that Alma Garret?" we gasp, seeing Molly Parker in jeans.) We watch with fascination as characters are dusted down with fullers' earth in an effort to make them look as if they had just emerged from a stagecoach or crawled out of the diggings ("The Wedding Celebration").

As characters and production staff comment on these transformations, they frequently marvel at Garret Dillahunt, who, with the aid of costume and prostheses, plays two stunningly different characters: Jack McCall in season 1 and Francis Wolcott in season 2. Makeup artist John Rizzo displays a photograph of the "real" Dillahunt in contrast to the character of Jack McCall ("Making Deadwood"). Dillahunt explains how he effected the physical transformation:

> There are some children who ask you a question and when you answer them, they look around at everything in the room except for you. That's part of what I was trying to do with Jack McCall.

> People described him as the ugliest man they'd ever seen. He had a crossed eye. I stuffed the tip of a baby bottle up one of my nostrils to make it deformed, as if his nose got broken and healed badly. (Milch, *Deadwood* 172)

Indeed, part of the fascination of Dillahunt's transformation involves the presence and absence of signifiers of disability. As McCall his physical deformity signals the moral blankness of his character; as Wolcott, however, his dandified, tidy, and altogether normal appearance adds horror to the great evil he embodies.

Follow-up interviews featuring Keith Carradine emphasize how closely his makeup for the series followed the apparent dress and physical appearance of Wild Bill Hickok. With Carradine Milch muses on the intermixing of historically verifiable characters with those invented for the narrative force of the series. His focus here is on Alma Garret, whose story seems crucial to the narrative arc of the series. Milch suggests that in introducing such characters, who lack identifiable historical referents, his "job [was] to be true to the character," noting, "If I've done that, then the viewer gets his or her chance to engage a larger reality than he might ordinarily recognize as reality" ("Making Deadwood").

This comment might fruitfully also apply to Jewel, for her character works in a doubled fashion to "engage a larger reality." Significantly, we do not see Geri Jewell's prosthetic transformation into a "gimp" in any of *Deadwood*'s special features. The homology between Geri Jewell in real life and Jewel, the character she performs in *Deadwood*, suggests that we should read her performance with a difference. Lacking a historical referent, her character can take a broader valence, reminding us of the heretofore erased presence of disabled characters in the historical record; expanding our imaginative understanding of that world as well as of the world of Deadwood.[21] Her simultaneous contemporary performance of disability is an absent presence on the screen: that is to say, we silently acknowledge to ourselves every time she appears that her disability is not the result of a makeup artist's skill. Jewell's physical condition persists after she has left the set. Jewel does not become "cured" over the course of the series. Acting as her own agent, she enlarges the vision of other characters within that filmic world. She cavorts nimbly as a forest animal through the nonvisual but absolutely necessary imaginary spaces of Deadwood, as she does in her life off the screen, asking us to join her in the dance of an enlarged reality, offscreen and in our present world.

Notes

1. Lennard J. Davis writes eloquently about "Nude Venuses" and disability: "In short, we cannot have Sharon Stone without Linda Hunt; we cannot have Tom Cruise without Ron Kovic; we cannot have the fantasy of the erotic femme fatale's body without having the sickened, disabled, deformed person's story testifying to the universal power of the human spirit to overcome adversity" (66).
2. These scholars seem unaware of the negative connotations of the dismissive adjective. According to Robert McRuer, "As an appropriation and revaluation of the derogatory term 'cripple,'" disability activists use the term "crip" (210n5). See also Linton 164–65.
3. Anne Helen Petersen also begins her essay with an analysis of this scene. After noting Trixie's abuse, Petersen immediately shifts her focus to Alma Garret, who is "obviously hopped up on dope," and declares, "Such is our dismal introduction to the women of *Deadwood*: as punching bags or as bored drug addicts" (267). Peterson does not include Jewel among "the women of *Deadwood*" in her essay.
4. See also the work of Robert McRuer, Michael Davidson, David Serlin, and Rosemarie Garland-Thompson (especially *Extraordinary Bodies*). For a productive exploration of the promises, possibilities, and threats of prosthesis as a figure that has "begun to assume an epic status that is out of proportion with its abilities to fulfill our ambitions for it," see the essays collected by Smith and Morra in *The Prosthetic Impulse* (Smith and Morra 2).
5. See, for example, Garland-Thomson, whose well-known quotation serves as epigraph to this paper. See also Davis, *Enforcing Normalcy* xv; and Davidson 118, among many others.
6. Disability, broadly defined, drives many a Western plot, as heroic protagonists overcome obstacles ranging from the physical to the psychological. *Permanently* disabled characters, such as Chester of *Gunsmoke*, are, however, usually relegated to the status of sidekick and played by so-called character actors. Because women's roles in typical Westerns are

limited, I consider the role of a permanently disabled woman to have special valence. Stella, the saloon keeper in Lawrence Kasdan's *Silverado*, for example, is a nod to *Gunsmoke*'s Miss Kitty, but Hunt's physical appearance helps mark *Silverado* as a hip—if respectful—parody of Western film stereotypes.

7. In the Deadwood Dick dime novel series, Calamity Jane is presented as a rape survivor. See, for example, *Deadwood Dick on Deck*, which establishes that Jane's "maiden name" has been defiled (Wheeler 174).
8. See Kyle Wiggins and David Holmberg for an extended analysis of this scene as a symbolic castration (288).
9. According to Robin Weigert, the backstory she was given for Wild Bill "said he's sort of a corpse in state already" (Milch, *Deadwood* 69). In season 3 George Hearst suffers an unnamed affliction that forces him to assume the same pose. See, for example, "Tell Your God to Ready for Blood," which presents Hearst supine on the floor behind his bed in a darkened room (3.1; see also 3.12).
10. According to Milch's audio commentary, "the death of Wild Bill Hickok allows Bullock to grow into manhood. It allows Deadwood to exist outside the shadow of Western myth." "Once Wild Bill Hickok dies, ... that's when the show can properly begin" (179, 201). Douglas L. Howard sees Hickok's death as the signal that "the days of frontier justice and street duels and lawmen maintaining order largely with their guns are over. . . . Bill allows himself to be killed . . . so that Bullock . . . can take over for him" (51; see also Howard 47).
11. Ian McShane calls Smith a "holy fool" at least twice in his audio commentary to "Sold under Sin" (1.12). Smith's function is taken over in the following seasons by Andy Cramed, who is a fool but not holy, and by Richardson, a grotesque and pagan fool.
12. In season 2's initial episodes, the bodily effects of Swearengen's stroke emphasize his fraternity with Smith: both are paralyzed on the right side of the body and walk only with difficulty, dragging a foot; each suffers a distortion of his face and eye. In fact, Cochran's description of the nearly dead Smith as he delivers him to Swearengen at the end of episode 11 anticipates Al's stroke: he is "damn near blind, mostly paralyzed, [and] past controlling his functions" (1.11).
13. Another near echo of this gesture is Trixie's care of Al's feet. In "Reconnoitering the Rim," she is shown "scraping Al's feet with a straight razor," and his first speech of the scene begins, "Trust. Hell of a way to operate, huh?" (1.3).
14. See also Mitchell and Snyder, *Narrative Prosthesis* 28. The so-called Palmer leg, introduced in the early 1860s, was a realistic prosthesis with a functioning knee joint, designed to replace the earlier simple peg legs.

Yuan's essay makes fascinating connections among the technologies of war that resulted in the increasing number of wounded soldiers needing such prostheses, the techniques of high-speed photography that enabled the design of an artificial limb that would mimic the processes of walking, and the rise of assembly-line manufacturing. For another insightful investigation of war, prosthesis, and industrial economies in the 1940s, see Serlin.

15. This is the only time Swearengen personally transports a dead body; more usually such tasks are left to Dan and Johnny. I thank Melody Graulich for this insight.
16. One of the many versions of the lyrics of this song is suggestive in the context of a season whose theme is fraternal reunion: "And change the green lilacs to the Red, White, and Blue."
17. See Natalie A. Dykstra's essay on Alice James's "[insistence] on a distance between what disabled her and what she understood to be her real life" (107).
18. As a motivational speaker in her off-camera career, Geri Jewell is noted for "her uncanny ability to captivate the hearts of her audiences by using humor to facilitate attitudinal change" ("Geri Jewell").
19. For a fuller examination of Swearengen's crucial explanation of his abandonment by his mother, which, significantly, occurs in the same episode as Jewel's receiving her prosthetic boot, see Akass.
20. In this episode from season 3, Al repeats the words with which he has described Trixie at the beginning of the series. I am indebted to Petersen for this insight (279).
21. According to Milch: "You don't create a character who could not live in that world" ("Imaginative Reality").

BIBLIOGRAPHY

Abbott, Carl. *How Cities Won the West: Four Centuries of Urban Change in Western North America.* Albuquerque: University of New Mexico Press, 2008.
Adams, James Luther, and Wilson Yates, eds. *The Grotesque in Art and Literature: Theological Reflections.* Grand Rapids MI: Wm. B. Eerdmans, 1997.
Adams, Ramon F. *Six-Guns and Saddle Leather: A Bibliography of Books and Pamphlets on Western Outlaws and Gunmen.* Norman: University of Oklahoma Press, 1969.
Agamben, Giorgio. *Homo Sacer: Sovereign Power and Bare Life.* Trans. Daniel Heller-Roazen. Palo Alto CA: Stanford University Press, 1998.
Akass, Kim. "Motherfucker: Al Swearengen's Oedipal Dilemma." Lavery 23–32.
Altman, Rick. *Film/Genre.* London: British Film Institute, 1999.
Austen, Jane. *Northanger Abbey.* 1818. London: Penguin, 1995.
Barra, Allen. "Goodbye *Deadwood*? David Milch Speaks Candidly about the Last Season of HBO's Hit Western Series." *True West* Dec. 2006: 18–22.
———. *Inventing Wyatt Earp: His Life and Many Legends.* New York: Carroll & Graf, 1998.
———. "The Man Who Made 'Deadwood.'" *American Heritage* June/July 2006: 50–55. Available online at http://www.americanheritage.com/entertainment/articles/web/20060608-deadwood-hbo-david-milch-television-westerns.shtml. Accessed May 15, 2007.
Bazin, André. *What Is Cinema?* 1971. Trans. Hugh Gray. Berkeley: University of California Press, 2005.
Benshoff, Harry M. *Monsters in the Closet: Homosexuality and the Horror Film.* Manchester: Manchester University Press, 1997.
Benz, Brad. "*Deadwood* and the English Language." *Great Plains Quarterly* 27.4 (Fall 2007): 239–51.
Berrettini, Mark L. "No Law: *Deadwood* and the State." *Great Plains Quarterly* 27.4 (Fall 2007): 253–65.
Bird, Robert Montgomery. *Nick of the Woods, or, Jibbenainosay; a tale of Kentucky.* 1837. New York: American Book, 1939.
Booth, Wayne. *The Rhetoric of Fiction.* Chicago: University of Chicago Press, 1961.

Botting, Fred. "Aftergothic: Consumption, Machines, and Black Holes." In *The Cambridge Companion to Gothic Fiction*. Ed. Jerrold E. Hogle. Cambridge: Cambridge University Press, 2002. 277–300
Brockway, Christi H. *Deadwood: The Complete Transcripts*. http://members.aol.com/chatarama/. Accessed Feb. 2, 2008.
Brooks, Cleanth, R. W. B. Lewis, and Robert Penn Warren. *American Literature: The Makers and the Making*. Vols. 1 and 2. New York: St. Martin's Press, 1973.
Brown, Norman O. *Life against Death*. 1959. Middletown CT: Wesleyan University Press, 1977.
Buffalo Girls. CBS-TV, 1995.
Burke, Kenneth. "Catharsis—Second View." *Centennial Review* 4 (1961): 107–32.
———. "Dramatism." *International Encyclopedia of the Social Sciences*. Vol. 7. Ed. David L. Sill. New York: MacMillan, 1968.
———. *Dramatism and Development*. Barre MA: Clark University Press, 1972.
———. *Essays toward a Symbolic of Motives, 1950–1955*. Ed. William H. Rueckert. West Lafayette IN: Parlor Press, 2007.
———. *A Grammar of Motives*. 1945. Berkeley: University of California Press, 1969.
———. *Language as Symbolic Action*. Berkeley: University of California, 1966.
———. "On Catharsis, or Resolution." *Kenyon Review* 21.3 (Summer 1959): 337–74.
Buscombe, Edward. *Stagecoach*. London: British Film Institute, 1992.
Butler, Judith. *Bodies That Matter: On the Discursive Limits of "Sex."* New York: Routledge, 1993.
Calamity Jane. Warner Brothers, 1953.
Caso, Maria. "Deadwood—Behind the Scenes: Star and Bullock Hardware." HBO. http://www.hbo.com/deadwood/behind/sets_and_costumes/sets_hardware.html. Accessed May 15, 2007.
Cassuto, Leonard. *Hard-Boiled Sentimentality: The Secret History of American Crime Stories*. New York: Columbia University Press, 2009.
Cawelti, John G. "The Gunfighter and the Hard-Boiled Dick: Some Ruminations on American Fantasies of Heroism." *American Studies* 16.2 (1975): 49–64. Rpt. in *Mystery, Violence, and Popular Culture*. Madison WI: Popular Press, 2004. 173–92.
Chandler, Raymond. "The Simple Art of Murder." *Atlantic Monthly* Dec. 1944: 53–59.
Charters, Samuel. *The Blues Makers*. New York: Da Capo Press, 1991.
Chisholm, Dianne. *Queer Constellations: Subcultural Space in the Wake of the City*. Minneapolis: University of Minnesota Press, 2005.
Cohen, Hubert. "'Men Have Tears in Them': The Other Cowboy Hero." *Journal of American Culture* 21.4 (Jan. 1, 1998): 57–78.

Comer, Krista. *Landscapes of the New West: Gender and Geography in Contemporary Women's Writing.* Chapel Hill: University of North Carolina Press, 1999.

———. "Literature, Gender Studies, and the New Western History." *Arizona Quarterly* 53.2 (Summer 1997): 99–134.

Cook, Nancy. "The Only Real Indians Are Western Ones: Authenticity, Regionalism, and Chief Buffalo Child Long Lance, or Sylvester Long." In Handley and Lewis 140–54.

Davidson, Michael. "Universal Design: The Work of Disability in an Age of Globalization." In *The Disability Studies Reader.* Ed. Lennard J. Davis. 2nd ed. New York: Routledge, 2006. 117–28.

Davis, Lennard. J. *Enforcing Normalcy: Disability, Deafness, and the Body.* London: Verso, 1995.

———. "Nude Venuses, Medusa's Body, and Phantom Limbs: Disability and Visuality." Mitchell and Snyder 51–70.

Deadwood. DVD. Exec. prod. David Milch, executive producer. 3 seasons, 18 DVDs. New York: HBO, 2004–6.

Deadwood: The Complete First Season. Exec. prod. David Milch. DVD. HBO, 2004.

Deadwood: The Complete Second Season. Exec. prod. David Milch. DVD. HBO, 2005.

Deadwood: The Complete Third Season. Exec. prod. David Milch. DVD. HBO, 2006.

"Deadwood Officials Want Historical Bricks Back." In *Sioux Falls Argus-Leader,* April 4, 1992: sec.3.

Dean, Janet. "Calamities of Convention in a Dime Novel Western." In *Scorned Literature: Essays on the History and Criticism of Popular Mass-Produced Fiction in America* Ed. Lydia Cushman Schurman and Deidre Johnson. Westport CT.: Greenwood, 2002. 37–50.

DeLamotte, Eugenia C. *Perils of the Night: A Feminist Study of Nineteenth-Century Gothic.* New York: Oxford University Press, 1990.

Denning, Michael. *Mechanic Accents: Dime Novels and Working-Class Culture in America.* London: Verso, 1987.

Derrida, Jacques. "Paper or Myself, You Know . . . : New Speculations on a Luxury of the Poor": Interview with Marc Guillaume and Daniel Bougnoux. Trans. Keith Reader. *Paragraph* 21.1 (Mar. 1998): 1–27.

———. "Signature Event Context." In *Margins of Philosophy.* Trans. Alan Bass. Chicago: University of Chicago Press, 1982. Chap. 10.

———. "The Voice That Keeps Silence." In *Speech and Phenomena.* Trans. David B. Allison. Evanston IL: Northwestern University Press, 1973. Chap. 6.

Désert, Jean-Ulrick. "Queer Space." In *Queers in Space: Communities, Public Places, Sites of Resistance.* Ed. Gordon Brent Ingram, Anne-Marie Bouthillette, and Yolanda Retter. Seattle: Bay Press, 1997. 17–26.

Dickens, Charles. *Bleak House.* 1853. New York: Penguin, 2006.
Diffrient, David Scott. "*Deadwood* Dick: The Western (Phallus) Reinvented." In Lavery 185–200.
Dimendberg, Edward. *Film Noir and the Spaces of Modernity.* Cambridge MA: Harvard University Press, 2004.
Drysdale, David. "'Laws and Every Other Damn Thing': Authority, Bad Faith, and the Unlikely Success of *Deadwood.*" In Lavery 133–44.
DuFran, Dora. *Low Down on Calamity Jane.* 1932. Stickney SD: Argus, 1981.
Dykstra, Natialie. A. "'Trying to Idle': Work and Disability in *The Diary of Alice James.*" In *The New Disability History: American Perspectives.* Ed. Paul K. Longmore and Lauri Umansky. New York: New York University Press, 2001. 107–31.
Fielder, Leslie A. *Love and Death in the American Novel.* New York: Criterion, 1960.
Franklin, Benjamin. *The Papers of Benjamin Franklin.* Vol. 1. Ed. Leonard W. Labaree. New Haven CT: Yale University Press, 1959.
Freud, Sigmund. *Civilization and Its Discontents.* 1929. Trans. James Strachey. New York: W. W. Norton, 1961.
Gage, Carolyn. Introduction to *The Second Coming of Joan of Arc and Selected Plays.* Denver: Outskirts Press, 2008. i–xvi.
Gardner, Erle Stanley. "Getting Away with Murder." *Atlantic* Jan. 1965: 72–75.
Garland-Thomson, Rosemarie. *Extraordinary Bodies: Figuring Physical Disability in American Culture and Literature.* New York: Columbia University Press, 1997.
———. "Integrating Disability, Transforming Feminist Theory." In *The Disability Studies Reader.* Ed. Lennard J. Davis. 2nd ed. New York: Routledge, 2006. 257–73.
"Geri Jewell: Entertainer, Comedienne Diversity Intelligence." Great Women Speak Their Minds. http://www.greatwomenspeakers.com/Pages/Ger-Jewell.htm. Accessed Apr. 18, 2009.
Gilbert, Sandra M., and Susan Gubar. *The Madwoman in the Attic: The Woman Writer and the Nineteenth-Century Literary Imagination.* New Haven CT: Yale University Press, 1984.
Girard, René. *Violence and the Sacred.* Trans. Patrick Gregory. Baltimore MD: Johns Hopkins University Press, 1977.
Grafe, Ernest, and Paul Horsted. *Exploring with Custer: The 1874 Black Hills Expedition.* Custer SD: Golden Valley Press, 2002.
Graulich, Melody. "What if Wister Were a Woman?" In *Reading* The Virginian *in the New West.* Ed. Melody Graulich and Stephen Tatum. Lincoln: University of Nebraska Press, 2004. 198–212.
Haber, Matt. "Jewell in the Rough: How Did Sweet Cousin Geri from 'The Facts of Life' End Up Cleaning Up after the Ruffians of 'Deadwood'?"

http://dir.salon.com/story/ent/tv/feature/2005/05/09/jewell/. Accessed Jan. 25, 2008.

Halberstam, Judith. *Female Masculinity.* Durham NC: Duke University Press, 1998.

———. "Not So Lonesome Cowboys: The Queer Western." In *The Brokeback Book: From Story to Cultural Phenomenon.* Ed. William R. Handley. Lincoln: University of Nebraska Press, 2011. 190–201.

Hall, Barbara. "BarbaraHall20's Channel." YouTube. YouTube, n.d. http://www.youtube.com/user/BarbaraHall20. Accessed Sept. 2, 2012.

Hall, Donald E. *Queer Theories.* New York: Palgrave MacMillan, 2003.

Hamilton, Cynthia S. *Western and Hard-Boiled Detective Fiction in America: From High Noon to Midnight.* Iowa City: University of Iowa Press, 1987.

Handley, William R. *Marriage, Violence, and the Nation in the American Literary West.* New York: Cambridge University Press, 2002.

Handley, William R., and Nathaniel Lewis. Introduction to *True West: Authenticity in the American West.* Lincoln: University of Nebraska Press, 2004. 1–17.

Havrilesky, Heather. "The Gory Finish." *Salon.com.* http://www.salon.com/ent/tv/review/2006/08/28/deadwood_finale/index.html. Accessed Aug. 28, 2006.

Hawthorne, Nathaniel. *The Blithedale Romance.* 1852. New York: Norton, 1978.

———. Preface by the Author. *The House of the Seven Gables: A Romance.* 1851. New York: New American Library, 1961. vii–ix.

Helberg, Michelle. "HBO's 'Deadwood' Makes Room for Lesbians." AfterEllen.com. 17, August 2006. http://www.afterellen.com/TV/2006/8/deadwood.html?page=0%2Co. Accessed Aug. 2, 2009.

Hill, Erin. "'What's Afflictin' You?': Corporeality, Body Crises and the Body Politic in Deadwood." In Lavery 171–84.

Holmlund, Chris. "When Is a Lesbian Not a Lesbian? The Lesbian Continuum and the Mainstream Femme Film." In *Impossible Bodies: Femininity and Masculinity at the Movies.* London: Routledge, 2002. 31–50.

Hooper, Johnson Jones. *Some Adventures of Captain Simon Suggs, Late of the Tallapoosa Volunteers; Together with "Taking the Census" and other Alabama Sketches.* Philadelphia: Carey & Hart, 1845.

"How Firm a Foundation." 1787. Words attributed to John Keith. *The Hymnal of the Protestant Episcopal Church in the United States of America.* Norwood MA: Plimpton Press, 1940. No. 564.

Howard, Douglas L. "Why Wild Bill Hickok Had to Die." In Lavery 43–56.

Hussain, Nasser. "Thresholds: Sovereignty and the Sacred." *Law & Society Review* 34.2 (2000): 495–515.

"An Imaginative Reality." Special feature. *Deadwood: The Complete First Season.* Disk 6.

Irigaray, Luce. "The Sex Which Is Not One." In *New French Feminisms*. Trans. and ed. Elaine Marks and Isabelle de Courtivron. New York: Schocken Books, 1981. Repr. in *Feminisms: An Anthology of Literary Theory and Criticism*. Ed. Robyn R. Warhol and Diane Price Herndl. New Brunswick NJ: Rutgers University Press, 1997. 363–69.

Irwin, John T. *Unless the Threat of Death Is behind Them: Hard-Boiled Fiction and Film Noir*. Baltimore MD: Johns Hopkins University Press, 2006.

Jacobs, Jason. "Al Swearengen, Philosopher King." In Lavery 12–21.

James, Henry. *The Art of Fiction*. 1907. New York: Scribner's, 1962.

———. *The Turn of the Screw*. 1898. New York: Signet Classic, 1995.

Johnson, Michael K. *Black Masculinity and the Frontier Myth in American Literature*. Norman: University of Oklahoma Press, 2002.

Johnson, Susan Lee. *Roaring Camp: The Social World of the California Gold Rush*. New York: Norton, 2000.

Kalinak, Kathryn. *How the West Was Sung: Music in the Westerns of John Ford*. Berkeley: University of California Press, 2007.

Kamir, Orit. "Honor and Dignity in the Film *Unforgiven*: Implications for Sociological Theory." *Law & Society Review* 40.1 (2006): 193–233.

Kellar, Kenneth C. *Seth Bullock: Frontier Marshal*. Aberdeen SD: North Plains Press, 1972.

Klein, Amanda Ann. "'The Horse Doesn't Get a Credit': The Foregrounding of Generic Syntax in *Deadwood*'s Opening Credits." In Lavery 93–100.

Klein, Marcus. *Easterns, Westerns, and Private Eyes: American Matters, 1870–1900*. Madison: University of Wisconsin Press, 1994.

Kollin, Susan. "Race, Labor, and the Gothic Western: Dispelling Frontier Myths in Dorothy Scarborough's *The Wind*." In *Gothic and Modernism: Essaying Dark Literary Modernity*. Ed. John Paul Riquelme. Baltimore MD: Johns Hopkins University Press, 2008. 83–100.

Kristeva, Julia. *Powers of Horror: An Essay on Abjection*. Trans. Leon S. Roudiez. New York: Columbia University Press, 1982.

———. *Revolution in Poetic Language*. Trans. Margaret Waller. New York: Columbia University Press, 1984.

Kruse, Noreen. "The Process of Aristotelian Catharsis: A Reidentification." *Theatre Journal* 57 (May 1979): 162–67.

Lacan, Jacques. *Ecrits: A Selection*. Trans. Bruce Fink. New York: Norton, 2002.

———. *The Four Fundamental Concepts of Psychoanalysis: The Seminar of Jacques Lacan, Book XI*. Ed. Jacques-Alain Miller. Trans. Alan Sheridan. New York: Norton, 1998.

Lavery, David, ed. *Reading Deadwood: A Western to Swear By*. New York: I. B. Tauris, 2006.

Lawrence, Tom. "Swearengen Likely Murdered, Research Indicates." *Black Hills Pioneer* July 24, 2007: 2.

Lewis, Nathaniel. *Unsettling the Literary West: Authenticity and Authorship.* Lincoln: University of Nebraska Press, 2003.
Lewis, R. W. B. *The American Adam.* Chicago: University of Chicago Press, 1955.
———. *Edith Wharton: A Biography.* New York: Harper Colophon, 1975.
Lighter, J. E., ed. *Random House Historical Dictionary of American Slang.* New York: Random House, 1994.
Linton, Simi. "Reassigning Meaning." In *The Disability Studies Reader.* Ed. Lennard J. Davis. 2nd ed. New York: Routledge, 2006. 161–72.
"Making Deadwood: The Show behind the Show." Special Feature. *Deadwood: The Complete First Season.* Disk 6.
"Making of Episode 12: 'Boy-the-Earth-Talks-To'." Special feature. *Deadwood: The Complete Second Season.* Disk 6.
Marling, William. *The American Roman Noir: Hammett, Cain, and Chandler.* Athens: University of Georgia Press, 1995.
Marx, Leo. *The Machine in the Garden: Technology and the Pastoral Ideal in America.* 1964. New York: Oxford University Press, 1967.
McCabe, Janet. "Myth Maketh the Woman: Calamity Jane, Frontier Mythology and Creating (Media) Historical Imaginings." In Lavery 59–77.
McDonald, Tamar Jeffers. "Carrying Concealed Weapons: Gendered Makeover in *Calamity Jane.*" *Journal of Popular Film and Television* 34.4 (2007): 179–86.
McLaird, James D. *Calamity Jane: The Woman and the Legend.* Norman: University of Oklahoma Press, 2005.
McMurtry, Larry. *Buffalo Girls.* New York: Simon & Schuster, 1990.
McRuer, Robert. *Crip Theory: Cultural Signs of Queerness and Disability.* New York: New York University Press, 2006.
McShane, Ian. Audio commentary to "Sold under Sin" (1.12). *Deadwood: The Complete First Season.* Disk 4.
Michasiw, Kim Ian. "Some Stations of the Suburban Gothic." In *American Gothic: New Interventions in a National Narrative.* Ed. Robert K. Martin and Eric Savoy. Iowa City: University of Iowa Press, 1998.
Milch, David. Audio commentary to "Deadwood." *Deadwood: The Complete First Season.*
———. *Deadwood: Stories of the Black Hills.* New York: Bloomsbury USA, 2006.
———. Personal interview by Melody Graulich. Melody Ranch. February 6, 2007.
———. "Pilot." Script. *Deadwood.* HBO. Oct. 21, 2002.
———. "TV's Great Writer." Interview. MIT *Communications Forum.* April 20, 2006. http://web.mit.edu/comm-forum/forums/great_writer.htm. Accessed Jan. 21, 2006.
Milch, David, and Keith Carradine. "The New Language of the Old West." Special feature. *Deadwood: The Complete First Season.* Disk 6.

Millichap, Joseph. "Robert Penn Warren, David Milch, and the Literary Contexts of Deadwood." In Lavery 101–13.
Mitchell, David T., and Sharon L. Snyder. *The Body and Physical Difference: Discourses of Disability*. Ann Arbor: University of Michigan Press, 1997.
———. *Narrative Prosthesis: Disability and the Dependencies of Discourse*. Ann Arbor: University of Michigan Press, 2000.
Mitchell, Lee Clark. *Westerns: Making the Man in Fiction and Film*. Chicago: University of Chicago Press, 1996.
———. "What's Authentic about Western Literature? And, More to the Point, What's Literary?" In *Postwestern Cultures: Literature, Theory, Place*. Ed. Susan Kollin. Lincoln: University of Nebraska Press, 2007. 97–114.
———. "'When You Call Me That, Smile': Tall Talk and Male Hegemony in *The Virginian*." pmla 102.1 (Jan. 1987): 66–77.
Modleski, Tania. *Old Wives' Tales and Other Women's Stories*. New York: New York University Press, 1998.
Mogen, David, Scott P. Sanders, and Joanne B. Karpinski, eds. Introduction. *Frontier Gothic: Terror and Wonder at the Frontier in American Literature*. Rutherford nj: Farleigh Dickinson University Press, 1993.
Moran, Leslie J. "Law and the Gothic Imagination." In *The Gothic*. Ed. Fred Botting. Woodbridge, England: D. S. Brewer, 2001. 87–109.
"Mr. Wu Proves Out." In "Making of Episode 12: 'Boy-the-Earth-Talks-To'."
Naremore, James. *More Than Night: Film Noir in Its Contexts*. Berkeley: University of California Press, 1998.
Newcomb, Horace. "Deadwood." In *The Essential hbo Reader*. Ed. Garry R. Edgerton and Jeffrey P. Jones. Lexington: University of Kentucky Press, 2008. 92–102.
O'Connor, Flannery. *The Habit of Being: Letters Edited and with an Introduction by Sally Fitzgerald*. New York: Farrar, Strauss, Giroux, 1979.
Oldenburg, Ann. "Cussing on 'Deadwood' Sets Tongues A-wagging." USA Today.com. usa Today, 2 May 2004. Accessed Aug. 17, 2009.
Oliver, Kelly. *Reading Kristeva: Unraveling the Double-bind*. Bloomington: Indiana University Press, 1993.
———. "Women: The Secret Weapon of Modern Warfare?" *Hypatia* 23.2 (2008): 1–16. Project muse. Accessed July 20, 2011.
Oliver, Paul. *Blues Fell This Morning: Meaning in the Blues*. New York: Cambridge University Press, 1960.
Olyphant, Timothy. Audio commentary (1.12). *Deadwood: The Complete First Season*. Disc 5.
O'Sullivan, Sean. "Old, New, Borrowed, Blue: *Deadwood* and Serial Fiction." In Lavery 115–29.
The Paleface. Paramount, 1948.
Panek, LeRoy Lad. *The Origins of the American Detective Story*. Jefferson nc: McFarland, 2006.

Peek, Wendy Chapman. "The Romance of Competence: Rethinking Masculinity in the Western." *Journal of Popular Film and Television* 30.4 (Winter 2003): 206–19.

Petersen, Anne Helen. "'Whores and Other Feminists': Recovering *Deadwood*'s Unlikely Feminisms." *Great Plains Quarterly* 27.4 (Fall 2007): 267–82.

The Plainsman. Paramount, 1937.

Poe, Edgar Allen. "The Fall of the House of Usher." 1839. *The Fall of the House of Usher and Other Writings: Poems, Tales, Essays and Reviews*. Ed. David Galloway. New York: Penguin Classics, 1986.

Prassel, Frank Richard. *The Great American Outlaw: A Legacy of Fact and Fiction*. Norman: University of Oklahoma Press, 1993.

Prats, Armando José. *Invisible Natives: Myth and Identity in the American Western*. Ithaca NY: Cornell University Press, 2002.

Radcliffe, Ann. *The Mysteries of Udolpho*. 1794. Ed. Bonamy Dobrée. Oxford: Oxford University Press, 1998.

Ramazani, Vaheed. "The Mother of All Things: War, Reason, and the Gendering of Pain." *Cultural Critique* 54 (Spring 2003): 26–66.

Riebsame, William, et al., eds. *Atlas of the New West: Portrait of a Changing Region*. New York: Norton, 1997.

Robinson, Forrest. "Clio Bereft of Calliope: Literature and the New Western History." *Arizona Quarterly* 53.2 (Summer 1997): 61–98.

Rosowski, Susan. *Birthing a Nation: Gender, Creativity, and the West in American Literature*. Lincoln: University of Nebraska Press, 1999.

Schatz, Thomas. *Hollywood Genres: Formulas, Filmmaking, and the Studio System*. New York: Random House, 1981.

Sedgwick, Eve Kosofsky. *Between Men: English Literature and Male Homosocial Desire*. New York: Columbia University Press, 1985.

———. *The Coherence of Gothic Conventions*. 1980. New York: Methuen, 1986.

———. *Tendencies*. Durham NC: Duke University Press, 1993.

Serlin, David. "The Other Arms Race." In *The Disability Studies Reader*. 2nd ed. Ed. Lennard L. Davis. New York: Routledge, 2006. 49–65.

Sharp, Cecil J., and Maud Karpeles. *Eighty English Folk Songs from the Southern Appalachians*. Cambridge MA: MIT Press, 1968.

Sheller, Mimi, and John Urry. "Mobile Transformations of 'Public' and 'Private' Life." *Theory, Culture & Society* 20.3 (June 2003): 107–25.

"Show Gets Two Thumbs Up from Local Historians." *Black Hills Pioneer* Feb. 28, 2004: 17–19.

Simmon, Scott. *The Invention of the Western Film: A Cultural History of the Genre's First Half-Century*. New York: Cambridge University Press, 2003.

Singer, Mark. "The Misfit: How David Milch Got from *NYPD Blue* to *Deadwood* by Way of an Epistle of St. Paul." *New Yorker* February 14, 2005.

Singh, Frances B. "Terror, Terrorism, and Horror in Conrad's Heart of Darkness." *Partial Answers* 5.2 (June 2007): 199–218.

Slotkin, Richard. *The Fatal Environment: The Myth of the Frontier in the Age of Industrialization, 1800–1890*. Norman: University of Oklahoma Press, 1985.

———. *Gunfighter Nation: The Myth of the Frontier in Twentieth-Century America*. New York: Atheneum, 1992.

———. *Regeneration through Violence: The Mythology of the American Frontier, 1600–1860*. 1975. Norman: Oklahoma University Press, 2000.

Smith, Henry Nash. *Virgin Land: The American West as Myth and Symbol*. 1950. Cambridge MA: Harvard University Press, 2007.

Smith, Kathleen E. R. "Whores, Ladies, and Calamity Jane: Gender Roles and the Women of HBO's *Deadwood*. In Lavery 79–92.

Smith, Marquard, and Joanne Morra. Introduction to *The Prosthetic Impulse: From a Posthuman Present to a Biocultural Future*. Ed. Smith and Morra. Cambridge MA: MIT Press, 2006. 1–14.

Snauffer, Douglas. *Crime Television*. Westport CT: Praeger, 2006.

Solomon, Robert. "Sympathy and Vengeance: The Role of the Emotions in Justice." In *Emotions: Essays on Emotion Theory*. Ed. Stephanie H. M. Van Goozen, Nanne E. Van de Poll, and Joseph A. Sergeant. Hillsdale NJ: Lawrence Erlbaum, 1994. 291–312.

Sparks, Rennie. "Pretty Polly." In Wilentz and Marcus 35–49.

Staiger, Janet. "Film Noir as Male Melodrama: The Politics of Film Genre Labeling." In *The Shifting Definitions of Genre: Essays on Labeling Films, Television Shows and Media*. Ed. Lincoln Geraghty and Mark Jancovich. Jefferson NC: McFarland, 2008. 71–91.

Steckmesser, Kent Ladd. *Western Outlaws: The "Good Badman" in Fact, Film, and Folklore*. Claremont CA: Regina, 1983.

Stegner, Wallace. *The Sound of Mountain Water*. New York: Penguin, 1980.

Studlar, Gaylyn. "A Gunsel Is Being Beaten: Gangster Masculinity and the Homoerotics of the Crime Film, 1941–1942." In *Mob Culture: Hidden Histories of the American Gangster Film*. Ed. Lee Grieveson, Esther Sonnet, and Peter Stanfield. New Brunswick NJ: Rutgers University Press, 2005. 120–45.

Tatum, Stephen. "Postfrontier Horizons." *Modern Fiction Studies* 50.2 (Summer 2004): 460–68.

Taft, Michael. *Talkin' to Myself: Blues Lyrics 1921–1942*. New York: Routledge, 2005.

Thomas, David. "Destiny in My Right Hand: 'The Wreck of Old 97.'" In Wilentz and Marcus 159–74.

Thoreau, Henry David. *Walden* and *The Resistance to Civil Government*. Ed. William Rossi. 2nd ed. New York: Norton, 1992.

Thorburn, David. "TV's Great Writer, an Interview with David Milch." MIT

Communications Forum. http://web.mit.edu/comm-forum/forums/great_writer.htm. Accessed Mar. 20, 2010.

Tompkins, Jane. *West of Everything: The Inner Life of Westerns.* New York: Oxford University Press, 1992.

Traubel, Horace. Foreword to *An American Primer* by Walt Whitman. Boston: Small, Maynard, 1904: v–ix.

"Trusting the Process with David Milch." In "Making of Episode 12: 'Boy-the-Earth-Talks-To'."

Turner, Frederick Jackson. *The Frontier in American History.* New York: Henry Holt, 1921.

Turner, Matthew R. "Cowboys and Comedy: The Simultaneous Deconstruction and Reinforcement of Generic Conventions in the Western Parody." *Film & History* 33.2 (2003): 48–54.

Ursini, James. "Noir Westerns." In *Film Noir Reader 4: The Crucial Films and Themes.* Ed. Alain Silver and James Ursini. New York: Limelight Editions, 2004. 247–60.

Wallace, Jane. "Dear Lost Reader." http://www.deadwoodsoundtrack.com/adult.html. The "lost reader" addressed in the salutation of this open letter refers to Lost Highway Records, which issued the soundtrack CD and on whose website the letter originally was published.

Warner, Michael. *The Letters of the Republic: Publication and the Public Sphere in Eighteenth-Century America.* Cambridge MA: Harvard University Press, 1990.

"The Wedding Celebration." In "Making of Episode 12: 'Boy-the-Earth-Talks-To'."

Wheeler, Edward L. *Deadwood Dick on Deck; or, Calamity Jane, the Heroine of Whoop-Up. Dime Novels.* Ed. Philip Durham. New York: Odyssey, 1966.

Wiggins, Kyle, and David Holmberg. "'Gold Is Every Man's Opportunity': Castration Anxiety and the Economic Venture in *Deadwood.*" *Great Plains Quarterly* 27.4 (Fall 2007): 283–95.

Wild Bill. MGM/UA, 1995.

Wilentz, Sean, and Greil Marcus, eds. *The Rose and the Briar: Death, Love and Liberty in the American Ballad.* New York: W. W. Norton, 2005.

Williams, Doug. "Pilgrims and the Promised Land: A Genealogy of the Western." In *The Western American Literature Reader.* Ed. Jim Kitses and Gregg Rickman. New York: Limelight Editions, 1998. 93–114.

Williams, G. Christopher. "Pimp and Whore: The Necessity of Perverse Domestication in the Development of the West." In Lavery 145–56.

Wister, Owen. *The Virginian: A Horseman of the Plains.* 1902. New York: New American Library, 1979.

Witschi, Nicolas S. "Detective Fiction." In *A Companion to the Literature and Culture of the American West.* Ed. Nicolas S. Witschi. Malden MA: Wiley-Blackwell, 2011. 380–94.

Wolfe, Mark S. *Boots and Bricks: A Walking Tour of Historic Downtown Deadwood.* Deadwood SD: Deadwood Historical Preservation Commission, 1996.
Wolk, Josh. "How the West Is Run." *Entertainment Weekly* Mar. 11, 2005. http://www.ew.com/ew/article/0,,1033985,00.html. Accessed May 15, 2007.
Worden, Daniel. "Masculinity for the Million: Gender in Dime Novel Westerns." *Arizona Quarterly* 63.3 (2007): 35–60.
Yuan, David D. "Disfigurement and Reconstruction in Oliver Wendell Holmes's 'The Human Wheel, Its Spikes and Fellowes.'" In Mitchell and Snyder *The Body and Physical Difference*, 71–88.
Ziff, Larzer. *Writing in the New Nation: Prose, Print, and Politics in the Early United States.* New Haven CT: Yale University Press, 1991.

Sound Recordings

Burhans, Hilarie. "Pretty Polly." *Put on the Skillet.* Make 'Em Go Wooo, 2003. CD.
Coon Creek Girls. "Pretty Polly." 1938. Reissued on *The Rose and the Briar.* Columbia/Legacy, 2004. CD.
Deadwood: Music from the HBO Series. Lost Highway Records, 2005. CD.
Hurley, Michael. "The Hog of the Forsaken." *Long Journey.* Rounder 3011, 1976. CD. Also reissued on *Deadwood: Music from the HBO Series.*
Lovett, Lyle. "Old Friend." *I Love Everybody.* Curb, 1994. CD. Also reissued on *Deadwood: Music from the HBO Series.*
Margaret. "Creek Lullaby." *A Treasury of Library of Congress Field Recordings.* Rounder, 1997. CD.
New Coon Creek Girls. "Pretty Polly." *Ain't Love a Good Thing.* Pinecastle, 1995. CD.
"Pretty Polly." There are many differing transcriptions of this traditional ballad; Sparks refers to Dock Boggs's 1927 recording rereleased on *Country Blues: Complete Early Recordings.* Revenant 205, 1998. The lyrics excerpted in David Fenimore's essay derive from his memory, based on many years of performing the song.
"Row, Row, Row Your Boat." Sung by Robin Weigert ("Calamity Jane"). *Deadwood: Music from the HBO Series.*
Scott, Mark Lee. "Fallen from Grace." *Fallen From Grace.* Mark Lee Scott, 2002. CD. Also reissued on *Deadwood: Music from the HBO Series.*
Terry, Sonny, and Brownie McGhee. "God and Man." 1973. *Sonny & Brownie.* A&M Records, 1989. CD. Also reissued on *Deadwood: Music from the HBO Series.*
"The Unfortunate Rake." "Folk and Traditional Song Lyrics." http://www.traditionalmusic.co.uk/folk-song-lyrics/Unfortunate_Rake.htm. Accessed July 20, 2007.
White, Bukka. "High Fever Blues." 1940. *Aberdeen Mississippi Blues: Bukka White; The Vintage Recordings (1930–1940).* Document, 2003. CD. Also reissued on *Deadwood: Music from the HBO Series.*

CONTRIBUTORS

JOHN DUDLEY, associate professor and chair of the English department at the University of South Dakota, is the author of *A Man's Game: Masculinity and the Anti-Aesthetics of American Literary Naturalism* (University of Alabama Press, 2004). He is currently working on a study of African American literature and culture between 1890 and 1928, with an emphasis on the role of music, aesthetics, and material culture in developing notions of racial identity.

DAVID FENIMORE is a lecturer and director of undergraduate studies in English at the University of Nevada, Reno. His research and recently published articles focus on music and rhetoric. A musician, he is best known for dozens of Chautauqua presentations as Woody Guthrie, including a traveling exhibit on California labor history, as well as portrayals of Zane Grey, John Sutter, and Horace Greeley. He is currently at work on a teaching guide for using American song in the classroom.

MELODY GRAULICH is a professor of English and American studies at Utah State University, editor of the scholarly journal *Western American Literature*, and a recipient of the Wylder Prize for Distinguished Service to the Western Literature Association. Her recent books include the coauthored *Trading Gazes: Euro-American Women Photographers and Native North Americans* and three edited collections, *Reading The Virginian in the New West*, *In Search of a Common Language: Environmental Writing and Education*, and *Exploring Lost Borders: A Collection of Essays on Mary Austin*. She has published numerous essays on Western literature and culture. Her essay "Monopolizing *The Virginian*—or Railroading Wister" won the Palladin Prize for the best essay published in *Montana: A Magazine of Western History* for 2006.

MICHAEL K. JOHNSON is an associate professor of American literature at the University of Maine at Farmington. His book *Black Masculinity and the Frontier Myth in American Literature* was published by the University of Oklahoma Press. He has published articles on various aspects of the Western and the American West in *Quarterly Review of Film and Video*, *African American Review*, *Great Plains Quarterly*, and *Western American Literature*.

NATHANIEL LEWIS is a professor of English and English department chair at St. Michael's College in Vermont. He is the coeditor of *True West: Authenticity and the American West* and the author of *Unsettling the Literary West*, which won the Western Literature Association's 2004 Thomas J. Lyon Award for Best Critical Book in the field.

BRIAN MCCUSKEY is an associate professor of English at Utah State University, where he teaches courses on nineteenth-century British literature, critical theory, and film studies. He is currently researching and writing about pseudoscience, supernaturalism, and the humanities; portions of this work have appeared in the *Quarterly Review of Biology* and PMLA.

JENNILYN MERTEN directs and produces documentary films and nonfiction projects and is the founder of Perpetual Projects, a production company dedicated to telling uniquely American stories. Merten's work includes the feature documentaries *Sons of Perdition, First Position, The Spice Trade Expedition,* and *Lovesick*. She is also the producer of the off-Broadway play *The Eyes of Babylon*, the one-man show *This Too Shall Suck*, and short documentary projects for Discovery, HBO, and National Geographic. Merten writes about the American West, popular culture, and religion.

LINDA MIZEJEWSKI is a professor of women's, gender, and sexuality studies at the Ohio State University. She is the author of *Divine Decadence: Fascism, Female Spectacle, and the Makings of Sally Bowles* (1992), *Ziegfeld Girl: Image and Icon in Culture and Cinema* (1999), and *Hardboiled and High Heeled: the Woman Detective in Popular Culture,* (Routledge, 2004). Her most recent book, *It Happened One Night* (2010), is part of the Wiley-Blackwell Studies in Film and Television. She is currently working on a book about contemporary women comics.

TIM STECKLINE is an associate professor at Black Hills State University, where he teaches speech communication, mass communication, and film history. His training as a rhetorical critic engrosses him in issues of social change, social control, cultural forms and performances, and language use, both strategic and aesthetic. His western upbringing and midwestern schooling have made him especially appreciative of the influence of western culture, history, and geography on his character. He aspires to take an epic, multistate car ride with James Crumley someday. Burkean criticism is one of his special interests.

NICOLE TONKOVICH is a professor of literature at the University of California, San Diego. Her fields of study include nineteenth-century women writers, the history of photography, and the West. Her most recent book, *The Allotment Plot: Alice C. Fletcher, E. Jane Gay, and Nez Perce Survivance*, is forthcoming from the University of Nebraska Press.

WENDY WITHERSPOON received a PhD in English from the University of Southern California in 2007. Her essay, "The Final Stamp: Deadwood and the Gothic American Frontier," was a chapter of her dissertation, titled "The Haunted Frontier: Troubling Gothic Conventions in Nineteenth-Century Literature of the American West." She presented this essay at the Western Literature Association Conference in Boise, Idaho, in 2006. She was the recipient of the University of Southern California's Marta Feuchtwanger Fellowship for work on the historical novel in 2005–6 and the recipient of the University of Southern California's Graduate School Arnold and Oakley Fellowship in 2003–4. She has taught English at Los Angeles City College and at Los Angeles Valley College and has written book reviews for *Los Angeles* magazine and other publications.

NICOLAS S. WITSCHI is a professor of English at Western Michigan University. He is the author of *Traces of Gold: California's Natural Resources and the Claim to Realism in Western American Literature*, a Western Writers Series monograph, *Alonzo "Old Block" Delano*, and articles and essays on Mary Austin, John Muir, Sinclair Lewis, and Henry James. A past copresident of the Western Literature Association, he is also the editor of *A Companion to the Literature and Culture of the American West*.

INDEX

Page numbers in italic indicate illustrations.

Abbott, Carl, 139n6
abjection, 72–103, 188, 256, 259; and male homosexuality, 197
Adams, James Luther, xxxvi
Adams, Ramon F., 139n1
Adams, Silas (character), xxxvi, *xxxvii, xlii, 32,* 51, 56, 217
African Americans: represented in *Deadwood,* 11–12, 33, 96. *See also* Fields, Samuel "Nigger General" (character)
Agamben, Giorgio, 114, 115, 123n7
Akass, Kim, 268n19
Altman, Rick, 126
ambiguity: representation, meaning, and, xxiv–xxv, 11–12, 24–25, 26–31, 39, 131, 161–62, 264–65
American Literature: The Makers and the Making (Brooks, Lewis, and Warren), xiv–xvii, xviii, xxi, xxix, xxxii, xxxiv, xxxvii, xl, xlviiin1, lin7, 1; David Milch's work for, xv, xxix–xxx
Anderson, Sherwood, liin13
Aristotle, 45, 46–47, 154
Arthur, Jean, 185, 204
Austen, Jane, 120
authenticity, xiv, xix, xvii, xxii, lin9, liiin19, 166; and critics' focus on historical accuracy, xlv; and music, 170–71
Autry, Gene, 173

Back to the Future (Zemeckis), 137
The Ballad of Little Jo (Mansfield), 103n20, 164n3, 191
Barkin, Ellen, 185, 205n3
Barra, Allen, 97, 100n1, 127, 132, 139n1
Bazin, André, 113, 122n2
Benshoff, Henry, 215–16
Benz, Brad, xxxii, xlixn3, lin9, 100n1, 131–32, 139n5
Berrettini, Mark, 100n1, 234n1
The Big Lebowski (Coen), 138
Billy the Kid, 139n1, 152–53
Bloom, Harold, xxix
blues music, 171–72
bodies: representations of, 33, 44–71, 72–103, 193, 241, 268n15. *See also* catharsis: bodily; Mr. Wu: pigsty; sexuality
Booth, Wayne, xxxi
Botting, Fred, 121, 123n13
Bourjaily, Vance, 8
Brando, Marlon, 156
Brockway, Cristi H., xlviii
Brokeback Mountain, 164n3, 206n7, 220
Brontë, Charlotte, 107, 115
Brooks, Cleanth, xv, xxxviii, xliv–xlv, 5, 7, 14, 15. *See also American Literature: The Makers and the Making;* Lewis, R. W. B.; Milch, David: at Yale; Warren, Robert Penn

Broonzy, Big Bill, 183n
Brown, Charles Brockdon, 106
Brown, Norman O., 71n3
Buffalo Girls (McMurtry), 187, 197, 205n2, 205n3
Bullock, Martha (character), xx, xxvi, xli, 52–53, 116, 198–99
Bullock, Seth (character), xxii, xxv, xxvi, xxxiii, *xl*, xli, xliii, *xlvii*, 8–9, 36–38, 51, 52–53, 59, 106–7, 113–16, *137*, 154–56, 248–49, 260; and Alma Garret, xliii–xliv, *xliv*, 26, 85–86, 97, 219; fight with Sioux warrior, xxxviii, 78–79, 101n8, 155–56, 169; as hard-boiled hero, 133–34; marriage to Martha, 160; as writer, 18–20, 22, 26–27, 41–43, 134, 242. *See also* Olyphant, Timothy
Bullock, William (character): death of, 63, 64–66, 82, 96, *137*, 172, 198–99, 241, 260
Burhans, Hilarie, 182
Burke, Kenneth, 45–46, 49, 58, 61, 62, 65, 70, 70n2, 71n5
Burns, Johnny (character), xx, 56, *58*, *142*
Buscombe, Edward, 177
Butler, Judith, 206n6

Calamity Jane (Butler), 185, 186, 188, 204
Calamity Jane (character), xxii, xxiii, 16, 105, 146–48, 174–75, *176*, 185–207, 210–11, 243; and Joanie Stubbs, 196–205, *201*, 211, 233–34; and Wild Bill Hickok, 54–55, 186. *See also* Metz, Sofia (character); Weigert, Robin
Calamity Jane: legend of, 146, 185–91, 204
Caleb Williams (Godwin), 113

Canary, Martha Jane, xxiii, 45, 185, 187, 197. *See also* Calamity Jane (character); Calamity Jane: legend of
Carradine, Keith (Wild Bill Hickok), xxiv, 167
Cash, June Carter, 168
Cassidy, Butch, 145
Cassuto, Leonard, 132, 140n9
catharsis, 82; bodily, 45–46, 47; social, 61–67. *See also* Burke, Kenneth; Swearengen, Al: and kidney stone
Cather, Willa, liiin17
Cawelti, John, 139n2
Chandler, Raymond, 125, 138
Charters, Sam, 172
Child, Francis, 181
children, 199–202, 227; and innocence, xxxvi
Chinese Americans: represented in *Deadwood*, 117–18, 169, 219–20. *See also* Mr. Wu
Chisholm, Dianne, 208–9, 211
civilization: American West and establishment of (theme), 2–3, 21–22, 23, 42–43, 72–73. *See also* community: *Deadwood* and; frontier
Civil War, 245–46, 247, 249, 252, 255
Cochran, Doc (character), xix, xxii, xxvi, 49, 56, 57, *58*, 71n4, 73, 110, 149, 193, 241, 245–46; and Jewel, 252–57, 262
Cohen, Hubert, 152, 164n2, 164n7
Comer, Krista, liiin19, 139n6
community: *Deadwood* and, 101n6, 105, 112, 135–38, 143, 148–51, 174–75, 190–91, 199–202, 211, 213, 240, 245. *See also* civilization: American West and establishment of (theme); frontier

Conrad, Joseph, 13–14, 107
Cook, Nancy, 183
Coon Creek Girls, 182
Cooper, Chris, 157
Cooper, James Fenimore, 80
Copland, Aaron, 166
Corkin, Stanley, 164n1
Crane, Stephen, xvi–xvii, 164n5
Crawford, Joan, 191
"Creek Lullaby," 177
Crocket, Davy, xvi
"The Cruel Ship's Carpenter." *See* "Pretty Polly"
Custer, George Armstrong, 94, 96, 132, 179, 198–99, 211, 263

Dances with Wolves (Costner), 164n3
Davidson, Michael, 266nn4–5
Davis, Lennard J., 266n1, 266n5
Day, Doris, 185, 205n3
Deadwood SD, 44–45, 70n1, 95, 122n1, 132, 264
Deadwood Dick on Deck (Wheeler), 190, 237n7
Dean, Janet, 190
DeLamotte, Eugenia, 115, 119, 122n4
DeMille, Cecil B., 204
"The Demon Lover." *See* "Pretty Polly"
Denning, Michael, 139n1
Derrida, Jacques, 22, 25–26, 27, 29, 34, 40
Désert, Jean-Ulrick, 209, 213, 214, 232
detective fiction: conventions of, 126, 127–30, 132–39
dialogue, xvii, xl, 131–32, 194. *See also* homophobia; language; profanity
Dickens, Charles, xxxi, 107
Diffrient, David Scott, 192, 193, 239, 264–65

Dillahunt, Garret, xx, 264–65
Dimendberg, Edward, 128–29, 135
disability: representations of, 237–67. *See also* Jewel (character)
Dolly (character), 87, 90–91, 94–95, 98, 123n11, 150, 201. *See also* Swearengen, Al: fellatio performed on
Dority, Dan (character), xx, xxiv, xxvi, *xlii*, 9, 37, 40–41, 51, 55, 101n9, 120, 151–52, 156, 234
doubles: and marriages, 52–55; treatment of pairs and, lin11, 52–55, 83, 215–23, 224–25, 233–34
Down in the Valley (Jacobson), 138
Dreiser, Theodore, liin13
Drysdale, David, 107
DuFran, Dora, 197, 206n11
Dykstra, Natalie A., 268n17

Earp, Wyatt, 125, 129–30, 135, 139n1
Eastwood, Clint, 80, 113, 127, 128, 139n3, 143, 156
Eliot, T. S., 7, 11, 16n2
Ellsworth (character), xxv, 22, 237–38; first episode speech by, xxvii, 73, 100n2; marriage to Alma Garret, 23, 54, 66–67, 188
Emerson, Ralph Waldo, xix, xviii, xxxvii, 39
emotion: representation of, 141–64, 195–96, 208–35

"Falling from Grace" (Scott), 172
Farnum, E. B. (character), xx, xxiv, xxviii, xxxiii, 26, 34, 38, 48, 115, 194
Faulkner, William, xv, xxxiv–xxxv, xxxvi
Fiedler, Leslie, 106, 126
Fields, Samuel "Nigger General" (character), 63, 158, 206n4

INDEX 287

Fitzgerald, F. Scott, 4, 16
Fleck, Bela, 180
Flora and Miles incident, 83–85, 86, 110–11, 198, 210, 226–27, 230–31. *See also* innocence (theme); James, Henry: *The Turn of the Screw* as influence
Fonda, Henry, 123n8
Ford, John, 3, 113, 119, 139n3, 146, 151, 156–57, 164n5, 175, 178
Franklin, Benjamin, 40
Freud, Sigmund, 58–59
frontier, xxxviii, xlv, 13–14, 82, 94; and archetypal frontiersman, 78; as gothic narrative, 106–8. *See also* civilization: American West and establishment of (theme); community: *Deadwood* and

Gage, Carolyn, 186
Gardner, Erle Stanley, 139n7
Garland-Thomson, Rosemarie, 237, 244, 266nn4–5
Garret, Alma (character), xix, xx, xxv, *xl*, xli–xlii, liiinn16–17, 23, 41, 60, 115–17, 192; marriage to Ellsworth, 23, 54, 66–67, 188; and Seth Bullock, xliii, *xliv*, 26, 85–86, 97, 219; and Trixie, 50, 221–22. *See also* Parker, Molly
"Garry Owen," 179
gender: female masculinity, 188, 189–90; representations of, 31–35, 72–103, 127, 130–31, 144, 185–207; separate spheres ideology, 123n9. *See also* homosexuality; women
genre and hybridity, 104–23, 124–40, 185–207
ghosts: hauntings and, 9–10, 29, 104–5, 108–10, 258–59
Gilbert, Sandra, 31–32

Gilman, Charlotte Perkins, 106
Girard, René, 79–80, 82, 94, 101n8
Godwin, William, 113
gold, 11–12, 22, 39, 90
gothic: conventions of, 104–23
Grafe, Ernest, 246
The Great Gatsby (Fitzgerald), 4
Greenwald, Maggie, 103n20
Grey, Zane, 190
Griffith, Melanie, 197
grotesque, xxxiii–xxxvi, 73–74, 93
Gubar, Susan, 31–32
The Gunfighter (King), 111

Haber, Matt, 241
Halberstam, Judith, 189, 190, 206n7, 206n10, 220–21
Hall, Donald, 213
Hamilton, Cynthia, 126
Hammett, Dashiell, 130–31, 132, 138, 140n7
Handley, William, xxi, xlv, liiin19, 82, 101n8, 170–71
Harris, George Washington, xv–xvi, xxxii–xxxiii
Havrilesky, Heather, 118
Hawkes, John (Sol Star), xlv
Hawthorne, Nathaniel, xv, xvii–xviii, xxi, xxxvii–xxxviii, xli; preface to *The House of the Seven Gables*, xviii; preface to *The Scarlet Letter*, xviii
Hearst, George (character), xxiv, xxvi–xxvii, 11, 23–24, 32, 38, 48, 50, 120, 129–30, 162–63, 192, 235n1, 244–45, 260; distrust of language, 39–42; shooting by Trixie, 67–68, 97–98, 153
Heart of Darkness (Conrad), 121, 122n3
Heil, Reinhold, 167
Helberg, Michelle, 198
Hemingway, Ernest, 132

Hickok, James Butler "Wild Bill," 45, 146: and Martha Jane Canary, 186–87
Hickok, Wild Bill (character), xix, xvi, xxii, xxiii, 33–35, 78–79, 104–5, 108, 111–12, 129, 146–47, 191, 265; and Calamity Jane, 54–55, 186; death and funeral of, xix, xxii–xxiii, xxiv, 17n3, 79–81, 111, 147–48, 152, 172, *174*, 203, 209–10, 245, 246–47, 267n10. *See also* Carradine, Keith
High Noon (Zinnemann), 79, 111, 149
High Plains Drifter (Eastwood), 164n3
High Sierra (Walsh), 126
Hill, Erin, 241
Holmberg, David, 267n8
Holmlund, Chris, 206n12
homophobia, 194–95, 204, 209–10, 216–17
homosexuality: in cinema, 216; *Deadwood* and, 195, 197, 208–25. *See also* lesbians: representations of; Stubbs, Joanie (character)
Hooper, Johnson Jones, xvi
Hopkins, Lightnin', 168
Horsted, Paul, 246
Howard, Douglas L., lin10, 111, 191, 267n10
"How Firm a Foundation," 174–75
Hurley, Michael, 176–77
Hurt, Mississippi John, 168
Hussain, Nasser, 114
Huston, Angelica, 185, 205n3
Huston, John, 131

Ingres, Jean-August-Dominique, 228
interconnectedness: theme of, 15–16, 81, 150–51. *See also* St. Paul's letter to Corinthians
interpretation, xxiv, 119–21, 132–34; gothic narratives and theme of, 119–21
Irwin, John T., 132, 139n3, 140n9

Jacobs, Jason, 123n10
James, Alice, xxxix, 268n17
James, Henry, xviii, xxxix–xli, 6, 121; *The Turn of the Screw* as influence, xxxix, xlixn3, 83–85, 110. *See also* Flora and Miles incident
James, Henry, Sr., 6
James, William, xxxix, liin13, 6, 15
Jane Eyre (Brontë), 107, 115–16
Jen (character): as stand-in for Trixie, 63–64, 67–69, 98, 153, 223, 233–34, 260–62
Jewel (character), xxvi, xxxiv, xliii–xliv, 49, 223, 237–41, 251–67. *See also* Jewell, Geri
Jewell, Geri (Jewel), 268n18
"John Chinaman, My Jo," 169
"John Chinaman's Appeal," 169
Johnson, Susan Lee, 190–91, 194
Jones, Jeffrey (A. W. Merrick), xlvii
Joyce, James, 5

Kalinak, Kathryn, 175–76, 178
Kamir, Orit, 113
Karpelos, Maud, 181
Karpinski, Joanne B., 106
Kasdan, Lawrence, 267n6
Kellar, Kenneth, 113
Kierkegaard, Søren, 10–11
Klein, Amanda Ann, 136, 139n4
Klein, Marcus, 126, 139n1
Klimek, Johnny, 167
Koerner, Spider John, 168
Kollin, Susan, 106
Kristeva, Julia, 75, 76–78, 82, 88, 91–92, 93–95, 96, 100n3, 102n12, 103n19
Kruse, Noreen, 45

INDEX   289

Lacan, Jacques, 84, 92, 98, 102n12, 103n21
Langrishe, Jack (character), 39–40, 41, 135–37
language, xiv, xix, xvii, xxi, xxiv–xxxi, 18–43, 71n4, 72–73, 75–76, 88, 92–93, 94–96, 99, 103nn16–17, 108–9, 127, 130–32, 157–64, 209–10, 257; and intimacy, 161–62; and sexual violence, 76–77. *See also* Ellsworth (character): first episode speech by; homophobia; profanity
Lavery, David, 139n4, 239
Lawrence, Tom, 71n6
Le Bain Turc (Ingres), 228
Leone, Sergio, 127, 144, 164n2
lesbians: representations of, 196–205. *See also* homosexuality: *Deadwood* and; Stubbs, Joanie (character)
letter writing, 16, 34–36, 38–42, 152, 252
Lewis and Clark, 16
Lewis, Nathaniel, xlv, 170–71
Lewis, R. W. B., xv, xxx, xxxvi, xxxvii–xxxviii, xxxix, xlixn1, liinn15–16, 1–2, 3–7, 14, 15–16. See also *American Literature: The Makers and the Making*; Brooks, Cleanth; Milch, David: at Yale; Warren, Robert Penn
Linton, Simi, 266n2
literary history: *Deadwood* and, xiv–xlviii; and genre Westerns, 3, 77–79, 80, 127–39, 200. *See also* Westerns: genre conventions of
Little Big Man (Penn), 179
Lonesome Dove (McMurtry), 157
Lovett, Lyle, 173
The L Word, 198

Mad Men, 143
The Magnificent Seven (Sturges), 128
The Maltese Falcon (Hammett), 130–31
The Maltese Falcon (Huston), 131
The Man Who Shot Liberty Valance (Ford), 113, 146, 156–57, 164n5
Marling, William, 138, 139n3
Martin, Dean, 173–74
Marx, Leo, xxxviii
McCabe, Janet, 187, 191, 197, 204, 207n14
McCall, Jack (character), xvi, xxii, 62, 82, 111. *See also* Dillahunt, Garret
McCarthy, Cormac, xxi
McDonald, Tamar, 204
McGhee, Brownie, 176
McLaird, James D., 185, 186–87, 204, 205n1
McMurtry, Larry, 157, 187, 197, 205n2
McRuer, Robert, 241–42, 266n2, 266n4
McShane, Ian (Al Swearengen), xiv, xx, xxvii, xliii, xlvii, liiin18, 38, 167, 267n11
Melville, Herman, xix, xv, xvii, xx, xxx, xxxvii, lin6, 21, 39
Memphis Slim, 169, 183n
Merrick, A. W. (character), xxv, xxvii, xxviii, 25, 35–36, 37, 42, 241, 263. *See also* Jones, Jeffrey
Metz, Sofia (character), xxiii, *xl*, 66–67, 85–86, 96, 108–11, *109*, 177–78, 193, 243, 202–3. *See also* Calamity Jane (character)
Michasiw, Kim, 118
Milch, David: xiii–xiv, 2, 20–21, 48, 72–73, 103n21, 104–5, 108, 116, 128–29, 132, 145, 177, 239, 249, 267n10l; and addiction, xvi, 4; on the art of storytelling, 7–12, 90, 105, 122n1, 138, 268n21; *Dead-*

wood: Stories from the Black Hills, xvi, xx, xxii, xxxi, xlixn3, ln6, 38, 249, 264–65, 267n9; on genre Westerns, lin12, 3, 75–76, 94–95, 97, 119, 121, 127, 148, 150–51, 160, 164n5; on Hawthorne, xviii, xx; Hill Street Blues, xxxix, 100n1, 127, 132; interviews with, xxix–xxx, xxxvi, xxxix, lin8, liin13, liin15, 1–17, 94–95; John from Cincinnati, liin13, 121; on literary history, xviii–xxi, xxi–xxii, xxiii–xxiv, xxx–xxxi, xxxii, xxxiv–xxxv, xliv–xlv, xlvi, liin13, 7; NYPD Blue, 100n1, 127, 132; at Yale, xiv, xv, xxxix, 3–4, 8, 14–15

Miller, J. Hillis, 14

Millichap, Joseph, xlixn3, 139n5, 140n9, 239

Mitchell, David T., 240–41, 244, 267n14

Mitchell, Lee Clark, lin12, livn19, 79, 144–45, 157, 163, 164n5, 164n8, 190, 206n5

mobility: representation of, 212. *See also* Nuttal, Tom: bicycle

Modleski, Tania, 103n20

Mogen, David, 106

The Monk (Lewis), 110, 122n5

Moran, Leslie, 122n6

Morra, Joanne, 254, 258, 266n4

Morricone, Ennio, 166

Mr. Wu (character), xlii, xxv, xxvi, xxvi, 117, 169, 172; and Al Swearengen, xxiv, 120, 150, 163, 219–20; pigsty, 51–52, 82, 86, 176

Murdoch, David Hamilton, 126

music, 165–83; ballads, 179–82; and race, 169–70, 172; and transdiegesis, 176–78

My Darling Clementine (Ford), 79, 138, 123n8, 126

"My Rifle, My Pony, and Me," 174

myth: U.S. history and, 13–14

The Mysteries of Udolpho (Radcliffe), 112–13

Naremore, James, 128, 139n3

Native Americans, xxxviii, 13, 78, 80–81, 90, 108, 109, 119, 151, 155–56, 169, 177–78, 191, 246, 263. *See also* Bullock, Seth: fight with Sioux warrior; Swearengen, Al: talking to severed head

Nelson, Ricky, 173–74

Newcomb, Horace, xlixn3, xlvi

Nick of the Woods (Bird), 119

Northanger Abbey (Austen), 120

Nuttal, Tom: bicycle, 69–70. *See also* mobility: representation of

O'Connor, Flannery, xv, xxxiv

Oldenburg, Ann, 139n5, 140n8

Oliver, Kelly, 78, 96

Oliver, Paul, 171

Olyphant, Timothy (Seth Bullock), 124–25, 127

One-Eyed Jacks, 156

O'Neill, Eugene, xxi

order: theme of, xxxi, 97, 240. *See also* civilization: American West and establishment of (theme)

O'Sullivan, Sean, xlixn3, 100n1, 206n8

The Paleface, 188, 205n3

Panek, LeRoy, 139n1

Parker, Molly, xxxix

Pat Garrett and Billy the Kid (Peckinpah), 152

Peckinpah, Sam, 3, 152, 175

Peek, Wendy Chapman, 154

Petersen, Anne Helen, 74–75, 88, 234n1, 235n2, 244, 266n3, 268n20

Pinkerton Detectives, 51, 62, 125
The Plainsman (DeMille), 204
Poe, Edgar Allen, 109
pollution, 107, 117, 142–43, 198
Porter, Katherine Anne, xxx
Prassel, Frank Richard, 164n4
Prats, Armando, 178
"Pretty Polly," 180–82
profanity, xiv, xxvii, 39, 46, 75–76.
   See also Ellsworth (character): first
   episode speech by; language
purgation, 46–71
Pursued (Walsh), 126–27

queer: couples, 215–23; spaces and
   identities, 208–35

Radcliffe, Ann, 112
Ramazani, Vaheed, 96, 97–98
Red Harvest (Hammett), 132, 138
Rhodes, William, 177
Riders of the Purple Sage (Grey), 96
Riebsame, William, 139n6
Rio Bravo (Hawks), 174
Robinson, Forrest, xlv, liiin19
Rosowski, Susan, 96
Russell, Jane, 205n3
Rustler's Rhapsody (Wilson), 149

same-sex couples, 220–22
Sanders, Scott P., 106
Santayana, George, xxix, 5–6
scapegoats, 62–64
Scarborough, Dorothy, 106
Schatz, Thomas, 207n13
Schwartz, David, 168
Scott, Mark Lee, 172
The Searchers (Ford), 119, 151, 179
Sedqwick, Eve Kosofsky, 109, 122n5,
   214, 216–17
Seinfeld, 137
Serlin, David, 266n4, 268n14
Seven Samurai (Kurosawa), 128

sex, 32–33, 145, 215
sexuality, 185–207, 239
Shane (Stevens), 96, 111
Sharp, Cecil, 181
Sheller, Mimi, 209, 222, 211–12
signatures, 26–31. *See also* letter writ-
   ing
Silverado (Kasdan), 267n6
Simmon, Scott, 126–27, 139n3
Simon, David, xlvi
Singer, Mark, xv, xvii, xxxix, xlixn2,
   lin8, liin14, 97, 102n14, 123n12,
   132, 240
Singh, Frances B., 122n3
Slotkin, Richard, xxxviii, 78, 94, 96,
   111, 155–56, 164n1, 189, 206n5,
   168, 169
Smith, Henry Nash, xxxviii, 139n2
Smith, Kathleen E. R., 239
Smith, Marquard, 254, 258, 266n4
Smith, Reverend (character), 12–13,
   47–48, 68, 81, 173, *174*, 224,
   244, 247–50; and Al Swearengen,
   91, 118, 141–42, *142*, 217–19,
   233, 249–50. *See also* St. Paul's
   letter to Corinthians
Snyder, Sharon L., 240–41, 244,
   267n14
Solomon, Robert, 152–53
The Sopranos, 143
Southwest humor, xv–xvi, xxxi–xxxii
space: cinematic, 134–39, 212–13;
   queer, 210–14
Sparks, Rennie, 180
Staiger, Janet, 127
Stanwyck, Barbara, 191
Star, Sol (character), xxvi, xxvii, 20,
   22, 26, 37–38, 51, 102n15, 248–
   49; and Trixie, 53, 87–88, 215. *See
   also* Hawkes, John
Station West (Lanfield), 126–27
Steckmesser, Kent Ladd, 164n4

Stegner, Wallace, xxxix
Steinbeck, John, liiin18
St. Paul's letter to Corinthians, 17n3, 47–48, 68, 81
Stubbs, Joanie (character), 54, 191–92, 210, 214, 225–33, *229*, 243–44; and Calamity Jane, 196–205, *201*, 211, 233–34; and Flora and Miles, 83–85, 86. *See also* lesbians: representations of
Studlar, Gaylyn, 139n7
surveillance, xl–xliv, *xlii*, 24, 98–99, 125, 218, 222, 243
Sut Lovingood Tales (Harris), xvi, xxxii–xxxiii
Sutter's Mill, 90
Swearengen, Al (character), *xv*, xxv–xxvi, *xxvi*, xxxi, xxxiv, *xxxvii*, xl, *xlii*, xliii, *xlvii*, 8–9, 16n1, 21, 22–23, 73–74, *99*, 102n15, 145–46, 155, 156, 212, 237–38, 241, 246, *261*; fellatio performed on, 32–33, 87–90, 103n18, 123n11, 150, 201; as gothic villain, 118–21; and Jack Langrishe, 135–37; and kidney stone, xx, 55–61, *58*, 68–69, 96, 97, 120, 149, 159, 192, 242–43; and language, 24–25, 29, 30–32, *32*, 38–40, 59–60; and Mr. Wu, *xxvi*, 209, 219–20; mutilation of, xliii, 120, 163, 192; and Reverend Smith, 91, 118, 141–42, *142*, 217–19, 233, 249–50, 253; singing "The Unfortunate Rake," 179–80; talking to severed head, 62–63, 80–81, 101n5, 121, 151, 153, 178. *See also* McShane, Ian

Tarantino, Quentin, 128
Tatum, Stephen, xxi
telegraph: arrival in camp, 24, 59–60, 160–61, 206n8, 263

Terry, Sonny, 176
Thomas, David, 180
Thoreau, Henry David, 34, 35, 36, 37, 39
Tolliver, Cy (character), xvi, xxiv, xxvi, 23, 83–85, *99*, 129–30, 225, 227–31, 260
Tompkins, Jane, lin12, 144, 158, 189, 206n5
Traubel, Horace, xxiv
Trixie (character), xiv, xxv, xxvi, xxvii, xl, xlii, xliii, 33, 50, 56, *58*, 63–64, *74*, 223, 231, 243–44, 260; and Alma Garret, 50, 221–22; and Sol Star, 53, 87–88, 215; shoots a john, 73–74, 90–91, 237–39; shoots Hearst, 97–98, 153. *See also* Jen (character): as stand-in for Trixie
Turner, Frederick Jackson, 97, 106
Turner, Matthew R., 149
Twain, Mark, xv, xxviii, xxx, xxxi, xxxii, liin14, 5

Unforgiven (Eastwood), 80, 113, 119, 127, 139n3, 143, 156
"The Unfortunate Rake," 179–80
urban spaces: development of western American, 126, 134–39, 145
Urry, John, 209, 211–12, 222
Utter, Charlie (character), xxii, xxv, 20–21, 35, 37, 41, 51, *112*, 147–48, 194, 217

value: and paper, 22–24, 27–31
violence, 127, 148–58, 193, 239; against women, xiv, 117–18
Vizenor, Gerald, 106
Vonnegut, Kurt, 8

Walden (Thoreau), 36
Walker, Don D., xlv
Wallace, Jane, 166, 168, 172–73

Warner, Michael, 35, 36, 38, 213
Warren, Robert Penn, xv, xxix, xxx, xxxv–xxxvi, xxxviii, 1–2, 5, 7, 11, 14, 15, 132. See also *American Literature: The Makers and the Making*; Brooks, Cleanth; Lewis, R. W. B.; Milch, David: at Yale
Warshow, Robert, 157, 164n8
Wayne, John, 119, 135
Weigert, Robin (Calamity Jane), 200, 206n9, 267n9
Weil, Simone, xxxiv
West, Nathaniel, liiin13
western American literature, xvi, xxi. See also literary history: and genre Westerns
Westerns: characters in, 19; and disability, 236, 266n6; and gender, 186, 189–96, 221, 235n2; genre conventions of, 5, 75–76, 94–95, 100n4, 101n8, 105–6, 113, 119, 122n2, 126–30, 131–39, 142–64, 173, 191, 207n13, 238, 242, 245; music in, 166, 170
Wharton, Edith, liiin16
Wheeler, Edward, 190. See also *Deadwood Dick on Deck*
White, Bukka, 168, 171–72

Whitman, Walt, xiii, xxiv, xxviii, xxxvii, 39, 96, 253
Wiggins, Kyle, 267n8
The Wild Bunch (Peckinpah), 79, 175
Williams, Doug, 113, 119
Williams, G. Christopher, 192, 239
Wills, Bob, 168, 172
The Wire, xlvi, 143
Wister, Owen: *The Virginian*, xvi, ln4, 95, 145, 173, 190, 206n5
Wolcott, Francis (character), xiv, xxv, xxxiii, 23, 34–35, 40, 51, 53–54, 62, 113, 180, 162–63; and threat of sexual violence, 117–18. See also Dillahunt, Garret
Wolfe, Mark S., 45
women, 72–103, 115–17, 150, 185–207, 239
Worden, Daniel, 189–90
Wovoka, 13
writing, xxiv, 18–43, 99, 107, 132–34, 152, 242; and masculinity, 31–35. See also language, letter writing
Wu, Mr. (character). See Mr. Wu

Yates, Richard, 8
Yates, Wilson, xxxvi
Yuan, David D., 268n14

Ziff, Larzer, 21

In the Postwestern Horizons series

Dirty Wars: Landscape, Power, and Waste in Western American Literature
John Beck

The Rhizomatic West: Representing the American West in a Transnational, Global, Media Age
Neil Campbell

Positive Pollutions and Cultural Toxins: Waste and Contamination in Contemporary U.S. Ethnic Literatures
John Blair Gamber

Dirty Words in Deadwood: *Literature and the Postwestern*
Edited by Melody Graulich and
Nicolas S. Witschi

True West: Authenticity and the American West
Edited by William R. Handley and
Nathaniel Lewis

Postwestern Cultures: Literature, Theory, Space
Edited by Susan Kollin

Manifest and Other Destinies: Territorial Fictions of the Nineteenth-Century United States
Stephanie LeMenager

Unsettling the Literary West: Authenticity and Authorship
Nathaniel Lewis

María Amparo Ruiz de Burton: Critical and Pedagogical Perspectives
Edited by Amelia María de la Luz Montes
and Anne Elizabeth Goldman

To order or obtain more information on these or other University of Nebraska Press titles, visit www.nebraskapress.unl.edu.

www.ingramcontent.com/pod-product-compliance
Lightning Source LLC
Chambersburg PA
CBHW021817300426
44114CB00009BA/210